Education in East Asia

Available and Forthcoming Titles in the Education Around the World Series

Series Editor: Colin Brock

Education Around the World: A Comparative Introduction,
Colin Brock and Nafsika Alexiadou

Education in South-East Asia, edited by Lorraine Pe Symaco

Forthcoming volumes:

Education in Australia, New Zealand and the Pacific, edited
by Michael Crossley, Greg Hancock and Terra Sprague
*Education in the Commonwealth Caribbean and
Netherlands Antilles,* edited by Emel Thomas
Education in Eastern Europe and Eurasia, edited by Nadiya Ivanenko
Education in Southern Africa, edited by Clive Harber
Education in West-Central Asia, edited by Mah-E-Rukh Ahmed
Education in West Africa, edited by Emefa Amoako

Education in East Asia

Edited by Pei-tseng Jenny Hsieh

Education Around the World

B L O O M S B U R Y

LONDON • NEW DELHI • NEW YORK • SYDNEY

Bloomsbury Academic

An imprint of Bloomsbury Publishing Plc

50 Bedford Square	1385 Broadway
London	New York
WC1B 3DP	NY 10018
UK	USA

www.bloomsbury.com

First published 2013

British Library Cataloguing-in-Publication Data
A catalogue record for this book is available from the British Library.

ISBN: HB: 978-1-4411-4009-8
PDF: 978-1-4411-4971-8

Library of Congress Cataloging-in-Publication Data
A catalogue record for this book is available from the Library of Congress.

Typeset by Fakenham Prepress Solutions, Fakenham, Norfolk NR21 8NN
Printed and bound in Great Britain

Contents

Series Editor's Preface

The volumes in this series will look at education in virtually every territory in the world. The initial volume, *Education Around the World: A Comparative Introduction,* aims to provide an insight to the field of international and comparative education. It looks at its history and development and then examines a number of major themes at scales from local to regional to global. It is important to bear such scales of observation in mind because the remainder of the series is inevitably regionally and nationally based.

The identification of the regions within which to group countries has sometimes been a very simple task, elsewhere less so. Europe, for example, has multiple volumes and more than 50 countries. National statistics vary considerably in their availability and accuracy, and in any case date rapidly. Consequently the editors of each volume point the reader towards access to regional and international datasets, available online, that are regularly updated. A key purpose of the series is to give some visibility to a large number of countries that, for various reasons, rarely, if ever, have coverage in the literature of this field.

For this volume, *Education in East Asia,* it has been a relatively simple task to identify the region. The countries concerned share a combination of traditional Chinese culture and the influence of more recent Japanese occupation, both of which have had a strong influence on education. Major languages other than Chinese in the region have derived from it in different ways and are now distinctive. There are of course dialects in all places but in general the countries have a much greater linguistic homogeneity than in almost any other part of the world. This attribute was put forward by one of the founding fathers of comparative education, Nicholas Hans, as a particularly favourable one. Only in Hong Kong and Macau are there any significant legacies of European colonial languages.

The region is also notable for its rapid economic rise in recent decades. Japan is still one of the world's leading economies in terms of sophistication as well as size, while China (PRC) is now the world's second largest economy in absolute terms. Korea and Taiwan (ROC) are world leaders in the electronic and ICT fields, and Mongolia has the fastest growing economy in the world due to the recognition of its massive reserves of a variety of minerals. All of these things have a variety of connections with education that can be problematic and not always favourable, but they make for an important and complicated range of educational traditions, settings, demands and problems.

As Series Editor, I would like to thank Pei-Tseng Jenny Hsieh for all her hard editorial work, the outcome of which certainly repays its reading.

Colin Brock, Series Editor

The Contributors

Hsiao-Lan Sharon Chen is Professor of Education at the National Taiwan Normal University in Taipei, Taiwan, where she was formerly the Director of the Centre for Education Research and Evaluation. Her professional interests lie in the areas of curriculum and instruction, teacher professional development, and qualitative research methodology. Currently she heads several public policy research projects, including one on the construction of teacher professional standards, the establishment of a learning support system and a teacher empowerment programme.

Jeong-ah Cho is a Researcher at the Korea Institute for National Unification, a national research institute of the Republic of Korea government which conducts research and policy development on North Korea and the multidimensional issues related to the unification of the Korean peninsula. Her research interests include the education system and policies of North Korea. She is also interested in identity formation as well as the current social situation of ordinary North Koreans. Jeong-ah Cho received her PhD in the Sociology of Education from Seoul National University, South Korea.

Enkhzul Dambajantsan is a Lecturer at the University of the Humanities, Mongolia, with a mixed background in finance and education. She received a BSc in Finance and an MBA from the University of the Humanities, Mongolia, and an MSc in Education from the University of Oxford, UK. Her research interests are academic development, professional learning and the teaching and learning experiences of students in the fields of business and finance.

Hubert Ertl is Lecturer in Higher Education at the Department of Education, University of Oxford, UK. He is Director of the Department's MSc in Education (Higher Education) programme and Senior Research Fellow of the ESRC-funded Centre on Skills, Knowledge and Occupational Performance (SKOPE). He is also the convener of the Higher Education and Professional Learning Research Group and Fellow of Linacre College, University of Oxford, UK. Hubert Ertl's research interests include international aspects of higher education, vocational education and training, EU educational policies, transition processes to higher education and the world of work, and widening participation in higher education.

Jiyeon Hong has been an Associate Professor at Kyungmin College, South Korea, for the past 11 years. She became a full-time lecturer after she completed her Masters in Education from Ewha Woman's University, South Korea. She also obtained a Masters degree from the University of Edinburgh, UK, and a Doctoral degree from University of Oxford, UK, on the topic of Gender Inequalities in a Confucian Society in Korea. She was a visiting scholar at Harvard University, USA, before returning to Korea to further her academic career. In recent years, her research focus has been on theoretical and substantial approaches on early childhood education in both national and international contexts.

Pei-tseng Jenny Hsieh is a Researcher in the Department of Education, University of Oxford, UK. Her research interests are on assessment and evaluation for education policies in both developed and developing contexts. She has worked extensively on issues related to English-as-a-second-language education policy in East Asia, but in recent years her research focus has been on large-scale assessments in developing countries and how they contribute to progress in education. She has worked on education policy and national assessment issues in East Asia, South Asia and sub-Saharan Africa and is currently involved in research projects in India and The Gambia.

Yuki Imoto is an Assistant Professor at Keio University, Japan, where she teaches English and Research Methods for Social Science. She has been conducting research on Japanese education, childhood and youth from social anthropological perspectives, with particular focus on how individual educational routes are changing in the context of globalization. She is also co-editor of *A Sociology of Japanese Youth – from returnees to NEETs* (with Roger Goodman and Tuukka Toivonen), Routledge, 2012.

Takehiko Kariya is Professor of the Sociology of Japanese Society at the Nissan Institute of Japanese Studies and the Department of Sociology, and a Faculty Fellow of St Antony's College, University of Oxford, UK. His research interests include the sociology of education, social stratification, school-to-work transition, educational and social policies, and social changes in post-war Japan. Before he joined the University of Oxford, he taught sociology of education for two decades at the Graduate School of Education, University of Tokyo, Japan. Takehiko Kariya is co-editor of *Challenges to Japanese Education: Economics, Reforms, and Human Rights* (Teachers College Press, 2010), the author of *Education Reform and Social Class in Japan* (Routledge, forthcoming), and has published more than 20 books in Japanese.

Eul Sook Kim works at Handong Global University, South Korea. Before taking up her current position, she worked at the Korean Educational Development Institute (KEDI) as a researcher. She is in charge of admissions of foreign students, especially those from developing countries, as her interests are highly focused on education in developing countries and disadvantaged children. Kim has also been an evaluator for GKS (Global Korea Scholarship), which grants international students scholarships to pursue excellence in education.

Ki-Seok Kim is a Senior Professor in the Department of Education, Seoul National University, South Korea, where he is currently Chair of the Global Education Cooperation Program. His research interests include the social history of the Korean education system, questions related to social transformation through education, and educational development issues. He received his PhD in the Sociology of Education from the University of Wisconsin, Madison, USA.

Huang-kue Lee is currently a Research Professor at the Institute of Globalization and Multicultural Studies at Hanyang University, South Korea. Her current work involves curriculum development and policy design for the integration of North Korean refugees and other migrant populations into the South Korean education system. She has also worked as an Adjunct Professor at the Graduate School of North Korean Studies and a Research Fellow at the Korean Education Development Institute. Hyang-kue Lee received her PhD in the Sociology of Education from Seoul National University, South Korea, and was a Visiting Academic at the Institute of Education, University of London, UK.

Dr Soojeong Lee completed her doctoral studies at the Department of Education Policy Studies in Pennsylvania State University. She has been working as an assistant professor in the College of Education at Dankook University in Korea since 2009 and is the Director of the Center for Admission Counseling'. Her major research interest is in analyzing and evaluating educational policies such as accountability and evaluation of public schooling, shadow education (private tutoring services) and college admission systems. She is currently a member of the Committee for Policy Research Revie' in the Korean Ministry of Educational Science and Technology and the editor of three major journals in the programme of educational administration, which are published at the Korean Educational Administration Society, the Korean Society for the Economics and Finance of Education, and the Korean Society for the Politics of Education.

Alka Sharma is a PhD candidate in the Faculty of Education at the University of Hong Kong. Originally from India, she holds a Masters degree from Delhi University. Prior to enrolling for her PhD programme, Alka taught senior secondary students for almost ten years. Her research interests include ethnic minority education, citizenship and governance in education, multicultural education, sociological theories and research methods.

Shin'ichi Suzuki is Professor Emeritus of Waseda University, Tokyo, Japan, from which he retired in 2003 at the age of 70. He served as the Director of the British Studies Institute, Vice-Dean of the School of Education and Chair of the Department of Education at Waseda. He convened the Japan–UK Education Forum. Suzuki Shin' cihi was nominated by the Minister of Education as the senior member of the Advisory Council for Teacher Education from 1980 to 1990. His majoring fields are comparative education and teacher education and training. Nationally he served as the Secretary-General of the Association of the Private Universities for Teacher Education for more than ten years and has organized, as Chair, a series of Japan–UK Fora for Education since 1991. Internationally, Suzuki joined the World Council of Comparative Education Societies (WCCES) in 1984 as part of the Commission on Methods and Methodology and played the part of commissioner for the Commission of the Worlds of Childhood. He has worked closely with the Chinese Comparative Education Society, and convened the Comparative Education Society of Asia. He also successfully organized five International symposia for comparative and teacher education at Waseda between 1993 and 2003. Suzuki's articles in English have been published in the Komparatistische Bibliothek series (Peter Lang) and elsewhere.

Sou-Kuan Vong is currently Associate Professor and Director of the Educational Research Centre in the Faculty of Education, University of Macau, China. She has worked in the field of education for over 20 years. She holds a doctoral degree in the Sociology of Education awarded by the University of Nottingham, UK. Her research interests are diverse, including educational policy, curriculum issues, citizenship education, teacher education, and yet they are held together by an overarching commitment to social justice and an interest in questions of power/knowledge and discourse/practice in educational research.

Kai Yu is Associate Professor and Assistant Dean of the Graduate School of Education, Shanghai Jiao Tong University, China. His research focuses on higher education in China, graduate education, and higher education management. Kai Yu has published in leading journals in China including *Educational Research*, the *Journal of Higher Education*, and *Peking University Education Review*. He has also written for newspapers such as the *China Education Daily*. Kai Yu obtained his Doctor of Philosophy and Master of Science degrees from the University of Oxford, UK, in the field of educational studies. Before that he studied computer science at Queen's University Belfast, Northern Ireland, where he received a Bachelor's degree in Engineering.

Zhou Zhong is Associate Professor at the Institute of Education, Tsinghua University, China. Zhou graduated from Peking University, China, with a degree in English Language and Literature (BA), and the University of Oxford, UK, with degrees in Comparative and International Education (MSc) and Educational Studies (DPhil). She has worked at the Tsinghua Institute of Education since 2005. The main courses Zhou teaches are Comparative and International Education, the History of Chinese Education, and the History of Western Education. Her research interests focus on higher education studies, with special references to internationalization, regional development and skills development. In 2008 Zhou worked full-time for the Organising Committee for the 29th Olympic Games (Beijing) as a Manager of Venue Operation and Volunteer Training and Management in the International Broadcast Centre.

Introduction

Education in East Asia: A Regional Overview

Pei-tseng Jenny Hsieh

After World War Two, economists around the world had predicted it would take a substantial amount of time before Asia could revive. They put greater emphasis on aid and development elsewhere, mostly in sub-Saharan Africa. Few would have thought that after just three decades, the East Asian economies would have expanded so substantially. The co-called miracle of the 'East Asian Tigers' became a frequently used term as this region became the home of some of the major economic powers of the world by the turn of the millennium.

Education is hugely important in these East Asian societies, with parents and families willing to endure hardships to support their children's education. Educational qualifications became vital for one's social status, and that of the family. When trying to explain the economic and social development of East Asian societies, a simplified version of human capital theory with its call for investment in education is almost always given as the answer. Education is recognized as a major factor in development. It delivers values and attitudes supportive of development and prepares a workforce able to make changes possible. This claim is especially rooted in the academic disciplines of economics (Rodrik, 1995; Hanushek and Welch, 2006). Education is viewed, almost without question, as a crucial driving force for the rapid economic growth of nations, even though the complex relationship between educational investment and economic growth involves many more confounding factors and is not yet fully understood.

Near universal access to primary education is considered a key characteristic of the East Asian economies prior to their exponential growth. Although such a view is in danger of oversimplification, given the complex contextual background of this region, one can hardly deny that the most valuable source of comparative advantage of these nations is their well-educated workforce

(Morris and Sweeting, 1995; Morris, 1996). The East Asian experience has gradually become an exemplary model to those societies suffering from low or declining levels of economic growth (Berger, 1988; Applebaum and Henderson, 1992; Cummings, 1995). However, the story of East Asia is not only the outcome of successful education policy and practice, but also derives from the histories and cultures that have long shaped the ideologies of the peoples concerned.

The countries in this region exhibit many similarities in their education systems and non-formal experiences, from the examination systems they employ to the private supplementary classes dedicated to achieving success (Bray, 2009). While being humble, understated and respectful are crucial rituals in the cultures of the region, the education systems encourage competition and ranking of ability at a very early stage. This approach, and its mentality, history and philosophy, underpin the successes achieved, despite the downsides as researched by Zeng (1999).

This volume aims to present a general picture, and some contemporary issues, of education in the following countries: China and its two Special Governance Regions – Hong Kong and Macau; Japan; Mongolia; North Korea; South Korea; and Taiwan. All of them represent a strong link to the underlying education values of Confucianism. The types of teaching and learning contexts prevailing in these countries are different from conventionally accepted Western norms. These countries also exhibit achievement-orientation, collectivism, high expectation of the parents, and attribution of success to effort in their attitudes towards teaching and learning and other educational dimensions (Biggs, 1998; Leung, 2002).

However, this volume exhibits variation as well as generalization with regard to East Asia as a whole and each country within it. The allocation of resources to education, both physical and human, cannot be homogeneous within any country or region. While most of the countries exhibit a long-term influence of Confucianism and Chinese cultures, it is clear that the diversities between and within those countries are more than significant due to their evolving and divergent social, cultural and economic contexts. Such variations necessarily exist, and one must be aware of disparities within all these countries at the local scale. Consequently, the 13 chapters in this volume cover a wide range of topics and experiences under the overarching Confucian umbrella.

The first is Zhong's chapter, an overview of education in the People's Republic of China. It explains the influence of Confucianism on the ideology and system of education, not just in China but in most of the Confucius heritage countries. She also describes the conflicts and difficulties brought about by the implementation of the modern, often foreign, derived education model of formal education, their structures and modes of provision. Yu and Ertl's chapter focuses on the role of independent colleges in the ever-growing higher education market in China. The admission to higher education institutions (HEIs) is extremely competitive in China, with around 50 per cent of pupils gaining access to senior secondary schools (Grades 10–12) and just around 20 per cent of all pupils entering higher education. While these colleges contribute a large pool of degree-seeking students, it is a fairly new phenomenon and often overlooked by scholars interested in the tertiary sector in China. In a case study, the authors compare independent college, public university, public college and private college. They suggest that there are often socioeconomic factors involved in student choices among these different types of higher education institutions. They show that the variety of the HEIs does not in reality cater for the promotion of educational diversity.

In the first chapter on Japan, Suzuki provides a detailed profiling of the country, especially the demographic, social and cultural changes in recent decades that help to explain educational trends. Japanese society is well known for its sophistication and pursuit of perfection in many aspects. From an anthropological point of view, Suzuki tries to explain how the deeply rooted historical, conceptual and cultural elements shape both choices and developments in Japanese education.

Kariya, in his chapter, examines education resource allocation in post-World War Two Japan. He discusses in detail how funding schemes were decided and implemented after the war, and the contextual and circumstantial constraints operating. The more individualistic American scheme of resource allocation was introduced as a comparison to the traditional Japanese approach that seeks more even distribution in resources. The author argues that the Japanese model has led to a more progressive approach in resource allocation and a more collaborative and collectivistic learning environment.

Imoto's chapter on Japan discusses the development of international education within Japan and the 'internationalization' and 'globalization' in the country's higher education. She points out that Japanese youth, as compared to those in neighbouring East Asian countries, are more inward-looking in terms of their choices in education, work and lifestyle. She also sees the significant reduction of Japanese students in foreign universities as a serious problem, and discusses how the government, and Japanese society as a whole, react to this phenomenon.

Hong Kong and Macau, both Special Administrative Regions of the People's Republic of China, are strongly influenced by their European colonial past.

They are often discussed together due to the seemingly similar contextual background, but this can be misleading. Sharma's chapter on Hong Kong stresses the inequalities caused, or reproduced, by streaming at various education levels. It also addresses the dilemma in choices of schools and languages of instruction after the 1997 reunification with the PRC.

Compared to Hong Kong, Macao's return to Chinese sovereignty seemed a more tranquil transition. Possibly most well known for its gaming industry, Macao is very much a market-oriented society where government policies often become more symbolic than practical. Vong in her chapter analyzes the role that local and central government played in a series of education reforms post-1999. The chapter centres on the notion of governmentality and provides a distinctive perspective in the discussion of education development in Macao.

In the last century, education in Mongolia has experienced a number of phases with regard to its educational experiences. It moved from the traditional and informal ways of teaching and learning in a nomadic social inheritance to having to adhere to the Soviet model of the USSR under communist rule, and then to a distinctively modernized system in recent years in keeping with experiencing the most rapid economic growth within the whole region (Kaiman and Macalister, 2012). Dambajantsan in her chapter provides an overview of the contemporary education system of Mongolia, the former land of Genghis Khan, and its numerous nomadic tribes. In particular she examines the mismatch between the current demand of a labour market related to a range of extractive industries and government strategies in education designed to respond to this problem.

The chapter on North Korea unveils the education system and practice in one of the most closed national communities of the modern era. The country is in desperate need of economic and social development to solve the immediate problem of basic survival. Yet the North Korea authorities face the dilemma of having to maintain a political and ideological communist system in an era when creative thinking, problem solving and access to the latest information are normal everywhere else, including their only ally, the PRC. Challenging existing ideologies and methodologies is an important part of learning and achieving progress in the contemporary globalized world.

Jiyeon Hong writes about the multicultural society in present day South Korea and discusses the problems that children from multicultural backgrounds face in daily life and in schooling. Unlike its northern neighbour and ethnic twin, South Korea is at the forefront of the modern world economy, and the related changes in skills distribution are an educational challenge to its increasingly multicultural society. This is despite the country being a leader in ICT and PISA (Programme for International Student Assessment) scores. Lee and Kim's chapter deal with the higher education sector in South Korea. Like many other countries in East Asia, challenging entrance examinations are the gatekeeper for the tertiary level of education and enhanced opportunities in society. The authors investigate the reforms of the college admission process and the driven forces behind that movement.

Chen's chapter introduces the various education reform acts that have been introduced in Taiwan in the decades before and after the millennium. She examines the major education reforms in the context of significant social change, even crisis. Chen also discusses the difficulties in implementing reform policies at school level and suggests that such policies do not necessarily mandate what really matters. Indeed, neither do they necessarily guarantee improvement. The second chapter on Taiwan explores in further details the geopolitical background and international status of Taiwan. The need for individual Taiwanese, as well as the country as a whole, to be competitive underpins the mindset behind educational developments. Hsieh further focuses the discussion on the entrance examination systems and the phenomenon of credentialism, and how they drive the life chances of the people and the nation.

Regardless of the particular topics of each chapter, readers will find a few constantly emerging themes across the regions. High scores in international achievement surveys is probably the one that attracts the most attention from the outside world. China (with its non-representative sample of Shanghai), Hong Kong, South Korea and Taiwan occupied the top rank of the most recent league tables of school-level performance. With the release of international achievement surveys (PISA, TIMSS (Trends in International Mathematics and Science Study), PIRLS (Progress in International Reading Literacy Study)), scholars and governments from around the world try hard to explain the continued 'success' at the west of the Pacific Rim. In such an examination-oriented setting, it is probably not surprising to see East Asian countries continue to top these international achievement surveys. The parallel economic success attracts the attention of education and economic policy makers alike, and yet the evidence for correspondence between curriculum and economy is as elusive as ever. Hsieh has chosen to explore this topic further in her chapter on examinations in Taiwan.

The role of 'shadow education' or 'cramming' is also prominent in these countries. The term 'shadow' is derived from the fact that it is private supplementary tutoring in academic subjects beyond the hours of mainstream formal schooling. However, it co-exists only in relation to the mainstream system. A growing body of literature focuses on the influence cramming brings to general education (Zeng, 1999; Bray, 2006; 2009; Yoo, 2002; Kwok, 2004; Silova and Bray, 2006). Cramming is huge in this region, not only at the transition points at which students are selected for the next stage of education but also at almost every education level, as parents do not want their children to be disadvantaged at any stage of 'the education race'. Lower achievers in school fear being left behind if they do not receive extra tutoring, and higher achievers continue to attend cram schools in order to remain at the top of the game. Moreover, children of low-income families who could not receive such benefits may fail to keep up with their peers and are thus more likely to drop out of school at an earlier age. In such a process, major issues of equity are involved, with implications for social cohesion.

Under the competitive ethos, children are used to being ranked, sometimes weekly and monthly, in their test performance, especially when getting close to examinations. Examinations have become one of the most crucial components of the education system in Confucius heritage cultures. They embody the theory of Hopper (1968) that some form of selection is the major function of education systems, whatever the mode of selection may be. In East Asia the mode is clearly that of formal examination. Formal examination originated from this part of the world, in Imperial China. It is rooted in the cultures, despite the many criticisms of it in limiting initiative and constraining 'blue skies thinking'.

Another key issue is the choice in language of instruction in formal education, especially at school level but at other levels too. It has generated keen debates in some countries, especially those with longer colonial histories or stronger cultural connections with the West. Public schools in Hong Kong and Macao have introduced Chinese as the medium of instruction after the official handover of governance to China. Conversely, in Mongolia's new education system, most of the subjects are now taught in English. In other countries, English is a *lingua franca* and a tool to increase the global competitiveness of a nation. This also affects education policy and planning (Watson, 2001; Tollefson and Tsui, 2004; Hsieh, 2010). While there is always the urge for nations to maintain national identification through reinforcing the importance of national languages, especially as the medium of instruction in school, parents may often favour English as it represents higher status and better life chances. Even government officials strive to secure a place for their children in international schools or schools providing English medium of instruction for this reason.

Most of the topics relating to education in East Asia have already been highlighted both inside and outside the region. Here, in addition to providing basic information about systems and cultures of education, the intention is to provide readers with an understanding of some distinctive phenomena by immersing them in the socio-cultural setting that is unique to this region.

References

Applebaum, R. P. and Henderson, J. (1992). *States and Development in the Asian Pacific Rim*. Thousand Oaks, CA: Sage Publications.

Berger, P. (1991). 'Comparative perspectives on the state'. *Annual Review of Sociology*, 17: 523–49.

Berger, P. L. (1988). 'An East Asian Development Model'. In P. L. Berger and H. M. Hsiao (eds), *In Search of an East Asian Development Model*. New Brunswick: Transaction Books.

Biggs, J. (1998). 'Learning from the Confucian heritage: So size doesn't matter?' *Educational Research*, 29: 723–38.

Bray, M. (2006). 'Private supplementary tutoring: comparative perspectives on patterns and implications'. *Compare*, 36: 515–30.

—(2009). *Confronting the Shadow Education System: What Government Policies for What Private Tutoring?* Paris: UNESCO-IIEP, p. 130.

Cummings, W. (1995). 'The Asian resource approach in global perspective'. *Oxford Review of Education*, 21: 67–81.

Hanushek, E. A. and Welch, F. (eds) (2006). *Handbook of the Economics of Education*. London: Elsevier.

Hopper, E. I. (1968). 'A Typology for the Classification of Education Systems'. *Sociology*, 2: 29–46.

Hsieh, P. T. (2010). 'The Impact of Globalisation on Foreign Language Education Policy in Taiwan: Policy Initiatives and Industrial Demand'. *International Journal of Educational and Psychological Assessment*, 5: 76–100.

Kaiman, J. and Macalister, T. (2012). 'Mines Bring Steppe Change to Mongolia'. *The Guardian*, 21 August: 24.

Kwok, P. (2004). 'Examination-oriented knowledge and value transformation in East Asian cram schools'. *Asia Pacific Education Review*, 5: 64–75.

Leung, F. K. S. (2002). 'Behind the High Achievement of East Asian Students'. *Educational Research and Evaluation*, 8, 1: 87–108.

Morris, P. (1996). 'Asia's four little tigers: A comparison of the role of education in their development'. *Comparative Education*, 32: 95–110.

Morris, P. and Sweeting, A. (eds) (1995). *Education and Development in East Asia*. London: Garland Publishing, Inc.

Rizvi, F. (2007). 'Rethinking educational aims in an era of globalisation'. In P. Hershock, M. Manson and J. N. Hawkins (eds), *Changing Education: Leadership, Innovation and Development in a Globalizing Asia Pacific*. Hong Kong: Springer.

Rodrik, D. (1995). 'The dynamics of political support for reform in economies in transition'. *Journal of Japanese and International Economies*, 9: 403–25.

Silova, I. and Bray, M. (eds) (2006). *Education in the hidden market place: monitoring of private tutoring*. New York: Open Society Institute.

Tollefson, J. and Tsui, A. (eds) (2004). *Medium of Instruction Policies: Which Agenda? Whose Agenda?* Mahwah, NJ: Lawrence Erlbaum Associates.

Watson, K. (2001). 'The impact of globalization on educational reform and language policy: Some comparative insights from transitional societies'. *Asia Pacific Journal of Education*, 21: 2.

Williamson, J. W. and Morris, P. (2000). 'Teacher education in the Asia–Pacific region: a comparative analysis'. In P. Morris and J. W. Williamson (eds), *Teacher Education in the Asia–Pacific Region: a comparative study*. New York: Falmer Press.

Yoo, Y. H. (ed.) (2002). *Economics of Private Tutoring: In Search for its Causes and Effective Cures*. Seoul: Korea Development Institute.

Zeng, Kangmin (1999). *Dragon Gate: Competitive Examinations and their Consequences*. London: Cassell.

China: An Overview

Zhou Zhong

The rise of China as an important player in international economic competition and global politics over recent decades appears to have come as a surprise to the world. Such surprise is often accompanied by overestimations or underestimations of China's actual capabilities. A strong aspiration for the development has long been a goal of the Chinese government and people. This has involved modernization and industrialization of educational, scientific and technological capacity, and China has impressive records of policy intent, planning and resource commitment for meeting such goals. This chapter provides an overview of education development in modern China. Based on a discussion of selected legacies that have cast a profound influence on Chinese education today, this study describes and analyzes key trends and challenges of education development in China in 1990–2010, then discusses the main features of China's National Outline for Medium and Long Term Educational Reform and Development (2010–20).

Selected Legacies of Chinese Education

This section outlines the historical development of the Chinese education system over the twentieth century, and discusses three diverse traditions that shape Chinese education systems today. Those three forces have come together with creative tensions that have yet to be fully reconciled (Zhong, 2005). The first tradition is that of indigenous Chinese learning based on the thinking of Confucius and the millennia-old Mandarin system. The second tradition is an amalgam of modern Western-influenced education systems developed in China during the 1900s to the 1940s, and the third tradition is that of the Soviet-inspired system in the 1950s to 1960s. The influence of each of the three traditions can still be seen in China today, and have become caught up in the more recent influences of international interaction and globalization.

The legacy of Confucianism and the Mandarin system

If one is to characterize in one word the Chinese way of education for the last two millennia, the word would be 'Confucius' (about 551BC–479BC). No other individual in Chinese history has so deeply influenced the life and thought of his people, as a teacher, an educationist, a philosopher, a political theorist and creative interpreter of the ancient culture, and as a moulder of the Chinese character.

For Confucianism, since the time of its general acceptance, has been more than a creed to be pressed or rejected; it has become an inseparable part of the society and thought of the nation as a whole. It is fundamental to what it means to be a Chinese, as the Confucian classics are not the canon of a particular sect but the literary heritage of a whole people (De Bary et al., 1960, p. 15).

In the contemporary world, the global phenomena of the higher achievement of Asian students in schools and universities has generated much scholarly interest. Several studies have discovered that Confucian values on respect for education and learning are underpinning the diligence and motivation of such students (Volet & Remshaw, 1996; Flynn, 1991; Kim, 1988). These cultural values – such as the educatability of all, perfectibility for all, lifelong learning, learning through effort and willpower, and reciprocity of teaching and learning – all provide an intrinsic motivation for learning for self-realization (Oh, 2001).

If one is to characterize in one word the Chinese way of education today, the word would be '*Gaokao*', meaning national entrance examination to higher education. No other examination in Chinese society today has so deeply influenced the life and thought of students, parents, teachers, schools and universities. It is a mechanism to select or 'screen' people for higher learning, to safeguard equity and promote social mobility, to steer reforms in both general education before *Gaokao* and higher education and continuing education afterwards; to underpin a *Gaokao* economy of private tuition in the marketplace, and as a moulder of the character of Chinese intellectuals. Not surprisingly, of course, the idea of *Gaokao* has a Confucian underpinning, a 1300-year-long tradition of the Mandarin system of the civil service examination.

From year 605, in the Sui Dynasty, until 1905, the Confucian thinking of the education–state relationship was institutionalized through the Mandarin system, a civil servant recruitment examination, and its supporting education system that prepared students for that examination. This examination was a holistic educational and social mechanism for the cultivation, selection and recruitment of talents, social reproduction, and mobilization and distribution of scarce resources of status, power and wealth (Wu, 2002; Jin, 1990). It was hence an embodiment of Confucian thinking on education, learning and the ideal world governed by the scholars. The Mandarin system served to cultivate and integrate intellectual resources, and to maintain the socio-cultural ecological equilibrium of traditional Chinese society.

The extent and significance of social mobility through the Mandarin examinations have occasioned sustained debate both in the past (He, 1962; Kracke, 1957; Cressey, 1931) and in more recent years (Elman, 2000; Liu, 2002; He, 2009). In general, the meritocratic Mandarin system created a sustainable and inclusive social metabolic mechanism between the masses and the well-educated group, as well as within the educated group. Therefore human intelligence, the essence of social development, could be effectively identified and absorbed into the leadership with a sustainable supply of new blood.

Second, though only a small proportion of people could obtain the status and privileges bestowed by the Mandarin examinations, a far larger proportion of the population actually obtained significant education at various levels in attempting the process (Liu, 1996). Consequently there was a powerful incentive for learning and a respect for education as well as esteem for scholars and intellectuals. The result was a relative 'mass' education infrastructure throughout the country where people could pursue studies in their local community.

Third, the highly uniform education and examination systems disseminated relatively uniform social values, the Confucian ideology, which in turn reinforced the sustainability of the Mandarin system for over a millennium. Confucian intellectuals selected by the Mandarin system functioned in politics, in governing and managing family and society at all levels, in promoting filial respect and cultural inheritance, and in supporting educational and academic systems as a whole.

The Mandarin system was not without its problems, however. The highly uniform culture was accompanied by rigidity and conservatism. The curriculum became too narrow and too examination-oriented, and it tended not to encourage creativity but rather rote learning and uncritical thinking. It is possible that the system did not select the talent but only the most skilled in passing examinations (Miyazaki, 1981). In contrast to the mobile and open-structured society it underpinned, the Mandarin system in its last stages turned into a mental shackle for ideological submission. It was therefore not surprising that the gentry-literati produced by the Mandarin system and related education system collapsed in the face of the national crisis and challenge of modernization at the turn of the twentieth century.

The legacy of Western-influenced education in China

The emergence of Western-influenced education in China began in the late nineteenth century up to the establishment of the People's Republic of China (PRC) in 1949. It was a turbulent half-century of military and economic Western and Japanese aggression in China, plus continuous civil wars and socio-political disorder. This encouraged increasing rigidity in the Mandarin system, but also substantial growth in China's contact with Western learning. It was during this period that modern education in China proliferated in varied forms and with many types of foreign influence and participation (Sun, 1986). This led to the growth of a modern national system of education, of urban public informal education through the press, of Chinese students studying abroad, of the formal education of women, of a widespread functional literacy among the common people, and of the founding of educational institutions and associations as seedbeds of reform and revolution (Yang, 2004; Li, 1997; Borthwick, 1983).

The educational goal of this period was how to create the academic institutions needed for modernity, reconciling the Chinese and Western cultural traditions both intellectually and institutionally. There was a wide consensus among different interest groups that education was the way to save the nation from Western aggression and colonization (Rankin, 1971). From 1911 to 1927 China was characterized as a land of warlords with constant conflict between them. As a result, diverse cultures and movements flourished and there was a shift from the Japanese to German and French models of education. The higher education sector saw a growth in universities, university autonomy and academic freedom. As Japanese aggression grew, more Chinese turned towards Europe and the United States for inspiration. While the Japanese model laid more stress on primary and secondary schooling, the European-based models had shifted the focus to the higher education sector.

The USA soon became China's new authoritative reference between the 1920s and 1940s. In 1922, China adopted the American 6-3-3-4 education system which is still in use in China today. Dewey's pragmatism and experimentalism became a strong influence on China's educational policy and practice during this period (Yuan, 2001). The American influence was further strengthened by a growing number of Chinese students and scholars returning from the USA, who formed a central force in Chinese education (Wang, 1966). In higher education, China replaced the French model of a two-tier system with the American three-tier system, comprising the university, liberal college and specialist college, replaced collegiate governance with presidential governance, introduced the credit system, broadened specialized curricula into generalized and individualized curricula, and created a national network of specialist colleges, especially technical schools (Li, 1997).

In 1932 the Nationalist government commissioned the League of Nations' Mission Educational Experts with a comprehensive consultation of Chinese education at the time. Interestingly, many of the issues discussed in the consultation, *The Reorganisation of Education in China* (1932), are still relevant today: namely, elite–mass distinctions, urban–rural and regional disparities, and foreign borrowing and adaptation.

The legacy of Soviet higher education in China

Foreign influence on Chinese education culminated in a new and more penetrating mode after the founding of the People's Republic China on 1 October 1949. At that time China was a war-worn, backward, predominantly rural state isolated from most of the world. The Chinese Communist Party recognized that the key priorities in nation-building were political consolidation and rapid industrialization through 'learning from the Soviet Union'.

> The rationale was that since the best of Western science and technology had already been absorbed by the Russians, the quickest and best way was to take the distilled essence directly from the Soviet Union. And since education and industry are the main social institutions necessary for the application of science and technology, their organisation and management were also reshaped in the Soviet mould. (Pepper, 1987, p. 197)

Those most directly responsible for establishing a Soviet system in China involved 10,000 or more Soviet 'experts' who served in China during the 1950s, including some 700 who worked in higher education. Moreover, there were also more than 30,000 Chinese students, academics and professionals who went to the Soviet Union for study and training during the same period (Shen, 2009).

The Soviet-inspired education reconstruction in the 1950s revolved around wholesale transplantation of the Soviet system of institutional structure, curriculum content and job assignment. Then four decades later, in the 1990s, the same route, though in the opposite direction, was taken to reverse that restructuring. However, back in the 1950s the Soviet restructuring of Chinese education proved effective in overcoming China's serious personnel shortages in many key areas while increasing and widening educational opportunities (Yu, 1994).

A criticism common to all types of educational borrowing is that the model system would itself soon be in a state of transition. After the Sino-Soviet split in 1953, the Soviet model soon fell into disrepute in China. This was partly because the Chinese authorities tried to regain their balance after leaning so heavily 'to one side', and partly because the Soviet Union itself experienced important changes when the 'Stalinist Model' in education and in politics and economy at large were discarded after Stalin's death in 1953.

A principal criticism of Soviet education was against the narrow specialization of undergraduate programmes, especially in engineering. Such narrow specialization was only beneficial in the short term. It then became increasingly dysfunctional when a wider range of integrated skills and technologies were needed after the early stage of industrialization.

The success of Soviet engineering education was accompanied by serious neglect of the humanities and social sciences, which were also narrowly restructured on ideological grounds. Politics, sociology, psychology and anthropology faculties were closed, finance and economics faculties were downsized, and comprehensive universities were disintegrated and severely weakened. The number of comprehensive universities dropped from 49 in 1949 to 13 in 1953, and the proportion of enrolment in the arts dropped from 33.1 per cent in 1949 to 14.9 per cent in 1953, despite the fact that the total enrolment in higher education almost doubled during the same period (Yang, 1995).

The destruction of comprehensive universities had a far-reaching, negative impact on the nature, function and prospect of Chinese education. From the mid-1980s, China began to reconstruct her comprehensive universities through institutional rationalization and reinstallation of arts faculties with rapid enrolment expansion and large-scale investment. Such remedial efforts are indeed necessary, but the task is complex and long and involves much more than capital investment and political will.

It is worth noting that despite the overall 'mechanical copying' of the Soviet system, China managed to revive its unique tradition, the Mandarin examination system, which was reintroduced in 1952 in a 'modern guise' of national college entrance examinations, or *Gaokao*:

> The two [the Chinese and the Soviet] had come together most effectively in the college entrance examinations, which merged Soviet-style economic and

personnel planning with the old Chinese selection procedure to create a new unified enrolment and job assignment mechanism far more rigid than the Soviet counterpart. But this mechanism helped ensure that the restructured tertiary system with its newly designated prestige categories in the applied sciences would overcome inherited intellectual priorities to produce the talent needed for economic development. The mechanism would also go on to become an established feature of Chinese higher education. Restored with alacrity after each of the two massive irregular interruptions[1] to follow. (Pepper, 1996, p. 191)

Historical repetitions are abundant in Chinese higher education. During the first half of the twentieth century the reforms and reconstructions of higher education were generally aiming for China's modernization, but ideological agendas for a specific type of power reconstruction played a more determining role. The task of development was urgent, but the old and new regimes of China seemed to lack preparedness. Hence a foreign model was uncritically imitated by China through a top-down, wholesale approach, while the old model was discarded altogether. Soon the foreign model proved inappropriate, so another new model was introduced. But whatever the nature of the Western models, they were largely operated as a crude transplant in China. During this process, the Confucian and mandarin traditions managed to reproduce themselves under various modern guises, and the problems of the old and new coexisted and mutually reinforced one another.

Foreign educational borrowing in China resumed in the mid-1980s but it remained piecemeal. Contemporary concerns in Chinese education have been with regaining some connection with lessons and experience from the pre-1949 period: how to learn from both the traditional Chinese and latest international, and especially Western, education systems; how to maintain and promote scholarship in the face of financial crisis and marketization; how to balance the elite orientation of key schools while expanding the overall enrolment; how to promote the use of communication and information technology; and how to extend the benefit of higher education to the wider society.

Key Trends in Chinese Education in 1990–2010

China has developed the largest educational system in terms of student enrolment in the world. Entering the twenty-first century China has set itself the goal to transform the Chinese education sector from a big system to a strong system. Chinese education over the past two decades experienced increasing political commitment and funding resources available for a decreasing scale of school-age population. As a result, education attainment and participation achieved unprecedented improvement. This section presents characteristics of the Chinese education systems between 1990 and 2010 in terms of outstanding progress in demographic change, funding, attainment and participation.

Marco demographic and economic trends

As a country with the largest population in the world, China has managed to reduce its population growth under the one-child policy over the past three decades. As a result, while the total population continued to expand at a decelerating rate from 1.16 billion in 1990 to 1.34 billion in 2010, the scale of the school-age 0–14 cohort shrank by about one-third, from 316.6 million (22.7 per cent of the total population) in 1990 to 222.6 million (16.6 per cent of the total population) in 2010 (NSBC, 2011). In contrast, China's labour force of age 15–64 continued to grow in 1990–2010, presenting a 'population surplus'. As a result, the child-age dependency rate went down from 44.5 per cent to 22.3 per cent, signifying a larger labour-active population supporting a smaller dependent youth population. This reflects the larger picture of China's aging population which would not be welcome in the long run. Nonetheless, as far as formal education is concerned, it is a good sign that a smaller school-age population coupled with rising education capacity has led to a rapid increase and widening of education participation.

In the same period, as a country with the most rapid economic growth in the world, with double-digit average annual growth rate, China managed to achieve a twentyfold growth in terms of both gross domestic product (GDP) and GPD per capital. In 1990–2010, China's GDP rose from ¥1871.83 billion to ¥40,326 billion, and GDP per capita from ¥1,644 to ¥29,992. This means that China has generated a growing pool of resources available for education investment, both public and private, in the context of rising demand for boosting education capacity (NBSC, 2011).

Education expenditure

With a booming economy, China's education expenditure also soared since entering the twenty-first century (Figure 1.1). In 2000–10, China's total

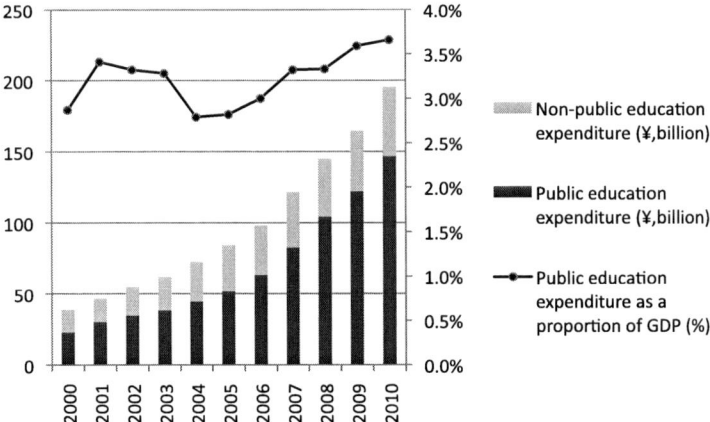

Figure 1.1 Public education expenditure in China, 2000–10

Source: MOE (2001–11).

education expenditure rose five times, from ¥384.91 billion (RMB yuan) to 1956.19 billion, while the public education expenditure rose at a faster rate of 6.4 times, from ¥22.8 billion in 2000 to ¥146.7 billion in 2010. It is worth noting that China's public education expenditure, as a proportion of GDP (per cent), fell in the first half of the decade to hit 2.79 per cent in 2004 before resuming a steady rise, reaching 3.66 per cent in 2010. It is projected to reach 4 per cent in 2012, with the public education expenditure budget of ¥2198.46 billion (Wen, 2012).

From the international perspective, China's attainment of this 4 per cent target in 2012 seems not to be a breakthrough, because in 2007 the OECD average level of public education expenditure as a proportion of GDP had already reached 4.8 per cent, with the USA at 5.0 per cent, the UK, 5.2 per cent, Brazil, 5.2 per cent, and Russian Federation, 6.0 per cent (OECD, 2010a). However, in terms of China's own preformance, reaching the 4 per cent target registers a milestone in education development. This is because the Chinese central government had set the 4 per cent goal by 2000 as early as 1993 in China's *Guidelines of Education Reform and Development*, before making two long decades of effort to achieve it. The difficulty of meeting this goal reflects the fact that China has marked regional and local disparities in economic and educational capacity (*Outlook Weekly*, 2011). Therefore statistics in national average terms are useful to make macro-level international comparisons but less so in terms of understanding the actual situation in China's many different regions.

Education attainment

China's average years of schooling of the age 25+ population grew by 2.7 years, from 4.85 to 7.55, in 1990–2010, representing a growth of 55.7 per cent. This trend is due to the expansion of upper-secondary education as well as that of tertiary education (Figure 1.2). The female age 25+ population in comparison has a lower level of average years of schooling, which rose from 4.42 to 6.87 in the same period. This signifies that China's adult male–female gap in education attainment widened in 1990–2010 from 0.86 years to 1.36 years of schooling (Barro-Lee Data set, 2011).

The two decades of 1990–2010 also witnessed a substantial reduction of illiteracy through the combined efforts the 'two basics': compulsory education and adult literacy education. This trend was accompanied by demographic change as the older, less-educated generations are passing away. China's illiteracy rate for the age 15+ population fell from 15.88 per cent in1990 to 6.72 per cent in 2000, and then to 4.08 per cent in 2010, signifying that China has 125 million fewer illiterate people over two decades (NSBC, 2011). However, in 2010 China still had over 50 million illiterate people, the majority of them being adult females living in poor and remote areas. According to the *Guidelines of China's Female Development (2011–2020)* (State Council, 2011), China aims to reduce illiteracy in the 15–50 age range female population to less than 2 per cent by 2020.

Outstanding progress in secondary and tertiary education in China is well observed in terms of highest education qualifications obtained per 100,000 inhabitants. In China in 1990–2010, people with lower or upper secondary education qualifications almost doubled while people with tertiary education qualifications grew over sixfold (NSBC, 2011).

China is among an increasing number of countries that aim for universal participation in secondary education (UNESCO, 2011). A World Bank study has showed that the social returns[2] on investment in school education are greater than in higher education regardless of the income level of the country (Psacharopoulos and Patrinos, 2002).

The above indicators of educational attainment summarize the rising level of education of the entire adult population in China and reflect the improved structure and performance of the education system and the growing capacity and quality of human capital which is one of the main determinants of economic growth in China.

Education participation

The improvement in education attainment in China reflects dramatic enrolment expansion over the past two decades. For the primary and lower secondary levels, China's ratios lie above 90 per cent, which means, according to UNESCO's standards, that the country is approaching universal access for these particular levels.[3] China's gross enrolment rate at the primary level remained higher than 100 per cent in 2000–10, which can be explained by late entrance and grade repetition.

The gross enrolment ratio at upper secondary level almost doubled, from 38 per cent to 71.3 per cent, while that of the tertiary sector more than tripled from, 8 per cent to 26 per cent (Figure 1.2). However, from the international perspective such levels of participation were still low compared to the most developed countries.

China's enrolment in regular undergraduate programmes has soared since 1999. In 2002, China passed the threshold of 15 per cent of the 18–22-year-old population enrolled in tertiary education (Figure 1.3). This threshold is generally considered to be a move away from an elite system into a mass system of tertiary education (Trow, 1973). China's new enrolment in regular undergraduate programmes achieved an elevenfold expansion in 1990–2010, and the total tertiary enrolment reached 31.05 million in 2010. Looking to the future, China has set the goal to achieve a 40 per cent tertiary gross enrolment rate by 2020. Hence, despite the fact that the cohort of people aged 18–22 will shrink substantially, the numbers of tertiary graduates will be growing in the next decade, though at a slower rate than over the last decade.

With regard to choices of pathways from upper secondary to tertiary education, Chinese students exhibited roughly equal preference for general and

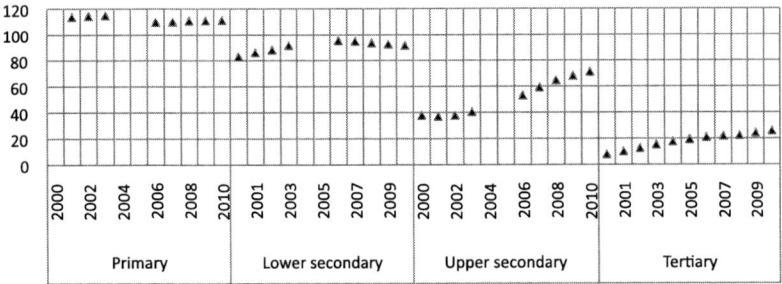

Figure 1.2 Gross enrolment ratio by level of education in China, 2000–10

Source: UNESCO Institute for Statistics (UIS) (2012).

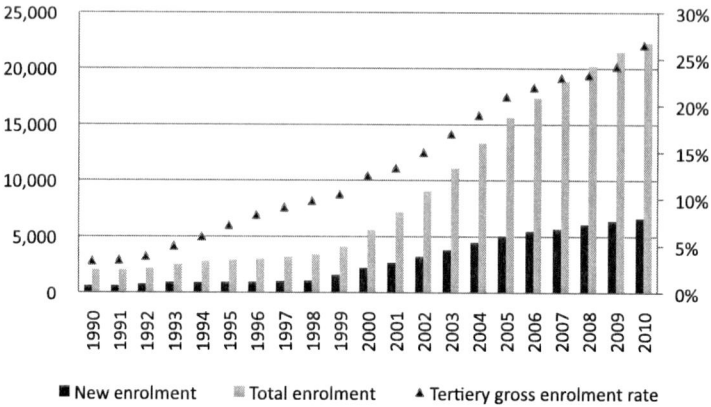

Figure 1.3 Regular undergraduate enrolment in China, 1990–2010 (Thousands)
Source: National Bureau of Statistics of China (1991–2011).

vocational education. In 2010, there were 17 million students in upper secondary education in China, comprising 49 per cent in the general route and 51 per cent in the vocational route. On the other hand there is a much stronger preference for technical studies at tertiary level: 41.6 per cent of Chinese students in tertiary education were enrolled in science and engineering in 2010, while 20.5 per cent were enrolled in management and business-related studies (NBSC, 2011).

From the international perspective, China over the past decade has produced far more graduates in natural and applied sciences, and especially engineering, than any other country in the world (OECD, 2010a). In 2008, the whole world produced 2 million first university degrees in engineering and 1.7 million in natural sciences, while China's share in the two categories were 34 per cent and 17 per cent respectively. This is in contrast to the USA figures of 4 per cent and 10 per cent respectively, and the EU's 17 per cent and 18 per cent respectively (OECD, 2010b).

This brief overview of the key trends in Chinese education in 1990–2010 shows that China has made substantial development in education. However, beyond the numbers lies the question of quality of education and its outcomes. The following section will outline the key challenges faced by education in China.

Key Challenges for Chinese Education, 1990–2010

The exponential growth in Chinese education, in association with economic and social transformation and economic transition, comes with a number of challenges for the education system. These challenges are faced by policy-makers at national and regional level as well as educational institutions themselves, and are affecting the quality and equity of educational outcomes. Ongoing transformations of the education system are not only driven by demographic change, labour market demand and socioeconomic pressure within China, but also by the increasing competitive 'race for talent' across the world (Ulicna et al., 2011). Current education reforms in China aim at making effective use of increased public budgets in education and eventually the need to enhance quality and safeguard equity.

General education

Developing a competence-based approach

China's political commitment to moving from a knowledge-based, examination-oriented education system towards a competence-based system dates back to the 1990s (State Council, 1993, 1999). From the late 1990s, China embarked on a new round of systematic national curriculum reform that has lasted to the present day. This curriculum reform was designed to move away from learning based on memorization of subject-specific knowledge towards the type of learning that encourages the holistic development of students for the twenty-first century (Yan and Ehrich 2009). A key feature of this reform is replacing a common set of national textbooks for the national curriculum. Instead, regional and local government and individual schools are given the autonomy to choose their own textbooks. The objectives, structure, content, delivery, assessment and management of this new curricular approach has adopted many internationally comparable ideas that are at the forefront of educational thinking.

In line with this reform, *Gaokao*, or the National Entrance Examination to Colleges and Universities, has also undergone reform in both structure and content to focus more on testing problem-solving capacity. Education in China has long been criticized for its narrow focus on examination content and examination skills at the expanse of fostering creativity, critical thinking and vocational skills (Zhang and Zhao, 2005; World Bank, 1999). This is because progression in the Chinese education system from as early as kindergarten through to postgraduate education is still largely determined by strongly competitive examinations. Education is therefore still dominated by examinations. As a result, the Chinese teaching style is largely teacher-centred, sometimes described as a 'spoon-feed model' – and this applies also to different levels of education (Wang and Morgan, 2009). Learning is still often limited to listening to lectures, reading and learning by heart. Curricula, tests and examinations concentrate on the knowledge of facts. Topics are taught one by one, with a relatively narrow scope, often at the expense of interdisciplinary implications, soft skills, complex work processes or the economic, social and environmental context of professional work. Again, such contemporary characteristics of Chinese education are deeply rooted in long Confucian traditions.

China's national curriculum reform is a long-term process. It needs to embrace teacher development, especially in terms of updating teaching methods and the concepts of student competences and skills required in the twenty-first century. At the same time, China is actively learning from international experience and is quickly building up its capacity to monitor student achievement from local to national level. The OECD Programme for International Student Assessment (PISA) in 2009 was China's debut in international standardized testing. Only Shanghai (in fact about 5,100 15-year-olds chosen as a representative cross-section of students of the city), participated in PISA (SAES, 2010). The result was that Shanghai outscored all other counterparts in more than 60 countries and regions across the world, in reading as well as in mathematics and science. A recent OECD study shows that Shanghai's success in PISA is due to a series of educational innovations:

> … the [Shanghai] government's abandonment of a system built around 'key schools' for a small elite and its development of a more inclusive system in which all students are expected to perform at high levels; greatly raising teacher pay and upgrading teacher standards and teacher education; reducing the emphasis on rote learning and increasing the emphasis on deep understanding; the ability to apply knowledge to solving new problems and the ability to think creatively. All of these are reflected in deep reforms to the curriculum and examinations. These changes have been accompanied by greater curricular choice for students and more latitude for local authorities to decide on examination content, which in turn is loosening the constraints on curriculum and instruction. (OECD, 2010b, p. 83)

However, Shanghai is by no means representative of all of China. Located in the most developed region in China, Shanghai is an industrial and financial powerhouse and a magnet for the best talents in the country. Shanghai's 20 million residents enjoy direct access to some of the nation's best schools and universities located in that city. To a large extent, Shanghai exhibits the way forward for reform and development in Chinese education as a whole. However, the privileged conditions that Shanghai enjoys are beyond the reach of the majority of Chinese regions except for a small number of powerful cities. A main challenge is how to enable the less developed parts of China to participate in innovations to enhance both quality and equity in education. There are several key issues to be faced in ensuring equity in opportunity and achievement.

- A main challenge to educational equity in China concerns the interconnected issues of access to upper secondary education and to tertiary education. Education institutions from kindergartens to universities in China are highly hierarchical in terms of academic merits, financial resources, and social and cultural capital. Key upper secondary schools and key universities in China have become increasingly interdependent on each other and more influential in society since the late 1990s. This is mainly due to China's efforts towards the massification of tertiary education and building towards more world-class universities.

- Competence-based education is often provided by 'key schools' in China. Access to key schools is closely related to school choice mechanisms and associated family expenditure. This is putting significant financial burdens on working-class families. The recent decade has seen a flourishing marketplace with intensified competition for places in secondary and, more recently, even in primary and pre-primary schools in urban China (Yang, 2006). Key schools have built up an 'education economy' by attracting talented and/or rich students from other cities or provinces, leaving students in local catchment areas in growing competition for already limited places. This is the Chinese version of market-oriented school choice policies in Western nations, but is even more thoroughgoing, creating growing disparities and tensions (Zhong, 2005). This creates inequality in education expenditure as well as gaps in provision as certain children whose parents cannot afford such school choice fees are left behind (Wu, 2009; Bray, 2009). Moreover, a major criticism of the students in key schools is that they are made into a distinctive elite, most of which tend to lose touch with the rest of the youth in the same age group and society at large (Zang, 2001).

- In consequence, equal access to tertiary education is preconditioned by access to key schools at secondary down to pre-primary stages. Students from high-income families, from families where parents have received at least upper secondary education, and from urban areas are over-represented among higher education students, while young women from rural areas are under-represented (Huang, 2005). It is also alarming to note that there are fewer students from rural areas participating in leading universities and in higher education in general.

Moreover, China also faces the challenge to increase the attainment of upper secondary education qualifications. In terms of participation, the progression rate from lower to upper secondary schools in China in 2009 was 85.6 per cent, signifying an influx of at least 2.67 million young people into the labour market with only lower secondary education qualifications (NBSC, 2010). China has set a goal to provide universal access (90 per cent) to upper secondary education by 2020. The main strategies to achieve this goal involve expanding and diversifying both general and vocational upper secondary education and strengthening the provision of vocational education in general schools.

Vocational education and training

Enhancing attractiveness and connecting tertiary education

As Chinese education is dominated by the academic-oriented *Gaokao* system, vocation education today, as well as in the past, has a poor image in China. It is difficult to recruit students. Well performing students will opt for the general pathway. Vocational education is regarded as a last resort for those who cannot make their way to higher levels of general education. In this context, maintaining and even increasing the interest and morale of young people in vocational learning pathways is one of the challenges of vocational education in China. As China has developed into a 'world factory' over the past two decades, there is an increasing need to equip people with medium-level qualifications. Moreover, there are also shortages of qualified blue-collar workers in a number of sectors because a growing number of elementary occupations tend to require medium-level qualifications. In this sense, having a vocational qualification in a number of fields is a better guarantee for access to the labour market than having only a general education qualification or incomplete higher education.

As part of the attractiveness of vocational education, it is important to ensure that young people who opt for these pathways are able to continue their studies in higher education if they wish to do so. Otherwise they may prefer general education pathways that do not constitute a termination of formal education.

Vocational colleges are new to the Chinese labour market even today. The vocational tertiary sector began with 120 institutions across China in the 1980s. The 1990s has witnessed increasing awareness and willingness to support the development of vocational colleges, and the 2000s has seen dramatic growth in the scale of vocational education both in terms of its enrolment and the number of institutions. In this way China's tertiary education has quickly become a bipartite system comprising two roughly equal halves of general and vocational sub-sectors. For example, in 2005 China had 1091 vocational tertiary colleges, representing 60.9 per cent of tertiary education institutions. New and total enrolment in vocational tertiary education reached 5 million and 15.6 million respectively, representing 53.1 per cent and 45.7 per cent respectively of total regular undergraduate education (MOE, 2006).

The expansion in vocational tertiary education is driven by both labour market demand and innovations in student recruitment mechanisms to create flexible and transparent pathways into vocational tertiary education from both general and vocational secondary education. China began to explore alternative pathways into tertiary vocational education besides *Gaokao* since the second half of the 2000s. In 2007 China first allowed four provinces in eastern and southern China to pilot their own province-wide entrance examinations, and only eight selected national key vocational colleges in those regions could recruit students based on new types of entrance examinations. In 2010, the pilot project expanded to provide 25,505 places in 73 vocational colleges in China (XinhuaNet, 2010a). In scale it only touched a tiny fraction (1 per cent) of new enrolment in vocational tertiary education. However, the vocational colleges involved represent the top institutions in their fields and are the future direction of vocational education reform and development in China.

The new examinations focus on vocational and technical aspects of knowledge and skills are outside the scope of *Gaokao*. They have less academic content and lower academic standards. In the new examinations the student chooses one of 13 specialized examinations such as business and management, building sciences, or agriculture, in addition to general subjects such as Chinese, English and mathematics. In comparison, *Gaokao* just has two categories, arts and sciences, in addition to general subjects. So far the students can only apply for those selected vocational colleges within their own province, but if they do not obtain an offer they can still opt to take *Gaokao* and use its scores to apply for all other vocational colleges in China.

Moreover, a growing number of vocational colleges have also obtained permission from regional governments to recruit students directly from vocational secondary schools and adult learners already in employment through institutional-based examinations. Looking into the future, many regions are using their autonomy and creativity to design new policies such as open enrolment to vocational tertiary education available for all people with general or vocational upper secondary qualifications (*China Education Daily*, 2012).

At present, however, general upper secondary schools and *Gaokao* still form the main pathway to both academic and vocational tertiary education. In this context, the students applying for vocational colleges are still those who performed poorly in *Gaokao*, because with higher scores they may well apply directly to general universities or colleges. Therefore a main challenge here is that the general upper secondary schools are under increasing pressure to diversify their curriculum and provide more vocational preparation for students to be admitted into vocational colleges.

Teacher quality is another issue which undermines the attractiveness of vocational education in China. Vocational schools and colleges require teachers to have double competences in both teaching and professional expertise and experience in industry. Such teachers are in serious shortage in China (MOE, 2011a). It is currently difficult for good teachers to develop from within the vocational education sector. At the same time the different orientation of the general education system means that its graduates are unsuitable to teach in vocational schools and colleges, of which they themselves have little personal experience. The income and social status of vocational schools make its teaching posts relatively unattractive.

Among the latest responses to such teacher shortages, the Ministry of Education and Ministry of Finance of China jointly put forward a comprehensive *Plan to Enhance the Competence of Teachers in Vocational Education* in 2011 (MOE, 2011b). The plan set the key tasks as a) to establish a national network of centres of excellence for teacher education and training for vocational education in both vocational colleges and enterprises; b) to invest in the infrastructure of those centres; c) to develop 100 sets of innovative undergraduate-level teacher education programmes targeted at vocational education (including developing educational plans, core curricula and related textbooks and learning materials); d) to provide nationwide professional upgrades for 450,000 in 2011–15; e) and to provide fellowships for 20,000 young teachers to have short-term working experience in industry and personnel from industry to teach in vocational institutions. The implementation of the plan was backed up by strong political commitment, a large sum of concentrated investment over the first five-year phase, systematic action plans and a series of mutually supported policies. As a first step, in June 2012 China launched the first group of such national centres in 33 vocational colleges and two large-scale enterprises (MOE, 2012). It remains a challenge to develop more industry-based national teacher development centres, and align those centres with corresponding centres in vocational colleges and also with other types of government-accredited, industrial-based national centres, such as national innovation centres and enterprise technology development centres.

Higher education

Creating excellence by greater autonomy and strengthening quality

The quantitative growth of Chinese higher education has raised a quality issue. As more and more students are recruited to universities, there is a concern that lower standards will be applied, allowing less able students to enter. The ability of universities to maintain their quality standards while absorbing so many students is seen as problematical. Universities have experienced difficulties with recruiting qualified professors and the average class size has been increasing accordingly. The quality issue has been taken on board by the Chinese government, as illustrated by the Higher Education Teaching and Learning Quality and Reform Project launched by the MOE in 2003 and which will last until 2020.

In China, the American model of university is being adopted in research-intensive universities and research-teaching universities. The focus here is on research rather than teaching, and it has seen increasing drawbacks in terms of compromising teaching quality (Shi and Englert, 2008). At the same time the quest for world-class status goes hand in hand with the internationalization of Chinese higher education. Top universities have concentrated their efforts on attracting talents, especially from overseas, as well as accelerating the international mobility of their students and scholars (Ulcina et al., 2011).

Another major challenge in Chinese higher education is institutional autonomy (XinhuaNet, 2010b). Although the Chinese higher education system had been restructured towards greater autonomy in the 1990s, the Chinese Ministry of Education is still responsible for the direct administration of more than 70 key universities which restricts the autonomy of institutions. In addition, the government is responsible for the accreditation of academic programmes and for the organization of a large number of key research projects leading to the delivery of awards. These are used as a basis for the promotion of scholars, so universities have strong incentives to maintain good relationships with government officials. Moreover, internally, university autonomy is closely related to academic freedom. In many universities and colleges in China, the balance between faculties and administrative staff tend not to favour the academic community (Ngok, 2008). Key decisions regarding the admission of students, curricula, content of the examinations, promotion of academic staff and allocation of resources all lie in the hands of non-academic staff or of professors with senior administrative titles.

China's bid to build world-class universities began in 1998, at the centennial celebration of Peking University, when the Chinese government initiated Project 985. This project concentrated an unprecedentedly large amount of funding from central and regional government to strengthen the best of China's national research universities, with the aim of building world-class excellence (Zhong, 2010).

In 1998–2011, the two phrases of Project 985 provided a concentrated investment of ¥30 billion to 39 of China's leading universities. There are three tiers of excellence with matched levels of funding support in Project 985: a) world-class status – Peking University and Tsinghua University, each with ¥1.8 billion from the MOE; b) first class in China, and world renowned – seven universities, each with ¥0.9 to ¥1.4 billion from both the MOE and their regional governments; c) first class in China, and with an international reputation – the remaining universities, each with ¥0.3 to ¥1.2 billion jointly provided by the MOE and their regional governments.

The two plus seven universities in the first two tiers comprise the C9 group, a Chinese version of the USA Ivy League or the UK Russell Group. The formal establishment of the C9 group in 2009 has been welcomed by Chinese public opinion. Its central idea of building China's world-class universities has been well supported by both government and society. Many challenges remain, however, such as how to share the benefits of the C9 with other universities in China, and how to make Project 985 sustainable.

At the same time as Chinese higher education has been in a dramatic expansion since 1999, the government alone no longer has adequate means to finance the whole system, as it did during the previous phase when higher education engaged fewer students. Consequently, tuition fees have soared, and this means increased financial burdens on individuals and their families. There has been a growing need for student loans, grants or scholarships in China, which are often beyond the availability and desirability of national student loan schemes introduced in 1999 (Shen, 2009). Moreover, an equity issue arose relating to the decentralization policy, as poorer regions and provinces encountered difficulties in attracting investment in their higher education systems.

Enhancing graduate employability

In China, the growing numbers of university graduates have made the transition from school to work less smooth. In 2009, China had 5.3 million graduates emerging from undergraduate general higher education. According to one study, more than 30 per cent of those graduates failed to find a job after graduation in 2009. This was mainly due to skills mismatch and the inappropriate expectations of graduates (*Southern Weekly*, 2006). Moreover, unemployment is lower for graduates from China's top universities. This means that as participation in higher education increases, a major fault line in social stratification is shifting from between secondary and higher education to within higher education, that is, between the top universities and the rest.

Another challenge for the Chinese education system is that there are various employers placing different demands on the education system, including Chinese employers (state-owned enterprises and private domestic employers), foreign-owned enterprises and joint ventures. Organizations seeking skills for global competition, such as foreign-owned enterprises and joint ventures, appear most dissatisfied with Chinese graduates, as they want 'work-ready' graduates with prior work experience. On the other hand, Chinese employers tend to value 'appropriate attitudes and aptitudes' and assigned a low rating to 'work experience'. However, they also valued 'problem solving and creativity' which can be explained by a higher exposure to international markets (Velde, 2009).

In this context, Chinese higher education today shares many challenges that face higher education in general across the world, such as, a) enhancing quality and equity in a massified system while creating a tier of world-class universities and centres of excellence; b) creating an appropriate teaching–research balance, as well as an academic–administrative balance; c) encouraging internationalization through greater mobility, graduate unemployment and underemployment; and d) funding diversification. On top of all these challenges is China's unique challenge of reforming the *Gaokao* system in such a way as to foster creativity throughout the education sector while maintaining the tradition and significance of *Gaokao* in Chinese society and culture.

Looking Forward to Chinese Education in 2020

China's latest national strategy for education system reform and development is set in the *National Outline for Medium and Long Term Educational Reform and*

Development (2010–2020). It was put forward by the State Council in July 2010 after in-depth debate and consultation.[4] The *Outline* is China's first national plan for medium and long-term education reform and development in the twenty-first century, taking into account the full lifelong learning spectrum, spanning pre-school education and workplace learning for adults. Based on a critical assessment of the entire education system in China, the *Outline* put forward a series of themes that are rather unconventional in the Chinese context but which were broadly welcomed. For example, the *Outline* gives a strong emphasis to individual needs in learning, institutional autonomy and academic freedom in higher education. It advocates reducing the homework load for primary and secondary students, while experimenting with comprehensive senior secondary schools to provide both general and vocational education. Free secondary vocational education and admission to higher vocational education through national rather than regional entrance examinations is on the agenda. This enables public funding to support non-government kindergartens, and raises the portion of public expenditure on education to 4 per cent of GDP in 2012. Table 1.1 presents selected targets for all levels of education and training as set in the *Outline*.

Both Chinese society and the international community commended the *Outline's* focus on both quality and equity of education and the need for educational innovation in the context of rapidly changing economic and social conditions in China and the world at large. Among a diversity of themes that have sustained continuous debates since the formal publication of the *Outline*, one of the major issues has been international transparency and comparability of the goals and targets set in the document. It is suggested by both Chinese and international experts that those goals and targets be brought in line with international definitions such as those in UNESCO's Global Monitoring Reports, and that more detail be provided, such as how the goal of 4 per cent of GDP for investment in education should be allocated across the different levels and types of education and across regions and localities. In order to enable better monitoring and comparison of China's educational progress in the international context, it is also suggested that more systematic educational data be provided in a more timely fashion. How to utilize the goals and targets to support research and evidence building for policy and programme delivery should be clarified, and knowledge exchange to bring in global ideas and showcase China's experiences to the world should be promoted.

With regard to the targets and priorities set by the *Outline*, it is clear that Chinese education is heading towards a lifelong learning for all, with a real

Table 1.1 Selected major targets for China's education development from 2009 to 2020 (millions and percentage)

	2009	2015	2020
Pre-school education			
Total enrolment	26.6 m	34 m	40 m
3-year gross attendance rate	50.9%	60.0%	70.0%
1-year gross attendance rate	74.0%	85.0%	90.0%
9-year compulsory education			
Total enrolment	157.7 m	161 m	165 m
Retention rate of students	90.8%	93.5%	95.0%
Senior secondary education			
Total enrolment	46.2 m	45 m	47 m
Gross enrolment rate	79.2%	87.0%	90.0%
Vocational education			
Total enrolment in secondary vocational education	21.8 m	22.5 m	23.5 m
Total enrolment in higher vocational education	12.8 m	13.9 m	14.8 m
Higher education (including both general and vocational routes)			
Total enrolment	29.8 m	33.5 m	35.5 m
Gross enrolment rate	24.2%	36.0%	40.0%
Continuing education			
Number of on-the-job learners	166 m	290 m	350 m
China workforce			
Average years of education for new workforce	12.4 years	13.3 years	13.5 years
Proportion of new workforce who received upper secondary or higher education	67.0%	87.0%	90.0%
Number of people with higher education qualifications	98.3 m	145 m	195 m

Source: State Council (2010).

'step-change' in awareness of and access to pre-school education, a strong basic education for all, at least an upper secondary qualification for the vast majority of the workforce, a large proportion of highly qualified young people, and an increase in adult participation in continuing education and training.

In conclusion, Chinese education has made significant progress over the past two decades. At the same time, it is as much a product of Chinese society as a contributor as the Chinese education system continues to transform and be transformed. In addition, Chinese education has sustained certain features which exert both positive and negative influence in the building of a strong education system for the twenty-first century, which some predict will be 'China's century' (Brahm, 2001; Liu, 2010; Kissinger et al., 2011).

References

Barro-Lee Data set (2011). *Country Profile of China*. http://www.barrolee.com/

Borthwick, S. (1983). *Education and social change in China: the beginnings of the modern era*. Stanford, CA: Hoover Institution Press.

Brahm, L. J. (ed.) (2001). *China's Century: The Awakening of the Next Economic Powerhouse*. Chichester: Wiley.

Bray, M. (2009). *Confronting the Shadow Education System: What Government Policies for What Private Tutoring?* Paris: UNESCO-IIEP, p. 130.

China Education Daily (2012). 'Diversified pathways: reforms in student recruitment mecahnisms in vocational higher education'. 10 March.

Cressey, P. F. (1931). 'The Influence of Civil Service Examination on Chinese Culture'. Translated into Chinese by Z. Lei. *Journal of Historical Studies*, 1(1).

De Bary, W. T., Bloom, I. and Adler, J. (1960). *Sources of Chinese Tradition*. New York: Columbia University Press, p. 15.

Elman, B. A. (2000). *A Cultural History of Civil Examinations in Late Imperial China*. Berkeley, CA: University of California Press.

Flynn, J. F. (1991). *Asian Americans: Achievement Beyond IQ*. Hillsdale, NJ: Erlbaum.

He, Bingdi (1962). *The Ladder of Success in Imperial China: Aspects of Social Mobility, 1368-1911*. New York: Columbia University Press.

He, Zhongli (2009). *History of Civil Service Examination in South Song Dynasty*. Beijing: People's Publishing House.

Huang, Lihong (2005). *Elitism and Equality in Chinese Higher Education: Studies of Student Socio-economic Background, Investment in Education, and Career Aspirations*. Stockholm: Institute of International Education, Stockholm University.

Jin, Zheng (1990). *Civil Service Examinations and Chinese Culture*. Shanghai: Shanghai People Press.

Kim, K. D. (1988). 'The Distinctive Features of South Korea's Development', in P. L. Berger and H. M. Hsiao (eds), *Search of an East Asian Development Model*. New Bruswick: Transaction Publishers, pp. 197–219.

Kissinger, Henry, Ferguson, Niall, Li, David Daokui and Zakaria, Fareed (2011). *Does the 21st Century Belong to China?: The Munk Debate on China*. Toronto: House of Anansi Press.

Kracke, E. A. (1957). 'Religion, Family and Individual in the Chinese Examination System', in John K. Fairbank (ed.), *Chinese Thought and Institutions*. Chicago: University of Chicago Press, pp. 252–68.

League of Nations' Mission Educational Experts (1932). *The Reorganisation of Education in China.* Paris: League of Nations' Institute of Intellectual Co-operation.

Li, Xinghua (ed.) (1997). *History of Education in Republican China.* Shanghai: Shanghai Educational Publishing House.

Liu, Haifeng (1996). *Chinese Civil Service Examination and its Educational Dimensions.* Wuhan: Hubei Educational Publishing House.

—(2002). 'Multi-disciplinary perspectives on civil service examination system'. *Journal of Xiamen University (Philosophy and Social Sciences Edition)*, 6: 19–26.

Liu, Tao (2010). *China's Century.* Beijing: Xinhua Publishing House.

Miyazaki, I. (1981). *China's Examination Hell: the Civil Service Examinations of Imperial China.* Translated by Conrad Schirokauer. New Haven, CT: Yale University Press.

Ministry of Education (MOE) (2001–11). *Statistics of Education Expenditure in China, 2000–2010.* Ministry of Education, China.

—(2006). *Educational Statistics Yearbook of China 2006.* Beijing: People's Education Publishing House.

—(2011a). *The MOE's Policy to further improve teacher education and training system for vocational education, Department of Vocational and Adult Education [2011]16.* Ministry of Education, China, 24 December.

—(2011b). *The Plan to Enhance the Competence of Teachers in Vocational Education, Department of Vocational and Adult Education [2011]14.* Ministry of Education, China, 21 November.

—(2012). *MOE approved to establish 33 national centers of excellence for faculty development for vocational colleges.* Ministry of Education, China, 18 June.

National Bureau of Statistics of China (NBSC) (2010). *China Statistical Yearbook 2009.* Beijing: China Statistics Press.

—(2011). *China Statistical Yearbook 2011.* Beijing: China Statistics Press.

Ngok, Kinglun (2008). 'Massification, bureaucratization and questing for 'world-class' status Higher education in China since the mid-1990s'. *International Journal of Educational Management*, 22 (6): 547–64.

OECD (2010a). *Education at a Glance 2010: OECD Indicators.* Paris: OECD.

—(2010b). *Strong Performers and Successful Reformers in Education: Lessons from PISA for the United States.* Paris: OECD.

Oh, Su-Ann (2001). *From 'Ivory Tower' to 'Knowledge Factory'?: the impact of university–industry links on universities in China and England.* DPhil thesis, University of Oxford.

Outlook Weekly (2011). 'Why the goal of public education expenditure 4% of GDP is difficult to reach'. http://www.edu.cn/zong_he_429/20110315/t20110315_588092. shtml (Accessed 15 March 2011).

Pepper, S. (1987). 'New directions in education', in R. MacFarquhar and J. K. Fairbank (eds), *Cambridge History of China.* Cambridge: Cambridge University Press, pp. 197, 398–431.

—(1996). *Radicalism and Education Reform in 20th Century China*. Cambridge: Cambridge University Press, p. 191.

Psacharopoulos, George and Patrinos, Harry (2002). *Returns to Investment in Education: A Further Update* (Vol. 2881). Washington, DC: World Bank.

Rankin, M. B. (1971). *Early Chinese Revolutions: Radical Intellectuals in Shanghai and Chekiang, 1902–1911*. Cambridge, MA: Harvard University Press.

SAES (Shanghai Academy of Educational Sciences) (2010). *Shanghai completed PSIA 2009*. http://www.cnsaes.org/homepage/html/SHPISA/SHPISAnews/432.html (Accessed 8 February 2010).

Shen, Hong (2009). 'Access to higher education by student aid in China: results from the national survey of 100,000 students'. *Evaluation & Research in Education*, 22 (2): 145–66.

Shen, Zhihua (2009). *Soviet Experts in China (1948–1960)*. Beijing: Xinhua Publishing House.

Shi, Xiaoguang and Englert, Peter (2008). 'Reform of teacher education in China'. *Journal of Education for Teaching*, 34 (4): 347–59.

Southern Weekly (2006). 'An in-depth study of College graduates job hunting in 2006'. 6 April.

State Council (1993). *Guidelines of China's Educational Reform and Development*. State Council of China. 13 February.

—(1999). *Decision on Deepening Education Reform and Promoting System-wide Quality Education*. State Council of China, 13 June.

—(2010). *National Outline for Medium and Long Term Educational Reform and Development (2010–2020)*. State Council of China, 27 July.

—(2011). *Guidelines of China's Female Development (2011–2020)*. State Council of China, 30 July.

Sun, E. T. Z. (1986). 'The growth of the academic community 1912–1949', in J. K. Fairbank and A. Feuerwerker (eds), *The Cambridge History of China, Vol. 13, Republican China 1912–1949, Part 2*. Cambridge: Cambridge University Press.

Trow, M. (1973). 'Problems in the Transition from Elite to Mass Higher Education'. *Policies for Higher Education: General Report on the Conference on Future Structures of Post-Secondary Education*. Paris: OECD, pp. 55–101.

Ulicna, D., Zhong, Z., Irving, P., Li, Y., Mathis, J., Feng, L.Y., Bonneau, M., Guan, L. S., Cao, Y. and Jin, Y. Y. (2011). *EU and China: Race for Talent Relevance and Responsiveness of Education and Training – Joint Study of the European Commission and Ministry of Education of China*. Written by GHK Consulting and Tsinghua University. http://ec.europa.eu/education/external-relation-programmes/china_en.htm

UNESCO (2011). *Global Education Digest 2011: Comparing Education Statistics across the World*. UNESCO. http://unesdoc.unesco.org/images/0017/001787/178740e.pdf

UNESCO Institute for Statistics (UIS) (2012). *UNESCO Institute for Statistics Data Centre*. http://stats.uis.unesco.org/

Velde C. (2009). 'Employers' perceptions of graduate competencies and future trends in higher vocational education in China'. *Journal of Vocational Education and Training*, 61 (1), March: 35–51.

Volet, S. and Remshaw, P. (1996). 'Chinese students at an Australian University: adaptability and continuity', in D. A. Watkins and J. B. Biggs (eds), *The Chinese Learner: Culture, Psychological and Contextual Influences*. Hong Kong: University of Hong Kong.

Wang, Naixia and Morgan, John W. (2009). 'Student motivations, quality and status in adult higher education (AHE) in China'. *International Journal of Lifelong Education*, 28 (4), July–August: 473–91.

Wang, Y. (1966). *Chinese intellectuals and the West, 1872–1949*. Chapel Hill, NC: University of North Carolina Press.

Wen, J. (2012). *Report on the Work of the Government*. Delivered at the Fifth Session of the Eleventh National People's Congress on 5 March 2012 by Wen Jiabao, Premier of the State Council of China.

World Bank (1999). *Strategic goals for Chinese education in the 21st century*. Washington, DC: World Bank.

Wu, G. (2002). *Knowledge Evolution and Social Control: A Comparative Sociological Analysis of History of Education and Knowledge of China*. Beijing: Education Science Publisher.

Wu, X. (2009). 'The power of positional competition and market mechanism: an empirical study of parental choice of junior middle school in Nanning'. *P.R. China in Research Papers in Education*, 26 (1), March: 79–104.

XinhuaNet (2010a). *73 National key vocational colleges pilot new entrance examination in 2010*. http://news.xinhuanet.com/edu/2010-04/01/content_13281334.htm (Accessed 1 April 2010).

XinhuaNet (2010b). *Wen Jiabao: university should have institutional autonomy*. http://news.xinhuanet.com/edu/2010-02/02/content_12917065_3.htm (Accessed 2 February 2012).

Yan, W. and Ehrich, L. C. (2009). 'Principal preparation and training: a look at China and its issues'. *International Journal of Educational Management*, 23 (1): 51–64.

Yang, D. P. (1995). 'The university: intellectual reconstruction and institutional innovation'. *The Orient*, 1.

—(2006). *Ideal and Reality of Education Equity in China*. Beijing: Peking University Press.

Yang, J. (2004). 'Modernisation of women's education in Shanghai', in Chengxian Du and Gang Ding (eds), *Modernisation of Chinese Education in the 20th Century*. Shanghai: Shanghai Educational Publishing House.

Yu, L. W. (1994). *History of Chinese Higher Education* (Vol. 2). Shanghai: East China Normal University Press.

Yuan, Q. (2001). *John Dewey and China*. Beijing: People's Press.

Zang, X. W. (2001). 'Educational credentials, elite dualism and elite stratification in China'. *Sociological Perspectives*, 44 (2): 189–205.

Zhang, W. C. and Zhao, Y. D. (2005). *The Transformation of Regional Innovation System in Western China: A Case Study on Small and Medium Sized Enterprises*. Paper presented at the 5th Triple Helix Conference, Toruin, 18–21 May 2005.

Zhong, Z. (2005). *A Critical Analysis of Chinese Higher Education in the Context of its Contribution to China's Development*. DPhil thesis, University of Oxford, 2005.

—(2010). 'Beijing banks on C9 to break into higher education's elite'. *QS Showcase Asia 2010*. QS WorldClass Asia. http://www.qsshowcase.com/asia/

Notes

1   'Two massive irregular interruptions' refer to the Great Leap Forward (1958–60) and the Great Proletarian Cultural Revolution (1966–76).

2   According to Psacharopoulos and Patrinos (2002), social returns are defined on the basis of private benefits and total (private plus external) costs, because typical social rate of return estimates do not include social benefits.

3   Assuming there are enough places for the pupils from the expected age-group and that overaged pupils are not over-represented

4   The *Outline* publication followed about two years of drafting in 2008–10, five rounds of high-level consultations chaired by the Chinese premier, and two rounds of wide public consultations that received 1.1 million feedbacks.

2

China: The Role of Independent Colleges in the Expanding Higher Education System

Kai Yu and Hubert Ertl

Introduction

In 2008, the number of students studying in higher education in China reached 29 million, representing a 23 per cent participation rate of the 18–22-year-olds (Ministry of Education, 1978–2009), increasing from the 9 per cent participation rate in 1998. In quantitative terms, during this period the country experienced a dramatic shift from 'elite' to 'mass' higher education as classified by Trow (1973), and an unprecedented expansion of opportunities for people to participate in higher education.

With the rapid expansion in student numbers came the introduction of a new type of the degree-granting institution. Since 2000 over 300 new independent colleges have been created. During the same period, 172 existing public and private vocational colleges have been promoted to the *Benke* (the academic track of undergraduate education) level, and dozens of existing public *Benke* colleges have been granted university status (Ministry of Education, 1978–2009).

The high fee levels charged at independent colleges – at least double the level of public universities and colleges – make independent colleges an expensive option. The lower overall prestige of these institutions compared to their less expensive parent public institutions cannot justify the high level of tuitions. This raises questions that have not been systematically addressed in the literature, about who actually attends these independent colleges. This chapter aims to provide some insights into these issues, through the exploratory study of one case independent institution and through comparing the case institution with three other public and private institutions on students' characteristics. It will examine whether the independent colleges differ from other types of institutions on the student body. This exploratory study concludes with suggestions for future research.

Given their institutional set-up, independent colleges in China can be regarded as one particular way in which private money is brought into the higher education sector; a challenge faced by many systems around the world. The foundation of independent colleges also represents an example of a government-led reaction to rapidly expanding demand for higher education places – a phenomenon that can be observed in other countries with rapidly growing economies (Altbach, 1999; Levy, 1986b). Therefore, the lessons that can be learnt from the investigation of independent colleges in China seem relevant internationally.

Setting the Scene: The Diversity of Institutions

The Chinese higher education system is complex and comprises various types of institution that offer these study tracks. In this context, the university status/college status distinction is long established. In 2009, 337 of the 770 registered *Benke* institutions were named as 'universities' and 433 as 'colleges' (including public and private institutions, but not independent colleges) (Ministry of Education, 2009a). Whereas a university is usually accredited for postgraduate and doctoral studies, and has a longer history and offers a more comprehensive range of subjects in general, most colleges are only accredited for teaching undergraduate students and focus on particular subjects (State Council, 2002).

However, the distinction according to ownership is a much more recent phenomenon. In China, at present, the ownership of higher education institutions that can enrol *Benke* students can be categorized into three groups: *Gongban* (public), *Minban* (private) and *Duli* (independent). In the public category, there are public universities and colleges, but so far only colleges are in the private and independent categories because no private or independent college has been approved to offer postgraduate education (with the exception of a few international postgraduate programmes).

A main difference between public and non-public institutions is that public institutions receive general funding from government while non-public institutions do not. Public institutions also collect tuition fees from students (at levels set by the government). Private higher education institutions have been re-emerging since the 1980s, and today they have a significant market share in

Zhuanke (the vocational track of undergraduate education) education but are still marginal players in the *Benke* market. Most of the independent and private colleges rely almost exclusively on tuition fees as income.

The development of independent colleges

Another new type of higher education institution, the independent college, was introduced in 2000 as a measure to increase the supply of higher education places quickly. The underpinning philosophy was that by combining the prestige and teachers of public institutions and the investment of private enterprise, large numbers of high-quality institutions could be established in a short period of time and therefore provide a large quantity of student places. It is also considered as a way of allowing private forces to invest in higher education. These independent colleges are established under the name of a prestigious *Mutixuexiao*, or (public) parent institutions, but with private funding; the *Mutixuexiao* may share its teachers and equipment with its independent college to enhance the independent college's academic expertise. Since all the initial investment and daily running costs come from private sources, rather than public expenditure, independent colleges do not receive governmental funding and therefore can be considered 'quasi-private'. They are allowed to charge variable tuition fees, not limited by the restrictions applicable to public institutions (Yang, 2003). Through individual arrangements, independent colleges usually pay the *Mutixuexiao* and their private investors a pre-agreed amount or percentage from the tuition fee income or operating surplus to make financial returns to the *Mutixuexiao* and investors.

In 2008, 20 per cent of the undergraduate students in China were enrolled in non-public institutions. This figure had doubled since 2004. Of the 20 per cent of students studying in non-public institutions, about half were studying in independent institutions while the other half were studying in private institutions. Most of the students at independent institutions were studying *Benke* programmes while most students in private institutions were studying *Zhuanke* programmes. *Benke* students constituted 84 per cent of the student population in independent institutions but only constituted 10 per cent in private institutions (Yu, Stith, Liu and Chen, 2010), this is primarily because only a small fraction of the private tertiary institutions are accredited to offer *Benke* programmes. On the other hand, most independent institutions are accredited to offer *Benke* programmes.

Unlike private institutions, which must develop for a number of years before they can be approved to open *Benke* courses and confer degrees, independent colleges usually become degree-conferring institutions upon establishment (Hu and Xie, 2003). Since they enjoy the prestige of their *Mutixuexiao*, but with significantly lower admission requirements on students, their places are in good demand, even though their tuition charges are two or three times higher than those of their *Mutixuexiao*. Therefore, both private and independent colleges in China mostly fit the demand-absorbing (non-elite) type as classified by Levy (1986a).

As tuition fees at public institutions are kept by the government at a relatively low level, the capacity of public institutions to improve their financial position is severely limited. With the introduction of independent colleges, public institutions have found a way to generate significant and continuous income. Not surprisingly, public institutions were enthusiastic about establishing independent colleges. Within just six years, 2000 to 2006, 318 independent colleges were established. Almost all PhD-granting public institutions have established independent colleges, and many have established more than one (Ministry of Education, 2009b).

In the past, some independent colleges were established by *Mutixuexiaos* themselves through their business arm without an outside private investor and using the *Mutixuexiao*'s campus and facilities, teaching staff, enrolment quota and/or financial accounts, and conferred degrees in the name of the *Mutixuexiao*, while charging higher fees than the parent institution. This practice has been prohibited by regulations implemented in 2003, and today independent colleges are expected to meet a range of regulatory requirements which include having their own 'campus and educational facilities, implementing relatively independent organisation and management of teaching, recruiting students independently, conferring study certificates independently, maintaining independent financial accounts, and having independent legal status' (Ministry of Education, 2003). However, the 'private investor' of some independent colleges today is actually a company that is owned by its co-operating *Mutixuexiao*, or in some cases, the local government, therefore, these colleges are de facto entirely publicly owned. Although these independent colleges are in this sense 'public' institutions, the state regulations have made no provision for this indirect public ownership and therefore it seems that the government has tacitly approved this practice (Yang, 2003).

For prospective students, the crucial difference the new regulations have made is that degrees have to be conferred by the independent colleges themselves, rather than by the *Mutixuexiao*. This reduces the attractiveness of the degrees to students to a certain extent, as the full institutional title indicates that it is an independent college, which is known to impose lower admission requirements than the *Mutixuexiao*. However, the *Mutixuexiaos'* names are still included in the independent colleges' names, for example, Zhejiang University City College, which is the independent college of the highly prestigious Zhejiang University.

As public universities are often organized into subject or administrative units that are referred to as 'colleges' or 'schools' (or *xueyuan* in Chinese), people outside academia, or even within academia, are often unable to distinguish between a regular college (as a unit of the university) and an independent college. Therefore, it can be assumed that in the eyes of many not directly involved in higher education, independent colleges are considered to have a superior reputation to normal private institutions, as an independent college bears the name of an established institution. This situation has contributed to the attractiveness of independent colleges among students. Students who were admitted to an independent college hoping to gain a qualification from the prestigious *Mutixuexiao* were disappointed by the regulatory changes introduced in 2003 and many students were therefore opposed these changes. The fierce opposition from independent college students against the changes brought about by the new regulations of 2003 is an indication of the, arguably undeserved, reputational advantage of independent colleges (*The Economist*, 2006).

Institutional status and fee levels

In terms of institutional prestige, most of the expansion within the higher education system has taken place in its lower echelons, that is to say, in the lower-level public institutions and the newly emerged private and independent institutions. The 'elite university' schemes in China, the '985' project (to build a number of 'world-class' and 'world-renowned' universities) and '211' project (to strengthen 100 of the most prestigious institutions and certain key fields of study), have greatly strengthened the elite status of a relatively small number of public institutions (Ministry of Education, 2004a, 2004b).

Although the newly established independent and private colleges in general enjoy less prestige than public institution, they charge substantially higher fees. According to relevant national and provincial guidelines, the maximum fee levels for independent colleges are usually two to three times higher than for public universities and colleges. For example, for most *Benke* subjects in arts and humanities, science, and engineering, the tuition fees at public institutions range from ¥4500 to ¥6000 (equivalent of US$676 to US$901) per annum depending on the subject and province, but at independent colleges the fee levels range from ¥8000 to ¥20,000 (US$1202 to US$3006) depending on subject and institution, with an average of around ¥12,000 (US$1803) (CUAA, 2008b). Private institutions are usually free to set their own fee levels but still need to report to the educational and price control bureaux and sometimes need to gain approval from the authorities (see, for instance, Guangdong Prices Bureau, 2003). According to a survey, the fee levels at private colleges range from ¥5600 TO ¥16,000 (US$841 to US$2404) per annum, depending on subject and institution, with an average of around ¥11,000 (US$1653) (CUAA, 2008a).

The literature on independent colleges before 2006 mainly concentrated on the property rights of the institutions (Xu, 2004; Qin and Wang, 2005; Zhu, 2004) and on the context and rationale of independent colleges (Pan and Wu, 2004). After 2006, when a large number of independent colleges had been created, the research topics had been diversified and there have been studies on curriculum, library services, internationalization, personnel and almost every aspect of the independent institutions (Dai and You, 2006; Li, 2007; Mu and Yang, 2010; Wei and Han, 2010). However, the existing studies on the students and curricula of independent colleges often focus on independent colleges as individual institutions, and not in comparison with other public and private institutions (Li, 2007). There has been little understanding of students and education at independent colleges in relation to other types of institutions.

Case study

Scope and methods

The international academic community has had constant interest in private higher education in China ever since it re-emerged after the establishment of the communist government in 1949. A considerable number of articles published in English language journals have studied private higher education in China (Law, 1995; Levy, 1999; Lin, 2004; Mok, 1999; Yan and Levy, 2003; Yin and White, 1994). However, independent colleges have often been overlooked in the studies of private higher education. None of the above-mentioned studies have looked at independent colleges, even though in terms of the number of degree-granting institutions and the number of degree-seeking students, the independent college group is much larger than the private college group. This is partly due to the fact that independent colleges are a relatively new phenomenon, but the ambiguity of the ownership status of independent colleges may also have contributed to this situation.

Therefore, although independent colleges take a significant share in the higher education market in China, very little is known about their students, especially in comparison to their *Mutixuexiao*, and to other public and private institutions. A small-scale exploratory study was therefore conducted with the hope that its findings would shed light on the issue.

This investigation is an exploratory study into students' characteristics at one independent college in relation to other types of institutions. The sampling of these institutions deliberately included the four major ownership and qualification level types outlined earlier, and the four institutions selected are referred to in this study as Independent College, Public University, Public College and Private College. The study explores differences and similarities between these higher education institutions and offers potential explanations for them.

The Independent College is affiliated with the Public University in the study and was officially granted independent college status in 2003. As an approved independent college, it manages its campus, financial accounts and legal matters independent of the Public University. The Independent College is, in fact, owned by the business arm of the Public University and was moved to one of the Public University's old campuses after a new one was built for the *Mutixuexiao*. This is not an unusual scenario among independent colleges. The Public University, which is the *Mutixuexiao* of the Independent College, is considered to be the flagship university in the province under study. Like most other institutions of its size and status, it offers undergraduate and graduate courses that encompass virtually all academic subject fields. The tuition fees, as with all public universities and colleges in the country, are set by the administering authority, in this case the provincial government. The Public College was founded in the 1950s as a vocational college and was promoted to the *Benke* level in 2003. The college traditionally focused on engineering subjects, but has expanded to include English, economics, management, literature, science and agriculture in recent years. The Private College was established in the 1990s and promoted to *Benke* level in 2005. However, the vast majority of the Private College's students are enrolled in *Zhuanke* programmes. Although the government quota for the *Benke* enrolment of this Private College has been growing steadily since 2005, it started from a very small base and is still small compared to that at other institutions in this respect. The Private College itself determines its tuition levels. These characteristics are in line with other private colleges in the country. Table 2.1 presents the enrolment sizes and tuition charges of the four institutions.

Table 2.1 Sample institutions: *Benke* enrolment and tuition charges for representative programmes

Institution	Enrolment Quota in 2008	Tuition Fees for English Language Programme per annum	Tuition Fees for Computer Science Programme per annum
Independent College	3000	¥8000 (US$1202)	¥10,000 (US$1503)
Public University	9000	¥4950 (US$743)	¥5500 (US$826)
Public College	2000	¥4950 (US$743)	¥5500 (US$826)
Private College	800	¥8000 (US$1202)	¥10,000 (US$1503)

The major limitation of this method, as with all case studies, is its small sample size, which affects the quality of the representativeness of the data. However, since no studies of this kind exist, it is appropriate to conduct an exploratory study even with a small sample of institutions.

The study conducted a survey of students to gather factual and perceptual data. The data was collected with a sample of students, specifically those in their third year (of four-year programmes) and those studying in two *Benke* disciplines, namely engineering and languages, as these were the largest disciplines in the surveyed institutions.

The survey was conducted on-site at the institutions in a classroom setting. Questionnaires were distributed to students at their evening self-study sessions, with permission from their teacher and the director of studies at each institution. This direct contact with students helped to yield a high response rate: 1,345 questionnaires were distributed to students of the four institutions, and of these, 1,264 non-empty questionnaires were returned, representing a response rate of about 94 per cent. At the same time, students were assured of their anonymity and it was ensured that teachers did not put any pressure on students to fill in the questionnaire. Participation was voluntary; they were able to withdraw without penalty, and any information provided was not related to their institutional records in any way. The study results will be shown in summary form only and the institutions and course tutors do not have access to any individual responses provided by students taking part in the study.

Gaokao score

Gaokao, the National College Entrance Examination, is the principal route for students to access state-recognized on-campus higher education in China. An examination of the *Gaokao* scores of the students can indicate the selectivity and to some extent the reputation of an institution. As a result of the national requirement, every student in this survey took *Gaokao* before entering higher education.

Since many provinces design and implement their own examinations, the test contents and evaluation standards vary between provinces. This makes the comparison of *Gaokao* scores between provinces problematic. Because most of the students at these four institutions are from the local province, this section considers *Gaokao* results only from local students. It is possible that institutions' quality of student intake varies between provinces, but in general these variations are considered to be small, and the quality of student intake in the local province can be seen as fairly representative of the institutions overall.

In most provinces, students need to choose their track of study while still in senior secondary school, usually in the second year, or two years before graduation. Most students choose between natural science (*Like*) and social science (*Wenke*) tracks. Students in different tracks take different classes and different *Gaokao* test subjects. Because the test subjects are different, it is not possible to directly compare the *Gaokao* scores between tracks. As a result, colleges and universities usually set different admission standards for natural science and social science students.

Of the analytical sample, a total of 719 students indicated that they were from within the province, of whom 619 provided their *Gaokao* score and *Gaokao* track. Table 2.2 presents the *Gaokao* score of the respondents, grouped by *Gaokao* track and institution. The scores are classified into four groups: above 549, 500 to 549, 450 to 499, and below 450.

Table 2.2 shows that the four institutions had different distributions of *Gaokao* scores. The Independent College admitted students with lower scores than that of the Public University and Public College, but with similar scores to that of the Private College. This trend was evident in both the natural science and social science tracks.

For both *Gaokao* tracks, almost all (99 per cent and 100 per cent) of the Public University's students had a *Gaokao* score of 500 or higher. The Public College's distribution of student scores was somewhat lower than that of the Public University, but was still concentrated in the higher ranges: around 75 per cent students in the natural science track and 65 per cent students in the social science track had a score of 500 or higher.

Table 2.2 Survey respondents' *Gaokao* scores, by *Gaokao* track and institution

Track of *Gaokao* (*Gaokao* Score Range)	Institution				
	Independent College	Public University	Private College	Public College	Total
Natural Science					
Above 549	–	43.9%	.8%	3.3%	9.2%
500–549	4.9%	55.1%	2.5%	72.7%	29.4%
450–499	89.6%	1.0%	94.3%	20.7%	58.1%
Below 450	5.5%	–	2.5%	3.3%	3.3%
Social Science					
Above 549	–	33.3%	–	3.8%	11.5%
500–549	–	66.7%	17.9%	61.5%	42.7%
450–499	100.0%	–	82.1%	30.8%	44.8%
Below 450	–	–	–	3.8%	1.0%

The figures suggest that the Independent College, along with the Private College, mainly enrol those who do not make the cut-off for admission to public institutions, while the public institutions mainly cater for high achievers. Previously these low-achieving students would have been denied access to higher education due to the limited places available in the public institutions. The *Gaokao* scores of the student intake is certainly one factor in the status of different types of institutions. Independent colleges charge higher levels of fees and impose lower admission requirements to students. This indicates that the creation of independent colleges has increased the supply of higher education places through providing opportunities mainly to those with lower *Gaokao* scores.

Where students come from

In the questionnaire, students were asked to indicate the type of the place they come from. Students were requested to select one of five categories, namely *Shenghui Chengshi/Zhi Xiashi* (provincial capital or municipality), *Dijishi* (prefecture-level city), *Xianjishi*, *Xiangzhen* (township) and *Nongcun* (rural area).

As seen in Figure 2.1, the Independent College under study recruits more students from urban areas than the other institutions. Its intake of students from rural areas was significantly lower than at the other three institutions. At the Independent College, students from rural areas accounted for just 18.3 per cent, while at the Public University and Public College, students from rural

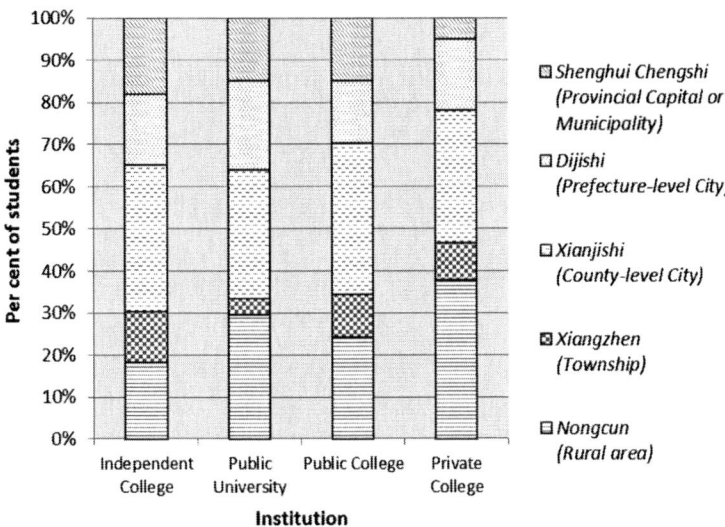

Figure 2.1 Where students come from, by institution

areas accounted for 29.6 per cent and 24.2 per cent respectively, and the Private College had the largest percentage of students from rural areas at 37.6 per cent.

This is significant, since the rural–urban divide in China is stark and closely correlated not only with the educational achievements of students at high school level (with students at urban high schools on average achieving higher *Gaokao* scores) but also with family income levels (with families in rural areas being overall poorer than families in urban areas) (Lu, 2002, 2004). The average disposable income of urban households per capita is ¥15,780 and the average net income of rural households per capita is ¥4760 in 2008 (Yu, Stith, Liu and Chen, 2010). According to the national statistics, in 2005, 57 per cent of the Chinese population were rural residents. In the fieldwork base province, over 60 per cent of the population resided in rural areas (National Bureau of Statistics of China, 2005).

Parental education

Of the analytical sample, 1191 respondents (94.2 per cent) indicated their father's educational level, and 1187 (93.9 per cent) provided their mother's educational level.

Table 2.3, above, shows that most of the students in the sample were first generation higher education students. This is consistent with the fact that

Table 2.3 Father's education level, by institution

| Father's Education Level | Institution (% within Institution) | | | | |
	Independent College	Public University	Private College	Public College	Total
Postgraduate	1.1%	1.7%	0.4%	0.3%	0.9%
Undergraduate – *Benke*	5.5%	6.1%	1.3%	4.8%	4.6%
Undergraduate – *Zhuanke*	12.1%	8.5%	2.1%	14.3%	9.8%
Senior Secondary School	42.2%	30.6%	27.8%	42.2%	36.5%
Junior Secondary School	24.7%	35.0%	39.3%	22.9%	29.6%
Primary School	7.2%	10.2%	17.9%	7.6%	10.2%
No Formal Education	7.2%	7.8%	11.1%	7.9%	8.3%
Total	100.0%	100.0%	100.0%	100.0%	100.0%

universities and colleges in China only resumed enrolment in 1978 after the Cultural Revolution, and the number of students enrolled was quite small in the earlier years. This was about the time when many of the parents of current university students were themselves at university-entering age.

The university participation rate in the late 1970s and earlier 1980s is estimated to be 5 per cent or lower nationally, and so the father's educational level of students at the Public University, Independent College and Public College was many times higher than the average in the overall national population.

Broadly speaking, the parents of Independent College students had the strongest educational backgrounds in the four institutions, and the parents of Private College students had on average the weakest; the Public University and Public College's profiles were somewhere between the two, but much closer to the Independent College. The trend in mothers' educational levels was broadly similar to the trend of fathers' educational level at the four institutions. The difference was that, in general, mothers' educational level appeared to be lower than fathers' educational level.

Parental occupation

The questionnaire adopted the ten-class scale developed by the Chinese Academy of Social Sciences (Lu, 2002, 2004) and asked students to choose their parental occupations from the scale. The scale is based on occupation. Although there is no absolute connection of occupation and socioeconomic status, in general it is considered that an occupation higher in the scale corresponds to higher socioeconomic status. Of the analytical sample, 1185 respondents (93.7 per cent) indicated their father's occupation and 1172 (92.7 per cent) provided a valid answer to the mother's occupation item.

The father's occupation figures were again consistent with the previous results on family residence and parents' educational background: on average, the Independent College father's socioeconomic status was higher than at the other three institutions, particularly the Private College. Compared with fathers of students at the Private College, fathers of students at the Independent College were 9.5 times more likely to be managers in a business, four times more likely to be administrative personnel at a public authority, twice as likely to be clerks

Table 2.4 Father's occupation of the survey respondents, by institution

	Institution (% within Institution)				
	Private College	Public University	Independent College	Public College	Total
Father's Occupation					
Public Authority Administrative	1.3%	3.8%	5.2%	7.6%	4.7%
Managerial	.4%	1.0%	3.8%	1.9%	1.9%
Public Authority Clerk	6.9%	11.3%	14.0%	14.2%	12.0%
Professional	3.0%	4.4%	3.5%	4.4%	3.9%
Home/Small Business Owner	8.6%	8.9%	12.8%	5.7%	9.1%
Staff in Business/ Service Industry	2.1%	1.4%	2.0%	.6%	1.5%
Private Business Owner	6.0%	6.1%	6.4%	4.7%	5.8%
Industrial Worker	13.7%	12.3%	11.1%	12.7%	12.3%
Farmer-worker	9.9%	4.4%	2.3%	6.6%	5.5%
Farmer	36.9%	32.8%	20.7%	28.5%	28.9%
Retired	2.1%	3.1%	2.0%	3.5%	2.7%
Unemployed	6.4%	6.8%	9.9%	4.1%	6.9%
Other	2.6%	3.8%	6.1%	5.4%	4.6%
Total	100.0%	100.0%	100.0%	100.0%	100.0%

at a public authority, and 48 per cent more likely to run a home/small business, while fathers of students at the Private College were more likely to be industrial workers, off-farm workers or farmers.

Fathers of students at the Independent College were more likely to be unemployed than fathers at other institutions. However, being unemployed does not necessarily indicate low socioeconomic status; in fact, it could imply that the person has income from other business, family or personal channels to support them without the need to work, and in this case unemployment actually means high economic status.

The trend of mothers' occupation was broadly similar to the trend of fathers' occupation. The difference was that, in general, mothers' socioeconomic status in terms of occupation seemed to be somewhat lower than fathers' occupation.

Concerns about finance

The fee-paying ability item in the questionnaire asked whether students were concerned about their or their family's ability to finance their current education. Of the analytical sample, 1,143 respondents (90.4 per cent) gave a valid answer to this question.

The differences in socioeconomic background of students are also reflected in the levels of concern students have with regard to the cost of their studies. Despite the fact that students of independent colleges pay significantly higher tuitions, their levels of financial concern are not higher than for students studying at the two public institutions which charge much lower fees. However, students at the Private College are on average much more concerned about finances: although the four institutions have similar proportions of students who are 'somewhat concerned about finance', 45 per cent of students at the Private College state that they are very concerned about their cost of their studies, which is double the level of concern of students at the other three institutions (see Figure 2.2 below).

This means that the higher level of tuition fees at the non-public institutions does not affect students at the Independent College because of their better-off family background, whereas for students at the Private College fee levels are a real concern.

Discussion and Conclusions

An interesting pattern has emerged from the findings: the Independent College seems to attract lower-achieving students from wealthy backgrounds. This

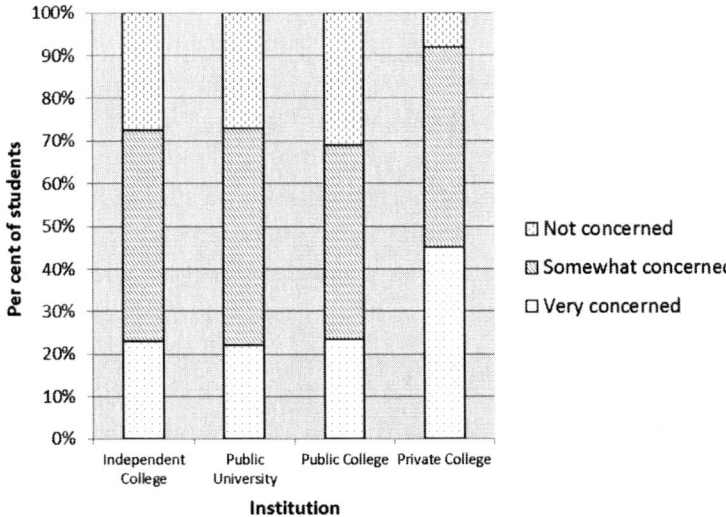

Figure 2.2 Survey respondents' concerns about finances, by institution

differs markedly from the Private College which also attracts low-achieving students but from significantly poorer backgrounds. This may be because the wealthier urban applicants have better information and prefer to enrol in independent colleges that have the 'good name' of their parent institution.

Further investigation shows that, compared with the Private College, the Independent College has a higher proportion of students who applied to their college as their first choice. Over 50 per cent of the Independent College students chose this independent college as their 'first choice' in their selection of institutions, but for Private College students the figure was less than 15 per cent. This suggests that the Independent College students are more likely to be lower achieving but wealthy students who decided to enrol in expensive independent colleges in the first place, while the Private College students are more likely to be lower achieving and poorer students who initially applied to a cheaper public institution but were forced to go to the more expensive Private College because of their failure to meet the admission requirements of that public institution.

The data from this exploratory case study show that institutions of different types, as classified by ownership and prestige, have very different student compositions. This finding has important implications. With regard to issues of equity, it suggests that low-achieving students from wealthier backgrounds can exercise more choices.

The creation of independent colleges could therefore be regarded as dispro-portionately beneficial to students from higher socioeconomic groups. The ability to exercise choice depends on the possession of economic, social and cultural capital which is disproportionately held by higher socioeconomic groups (see Reay et al., 2005).

The recent establishment of independent colleges has resulted in a signif-icant new 'non-public' sector in higher education in China. However, in terms of programme provision and student experience, research indicates that the new types of institutions seem to operate in a way that does not differ substantially from either the public college or the public university (Yu, 2010). Existing literature compared the educational orientation, curriculum structure, course offerings and students' experience of learning, and concluded that few systematic differences could be found between different types of institutions. Where there are differences, there are greater differences between disciplines *within* institutions than within disciplines *between* institutions (Yu, 2010). In a seminal study that analyzed the structure, function and changes of private higher education in eight countries, Geiger (1986) developed a taxonomic, analytic description of the functions of the private sector of higher education. He identified three roles for private higher education providers: providing more, different, or better higher education. Levy suggests that private higher education is often, but not always, about something different and innovative; due to isomorphism, private higher education may closely resemble public higher education and fail to contribute diversity to the system. The literature has pointed out that the rationales and functions of the private higher education sector are highly dependent on higher education policies (Levy, 1986; Zumeta, 1992). For instance, the government may require private providers to conform to the model of the public institution, an action Levy terms 'coercive modelling', which serves as a significant source of homogeneity (Levy, 1999, p. 24). This is considered to be the case for the independent institutions: they face limitations in their ability to be distinctive, most notably in ways that the government is not inclined to approve.

It appears that the establishment of independent institutions in China primarily served the goal of providing more spaces in higher education, though independent colleges' features of reputation and high tuition fees have attracted a different group of students than those at existing public and private institu-tions. Although the introduction of independent colleges has added diversity to the institutional structure of higher education in China, the purpose was not to offer a different kind of education.

For all the ideological notions associated with the distinctiveness of private and independent institutions, it appears that much of the practical drive for establishing these institutions concerns a desire to reduce the costs for government, and to increase revenue for public institutions, rather than to promote educational diversity. The hierarchy of reputation of different types of *Benke* institutions implies that the sector reflects many of the features of Teichler's (2007) 'vertical' form of diversity, with strong differences in the reputation of the institutions, but not many of the features of the 'horizontal' form of diversity.

These complexities highlight some of the difficulties of establishing a quasi-private higher education sector when a system attempts to attract private capital. The establishment of independent colleges in China can also be regarded as an attempt to introduce market forces into the system. This exploratory case study reveals consequences which can provide valuable lessons for policy initiatives in other countries.

This study has shed light on the distinctiveness of independent colleges as compared with other types of institutions in student compositions. Future studies of these independent colleges should more systematically assess the impact of independent college education on students as compared with other types of institutions, and extend the study to a larger and more diverse sample of public, independent and private institutions, as well as to a more diverse set of disciplines and subjects. Such research would help to facilitate a more in-depth understanding of independent colleges in China.

References

Altbach, P. (1999). 'Comparative Perspectives on Private Higher Education', in P. Altbach (ed.), *Private Prometheus: Private Higher Education and Development in the 21st Century*. West Port, CT: Greenwood, pp. 283–92.

—(2002). *Private Prometheus: Private Higher Education and Development in the 21st Century*. Charlotte, NC: Information Age Publishing.

Archer, L. (2007). 'Diversity, equality and higher education: a critical reflection on the abuses of equity discourse within widening participation'. *Teaching in Higher Education*, 12 (5): 635–53.

Axinn, W. G. and Pearce, L. D. (2006). *Mixed Method Data Collection Strategies*. Cambridge: Cambridge University Press.

Chen, D. Y. (2004). 'China's mass higher education: problem, analysis, and solutions'. Asia Pacific Education Review, 5 (1): 23–33.

CUAA (2008a). *2008 中国民办大学学费排行榜* [*Ranking table of tuition fees at private higher education institutions 2008*]. http://cuaa.net/cur/2008mb/13.shtml

—(2008b). *2008 中国独立学院学费排行榜* [*Ranking table of tuition fees at independent colleges 2008*]. http://cuaa.net/cur/2008mb/14.shtml

Dai, L. and You, J. (2006). 创新独立学院人才培养模式刍议 ['Discussion on innovating education in independent colleges']. *China Higher Education Research*, 2006 (01).

The Economist (2006). 'Chaos in the classrooms: an education policy torn between the market and the state'. 10 August.

Geiger, R. (1986). *Private Sectors in Higher Education: Structure, Function, and Change in Eight Countries.* Ann Arbor, MI: University of Michigan Press.

Guangdong Prices Bureau (2003). *Higher Education Institutions Charging Policy.* Guangzhou: Guangdong Prices Bureau.

Hu, W. and Xie, X. (2003). 'System environment for the development of China's private education', in D. Yang (ed.), *China's Education Blue Book 2003.* Beijing: Higher Education Press, pp. 76–197.

Law, W.-W. (1995). 'The role of the state in higher education reform: Mainland China and Taiwan'. *Comparative Education Review*, 39 (3).

Levy, D. C. (1986a). *Private Education: Studies in Choice and Public Policy.* New York: Oxford University Press.

—(1986b). *Higher Education and the State in Latin America: Private Challenges to Public Dominance.* Chicago: University of Chicago Press.

—(1999). 'When private higher education does not bring organizational diversity: Argentina, China, Hungary', in P. A. Altbach (ed.), *Private Prometheus: Private Higher Education and Development in the 21st Century.* West Port, CT: Greenwood Press.

Li, P. S., Li, L. and Zong, L. (2007). 'Postgraduate educational aspirations and policy implications: a case study of university students in western China'. *Journal of Higher Education Policy and Management*, 29 (2): 143–58.

Li, Q. (2007). 三年来独立学院研究综述 ['Summarization on the study of independent colleges in the last three years']. *Heilongjiang Researches on Higher Education*, 2007 (10).

Lin, J. (2004). 'Private higher education in China: a contested terrain'. *International Higher Education*, 2004 (Summer).

Lu, X. (ed.) (2002). *Research Report of Social Classes in Contemporary China.* Beijing: Social Sciences Documentation Publishing.

—(ed.) (2004). *Social Mobility in Contemporary China.* Beijing: Social Sciences Documentation Publishing.

Ministry of Education (1978–2009). *National Statistics on Educational Development.* Beijing: People's Education Press.

—(2003). 关于规范并加强普通高校以新的机制和模式试办独立学院管理的若干意见 [*Views on regulating and strengthening regular higher education institutions establishing independent colleges with new mechanisms and model*]. Beijing: Ministry of Education.

—(2004a). *211工程简介 [Introduction to the 211 project]*. Beijing: Ministry of Education.

—(2004b). 教育部 财政部关于继续实施'政部关工程'建设项目的意见 [*Ministry of Education and Ministry of Finance's views on the continuing implementation of the 985 Project*]. Beijing: Ministry of Education.

—(2008). 中华人民共和国教育部令第26号: 独立学院设置与管理办法 [*The 26th Order of the Ministry of Education, P. R. China: provisions on the establishment and administration of independent colleges*]. Beijing: Ministry of Education.

—(2009a). *2009 年具有普通高等学历教育招生资格的高等学校名单 [List of higher education institutions accredited to enrol regular students 2009]*. Beijing: Ministry of Education.

—(2009b). *2009 年具有招生资格独立学院名单 [List of independent colleges accredited to enrol students 2009]*. Beijing: Ministry of Education.

Mok, K.-h. (1999). 'Education and the market place in Hong Kong and Mainland China'. *Higher Education*, 37 (2).

Mu, Y. and Yang, Y. (2010). 独立学院管理运筹学课程教学内容与方法探讨 ['Study on teaching contents and methods of management operation research in independent college']. *Higher Education Forum*, 2010 (10).

National Bureau of Statistics of China (2005). *China Statistical Yearbook 2005*. Beijing: China Statistics Press.

Pan, M. and Wu, M. (2004). 独立学院的兴起及前景探析 ['Study of the rise and future of independent colleges']. *China Higher Education*, 2004 (Z2).

Qin, H. and Wang, D. (2005). 关于'独立学院'属性及其相关问题的思考 ['Reflections on the properties and problems of independent colleges']. *China Higher Education Research*, 2005 (4).

Reay, D., David, M. and Ball., S. (2005). *Degrees of Choice. Social Class, Gender and Race in Higher Education*. Stoke-on-Trent: Trentham.

State Council (2002). 普通高等学校设置暂行条例 [*Provisional regulations on establishment of regular higher education institutions*]. Beijing: Ministry of Education.

Tashakkori, A. and Teddlie, C. (1998). *Mixed Methodology: Combining Qualitative and Quantitative Approaches*. Thousand Oaks, CA: Sage Publications.

Teichler, U. (2007). *Higher Education Systems: Conceptual Frameworks, Comparative Perspectives, Empirical Findings*. Rotterdam: Sense Publishers.

—(2008). 'Diversification? Trends and explanations of the shape and size of higher education'. *Higher Education*, 56: 349–479.

Trow, M. (1973). *Problems in the transition from elite to mass higher education*. Berkeley, CA: Carnegie Commission on Higher Education.

Wei, L. and Han, D. (2010). 独立学院师资队伍建设的策略 ['Personnel strategy at independent colleges']. *Heilongjiang Researches on Higher Education*, 2010 (5).

Xu, W. (2004). 独立学院的产权关系分析 ['Analysis of property rights of independent colleges']. *Theory Monthly*, 2004 (6).

Yan, F. and Levy, D. C. (2003). 'China's new private education law'. *International Higher Education*, 2003 (Spring).

Yang, D. (2003). 'China's education in 2003: from growth to reform', in D. Yang (ed.), *China's Education Blue Book 2003*. Beijing: Higher Education Press, pp. 1–71.

Yin, Q. and White, G. (1994). 'The "marketization" of Chinese higher education: a critical assessment'. *Comparative Education*, 30 (3).

Yu, K. (2010). *Diversification to a Degree: An Exploratory Study of Students' Experience at Four Higher Education Institutions in China*. Bern: Peter Lang.

Yu, K., Stith, A., Liu, L. and Chen, H. (2010). *Tertiary Education at a Glance: China*. Shanghai: Shanghai Jiao Tong University Press.

Zhu, J. (2004). 新制独立学院概念及其本质特征:基于产权的分析 ['The analysis of concept and essential feature of private college in public university based on property rights']. *Fudan Education Forum*, 2004 (5).

Zumeta, W. (1992). 'State Policies and Private Higher Education: Policies, Correlates, and Linkages'. *Journal of Higher Education*, 63 (4): 363–417.

3

Hong Kong: Structuring the Education System for a Diversified Society

Alka Sharma

Introduction

All young residents of Hong Kong have to go through an extremely competitive and selective education system to establish themselves as academically successful individuals. The present education system exhibits the impact of both colonial and native traits and rules, although the latter has tried to minimize the effects of the former through reforms. Since July 1997, although being politically part of the People's Republic of China, Hong Kong is officially considered a distinct 'political unit'. Although 95 per cent of the population are ethnic Chinese, Hong Kong is a highly Westernized and diversified society. This could be attributed largely to the modern Western-style education system introduced in the old Hong Kong colony in 1861 by Fredrick Stewart (Sweeting, 1990). Previously, as part of Imperial China, the impact of the Han Dynasty on education was felt in various forms. It comprised basic reading and writing in village schools, vocational education in monastery schools, and halls and colleges which prepared students for the most elite civil service examination of China. The beginnings of the modern education system can be traced to provision by Protestant and Catholic missionaries followed by Italian missionaries who provided schooling to Chinese and British boys in 1843. After the 1939–45 war, reorganization of the education system began in 1949. In 1965 a White Paper on Education Policy was crafted. It announced the redevelopment of the primary and secondary school structure and set universal primary education as the immediate aim. During British rule, education seemed a privileged commodity characterized by standard curricula, high-pressure standardized tests and hardly any freedom to schools, teachers and students. Prior to 1978, student places in government-aided secondary schools and universities were limited. About half of the primary graduates could enter government-aided secondary schools, and the rest were children belonging to families who could afford to send their children to private secondary schools with higher fees. Only 2 per cent of secondary school leavers were admitted to university degree programmes in 1975 (Poon and Wong, 2008).

After 1978 everyone had access to free and compulsory school education for nine years, and since the 1990s the number of secondary school and university places has increased. The high pressure of standardized tests at school level continued, with those taken at the end of primary 6 to get an admission to higher-band schools being especially stressful. They were followed by HKCEE (Hong Kong Certificate of Education Examination, equivalent to the UK's General Certificate of Secondary Education O levels) at the end of secondary 5, and HKALE (Hong Kong Advanced Level Examination, equivalent to UK's General Certificate of Education A levels) at secondary 7. It was a continuous challenge. Such a highly competitive examination-oriented education system had its downside (Zeng, 1999), including leading to a highly stratified society.

Although the new secondary school reforms have decreased the pressure of public examinations, as from the year 2012 students will only take one examination at the end of secondary 6 which would act as the qualifier for university entrance. Nonetheless it still seems it would be difficult to reduce the influence of social class on the achievement gap. The highly stratified structure of society to a great extent is a consequence of school system which reflects diversity through social class composition, medium of instruction, academic ability and ethnic status. According to the ecological model of Bronfenbrenner (1979), such a diversified school system may contribute a 'risk factor' for the positive academic achievement of all students, as it places only a few as privileged students whereas the majority are placed as disadvantaged in different ways and to different degrees. Furthermore, research has also shown that risk factors combine with the individual characteristics to act in a cumulative manner (Evans, 2003; Burchinal et al., 2000). This chapter will discuss how the needs of school-going children representing different social classes, ethnic groups and academic abilities are being recognized by the Hong Kong school system. This discussion will highlight various factors, or cumulative risk measures, acting behind the differentiation in academic attainment (Aztaba-Poria et al., 2004; Deater-Deckard et al., 1998). First, however, it is necessary to provide some background information, beginning with a brief review of the Hong Kong education system. The major highlight of this discussion will be the post-1997 reforms introduced in various stages of formal education.

The Present Education System

Hong Kong has a population of around 7 million living in a small area of 1000 square kilometres (Census and Statistics Department, 2012). It has remained as the world's freest economy according to the Index of Economic Freedom since its inception in 1995 (Heritage Foundation and *Wall Street Journal*, 2012). According to the *CIA World Fact Book 2012* its GDP (gross domestic product) per capita at purchasing power parity ranks 36 globally. The service sector of the economy accounts for almost 90 per cent of Hong Kong's economic growth. Education is seen as a major path to climb the social ladder and upgrade one's social status. Such social emphasis on education requires an education system that is within the reach of all citizens of the state. According to the Education Bureau (EDB), children between the ages of three and six attend kindergartens which are privately run. Thereafter, eligible children between the ages of six and 18, irrespective of sex, ethnic origin, religion or ethical belief, family status and physical or mental ability, have the right to enjoy education in public sector primary and secondary schools (up to secondary 6). The government's language policy in education is to enable students to be biliterate (to master written Chinese (Cantonese, a dialect of the Chinese language and mother tongue of the majority of the Hong Kong citizens) and English), and trilingual (to speak fluent Cantonese, Putonghua and English). Chinese is the medium of instruction in most primary and secondary schools, with English taught as a core subject from primary 1. The present school structure consists of six years of primary school, three years of junior secondary, and three years of senior secondary leading to HKDSE which would qualify students for four years of various undergraduate courses (i.e. 6+3+3 +4). A consultation paper on *Reforming the Academic structure for Senior Secondary Education and Higher Education – Actions for investing in the Future* considered that an additional year of senior secondary and university education will raise the overall quality of young people.

The present education system can be traced to significant policy changes introduced under the status of Hong Kong as 'one country, two systems' after the return of its sovereignty to the People's Republic of China in 1997. Right after the beginning of native rule, the government realized that inadequacies within the existing (at the time of the 1997 handover) education system had to be addressed to enable the majority of Hong Kong people to achieve all-round education to meet the challenges at local as well as at global level (Poon and Wong 2008). Blame was put on 'lack of learning effectiveness' as classroom learning seemed largely examination-driven, creating a monotonous school life where students were given very little room to explore, think and create. The local policy-makers realized that Hong Kong was also transforming from an industrial society to an information society under the influence of globalization. Hence, a knowledge-based society was needed with a pool of talented individuals reflecting creativity and critical thinking. This meant that not only appropriate schooling but also lifelong learning was considered necessary for the future stability and prosperity of Hong Kong. To achieve these aims, the Education Commission proposed an education reform covering the entire education system: admissions system, academic structure, curriculum, medium of instruction, assessment methods and teacher certification and training (Education Commission, 1999). With a key aim to prepare citizens for the twenty-first century, the Hong Kong government put forward the education reform proposal entitled *Learning for Life and Learning through Life: Reform Proposals for the Education System in Hong Kong* in September 2000 (Education Commission, 2000). The Education Commission adopted a 'student-focused', 'no-loser', 'quality', 'life-wide learning' and 'society-wide mobilisation' approach while formulating new proposals . Reforms covered all areas, including the academic structure, the examination and assessment systems, the school places allocation system, the curriculum, the university admissions system, language requirements of teachers, the required qualifications of teachers at all levels of education and lifelong learning at senior secondary level and beyond. The most significant reform has been the introduction of the new secondary school (NSS) system in 2009 with the redefinition of the secondary stage in terms of number of years, curriculum and public examination. Under the NSS, school education has been reduced to 12 years, so that the secondary stage consists of six years instead of seven, one extra year has been added to the university undergraduate programme, and the two public examinations (HKCEE and HKALE) are combined into one called HKDSE. This would act as a qualifier for undergraduate studies to be taken at the end of secondary 6. Since 1997, mother tongue education has been adopted at the school stage, but university programmes are mostly conducted through the medium of English.

Figure 3.1 Structure of the education system

Postgraduate	Postgraduate Study
Year 4 Year 3 Year 2 Year 1	4 Year college/University OR 2 Year Associate Degree/ Vocational Education
S6 S5 S4	Hong Kong Diploma of Secondary Education (HKDSE) Higher Secondary School
S3 S2 S1	Lower Secondary School
P6 P5 P4 P3 P2 P1	Primary School
Kindergarten	Pre-primary Education

Note:
1) In the Hong Kong education system, P refers to primary whereas S refers to secondary. P1 is primary 1 and S1 is secondary 1, equivalent to grade 7 of other education systems.
2) Graduates of associate degrees or vocational colleges can either join the labour market or pursue higher education.

Pre-primary or early childhood education

Pre-primary services in Hong Kong comprise provision of education and care to young children by kindergartens and child care centres. Most kindergartens provide bi-sessional classes of around three hours each whereas most day care centres offer whole-day programmes (Wong Ngai Chun and Rao, 2004). Kindergartens are registered with the Education Bureau and provide services for children from three to six years old. Child care centres are registered with the Social Welfare Department and provide nurseries and crèches. The medium of instruction is mainly Chinese.

The reform proposal suggested in 2000 acknowledged early childhood education as the foundation for lifelong learning. To raise the quality of early childhood education, five initiatives were recommended: a) raising the qualifications for early childhood staff; b) improving ways of assuring quality; c) reforming the regulatory system to further harmonize the care and education provisions; d) enhancing continuity between early childhood and primary education; and e) giving the priority of resource allocation to parents to promote choice and hence raise the quality of early childhood education (Wong Ngai Chun and Rao, 2004). According to Yuen and Grieshaber (2009), prior to this there were no defined guidelines except for a framework that was continuously repeated in all recommendations for pre-primary education: 'to promote the development of high quality kindergarten education in the private sector by professional upgrading, curriculum advice, and miscellaneous subsidy schemes for operators and parents' (p. 264). Such a laissez-faire policy in the absence of clearly defined guidelines and measures saw early childhood education being provided by non-profit-making institutions as well by kindergartens running solely with aim of maximizing profit (Yuen, 2008). Furthermore, these early childhood institutions were not obliged to follow either the national curriculum guidelines or official recommendations (Ho, 2007). In December 2006, the government approved the HK$2 billion pre-school scheme to subsidize early childhood education to decrease the burden of raising children, especially for lower income parents, through a voucher scheme. It is considered an attempt to improve the quality of early childhood education via parents. It aims not only to reduce the financial burden on parents, but also provides them with a 'choice of services'. For example, on the official school website are the qualifications of teachers, fees and other financial information (Yuen and Grieshaber, 2009). The most significant development has been the raising of pre-primary teacher qualifications, so that as from now all pre-primary teachers require five parts of the standardized tests (including tests in both English and Mandarin) of the Hong Kong Certification of Education Examination (HKCEE). Previously only two parts of the HKCEE were the threshold to be a kindergarten teacher.

Primary education

Primary education in Hong Kong is compulsory for all children and free to those attending public sector schools. Emphasis is on the 'all round development of children' through exposure to a wide range of knowledge and skills in all public sector primary schools (Adamson and Pang, 2004). The core subjects include Chinese, English, mathematics and general studies, with a broad emphasis on music, physical education, arts and religious education (Education Bureau, 2009). The medium of instruction in most primary schools is Chinese, with English as a second language (Evans, 2000). These are known as Chinese medium instruction schools, or CMI schools. A few schools provide learning instruction through English (EMI schools) (Gao, 2011). To raise the quality of primary education, the first step taken by the government was implementation of whole-day school to promote the all-round development of students. This policy was emphasized to enable a learning environment with more scope for a diversified range of learning activities. Provision of relief from the tight learning schedule was also a feature, leading to more opportunities for better communication between teachers and students. Other steps were the promotion of the use of information technology (IT) and small class teaching (SCT).

The introduction of a centralized Primary One Admission System aimed to eliminate the pressure imposed on young children by the intense competition to enter popular primary schools. The Primary One Admission System is divided into two stages: the Discretionary Places Admission (DPA) stage and the Central Allocation (CA) stage. During the stage of Discretionary Places Admission, parents may apply to only one government or aided school which may be in or outside the school catchment area in which they reside. Critics of this system believe that it doesn't ensure quality, as all students irrespective of their ability from the same district are randomly allocated to primary schools through the central allocation system. It does not prove fair to the poor students, anyway, as the elite schools are located in the expensive districts and ability to reside in such districts is completely beyond the reach of the poor families. According to Poon and Wong, in the past academically able students from poor backgrounds had chances of entering the elite schools when the quota at the principals' discretion was larger, and the process of admission was based on 'human understanding' (Poon and Wong, 2008). So the central allocation system which was developed to reduce inequalities seems to be working towards widening the gap between the rich and the poor.

Secondary education

A new senior secondary (NSS) school system and curriculum was introduced in the school year of 2009–10. The secondary stage moved away from the English model of five years of secondary schooling and two years of university matriculation to the Chinese model of three years of junior secondary plus three years of senior secondary and four years for university. In an effort to improve senior secondary education, the government planned to make it a three-year process open to all students who wished to continue their education. Although senior secondary education would remain non-compulsory, the NSS reforms aim to provide 'an opportunity' of higher education for every student of the city-state (Education Commission, 2000). For this, two public exams, HKCEE and HKALE, have been merged into one public examination called the Hong Kong Diploma in Secondary Education, and school-based assessment has been increased. Under the NSS curriculum, the secondary school curriculum is designed according to what learning experiences students need, rather than being guided by the manpower needs in the economy. It is framed around eight key learning areas (KLA), rather than subjects: Chinese language, English language, mathematics, science and technology, social science and humanities, sports and arts, applied learning (to allow students to gain real-life workplace experiences) and other learning experiences (including service learning, workplace visits and overseas experiences). The latter two are new to schools and teachers. All students take four core subjects, including English language, Chinese language, mathematics and liberal studies. Liberal studies has introduced a new learning experience as it only provides an outline of broad topics instead of a carefully defined syllabus. In effect, teachers are expected to enable students to design their own learning schemes based mostly on current affairs and non-textbook information. The idea is to develop high-order critical thinking. Furthermore, students can choose two elective subjects from the remaining 20 applied learning courses. The NSS curricula include more work-related experiences to better prepare students for the world of work. Streaming of classes on the basis of various subjects has been abolished to ensure 'uniform learning' and that life-based experiences are more incorporated in the curriculum. Through the introduction of subjects like applied learning and other learning experiences in the curricula, it is ensured that students develop personal capabilities that not only prepare them for life beyond jobs, but also for the various personal, social, political and natural uncertainties of life. Policy-makers believe that satisfaction would not come as result of 'doing more' and 'with better results' in the existing system; instead, in order to maximize results, formal education has to be developed differently. Their belief rests on the perspective that at present 'academic credentials' do not last long, hence children need broader learning experiences emphasizing more the 'development of ability' than acquiring a 'stock of information'.

Another significant change in secondary education is the medium of instruction (MOI) guidelines for secondary schools, which was introduced in September 1997, ahead of the NSS. These guidelines provided that all secondary schools should adopt Chinese to teach all academic subjects, starting with their secondary 1 intake in the 1998–99 schools year, and progressing each year to a higher level of secondary education, unless a school has obtained approval to use English as the medium of instruction. In the 1998–99 school year, the number of secondary schools that adopted Chinese as the MOI increased by 223, from 77 to a total of 300. Secondary schools using Chinese as the MOI for their secondary 1 to secondary 3 classes may opt to use English as the MOI for certain subjects in some classes. In addition, since the 1998–99 school year, secondary schools using Chinese as the MOI have been given several privileges such as an average of two additional language teachers or native English teachers (NET) according to the requirements of the school (Education Bureau, 2009).

Entry to secondary schools involves two procedures addressed as 'through train' and 'central allocation'. Through-train schools offer a continuity of education from primary to secondary either at one integrated institution or by linking up with another school. The through-train model allows some primary and secondary schools to link (Education Commission, 2000). The linked secondary schools are supposed to accept all primary 6 graduates of their partner primary school. In this process both primary and secondary schools are not only expected to maintain similar financial models but are also expected to maintain some consistency across their curricula and teaching methodology. In addition, secondary schools linked to primary schools must have the capacity to accept all primary school students in addition to others who may wish to apply. The central allocation secondary school (SSPA) system is divided into two stages: Discretionary Places (DP) and Central Allocation (CA). All secondary schools participating in the SSPA system are allowed to reserve not more than 30 per cent of their secondary 1 (S1) places as discretionary. Schools may admit suitable students under DP, according to their educational philosophy and characteristics. However, they must make public the admission criteria and weightings prior to admission. Schools may arrange interviews, but no written test should be conducted. For CA, the Education Bureau will match students' preferences against schools' successful and reserve lists. If a student is successful in both schools to which he or she has applied, allocation will be based on the student's order of preference. CA is based on a student's allocation band, parental choice of schools and random number. Students' internal assessment results at the end of primary 5 and both in mid-year and at the end of P6 are used for the calculation of allocation bands. At present there are three levels with Band 1 at the top admitting students with the higher scores, followed by Band 2 and then Band 3. In the old admissions system, students were categorized into five bands (i.e. Band 1 being the top, and Band 5 the bottom), and all primary 6 students had to go through the Academic Aptitude Test (AAT) for selection. The Education Commission reduced the number of bands from five to three, on the basis that categorizing students into five bands was unfair to the less able students. Further, the AAT was also abolished in the year 2000 to reduce the pressure on the students. However, the gap has not been reduced. Rather, more competition has been created, with increased pressure among students to achieve a place in the higher-band schools (Poon and Wong, 2008).

Tertiary education

The higher education sector in Hong Kong is a relatively small and exclusive group catering for about 18 per cent of the eligible age group within Hong Kong's population of 7 million. The University Grants Committee (UGC) was formed by the Hong Kong government to safeguard and promote quality among these publicly-funded institutions. Hong Kong has 13 degree-awarding higher education institutions, including eight institutions funded by the public through the UGC – namely, City University of Hong Kong (City), Hong Kong Baptist University (HKBU), Lingnan University (LU), the Chinese University of Hong Kong (CUHK), the Hong University of Hong Kong (HKU) – and four self-financing institutions – namely, the Open University of Hong Kong, Hong Kong Shue Yan University, Chu Hai College of Higher Education and Hang Seng Management College – and the publicly-funded Hong Kong Academy for Performing Arts (the Education Bureau, The Government of the Hong Kong SAR). With public sector funding, the UGC, being responsible for the higher education sector, has come to the conclusion that Hong Kong's higher education sector should be viewed as a key force in the regional and international higher education arena. The UGC emphasizes that Hong Kong needs a higher education sector with institutions operating in distinctive but collaborative and complementary roles. This belief rests on the fact that Hong Kong is too small a place to afford excessive overlapping of efforts in higher education. In addition, the fiscal environment also calls for a very effective use of public money to enable the entire higher education system to advance as a 'single unit' in order to maximize the efficiency of the system.

A comprehensive review of the higher education system launched by the UGC in May 2001 covered major aspects of higher education provision, including an administrative framework for a much expanded post-secondary sector and the governance of universities. This led to the call for quality education and the launch of university-based management through a decen-tralization policy framework. This allocated each university more autonomy and power in deciding its routine work policies. Still, this development does not necessarily mean deregulation and absence of state control. Rather, it showed that the state could exercise control through the UGC, its executive body. The approach towards change in the higher education system is based on a managerial or executive-led model emphasizing efficiency, effectiveness and economy in education. In following the 'market model of privatisation and marketisation' in the midst of economic crisis, coupled with pressing demand for higher education, the government announced the adoption of a privatization policy to create more learning opportunities for higher education in the year 2001. This was marked by shedding the civil service salary structures of the UGC-funded higher education institutions to allow salaries to reflect performance and market forces. Unlike other countries where such policies were adopted to reduce the state's financial burden, in Hong Kong the reform strategies along the line of marketization are designed to improve the efficiency and performance of the university sector rather than purely resolve financial difficulties (Mok, 2000, 2003). Since its inception, the UGC has conducted a number of reviews of universities, such as the Management Review (1998–9), the Teaching and Learning Quality Process Reviews (TLQPR) (1995–7 and 2001–3), the Performance and Role-Related Funding Scheme (2004), and, more recently, the first round of Quality Audits (2008–11). As their names suggest, each review has a different focus and emphasis: the Management Review focused on management structure and effectiveness, the TLQPR scrutinized the processes of teaching and learning, and the Performance and Role-Related Funding Scheme and Quality Audits looked into the roles and fitness for purpose of each institution (Yung Man-Sing, 2004).

Over the last decade, higher education has also moved from the education of 'elites' to the education of 'the masses'. The relatively low-cost tuition fees due to heavy government subsidies are considered the main reason behind this. From 1911 (the beginning of higher education with the establishment of the University of Hong Kong) to 1984, the colonial government controlled the development of higher education by restricting financial support for private tertiary institutions and denying recognition of their qualifications. Even by 1984, only 2 per cent of the age-appropriate population was admitted to the local tertiary institutions. Large-scale expansion of higher education began after 1984 when colonial rulers realized that their political rule over Hong Kong would end by 1997 (Hui and Poon, 2004). Higher education in Hong Kong is renowned for its quality. According to the QS World University Rankings 2011–12 of top universities, HKU is ranked 22nd in the world, the best in Hong Kong and Asia. CUHK was ranked 37th, and HKUST 40th (QS World University Rankings, 2011–12). The MOI of tertiary education in Hong Kong is English, except for the CUHK which was established in 1963 to serve the Cantonese-speaking Hong Kong residents. According to *the Report of the Committee on Bilingualism* (2007), 'in the 1950s, demand for more school places in Hong Kong was caused not only by the increase of population but also by the fact that among the incoming refugees, there was a large number of students ranging from primary to university levels who wanted to continue their education in Hong Kong'. This social change led to the student population expanding greatly in Chinese middle schools. Due to the pressure from the mass of high school students who wanted to be well educated, the colonial government had to establish a university adopting Chinese as the language of instruction. As an international city, Hong Kong's tertiary institutions also attract many foreign exchange students. The mainland Chinese students are an integral part of all Hong Kong tertiary institutions. Until now the Joint University Programme Admissions System (JUPAS) determined admission for local students largely based on HKALE and HKCEE results, but from year 2012, performance at HKDSE replaces these two examinations. At present the biggest challenge for this sector is preparing for a major overhaul of its curriculum, which will revert from a three-year to a four-year system in the 2012–13 academic year. This curriculum change brings with it, among other things, the adoption of new assessment methods in line with the government's aim for an outcomes-based approach in teaching and learning. This means all staff and students of universities have to refamiliarize themselves with the new aims and policies. While, for staff and administration, there is the added challenge of having both student cohorts from the old school system (studying within the three-year curriculum) and those from the new system (within the four-year curriculum) simultaneously attending classes, using university facilities and requiring faculty manpower for at least three years until those in the former curriculum graduate.

Vocational education/higher diploma

According to the Education Bureau, the statutory Vocational Training Council (VTC) was established in 1982 to provide and promote a cost-effective and comprehensive system of vocational education and training to meet the needs of the economy of Hong Kong. The VTC provides a full range of pre-employment and in-service courses to over 170,000 students. All institutes of vocational education (IVEs) offer higher diploma, diploma, foundation diploma, vocational certificate and craft level courses which are designed to enable the young people to build a successful career. Courses are offered in disciplines such as applied sciences; business administration; child education and community services; construction; design, printing, textiles and clothing; electrical and electronic engineering; hotel, service and tourism studies; information technology and mechanical, manufacturing and industrial engineering. The VTC also operates training and development centres to provide basic skills training and upgrading training relating to the automobile, electrical, electronics, gas, jewellery, machine shop and metal working, maritime services, plastics and tooling technology, printing, textile and welding industries (Education Bureau, 2009). In order to strengthen vocational education, the government launched the Hong Kong Quality Framework in May 2008. It is a seven-tier hierarchy of qualification utilizing a set of generic level descriptors describing the different standards required at different levels.

Associate Degree

The Associate Degree, introduced in 2000, follows the pattern of Associate Degree programme of the USA. This programme has been designed to prepare students for both employment and further studies. It includes two-year programmes, providing chances to students who failed to gain entry to the undergraduate degree programmes offered by universities. This degree programme is mainly considered a stepping stone for further education. Many existing colleges began offering such degrees in an effort to increase enrolment to meet the government's educational mandate of increasing the post-secondary participation rate (Steering Committee, 2008). It can be compared with the Higher Diploma programme in terms of qualifications required on entry and value of qualification achieved on completion. Still, we find the focus of both the programmes in conflict with each other as Associate Degree programmes tend to contain more general education course work than Higher Diplomas which aim more for practical training.

'One challenge the Hong Kong government seeks to address in the future is a lack of a clear distinction between both the programmes. Currently individual schools can decide their own criteria for what constitutes the difference between these two' (McLoughlin et al., 2010, p. 32).

Special education

The aim of special education in Hong Kong is to provide special needs children with appropriate education to help them develop their potential to the full, achieve as much independence as they are capable of, and become well-adjusted individuals in the community. The Education Bureau is responsible for the planning, development, monitoring and operation of all special education facilities. It advises on organization, curricula, teaching methods and educational placement. Relevant officers of the Education Bureau have received training in their specialized fields and can provide professional advice in these fields to public-sector ordinary schools and special schools, non-governmental organizations and other government departments. The Bureau conducts a territory-wide early identification and intervention programme at primary 1 (Heung, 2006). Under the existing education policy, students with severe special educational needs (SEN) are referred to special schools for intensive support services subject to the assessment and recommendation of specialists and parents' consent. Other students with SEN are placed in mainstream schools as part of inclusive education policy. That is, students with SEN should be provided with opportunities to participate in all activities in the society (Education Department, 2010, p. 1). According to Lian (2004), a policy of placing SEN with the larger student population has been in existence since 1997 but its implementation has been very slow, as large numbers of SEN still attend special schools.

Another significant step in this direction has been two-year pilot Project of Integrated Education initiated in 1997. But the two main initiatives in this field are the 'Whole-School approach to integrated education' and the 'new funding mode'. The Whole-School Approach consolidates and redeploys all available resources – including school management, parents and other resources – whereas the new funding scheme was implemented in 2003 to test the feasibility of implementing inclusive education in mainstream schools and showed positive results (Heung, 2006). More than 800 students with special education needs are studying in mainstream schools. At the same time, teachers, whose role is critical to the success of inclusive education, experience certain barriers, such as insufficient training relating to the challenges of inclusive education, limited training for curriculum design in relation to inclusion and a lack of information about children with special needs (Forlin, 2010).

Challenges Faced by the Hong Kong Education System

Although several issues pose challenges to the government, the Education Bureau and educators, when asked to classify them on the basis of factors such as 'obvious' and 'urgent', the following matters are frequently raised.

The gap in school – higher education language policy

There is a gap between the MOI at school and tertiary level. The Chinese medium of instruction has become mandatory at the school stage whereas all universities have English as the MOI, except for the Chinese University of Hong Kong, which is bilingual. Although the government presents its educational agenda to justify this policy, in reality the language policy at the school stage is influenced by political motives, whereas economic and international image guides the MOI at tertiary level. Li, Leung and Kember (2001) point out that 'The medium of instruction, and its impact on teaching and learning, is amongst the most contentious and most widely discussed educational issues in Hong Kong. Debate has encompassed all levels of education from pre-primary to universities' (p. 293). For more than two decades prior to 1997, the choice of the MOI at the primary and secondary stage was left to schools. However, in 1997 the government announced that Chinese would be the default medium of instruction in schools. Those schools who wanted to use English as the MOI had to apply to the EDB for approval. By contrast, MOI policy in higher education aims to meet the requirements of economic development in a globalized world. Nunan concludes that 'Hong Kong is a major international trading, business, banking, and communications center, and English is seen as a key to maintain its position in these areas' (Nunan, 2003, p. 597). The Basic Law (Constitution) of Hong Kong SAR determined the principle of bilingual education policy in Hong Kong, but universities still have the right to formulate and adjust the specific policies based on bilingual education.

Moreover, the promotion of English as the MOI at universities is also related to the management system. As Li (2008) pointed out, 'Although almost entirely financed by the government, each university had its own governing bodies, a board and senate, responsible for the institution's own governance and quality control. Universities in Hong Kong had always been able to chart their own course and determine their output and standard, just like their counterparts in the free West' (p. 63). All universities see themselves as neither state nor business institutions but modern tertiary institutions with characteristics such as university autonomy, which means that universities a) have the right to manage all matters based on the national constitution and laws; b) operate faculty governance which means that self-management is carried out by groups of scholars and researchers in teaching and research; and c) they have academic freedom, specifically the freedom of study and research by faculty members and students is essential to the mission of the academy, and scholars and researchers should have freedom to communicate or teach facts or ideas without political repression and official obstruction.

Last but not the least, the MOI policy of higher education is also influenced by the societal development needs of Hong Kong. English as the international language not only helps in recruiting outstanding talents including students, teachers and researchers, but also consequently promotes the academic and teaching capabilities of Hong Kong higher educational institutions on the international map. One simple reason for successful continuation of this policy can be attributed to Hong Kong's bilingual status. Hong Kong became a bilingual society gradually under the colonial rule of the British, when English was adopted as the official language. Hong Kong developed its economy mainly through international finance and trade because it lacked natural resources. English was used not only as the communication language of business but also the working language of government. The 2006 population census, carried out by the Census and Statistics Department of the Government of Hong Kong SAR, shows Cantonese as the most commonly used language at home (for 91 per cent of the population aged five and over). The proportion of the population who could speak English either as the 'usual language' or as another language was 45 per cent in 2006. Another reason for the tradition of bilingualism is classroom practice at both school and university level. Research conducted at the classroom level has shown that some form of native languages is used in the English medium schools. This has been termed 'code switching', referring to the act of switching from one language to another. Officially, code switching gained momentum in 1978 when bilingual schools increased in number, as many Chinese middle schools changed to English or a bilingual MOI pending acquisition of full status when the Sino-British Joint Declaration was proclaimed. This is also the pattern at the universities where only English or mixed-code (combining English and Chinese) is used as the medium of instruction. Students and local teachers communicate in Cantonese on campus while switching to English for most of the classes. According to the *Report of the Committee on Bilingualism* of CUHK, published in 2007, the language of instruction should be understood in the context of different teaching and learning activities: 'It refers not only to the language used at lectures, but also to the language employed in reading and reference materials; discussions at tutorials; projects or class presentations; laboratory, practicum and clinical sessions; assignments and examinations; and individual supervision' (*Report of the Committee on Bilingualism*, 2007).

Education for ethnic minorities

The government of Hong Kong encourages non-Chinese-speaking children to study in public sector schools in order that they may integrate into the community as early as possible. The government also provides support services including initiation and induction programmes for newly arrived non-Chinese-speaking children to help them adjust to the local education system. All public sector schools can admit eligible non-Chinese-speaking children, but they need to establish their eligibility either directly with the schools, the Education and Manpower Bureau, the Regional Education Offices or the Placement and Support Section. Public sector schools are mainly attended by ethnic minority students from lower income groups, whereas their similar age peers attend ESF or international schools. Ethnic minority students attending public sector schools are mainly segregated in local public primary/secondary schools called designated schools. The Hong Kong Education Bureau nominates schools having large numbers of non-Chinese students (NCS) as 'designated schools' and provides these schools with focused support to enhance the learning and teaching of the NCS students, particularly in the subject of Chinese language. While admitting the problem of limited choice of schools possessed by ethnic minority students, the government introduced a policy of opening mainstream schools to ethnic minority groups in 2005. But this policy of 'integration' did not receive the support of ethnic minority parents, as more than 80 per cent of them did not want to send their children to Chinese schools. Also, 56 per cent of them said they would drop out and wait for the English medium schools.

The medium of instruction in designated schools is English. Until 1998, the majority of local secondary schools in Hong Kong used English as the medium of instruction but changed to the mother tongue teaching policy in 1998. Some 307 secondary schools switched from English to Chinese, and only 114 schools were allowed to continue to use English, resulting in a reduction in the number of secondary schools that ethnic minority students could attend. Teachers in designated schools do not have much experience in multicultural education and are not prepared to meet the learning needs of students with diverse ethnic backgrounds (Heung, 2006). Failure to assimilate with mainstream students, or in-group peers enjoying private education, decreases chances of upward social mobility for ethnic minority students belonging to lower income groups in the highly competitive Hong Kong society. Past trends show that large numbers of ethnic minority students drop out after secondary form 3 (Grade 9), with 300 to 400 ethnic minority students taking O-level (Grade 11) examinations every year, and only a handful of students becoming eligible to sit for A-level (Grade 13) examinations. While talking about the academic attainment of South Asian students, who contribute the majority of ethnic minority students in local schools, one of the studies highlighted that only 1 per cent of the South Asian students successfully complete secondary education (Sung, 2005).

A lack of competence in the Chinese language is considered the main reason behind the poor performance of ethnic minority students (Ku et al., 2005; Loper, 2004). In the past at HKCEE Chinese examinations there was no differentiation between Chinese and non-Chinese students. Since 2007, ethnic minority students can attain alternative Chinese language qualification(s) through the General Certificate of Secondary Education (GCSE) (Chinese) examination administered by the Hong Kong Examinations and Assessment Authority. Following this, the University Grants Committee-funded institutions have, from 2008, provided further flexibility for the acceptance of alternative Chinese language qualification(s) including GCSE (Chinese) for application under specified circumstances under the Joint University Programmes Admissions System.

Large class sizes in schools

Small class teaching (SCT) to enhance the quality of teaching and learning environments in secondary schools has not been implemented. EDB has introduced SCT only in primary schools on the assumption that SCT is more useful when students are younger. Its effectiveness diminishes as the age of students rises. Furthermore, after the implementation of SCT, a mixed method study exploring its effectiveness concluded that a small class setting alone would not necessarily bring about improvement in learning and teaching. Rather, schools and teachers need to consider how to better utilize a small class setting that is requiring a paradigm shift in pedagogy. According to EDB figures, the student-to-teacher ratio in public sector primary schools also is 14.9:1 in 2011–12. While defending a policy of not implementing SCT in secondary schools, EDB states that in public sector secondary schools' student–teacher ratio has improved from 18.5:1 in the 2000–1 school year to the estimated 15.3:1 in the 2011–12 school year. At present, there are no plans to implement SCT in secondary schools as EDB believes that the average class size of secondary schools in Hong Kong is generally not on the high side when compared with other developed economies in Asia. In support, EDB also adds that the teaching and learning environments of secondary and primary schools are different.

Hence any direct comparison between their class sizes is lacking in credibility. In support it is argued that at secondary levels, schools in general have adopted flexible timetables for the implementation of group teaching. In accordance with other educationally advanced locations, Hong Kong supports secondary school students, in particular those academically low achievers, through a whole-school approach and targeted guidance. This includes the provision of additional teachers to arrange subject-based group teaching to enhance students' learning effectiveness.

The School System

The school system of the Hong Kong Education Department (EDB – Education Bureau) can be divided into three main groups: government schools; subsidized schools, which are usually administered by charitable bodies; and private schools run by different organizations where admission is more often decided by academic merit. Aside from the government system, there are schools classified as English School Foundation (ESF) and international schools.

Government/government-aided schools

The majority of students attend government or government-aided schools. These schools are administered and funded by the government. According to an Education Bill Amendment approved in 2004, every school that receives economic support from the government must set up school management committees. The government maintains that this helps to allow greater transparency and democracy. This model is used in order to improve the teaching and management of schools. Since these schools receive government funds, they must admit their students according to the government's two-stage admissions scheme. This huge group of schools can be further divided into two major sub-categories. First, there are a number of truly 'government' schools run by the Hong Kong government itself and their names reflect this, for example Kowloon Tong Government Primary School. But most government-funded schools in Hong Kong are actually run by private organizations such as churches and community groups, and are called 'aided' schools. These schools receive full government funding and are required to follow the government's curriculum and rules for admitting students and have a limited degree of autonomy in the way they are run. Some of Hong Kong's most famous and reputable schools, such as Mary Knoll and LaSalle, are 'aided' schools. Admission to government/ aided schools is carried out in two stages. First, almost a year in advance, parents can apply for a 'discretionary place admission' to a single school of their choice. These schools do not need to be in the geographical catchment area of their residence. At the discretionary place admission stage, government/aided schools can fill half of their places; over half of these discretionary places are de facto reserved for siblings of children already in the school, and for the sons and daughters of teachers. The remaining places, which account for almost 20 per cent of a school's total places, are allocated according to a 'points system' that gives advantages for a range of factors, such as the first-born, to children whose parents are themselves graduates of the school, and several other categories. The rest of the places in government/aided schools are assigned by the infamous 'Central Allocation' that takes place in the January of the year in which the child has to start P1. The Education and Manpower Bureau (EMB) and general public regard government schools as 'de facto pioneers' or 'pilots' in trying out or testing government education policies at school level. In contrast, government-aided schools mainly operated by independent sponsoring bodies enjoy more financial freedom and flexibility.

Private schools

Private schools in Hong Kong fall into three categories: a) direct subsidy schools (DSS) receiving a direct subsidy from Hong Kong government; b) private independent schools; c) and English School Foundation schools (ESF) and international schools.

Direct subsidy schools (DSS)

The DSS scheme was launched in 1991, and ordinary 'aided' schools can apply to become DSS. The status of a school as DSS immediately transforms them from a government-controlled school to a quasi-private school. For example, they have complete freedom in admitting students as they are not expected to follow the government's catchment areas. They conduct their admissions via application forms and one or two rounds of interviews just like private schools. In relation to funding, they can charge tuition fees, within limits, and then the government donates the difference between the amount they've collected and the amount they would have received as ordinary aided schools for the number of students they have registered. The DSS schools are also granted fairly wide latitude in terms of setting their curricula and are considered 'alternative' to schools following a traditional style of teaching. A few DSS schools have English as the medium of instruction except for Chinese language/culture. At present more and more schools are changing their status to DSS and it is believed that this scheme will lead to schools competing against each other since they will accept more students in return for more subsidies. The present trend shows an increase in the number of DSS schools, hence limiting the choice of school and school places for students from lower income groups.

Private independent schools (PIS)

The system of PIS was launched in 1999 with the aim of fostering the growth of a quality private school sector. These schools were provided with capital assistance in the form of land and building grants. However, in return they are expected to admit at least 70 per cent of local students. The local independent schools form a distinct grouping from public sector schools and traditional local private schools in terms of curricula, admissions, management and charging of fees. Meanwhile, the orientation of these schools towards a more local student intake, and generally lower fees, separates their market position from ESF and international schools.

ESF and international schools

The educational needs of the children from expatriate families are met mostly by ESF and international schools. Many of these schools also have a significant proportion of local students from well-to-do families. Both groups of schools follow international curricula, hire expatriate teaching staff and charge very high fees. In Hong Kong, the term 'international school' covers all those schools that do not follow the local system of education. According to Bray and Yamato (2003):

> Some of Hong Kong's so called international schools are in fact national schools based on systems in foreign countries and almost exclusively serving nationals of those countries. The Japanese and Korean schools are in this category. Other schools adopt the curricula of particular foreign countries but accept many students from Hong Kong and other parts of the world. (p. 4)

On the contrary, ESF schools are run by a private body called the English School Foundation. Initially these schools were established to meet the needs of the children of colonial officers.

At the time of writing, the ESF foundation is facing a possibility of losing its government subsidy. In 2011 the government proposed reviewing the future of ESF schools, raising the possibility that the foundation should ultimately become self-financing. This poses questions on how the city will be able to maintain adequate opportunities for non-Chinese-speaking pupils who attend ESF schools. The government is considering whether funding should cease in the long term, while the ESF wants an increase to a level equivalent to the subsidies received by Direct Subsidy Schools in the government system. Direct Subsidy Scheme schools receive almost double the amount received by the ESF at present. In the academic year 2010–11, DSS schools received HK$35,200 for each primary pupil, and HK$43,890 for each secondary pupil. The ESF got HK$17,757 and HK$23,659 respectively, according to the ESF's own records.

Conclusion

Education enables individuals to develop their potential, construct knowledge and enhance personality. As an international city, Hong Kong, through its education provisions, tries to relate to development in other parts of the world. The world is experiencing rapid and unprecedented changes, and Hong Kong is no exception. Politically, reunification with China and democratization has influenced the policies of this city-state. The introduction of a new language policy emphasizing the learning of three languages is an indication of the new post-1997 political status. Otherwise, Hong Kong education seems endowed with a fine mix of Eastern and Western culture. The education system aims to preserve the basic element of traditional Chinese education while absorbing the most advanced concepts, theories and experiences from the more fluid Western educational trends. Nonetheless, this does not deny the impact of a strongly class-based society. Hong Kong citizens are socialized with the basic idea that capitalism is essential for the maintenance of its economic success, power and influence in the present globalized world. Overtly, the formal education process is a combination of fairness and merits which conveys success or failure to individuals rather than to the system as a whole. Upward mobility in this highly stratified society is more a class factor, signifying that the majority of Hong Kong Chinese residents, and most of its ethnic minority groups, are unable to perceive an upward mobility in socioeconomic terms during their adult life (Tan, 2008). In addition to Chinese from lower income groups and mainland immigrants, one is able to locate individuals from lower income ethnic minority groups like South and South-East Asians, such as Filipinos, at the lowest level. This is largely a consequence of the Hong Kong education system, which is geared to the highest success of 'the few', while the majority reside at various levels of the highly stratified society. Hong Kong's education system has provided nine years (Grades 1–9) of compulsory education to all children below the age of 15 years, with only 20 per cent of the total cost paid by the parents. Such a concept of utilitarianism projects continued discrimination among students through various categories associated with the school system. Mainstream, DSS, designated, local, English School Foundation (ESF), international and Band 1, 2 or 3 are terms that signify the divisions within the education system, divisions that may even become deeper in the future. Mainstream schools are mainly Chinese medium instruction schools, with very few offering English as a medium of instruction. Designated schools are meant for non-Chinese students and provide instructions in English. Few mainstream schools also provide learning instructions through English language solely for the Chinese students.

Local schools follow the local education system and have types of schools based on the size of the tuition fee and administrative independence. They include government as well as government-aided and private schools addressed as direct subsidy schools (DSS). Government schools, which are directly funded by the Education and Manpower Bureau (EMB), enjoy a relatively smaller degree of freedom over spending power. By contrast, aided schools, mainly operated by independent school sponsoring bodies, enjoy more financial freedom and administrative flexibility, though they also receive funding from the government. DSS schools can be compared with voucher systems in the USA. However, unlike Hong Kong, those are 'non-add-on' in nature. In Hong Kong, students have to pay additional school fees if they want to study in Direct Subsidy Scheme schools, and the amount of add-on is substantial, thereby creating more inequality through the admission process as students who enter DSS need to pay more school fees. This also leads to unfairness in the educational process, as students enjoy more facilities and a better learning environment. ESF schools are schools run by Hong Kong's leading international group, follow British/International Baccalaureate (IB) curricula, and charge high tuition fees as well as receiving government subsidies. Similarly, international schools are not part of the local education system, and follow various curricula preparing their students for the public examinations administered by the examination bodies of other countries.

Foreign students and local students from higher income groups are able to meet the requirement of high tuition fees demanded by ESF and international schools. Banding is the tracking system, or scaling tool, beginning in the secondary stage, whereby students are allowed access to schools categorized as Band 1, 2 or 3. Band 1 schools are considered the best secondary schools, while Band 3 schools are deemed to be the lowest quality secondary schools. The banding system is not applicable to ESF and international schools, otherwise the above discussed terms coexist, for example a designated school is also a local/government school and can be classified in any band on the basis of academic performance. The system is complex, and more likely to be manipulated by the already better off.

The categorization of schools as mainstream/designated also reflects stratification on the basis of ethnicity whereas local/ESF/international schools project the economic inequality of Hong Kong society more than the cultural differences. On the contrary, the banding system creates stratification through individual ability, mainly taking into consideration a child's cognitive skills although indirectly also reflecting income inequalities in society. It is believed that the secondary 1 admission procedure plays a key role in deciding students' chances of moving to higher education. Even the NSS curricula, which deny streaming of students on the basis of subjects, will not be able to reduce the negative impact of the banding system. Students in Band 1 or 2 schools are mainly those students who perform exceedingly well academically as a consequence not only of the teaching environment at school but also because of belonging to families who are able to provide them with private tutoring services. The competition for places in higher-band schools and limited university places has also resulted in the parallel school system addressed as 'Shadow education' (Kwo and Bray, 2011). Survey-based research in 2010 showed 72.5 per cent of upper primary school students relying on private tutors. According to the local social organization survey reports in 2010, 72.5 per cent, 82 per cent and 85.5 per cent of lower, middle and senior secondary school students respectively depended on private tuitions (cited in Bray and Lykins, 2012).

Furthermore, students in higher-band mainstream schools, ESF and international schools work to higher expectations from their teachers, and have successful peers on whom to model their behaviour. Overall, the Hong Kong education system projects and reinforces the profound inequities in its society. This is likely to increase in the context of international competition in the field of education, given that Hong Kong aspires to be, and to some degree already is, an education hub in the global network.

References

Adamson, B. and Lai, A.W. (1997). 'Language and the curriculum in Hong Kong: Dilemmas of triglossia'. *Comparative Education*, 33 (2): 236–46.

Adamson, B. and Pang, L. S. (2004). 'Primary and secondary schooling', in M. Bray and R. Koo (eds), *Education and Society in Hong Kong and Macao: Comparative Perspectives on Continuity and Change*. Hong Kong: Kluwer Academic Publishers, pp. 35–60.

Atzaba-Poria, N., Pike, A. and Deater-Deckard, K. (2004). 'Do risk factors for problem behaviour act in a cumulative manner? An examination of ethnic minority and majority children through an ecological perspective'. *Journal of Child Psychology and Psychiatry*, 45 (4): 707–18.

Bacon-Shone, J. and Kingsley B. (1998). 'Charting multilingualism: Language censuses and language surveys in Hong Kong'. In M. C. Pennington (ed.), *Language in Hong Kong at Century's End*. Hong Kong: Hong Kong University Press, pp. 44–91.

Bolton, K. (2003). *Chinese Englishes: A Sociolinguistic History*. Cambridge: Cambridge University Press.

Bray, M. (2001). 'Higher education and political transition: Market forces and state intervention in a small society', in M. Bray and W. O. Lee (eds), *Education and Political Transition: Themes and Experiences in East Asia*. Hong Kong: Comparative Education Research Centre and the University of Hong Kong, pp. 139–61.

Bray, M. and Lee, W. O. (Eds). (1997) *Education and Political Transition: Implications of Hong Kong's Change of Sovereignty*. Hong Kong: Comparative Education Research Centre and the University of Hong Kong

Bray, M. and Lykins, C. (2012). *Shadow Education: Private Supplementary Tutoring and Its Implications for Policy Makers in Asia*. Mandaluyong City, Philippines: Asian Development Bank.

Bray, M., and Yamato, Y. (2003). 'Comparative education in a microcosm: Methodological insights from the international schools sector in Hong Kong'. *International Review of Education*, 49 (1–2): 51–73.

Bronfenbrenner, U. (1979). *The Ecology of Human Development*. Cambridge, MA: Harvard University Press.

Burchinal, M., Roberts, J., Hooper, S. and Zeisel, S. (2000). 'Cumulative risk and early cognitive development: A comparison of statistical risk models'. *Developmental Psychology*, 36 (6): 793–807.

Census and Statistics Department (2012). *Hong Kong 2011 Population Census – Summary Results*. Hong Kong: Census and Statistics Department.

Cheng, K. M. (2004). 'Turning a bad master into a good servant: reforming learning in China', in I. Rotberg (ed.), *Balancing Change and Tradition in Global Education Reform*. Washington, DC: Scarecrow Education, pp. 3–19.

—(2007). *Facing the Knowledge Society: Reforming Secondary Education in Shanghai and Hong Kong*. World Bank Working Paper. Washington, DC: World Bank.

—(2007). 'Reforming education beyond education', in Y. M. Yeung (ed.), *The First Decade of the HKSAR*. Hong Kong: Chinese University Press, pp. 251–72.

—(2009). 'Education for all, but for what?', in J. E. Cohen and M. Malin (eds), *The Wise Child: International Perspectives on the Goals of Basic and Secondary Education*. Stanford, CA: American Association of Arts and Sciences/Stanford University, pp. 42–65.

—(2011). *Curriculum Reform: Why Bother?* Key-note address presented at C&I Conference 2011, Curriculum Matters: Policy, Implementation and Sustainability, Hong Kong Institute of Education, Hong Kong SAR, 19 November.

Cheng, K. M. and Yip, H. K. (2007). *Facing the Knowledge Society: Reforming Secondary Education in Shanghai and Hong Kong*. World Bank Working Paper. Washington, DC: World Bank.

Curriculum Development Council (2001). *Learning to Learn: Life-Long Learning and Whole-Person Development*. Hong Kong: Curriculum Development Council

Deater-Deckard, K., Dodge, K. A., Bates, J. E. and Pettit, G. S. (1998). 'Multiple risk factors in the development of externalizing behavior problems: Group and individual differences'.

Development and Psychopathology, 10 (3): 469–93.

EDB-Kindergarten, Primary and Secondary Education (2011). http://www.edb.gov.hk/ index.aspx?nodeID=74&langno=1.

Education Bureau (2009). *Education system: The Government of Hong Kong Special Administrative Region 2009*. Hong Kong: Education Bureau, HKSAR. http://www.edb.gov.hk/index.aspx?nodeid=2 (Accessed 23 August 2009).

—(2010). *Operation Guide on the Whole School Approach to Integrated Education*. Hong Kong: Education Bureau, HKSAR. http://www.edb.gov.hk/FileManager/EN/ Content_7385/ie%20guide_en.pdf

Education Commission (1997). *Education Commission Report No. 7*. Hong Kong: Education Commission.

—(1999). *Education Blueprint for the 21st Century: Review of Academic System in Hong Kong*. Hong Kong: Hong Kong Education Commission.

—(2000). *Learning for Life and Learning through Life: Reform Proposals for the Education System in Hong Kong*. Hong Kong: Hong Kong Education Commission.

Education Department (1997). *Medium of Instruction: Guidance for Secondary Schools*. Hong Kong: Education Department.

—(1999). *Lists of Dos and Don'ts for Kindergartens*. Schools Curriculum Circular No. 4/99. Hong Kong: Education Department.

—(2000). *Performance Indicators for Kindergartens*. Hong Kong: Education Department.

Education Department and Social Welfare Department (2002). *Working Party on Harmonisation of Pre-primary Services*. Consultation Document. Hong Kong: Government Printer Hong.

Education and Manpower Bureau (1998). *Consultation Document on the Review of* the Education-related Executive and Advisory Bodies. Hong Kong: Education and Manpower Bureau.

—(2003). *Direct Subsidy Scheme*. Hong Kong: Education and Manpower Bureau.

Evans, G. W. (2003). 'A multimethodological analysis of cumulative risk and allostatic load among rural children'. *Developmental Psychology*, 39 (5): 924–33.

Evans, S. (2000). 'Hong Kong's new English language policy in education'. *World Englishes*, 19 (2): 185–204.

Forlin, C. (2010). 'Developing and implementing quality inclusive education in Hong Kong: Implications for teacher education'. *Journal of Research in Special Educational Needs*, 10 (1): 177–84.

Gao, F. (2011). 'Linguistic capital: Continuity and change in educational language polices for South Asians in Hong Kong primary schools'. *Current Issues in Language Planning*, 12 (2): 251–63.

Heritage Foundation and *Wall Street Journal* (2012). '*Index of economic freedom*'. Heritage Foundation and Wall Street Journal. Washington, DC.

Heung, V. (2006). 'Recognizing the emotional and behavioral needs of ethnic minority students in Hong Kong'. *Preventing School Failure*, 50 (2): 29–36.

Ho, C. W. D. (2007). 'Policy of quality assurance in Hong Kong preschools'. *Early Child Development and Care*, 177 (5): 493–505.

Hui, K. F. and Poon L. M. (2004). 'Higher education, imperialism and colonial transition', in M. Bray and R. Koo (eds), *Education and Society in Hong Kong and Macao: Comparative Perspectives on Continuity and Change*. Hong Kong: Kluwer Academic Publishers, pp. 109–26.

Koo, R. D. Y., Kam, C. K. and Choi, B. (2003). 'Education and schooling in Hong Kong: Under one country, two systems'. *Childhood Education*, 79 (3): 137–44.

Ku, H. B., Chan, K. W. and Sandhu, K. K. (2005). *A Research Report on the Education of South Asian Minority Groups in Hong Kong*. Hong Kong: Centre for Social Policy Studies, Department of Applied Social Sciences, Hong Kong Polytechnic University and Unison Hong Kong.

Kwo, O. and Bray, M. (2011). 'Facing the shadow education system in Hong Kong'. *IIAS Newsletter* 56, 20. International Institute for Asian Studies, University of Leiden. http://web.edu.hku.hk/staff/mbray/docs/IIAS-Kwo-Bray.pdf

Lai, P. S. and Bryam, M. (2003). 'The politics of bilingualism: A reproduction analysis of the policy of the mother tongue education in Hong Kong after 1997'. *Compare: A Journal of Comparative Education*, 33 (3): 315–34.

Li, L. (2008). 'Does globalization lead to convergence in higher education? An empirical study of four East Asian university systems, 1946–1996: Hong Kong, Singapore, Taiwan, Thailand'. *Analytical Reports in International Education*, 2 (1): 49–75.

Li, N., Leung, D.Y.P. and Kember, D. (2001). 'Medium of Instruction in Hong Kong Universities: The Mis-Match between Espoused Theory and Theory in Use'. *Higher Education Policy*, 14, 4: 293–312.

Lian, M. G. J. (2004). *Alternative and Augmentative Communication: New Opportunities for Persons with Speech and Language Disabilities*. Hong Kong: INSTEP, University of Hong Kong.

Lin, A. and Detaramani, C. (1998). 'By carrot and by rod: Extrinsic motivation and English language attainment of Hong Kong tertiary students', in M. C. Pennington (ed.), *Language in Hong Kong at Century's End*. Hong Kong: Hong Kong University Press, pp. 285–302.

Loper, K. (2004). *Race and Equality: A Study of Ethnic Minorities in Hong Kong's Education System*. Hong Kong: Centre for Comparative and Public Law, University of Hong Kong.

McLoughlin, B., Paul, M. and Tan, G. (2010). *The Impact of the 334 Educational Reform on Caritas Institute of Higher Education (CIHE)*. Hong Kong: Worcester Polytechnic Institute.

Mok, K. H. (2000). 'Impact of Globalization: A Study of Quality Assurance Systems of Higher education in Hong Kong and Singapore'. *Comparative Education Review*, 44, 2: 148–74.

—(2003). 'Globalization and Higher Education: Restructuring in Hong Kong, Taiwan and Mainland China'. *Higher Education Research and Development*, 22, 2: 117–29.

Morris, P. (2002). 'Promoting curriculum reforms in the context of political transition: An analysis of Hong Kong's experience'. *Journal of Education Policy*, 17 (1): 13–28.

Nunan, D. (2003). 'The impact of English as a global language'. *TESOL Quarterly*, 37 (4): 589–613.

Poon, A. Y. K. and Wong, Y. C. (2008). 'Policy Changes and Impact of the Education Reform in Hong Kong'. *Journal of National Taiwan Normal University*, 53, 3: 47–65.

Poon, Y. K. (2000). *Medium of Instruction in Hong Kong: Policy and Practice*. Maryland: University Press of America.

Post, D. (2004). 'Family resources, gender, and immigration: Changing sources of Hong Kong educational inequality, 1971–2001'. *Social Science Quarterly*, 85 (5): 1238–58.

Postiglione, G. A. (1997). 'Schooling and Social Stratification', in G. A. Postiglione and W. O. Lee (eds) *Schooling in Hong Kong: Organization, Teaching and Social Context*. Hong Kong University Press, pp. 137–53.

QS World University Rankings (2011–17). *2012 Report*. http://www.itesm.la/archivos/ QS_World_University_Rankings.pdf (Accessed 14 January 2013).

Rao, N. (2002). 'Early childhood education in Hong Kong: Moving towards child-friendly policies, curricula and practices', in V. Sollars (ed.), *Curricula, Policies and Practices in Early Childhood Education Services*. Malta: P.E.G, pp. 76–88.

Shum, M. S. K., Gao, F., Tsung, L. and Ki, W. W. (2011). 'South Asian students' Chinese language learning in Hong Kong: Motivations and strategies'. *Journal of Multilingual & Multicultural Development*, 32 (3): 285–97.

Steering Committee (2008). *Review of the Post-secondary Education Sector*. Hong Kong: Hong Kong Education Bureau. http://www.edb.gov.hk/FileManager/EN/ Content_689/phase2reviewreport(eng).pdf (Accessed 30 June 2008).

Sun, C. F. (2002). 'Hong Kong's language policy in the postcolonial age', in M. K. Chan and Y. Alvin, *Crisis and Transformation in China's Hong Kong*. London: M.E. Sharpe, Inc. pp. 283–306.

Sung, H. M. (2005). *Approaching South Asians in Hong Kong*. M.Phil dissertation, Lingnan University, Hong Kong.

Sweeting, A. (1990). *Education in Hong Kong Pre-1841 to 1941 Fact and Opinion: Materials for a History of Education in Hong Kong*. Hong Kong: Hong Kong University Press.

—(1997). 'Education policy and the 1997 factor: The art of the possible interacting with the dismal science', in M. Bray and W. O. Lee (eds), *Education and Political Transition: Implications of Hong Kong's Change of Sovereignty*. Hong Kong: Comparative Education Research Centre and the University of Hong Kong, pp. 25–39.

Tan, J. (1997). 'Education and colonial transition in Singapore and Hong Kong: Comparisons and contrasts'. *Comparative Education*, 33 (2): 303–12.

Tan, K. B. (2008). *Colonialism, Sinicization and Ethnic Minorities in Hong Kong*. Paper read at (UN) Problematic Multiculturalism and Social Resilience conference, Singapore.

Tang, K. and Bray, M. (2000). 'Colonial models and the evolution of education systems: Centralization and decentralization in Hong Kong and Macao'. *Journal of Education Administration*, 38 (5): 468–85.

Wong, K. C. (1997). 'Organizing and managing schools', in G. A. Postiglione and W. O. Lee (eds), *Schooling in Hong Kong: Organization, Teaching and Social Context*. Hong Kong: Hong Kong University Press, pp. 81–94.

Wong Ngai Chun, M. and Rao, N. (2004). 'Preschool education', in M. Bray and R. Koo (eds), *Education and Society in Hong Kong and Macao: Comparative Perspectives on Continuity and Change*. Hong Kong: Kluwer Academic Publishers, pp. 15–34.

Yuen, G. (2008). 'Education reform policy and early childhood teacher education in Hong Kong before and after the transfer of sovereignty to China in 1997'. *Early Years: An International Journal of Research and Development*, 28 (1): 23–45.

Yuen, G. and Grieshaber, S. (2009). 'Parents' choice of early childhood education services in Hong Kong: A pilot study about vouchers'. *Contemporary Issues in Early Childhood*, 10 (3): 263–79.

Yung Man-Sing, A. (2004). 'Higher education', in M. Bray and R. Koo (eds), *Education and Society in Hong Kong and Macao: Comparative Perspectives on Continuity and Change*. Hong Kong: Kluwer Academic Publishers, pp. 61–72

Zeng, Kangmin (1999). *Dragon Gate: Competitive Examinations and their Consequences*. London: Cassell.

4

Macao: Governmentality and Education Development in the Post-1999 Era

Sou-Kuan Vong

The education system and its development in Macao differ from most Chinese societies where there is commonly the presence of a centralized system. The long-standing non-intervention approach adopted by the pre-colonial government, the Portuguese administration, left Macao a 'big market, small government' regime in which the government had limited participation in education and indeed in social matters overall (Vong and Wong, 2010, p. 65). Government policy was often reduced to a visible symbol rather than actual practice. Within the social milieu, education is one of the most contested terrains prior to, and following, the handover of Macao to Chinese sovereignty in 1999. 'Diversity' is a status quo both in the pre-tertiary and tertiary education sectors.

Since the political handover, Macao has undergone a certain degree of social change. In particular, the gaming industry has been opened to competition and has been thriving. While it has provided the local government with much more revenue, at the same time this industry has generated certain social pressures and problems, such as an extreme disparity between the rich and the poor. In order to resolve the conflicts and tensions in society and at the same time construct a 'harmonious society'[1] in line with the Chinese government, the Macao Special Administrative Region (Macao SAR), with abundant surplus generating from the gaming industry, has been adopting a money-driven policy for the last few years by giving direct subsidy to local permanent residents, supplementary subsidies on household electricity supply, individual public transportation, medical coupons and other benefits. The developments traced here demonstrate that there has been a significant shift of government rationality in governance, shifting from a *laissez-faire* policy to a *welfare state* policy. The Macao SAR has made considerable efforts to regain the space and discourse and to reparticipate in all social matters. This is especially so in the field of education, so as to effect direct changes in preparing good Chinese citizens who can better serve Macao under the 'One Country, Two Systems' principle. Nonetheless, by resuming its *state* responsibilities, the Macao SAR has also intended that its administration be one that would signify a strong governmental regime.

Situated in this particular historical, political, cultural and social context, this chapter draws on the notion of 'governmentality', a term coined by Michel Foucault (1926–84) and developed in the later years of his life to scrutinize the *shifting* governing principles and mentalities in education reforms in the post-1999 era in Macao. The reason for adopting the lens of governmentality is to explore and examine the emerging mentalities or govermental rationality in the parallel processes of post-colonialism and unprecedented economic growth in shaping the possibilities of education development in the post-1999 era in Macao. Governmentality, according to Foucault (1991), refers to the different mentalities of the government or 'government rationality' which involves 'the art of government' through a calculating preoccupation with activities aimed at shaping, challenging and guiding the conducts of others. Deriving from this notion, this study will focus on the analysis of texts, namely education policy that comes mainly from the Annual Chief Executive Policy Address, the Annual Policy Document of the Secretary for Social and Culture Affairs, and government administrative regulations promulgated in the *Government Gazette*.

The chapter will begin by presenting the context under study and provide a brief account of the social context in Macao and some if its recent developments. Next it will explore the changing educational landscape of Macao prior to and following its political transition in 1999. The main study will follow the description of the local background and will focus on the disclosure of governmentalities from the texts. Finally, the focus of analysis, involving discussion of the findings, will be on the shifting discourses of governance on education in the post-1999 era.

The Macao Context

Macao is a small city of 29.7 square kilometres (DSEC, 2010a) located at the southern tip of mainland China, at the exit of Pearl River Delta, with a population of 552,500, an increase of 26.9 per cent compared with the 2001 Census (DSEC, 2011). The Macao Special Administrative Region is composed of the Macao peninsula and two islands, namely Taipa and Coloane. According to the preliminary results of the census in 2011, with regard to age distribution, Macao is becoming an ageing society. The youth population, aged 0 to 14, totals 65,900, making up 11.9 per cent of the total population, a considerable decrease of 9.7 per cent compared with 21.6 per cent in 2001. The adult population, aged 15 to 64, occupies 80.8 per cent of the total, an increase of 9.7 per cent from 71.1 per cent in 2001. The elderly group, aged 65 and above, remains at a similar percentage of 7.2 per cent to that of the census in 2001.

Macao had been a Portuguese colony for more than four centuries before Portugal terminated her rule and handed the sovereignty of Macao to mainland China on 20 December 1999. In the contemporary history of Macao, the signature of the Sino-Portuguese Joint Declaration between Portugal and mainland China on the question of Macao on 13 April 1987 gave an impetus to social change and reform in the late colonial governance. This declaration delineated the parameters and schedule for the restoration of Chinese rule over Macao. After the political transition, Macao was designated a Special Administrative Region, like Hong Kong, and has since been administered under the principle of 'One Country, Two Systems'.

Social stability was one of the major concerns prior to and following the handover of Macao to the People's Republic of China (PRC). It is believed that social stability, 'implicitly defined as the presence of social harmony, citizen satisfaction with the quality of life, and the absence of political disturbances – is directly linked to economic success' (Scott, 2011, p. 1). Having suffered from the Asian financial crisis immediately before the political transition, Macao, as a city without any natural resources, has had largely to make its own way forward. Thus, the issue of the gaming industry was on the agenda in the 1990s as an unusual way to enhance social stability through economic development. In 2001, Edmund Ho Hau Wah, then the Chief Executive, deregulated the gaming laws and this has attracted a huge inflow of foreign capital, including some of the world's leading casino corporations, such as Steve Wynn and the Las Vegas Sands Corporation. In the following year, Ho declared the gaming industry as the lead industry in Macao with the aim of enhancing and restoring the economic position after financial recession and in order to improve the overall living standard of residents (*Governo de RAEM*, 2001, pp. 9–10). However, while the gaming industry has contributed to economic growth, it has also generated increased social pressures such as increasing the already extreme disparity between the rich and the poor.

In 2006, a large demonstration took place on May Day to protest against rising social inequality and unemployment. According to information from the Statistics and Census Bureau (DSEC, 2010b) in 2006, Macao's per capita GDP of $28,436 (227,508 patacas (MOP), Macao currency) surpassed the Hong Kong figure of $27,526 for the first time. But there is a deepening social divide. In the following years, protests have become a frequent and direct means to express dissatisfaction towards government. Demands have been made to relieve poverty and increase employment. In order to smooth the conflict and tension, the government has developed a 'Wealth Partaking in the Economic Development Plan' (*Plano de Comparticipação Pecuniária no Desenvolvimento Económico*), to give a direct subsidy to local residents. From 2008 to 2012, under this plan, permanent local residents have each received MOP 5,000 to 7,000 (equivalent to US$625 to 875) and non-permanent local residents MOP 3,000 to 4,200 (equivalent to US$375.00 to 525.00). However, some legislators and local scholars argue that the government merely provides local people with the equivalent of a palliative. In reality, without a long-term and more secure development plan, Macao will not become an economically and socially sustainable territory.

The Educational Landscape

A brief discussion of the birth of the educational reform in Macao is relevant before presenting educational development in the post-1999 era. The development of Macao, to a great extent, was shaped by the internal developments of both mainland China and Portugal. Long before 1974, both countries underwent internal political reforms and this left Macao unattended. Only through the Joint Declaration in 1987 did Macao recapture the extensive attention from both countries. Nonetheless, there is a consistent pattern of discontinuity in overall policies and practices in the territory, and the field of education is no exception.

Education reform and development

Education reform really began in the late 1980s as a product of political transition. The first Education Law, Law 11/91/M, which embraced both private and public education was only promulgated by the Legislative Assembly in 1991. During the years before the political handover, the Macao-Portuguese government took a more vibrant initiative in regulating the private education sector, by disciplining private schools through documentation (Niesche, 2010), creating a unified plan. Table 4.1 below shows the intensification of governance in the field of non-tertiary education prior to 1999.

Table 4.1 Legislation related to education development prior to 1999

Date	Legislation	Content
29 August 1991	L11/91/M	Definition of the orientation and policy of the education system for Macao.
18 July 1994	DL 39/94/M	Establishment of the curriculum framework for junior secondary education.
18 July 1994	DL 38/94/M	Establishment of the framework for organizing the curricula for pre-primary and primary education.
26 June 1995	DL 29/95/M	Establishment of norms for gradual universal free education and financial assistance to non-profit-making private institutes.
25 March 1996	DL 15/96/M	Definition of the Statute of Teachers for private institutes integrated in the Public School Net System.
16 September 1996	DL 54/96/M	Regulation of Technical and Professional Education. Removal of the DL 44/82/M legislation.
18 March 1997	DS 13/SAAEJ/97	Approval of the model of teacher training for the teaching of moral education and civic education, or moral education and civic education integrated in the area of personal and social development.
30 June 1997	DL 26/97/M	Definition of the juridical order of School Inspection.
22 September 1997	DL 41/97/M	Establishment of the juridical, assistance and coordination regime for the training of pre-primary, primary and secondary school teachers.
10 November 1997	DL 46/97/M	Establishment of the framework for organizing the senior secondary school curriculum.
26 January 1998	DL 4/98/M	Creation of norms in arts education.
16August 1999	DL 42/99/M	Definition of the scope and area of compulsory and free education.

Compiled and translated by the author based on the legislation on the DSEJ website. http://www.dsej.gov.mo/~webdsej/www/inter_dsej_page.php?con=grp_db/edulaw.htm (18 March 2012).

From Table 4.1, the Macao-Portuguese government's attempts to delineate the boundary of governance by means of legislation, particularly in certain domains such as curriculum development, teacher statute and school inspection, are clear.

Higher education began late in Macao. It was not until 1981 that the first private university – East Asia University – was founded. Coincidently, the development of the higher education sector took off in the late 1980s and early 1990s. Table 4.2 shows the development of higher education in Macao.

Unlike the development of non-tertiary education, the tertiary sector commenced late but has exhibited rapid and dramatic expansion in the last three decades. There are three notable phases of development, namely: a) from 1981 to 1988; b) from 1988 to 1996; and c) from 1996 onwards. In the first phase, there was no government commitment in higher education. It was in the hands of private enterprise. In the second phase, the government took an active role to build a public higher education sector, for instance in purchasing the private university and establishing four other public institutes. The third phase was dominated by the private sector, in which specialist institutions were established associated with the social and economic development of Macao. For instance, Macau Millennium College was founded by 'well-known educators

Table 4.2 Development of higher education in Macao

Year	Name of Institute	Type
1981	University of East Asia	Private
1988	University of East Asia	Government
1988	Macau Security Force Superior School	Government
1988	Open College of the University of East Asia	Private
1991	University of East Asia renamed as University of Macau	Government
1991	Macau Polytechnic Institute	Government
1992	United Nations University's International Institute for Software Technology	United Nations
1995	Institute for Tourism Studies	Government
1996	Institute of European Studies of Macau	Portuguese Enterprise Europe Network
1996	Inter-University Institute of Macau	Private
1999	Kiang Wu Nursing College of Macau	Private
2000	Macau Institute of Management	Private
2000	Macau University of Science and Technology	Private
2001	Macau Millennium College	Private
2009	Inter-University Institute of Macau renamed as St Joseph University	Private
2011	Open College of the University of East Asia renamed as City University of Macau	Private

Sources: Compiled by the author based on Bray et al. (2002) and the GAES website. http://www.gaes.gov. mo/big5/contentframe.asp?content=./mc_u_link.html (18 March 2012).

and businesses in Hong Kong and Macau' and the academic, research and professional fields were 'closely related to Macau's most important industry, namely, the Tourism and Gaming Industry' (Macau Millennium College, 2012).

Education system and provision

The education system in Macao is composed of two sectors, namely non-tertiary education and the tertiary sector. The Education and Youth Bureau (*Direcção dos Serviços de Educação e Juventude*, also known as the DSEJ) is in charge of the non-tertiary sector, while the Tertiary Education Services Office (*Gabinete de Apoio ao Ensino Superior*, also known as the GAES) is in charge of the tertiary sector. Non-tertiary education is governed by the Fundamental Law of Non-tertiary Education System, which is known as Law No. 9/2006. The higher education institutions are still governed by the Decree Law 11/91/M approved in 1991, with some minor and supplementary amendments in 1992.

The non-tertiary education system is composed of two parts: formal and continuing education. Formal education includes infant education, primary education, junior secondary education, senior secondary education, vocational-technical education and special education. Continuing education comprises family education, recurrent education, community education and vocational training. This embodies the notion of lifelong learning and 'it is the complement and development of formal education' (*Governo de RAEM*, 2006). This descriptive analysis will focus on formal education, and in particular policies concerning the schooling system. The structure of the system is 3-6-3-3, namely three years of infant education, six years of primary, and three years of junior and three years of senior secondary education. The DL 15/96/M passed in 1996 is a significant piece of legislation which marks the first step of ten years of universal free education, ranging from the last year of infant education to junior secondary education. With dramatic economic growth in the post-1999 era, the major development in the field of education has been the extension of ten years universal of free education to that of 15 years, which includes the first two years of kindergarten and three years of senior secondary education.

A key feature of the schooling system is that the major components are private rather than government. This is a very different situation to that in nearby regions, indeed worldwide, and dates from the former colonial government adopting a laissez-faire attitude toward the private sector (Adamson and Li, 1999). According to the so-called mini constitution of the territory, the Macao

SAR Basic Law, these private schools are entitled to enjoy much autonomy, as stated in Article 122, Chapter VI, Culture and Social Affairs:

> The existing educational institutions of all kinds in Macao may continue to operate. All educational institutions in the Macao Special Administrative Region shall enjoy their autonomy and teaching and academic freedom in accordance with law. Educational institutions of all kinds may continue to recruit staff and use teaching materials from outside the Macao Special Administrative Region. Students shall enjoy freedom of choice of educational institutions and freedom to pursue their education outside the Macao Special Administrative Region. (People's Republic of China, 1993)

This Article reflects the phenomenon of diversity prior to the political transition, as well as the commitment to safeguard the autonomy of private schools. It may also mean that private schools have a significant power of negotiation in this regard. The distribution of schools in Macao is another indicator of the imbalance of power between the government and the market (private schools). In the academic year 2010–11, a total of 75 schools registered under the DSEJ. Among these schools, 11 were government schools, 53 private schools that had joined the free education system and 11 were private schools that did not belong to this system (DSEJ, 2011a). All private schools are also divided into two categories: half have a religious background such as Roman Catholic, Protestant or Buddhist, and the remainder are patriotic schools run by traditional pro-China organizations. The schooling size in Macao is very small, too. The following table shows the population of formal education and its distribution:

As stated above, higher education developed late in Macao. The Tertiary Education Services Office was established in 1992. It is a governmental department in charge of higher education affairs in Macao, and is under the leadership of the Secretary for Social Affairs and Culture of the Government of the Macau Special Administrative Region. The main responsibilities of the Office (GAES, 2012a), as stated on its website, include to 'initiate and formulate policies'; to 'assist, follow-up and promote the higher education of Macao'; to 'organize inter-institutional activities for higher education students'; to 'provide information and counselling services for further studies'; to 'handle applications and examinations of joint admission to undergraduate and postgraduate programmes in Mainland universities'.

The tertiary sector in Macao contrasts markedly with that in Hong Kong, with more than ten times the population, where there are only eight higher

Table 4.3 Size of formal education and its distribution in academic year 2010–11

School Types	Government Schools	Private Schools		Total
		Free Education System	**Non-Free Education System**	
Number of Schools	11	53	11	75
Number of Students	2933 (4%)	57,473 (79%)	11,958 (17%)	72,364 (100%)

Compiled by the author, based on the DSEJ (2011b) website. http://www.dsej.gov.mo/~webdsej/www/statisti/2010/index-e.html (18 March 2012).

education institutions funded by the University Grants Committee and six self-funded higher education institutions (UGC, 2012). In Macao, according to information provided by the Tertiary Education Services Office (GAES, 2012b), there are currently ten higher education institutions, including the University of Macau (UM); Macao Polytechnic Institute (IPM); the Institute for Tourism Studies (IFT); Kiang Wu Nursing College of Macau (KWNCM); Macau Institute of Management (MIM); Macau University of Science and Technology (MUST); Macau Millennium College (MMC); St Joseph University (USJ); and the City University of Macau (CITYU). Most of the ten institutions are mono-technical, the notable exceptions being the University of Macau and the Macau University of Science and Technology, which are relatively comprehensive in nature. The remaining institutions are highly specific in cultivating certain kinds of professions, such as nursing, gaming and tourism. The following table shows the students registered by programmes in the academic year 2010–11.

The above table explicitly shows that, similar to that of the field of non-tertiary education, the field of higher education is also dominated by the private sector, which comprises up to 65 per cent of the total registered students. Among these, local students total 17,295, and non-local, 15,248 (GAES, 2011), another unusual feature.

Government, Policy, Governmentality and Disciplinary Power

After the political handover, the Annual Chief Executive Policy Address has become the signpost for the development of the territory. In the area of education, the policy is released in a form of *Linhas de Acção Governativa – Área*

Table 4.4 Students registered, by programmes, 2010–11

Institutions	Doctorate	Master	Post-graduate Diploma	Bachelor	Bacharelato (3-yr Degree)	Diploma	Total
UM	209	1614	151	5437	–	–	7411
IPM	–	–	–	1602	1049	–	2651
IFT	–	–	–	331	986	26	1343
ESFSM	–	–	–	74	–	–	74
CITYU	74	4621	1659	2073	–	18	8445
USJ	64	411	–	1247	–	–	1722
KWNCM	–	–	29	208	–	–	237
MUST	301	828	–	8734	–	–	9863
MIM	–	–	–	117	254	–	371
MMC	–	–	–	285	–	141	426
Total							
Percentage	648	7474	1839	20,108	2289	185	32,543
	1.99%	22.97%	5.65%	61.79%	7.03%	0.57%	100%

Source: GAES (Gabinete de Apoio ao Ensino Superior) (2011, p. 8). Data of Higher Education in Macao – Numbers of Staff and Students for the Academic Year 2010/2011. Macao: Tertiary Education Services Office.

dos Assuntos Sociais e Cultura, or in English, the *Annual Policy Address – Area of Social and Cultural Affairs*, which is announced by the Secretary for Social Affairs and Culture. In this study, the above two sets of texts, ranging from 2000 to 2012, are under analysis in order to disclose underpinning governmentalities in the area of educational development. The notion of governmentality is complicated and interwoven with a distinct conception of government, power, technology of self and disciplinary power.

Government and power

Foucault's key concept of 'government' and 'population' should be addressed here in order to gain a better understanding how governmentalities and technologies of self operate in this study. In Foucault's view,

> 'Government' did not refer to political structures or the management of states; rather it designates the way in which the conduct of individuals or state might be directed: the government of children, of souls, of communities, of families, of the sick. It did not cover only the legitimately constituted forms of political or economic subjection, but also modes of action, more or less considered, which were designed to act upon the possibilities of action of other people. To govern, in this sense, is to structure the possible field of action of others. (Dreyfus and Rabinow, 1982, p. 221)

In Foucault's perspective, government is not confined to a political structure. Rather, it delineates a scope and a domain able 'to act upon the possibilities of action of other people'. In this regard, policy is a political product that contributes to define a scope and domain to make the functioning of sovereignty or government possible (Foucault, 1991). Instead of referring to sovereign power, which is much associated with monarchical power, throughout his work Foucault is more concerned with two other forms of power, namely disciplinary power and bio-power. The former is a type of power invested in the nation-states with which to discipline individuals within a particular territory. The latter concerns the self-regulatory power that an individual employs to make himself/herself useful and productive in society. This is how 'population' or citizens come into existence as a distinct domain of 'governed and action'.

Furthermore, Foucault considers that government is the 'conduct of conduct' or 'government as activity' which involves 'a form of activity aiming to shape, guide or affect the conduct of some person or persons' (Gordon, 1991, p. 2). Miller and Rose (1990) and Rose and Miller (1992) summarize this as a programmatic form of power relations built on rationalities and technologies of government, which are embedded within discursive and other social and institutional practices. Similarly Hunt and Wickham (1998, p. 76) state that 'governmentality is the dramatic expansion in the scope of government, featuring an increase in the number and size of the governmental calculation mechanisms'. In short, there are a number of conditions making governmentality possible in modern societies, for instance a specific terrain of governance where people (population) are the targets to act upon 'governmental calculations' (technologies of government). It is in this way that technologies of the self serve as an interface connecting governmentality and the population to effect both disciplinary and bio-power in order to lead to a disciplined society. It is in this context that education has become an area of specific actions of investment during and beyond the political transition in Macao. In adopting a Foucauldian lens, this study aims to scrutinize the emerging governmentalities in the Macao education sector.

Policy, governmentality and disciplinary power

Policy is commonly understood as government intention. Kogan asserts (1975; cited in Ball, 1990, p. 3) that policy is a matter of the 'authoritative allocation of values', or 'statements of prescriptive intent'. There is a strong bond between government intent and policy. Furthermore, Gillies (2008) points out that policy has its symbolic value and spectacle effect so as to make governance possible.

By the term governmentality, Foucault suggests a different perspective on power. Foucault (1990) states that power is not always exercised in a form of repression and coercion by government. Likewise, as Tikly (2003, p. 165) suggests, 'education policy can usefully be seen as acting at the interface between programmes and technologies of government'. He further points out that 'education policies take the form of political programmes of government and attempt to use technologies of government to implement these programmes in a way that is consistent with the underlying rationality of government'. In short, education policy can be seen as a tool to make the governmentality explicit, in order to disseminate government's message and at the same time serve as an interface bridging the government and the governed.

Technologies of the self, also known as 'care of the self', are the techniques, according to Foucault, by which human beings constitute themselves. Technologies of self are the forms of knowledge and strategies that 'permit individuals to effect by their own means or with the help of others a certain number of operations on their own bodies and souls, thoughts, conduct, and way of being, so as to transform themselves in order to attain a certain state of happiness, purity, wisdom, perfection, or immortality' (Foucault, 1982, p. 225). According to this view, power no longer exists in a cohesive form. Rather, it is manifested through a self-technology and self-disciplinary mode 'to incite, reinforce, control, monitor, optimize and organize the forces' (Foucault, 1990, p. 136). This is in order to be more productive and to generate new forms of knowledge and *truths*. In order to make disciplinary power workable, several measures, such as surveillance, hierarchical observation, normalization and examination, are employed to ensure the mechanisms of discipline are achievable (Foucault, 1991a). In this study, there are two objectives: a) to reveal the (emerging) governmentalities in the area of education; and b) to analyze the what ways in which these governmentalities are delivered.

Emerging Governmentalities

As noted, prior to 1999 the Macao-Portuguese government did not develop a consistent pattern in policy. After the transition, the political atmosphere changed. Each year, the Annual Policy Address has developed a theme (or slogan) to maximize the symbolic value of the policy in order to enhance social cohesion (Gillies, 2008).

For the past 12 years, almost every year has had a specific theme, including 'Restoration of Institutions, Steady Development' (*Governo de RAEM*, 2000), 'Rely on Ourselves, Strive for Our Future' (2001); 'Solidarity, Self-confidence and Hard Work' (2002); 'Be Aware of the Overall Situation, Pace Up with Society' (2003); 'Pace Up with Society, Development with Coordination' (2004); 'Enhance Quality, Construct Our Future' (2005); 'Be Practical and Flexible, Construct Our Future' (2006); 'Brave to Innovate, Share Responsibilities' (2007); 'Strengthen Our Confidence, Embrace Challenges' (2009); 'Development with Coordination, Enhancement with Harmony' (2010); and 'Implementation of Scientific Policy, Plan the Blueprint for Macao' (2011). Regarding the year of 2008, there was no particular theme for the Policy Address but a number of significant points: 'to consolidate the economic base and to promote the appropriate level of economic diversity; to improve the living of residents and to share with them the economic growth; to develop humanistic spirit and to optimize cultural construction; to have greater commitment to improve governance standards; to promote public participation to foster civil society' (2008). These are clearly very much in the style of Chinese governmental exhortation.

The Chief Executive Annual Policy Address gives directions and guidance for the overall development of Macao. In reviewing past Annual Policy Addresses, five stages of governance and rationalities can be identified. These directive guidelines, indeed, have a direct impact on educational practices and developments. The first phase, from 2000 to 2002, focused on consolidation and restoration during which civic awareness was reinforced to re-establish the bond between Macao and her motherland. Thus, nation-state education was then the core value of education in all education sectors, bridging citizens and their motherland. The second phase, from 2003 to 2004, emphasized development and coordination. The outbreak of SARS (severe acute respiratory syndrome) in Hong Kong in November in 2002 also brought critical and negative impacts on the Macao economy. As such, the local government advocated social cohesion to overcome and redevelop the territory. Recovering from economic recession, in 2003, the government continued to provide four billion Patacas (around US$50,000,000) to subsidize unemployed people to join different training programmes in order to upgrade their competences and skills. This is one of the measures to safeguard social stability and maintain social cohesion. The third stage, from 2005 to 2008, initiated a period of reform. The year 2005 was the year of the Legislative Election. 'Reform' was the catchword during this phase of development. The original *Education Law* approved in 1991 was revised and replaced by the *Fundamental Law of Non-tertiary Education System* promulgated in 2006. In the sector of higher education, the higher education Decree Law 11/91/M was in the stage of revision. The fourth stage, from 2009 to 2011, endeavoured to place Macao in the international arena. First, the 11th National People's Congress Standing Committee authorized the Macao Special Administrative Region to exercise jurisdiction on the new campus of the University of Macau in Hengqin Island (*Va Kio Daily*, 2009). Then, the same year, the State Council authorized the reclamation of 361.65 hectares in Macao in order to build the new Macao City (State Council, 2009). At the end of 2010, the PRC Premier Wen Jiabao headed a central delegation to Macao. He recognized Macao's mixed Chinese and Western culture and positioned the future of Macao as a 'world travel and leisure centre' (*Macao Daily*, 2010). All these new developments have had a direct impact on education. The move of the University of Macau to Hengqin Island in particular has two major consequences. First, it is expected to enhance further cooperation between mainland China and Macao, in particular between Guangdong and Macao. Second, the new campus in Hengqin is 20 times bigger than the old campus. This means that the university has more capacity to recruit students from outside, becoming in other words a nascent international education hub.

In contrast to the period prior to the handover in 1999, the governmentalities of Macao SAR are now moving towards actively participating in social matters. This is a direct move to reposition the 'boundary of governance' (Vong and Wong, 2010). The state does not remain as a symbolic power, but now serves as 'a regulative idea' (Kivinen and Rinne, 1998) to normalize the diversity and uncoordinated in order to produce new dimensions of knowledge, such as development, quality, competiveness, excellence and sustainability. These new dimensions are grounded on two major aspects, namely the acquisition of Chinese identity and the achievement of social stability in terms of economic development. Regarding the former, as stated in the Policy Addresses, particularly in the first few years after handover, patriotism is the necessary condition to create and prepare Macao Chinese citizens under the 'One Country, Two systems' principle, in order to safeguard social harmony and cohesion. For the latter, social stability in the Macao context is closely associated with economic development and the government's interpretation of the redistribution of resources, that is, direct financial subsidies to residents. In view of these emerging governmentalities, education has become a domain of investment. Apple (1990, 1995, 2000) argues that education is so deeply imbedded in the politics of culture that it has lost sight of its own standing. Education then has become a mere vehicle to accomplish the political and economic goals of Macao, or more likely, it 'may be a mechanism for maintaining economic prosperity' (Bray et al., 2002, p. 15).

The caring state

Macao is a small place but it is fragmented in terms of educational practices. Private schools in particular enjoy a high degree of self-autonomy including the choice of curricula, textbooks and student admissions. Comparative educational researchers, Bray and Hui (1991), Bray and Packer (1993) and Bray et al. (2002), have criticized an absence of a territory-wide public examination and lack of a unified school system. De facto, prior to the political transition, the Macao-Portuguese government had developed several measures to frame a cohesive education system by passing a number of regulations, including the Education Law (Law No. 11/91/M), the Higher Education Decree Law (Decree Law No. 11/91/M), the Curriculum Framework (Decree Law No. 38/94/M and Decree Law No. 39/94/M), the Universal Free Education Decree Law (Decree Law 29/95/M), and the Statute of Teachers for Private Institutes (Decree Law 15/96/M). Nonetheless, private institutions continue to play a significant role in the entire education system. The diversity among these institutes is not limited to their respective curricula only but also includes their management systems, goals, cultures and student backgrounds. All these differences in the non-tertiary education sector make it even more difficult to deliver a common core curriculum for all schools in the territory. In the higher education sector, diversity is inevitable as most institutions are mono-technical.

Compared with the tertiary sector, school education in Macao has a longer history of government intervention and has a much larger student population. But with the private sector enjoying almost full autonomy, government has had little say in administering it. Bray and Packer (1993, p. 191) noted that 'no laws or regulations existed to control operation of the private schools' before the early 1990s. Even after the legislation concerning the curriculum had been promulgated in 1994, there was still little impact on private schools (Vong and Wong, 2010). Consequently the government employed a money-driven policy to advance interventions that seek to normalize and even regulate differences among schools in attempting to build a more cohesive schooling system. It has, for example, introduced a 'caring list' by: a) extending compulsory and free education from ten to 15 years; b) introducing a milk sponsorship programme for kindergarten pupils; c) enhancing lifelong education for all; and d) establishing a career ladder for private school teachers. Citizenship education is one of the key areas of government investment. This welfare rationale has been well received by private schools, and once they receive more money from the government, they become more public and have to be more accountable. Through this policy the government has been able to classify schools in three categories: government schools, private schools belonging to the free education system and private schools that do not belong to this system. This is a measure to regulate and enhance government administration over schools. This development is a kind of countercurrent governmentality compared to the developments in some other countries. Finland, a welfare state, has withdrawn from centralized state planning involving the adoption of mammoth evaluation and monitoring systems in order to exercise a more useful impact on the lives of individual schools, teachers, families and private individuals (Kivinen and Rinne, 1998, p. 50). Unlike the experience in most Chinese societies, where decentralization is the dominant discourse, the Macao government has moved to develop a more centralized schooling system, but has some way to go in order to achieve it.

In the higher education sector, the so-called 'caring' approach is less evident, though perhaps existing in a different form, as issues of political control or intervention are always sensitive, even taboo, in the academic world. So in effect the government's intervention in higher education is as yet relatively small in scale, Bray et al. (2002, p. 35) noting that only a small number of institutions are involved. Nonetheless, as early as 1992 the Tertiary Education Services Office was established, just one year after the University of Macau. However, Bray et al. argue that 'Macao has a greater need for coordination within the higher education sector than in the past, because of the considerable growth in the number of institutions' (ibid., p. 42). They go further, arguing that 'clear statements of long-term vision' in higher education are indispensable in relation to the future development of Macao. They also criticize the management of higher education as being 'over-centralised' and argue that the Tertiary Education Services Office is acting in an over-technical manner which is itself unfavourable to higher educational development (ibid.). Yet, in reality, higher education development in Macao is lagging behind that of the non-tertiary education sector, particularly in terms of planning and development. For instance, the proposal for revision of the Higher Education Decree Law was first raised in 2005 and is still at the stage of and consultation. With the rapid expansion in private higher institutions and increasing demand generated by economic growth, the government can no longer take a passive role in education planning. In 2008, the Tertiary Education Services commissioned the University of Macau to construct a 'Macao Tertiary Data Base System' (MOTERDS) to collect and organize higher education data including courses, staffing, students and other aspects in order to inform policy-making. This is the first time in the history of higher education in Macao that insightful ideas for managing/governing higher education has been accessed through informed databases. The Tertiary Education Services Office in 2012 also launched another initiative entitled the 'Books Subsidy Scheme' to encourage higher education students of Macao origins to undertake online registration in order to get MOP 2000 (US$250) subsidies. The idea of the database is to collect information on higher education students in Macao, including those from overseas.

In contrast to the practice in non-tertiary education where the government administers the schools, in the tertiary sector the government inclines to manage individuals. It is also notable that the government is making use of different 'technologies' to make this governance possible. For instance, in the area of non-tertiary education, money-driven school development and reforms are the programmes and technologies used to enhance improvement. In the tertiary education sector, the government is becoming aware of the significance of the collective data of institutes as well as the individual data of staff and students in the process of policy-making. This demonstrates how governmentality is shaped by both historical development and present conditions.

Quality as a disciplinary and self-caring technology

The notion of 'quality' was a prominent feature of past Chief Executive Annual Policy Addresses. Quality is believed to be both the end and means of Macao's sustainability. For instance, in 2004 the Chief Executive stated that 'either in tertiary education or non-tertiary education, we have to integrate all the components, including students, parents, school management, teaching staff, student recruitment, admission, curriculum, teaching, examination, graduation and further study and others to relate to the goal of quality in terms of knowledge and humanity' (*Governo de RAEM*, 2003, p. 18). He further stated that 'curriculum reform should be *localised* from kindergarten to university level in order to achieve this aim'. Higher education institutions should benchmark with international standards, at the same time, to 'enhance teaching and research in [the] needs of local society and in order to foster the quality of the whole society' (*Governo de RAEM*, 2003, p. 19). In 2006, the Chief Executive, Mr Chui Sai On, requested that all government officials bear in mind that the consent of society is 'the starting point on the road to achieving quality, as well as the cornerstone of sustainable development' (*Governo de RAEM*, 2005, p. 8). In 2010, he further pointed out that 'education is the force of social, economic and cultural development for enhancing moral and cultural quality and the competiveness of the Special Administrative Region' (*Governo de RAEM*, 2009, p. 14).

The government of Macao has adopted a number of measures that have been well received by the schools, and enhance teaching and learning quality. Two specific activities, namely improving teaching and learning conditions and emphasizing accurate assessment, have been at the forefront of development. The former has to do with input, while the latter is concerned with output. Small-class policies and the question of the teacher–student ratio have been key concerns. This is an effective means to 'normalize' the number of students as well as the teaching condition in diversified schools, and is what makes reforms possible.

The government also created auxiliary posts in schools with direct financial assistance, such as information technology auxiliary staff, reading promoters, extra-curricular promoters, and others. This is also a direct measure to 're-construct' the school personnel structure and the direction of school development. Likewise, launching this measure also helps to 'unify' and 'discipline' the school structure of each school. Parallel to the above measures, the government has also begun 'holistic school assessment' carried out by the Education and Youth Bureau. This is considered as 'internal assessment'. Another form of assessment is by means of the Programme for International Student Assessment (PISA) run by the Organization for Economic Co-operation and Development (OECD). The purpose of PISA is to assess students to see if they have acquired some of the knowledge and skills essential for full society participation near the end of compulsory education (age of 15) (OECD, 2012). In 2009, the government in its policy document explicitly stated that meeting the PISA challenge was one of the education priorities in the territory (*Governo de RAEM*, 2008). Torres (1989, p. 81) pointed out that 'international organisational cooperation, assistance and pressures' is one of the ways to shape the educational policies of any country. Similarly, the government is making use of international organizational cooperation to advance the quality of education in line with the best international standards. At the moment participation in PISA is an important and significant move to fill the current absence of a public examination and enables Macao to enter the cross-country and international assessment arena.

In the higher education sector, quality assurance is operated in a different manner but with the same rationality. The Tertiary Education Services Office is taking a more technical and administrative role in managing the higher education sector. As such, higher education institutions have more autonomy in initiating strategic plans. For instance, in 2002, the Macao SAR government took an initiative to revise the existing University Charter, approved in 1991, with the objective of helping the university to modernize its operation and internationalize its perspectives (UM, 2012). Some major and significant changes have been made in the new charter, including:

- a new governance structure with the University Council as the supreme governing body in lieu of direct supervision from the government, in keeping with prevailing international practices in higher education;
- academic autonomy on the development of courses subject to the financial control of the University Council, and revision of course content subject to the academic gate keeping of the Senate;
- open recruitment of the Rector and Vice Rectors at salaries above the ceiling of civil service salaries as recommended by the University Council, subject to the approval of the Chief Executive;
- open recruitment of professors at salaries above the ceiling of civil service salaries as approved by the University Council (UM, 2012).

In the first regard, contrasting with non-tertiary education, academic/self autonomy is a necessary condition for academic excellence, but it is only a relational concept to that of the external governing body, for instance, the Tertiary Education Services Office. The hierarchical observations and examinations, as revealed by Foucault (1991a), to safeguard the quality is for these evaluations to take place internally, that is, to switch from an external force to a self-disciplined management. In effect, the internal observation is no less intensive than any other external power, in terms of space and distance.

While Apple (2005) complained that audit had developed into a culture that had brought immense impact on all levels of education, it has been developed into an acceptable part of the academic package. Yet, as Foucault (1991a, p. 177) stated, this kind of disciplinary power is 'powerful enough to mould human beings to their will and to the will of the state'. But the state is not alone. Internationalization is now a principal rubric of good practice, applying to staff recruitment, student admission and publications. Internationalization creates comparison and competition in higher education on a global scale, comparisons that often lack credibility by failing to take account of local cultural, political and economic circumstances. Instead, the criteria of comparison take the form of quantifiable items, such as publications, citations in publications and, more importantly, international visibility in key Western-controlled journals. Research output always dominates the discourse of quality. Macao is catching this tide by attempting to boost the quality of higher education at the individual base, its academic staff. Foucault's (1983) notions of self-conduct and conduct of conduct come into play to discipline oneself to perform better and strive for excellence, but within what meaningful framework, local or international?

Some Concluding Remarks

Macao is a tiny place without any natural resources, but with the gaming industry as the leading business in the territory. Despite this contextual restriction, the GDP of the territory has surpassed Hong Kong, Korea and Japan, and has become the fifth economic dragon in Asia. The government has taken the decision to support the future development of Macao largely on this single industry, in association with tourism. It has positioned Macao as a 'world travel and leisure centre'. Education has to play its part as a key resource in accomplishing the goal. However, as stated, the government has inherited a weak tradition of governance, including with regard to education. This study has attempted to reveal the complexities of power struggles, negotiations and possible strategies in order that appropriate governance is made possible.

Drawing upon the historical context and moving from the political transition to the post-1999 era, this chapter has reflected on the emerging governmentalities, a Foucauldian notion, in the governance of education in Macao. The two sectors of education in Macao, pre-tertiary and tertiary, are at different stages of development in terms of governance, but the aim is similar, that is, to enhance self-discipline and technologies of the self in order to effect changes and reforms. Foucault's notion of governmentality in scrutinizing the education policy and development in Macao demonstrates in what ways the rationality of governance of the Macao SAR in education is shaped and how the art of government is emerging. From the above analysis and discussion, it is obvious that the government has made use of some external/global discourses, for instance, economic competitiveness, competencies, quality, excellence and standardization, to serve as the principal rubrics of governmentality. It is now deemed to be the responsibility of the state to effect a shift from a diversified mentality to a more regulated and normalized governmental rationality in order to effect relevant changes in education that will help to foster a sustainable future for Macao.

References

Adamson, B. and Li, T. (1999). 'Primary and secondary schooling'. In M. Bray and R. Koo (eds), *Education and Society in Hong Kong and Macau: Comparative Perspectives on Continuity and Change*. Hong Kong: Comparative Education Research Centre, University of Hong Kong, pp. 35–57.

Apple, M. (1990). *Ideology and Curriculum* (2nd edn). New York: Routledge.

—(1995). *Education and Power* (2nd edn). New York: Routledge.

—(2000). *Official Knowledge: Democratic Knowledge in a Conservative Age*. New York: Routledge.

—(2005). 'Audit cultures, commodification, and class and race strategies in education'. *Policy Futures in Education*, 3 (4): 379–99.

Ball, S. J. (1990). *Politics and Policy Making in Education: Explorations in Policy Sociology*. London and New York: Routledge.

Bray, M. and Hui, P. (1991). 'Curriculum development in Macau', in C. Marsh and P. Morris (eds), *Curriculum Development in East Asia*. London and New York: Falmer Press, pp. 181–201.

Bray, M. and Packer, S. (1993). *Education in Small States: Concepts, Challenges and Strategies.* Oxford: Pegamon Press.

Bray, M. et al. (2002). 'Changing nature of Macau's educational provision'. In M. Bray et al., *Higher Education in Macau – Growth and Strategic Development.* Hong Kong: Comparative Education Research Centre, University of Hong Kong, pp. 16–35.

Dreyfus, H. and Rabinow, P. (1982). *Michel Foucault: Beyond Structuralism and Hermeneutics.* Chicago: University of Chicago Press.

DSEC (Direcção dos Serviços de Estatística e Censos) (2010a). *Total Land Area of Macao.* http://www.dsec.gov.mo/TimeSeriesDatabase.aspx?KeyIndicatorID=11 (Accessed 16 March 2012).

—(2010b). *Gross Domestic Product 2010.* http://www.dsec.gov.mo/Statistic/ NationalAccounts/GrossDomesticProduct/GrossDomesticProduct2010Y.aspx (Accessed 16 March 2012).

—(2011). *Preliminary Results of the 2011 Population Census.* http://censos.dsec.gov.mo/ LatestNews.aspx?NewsGUID=a4a393ad-36bd-4608-9ee1-97e14a1f8cfe (Accessed 16 March 2012).

DSEJ (*Direcção dos Serviços de Educação e Juventude*) (2011a). *Basic Information of Schools Academic Year 2010/2011.* http://www.dsej.gov.mo/~webdsej/www/ statisti/2010/index-e.html (18 March 2012).

—(2011b). *Formal Education in Figures Academic Year 2010/2011.* http://www.dsej.gov. mo/~webdsej/www/statisti/2010/index-e.html (Accessed 18 March 2012).

Foucault, M. (1982). 'Technologies of the self', in P. Rabinow (ed.) (1994), *Ethics: Subjectivity and Truth.* London: Penguin, pp. 223–51.

—(1983). 'The subject and power'. In H. L. Dreyfus and P. Rabinow (eds), *Michel Foucault: Beyond Structuralism and Hermeneutics.* Chicago: University of Chicago Press, pp. 208–26.

—(1990). *The History of Sexuality. Volume 1: An Introduction.* London: Penguin.

—(1991). 'Governmentality'. In G. Burchell, C. Gordon and P. Miller (eds), *The Foucault Effect: Studies in Governmentality with Two Lectures by and an Interview with Michel Foucault.* London: Harvester Wheatsheaf, pp. 87–104.

—(1991a). *Discipline and Punish.* London: Penguin.

GAES (*Gabinete de Apoio ao Ensino Superior*) (2011). *Data of Higher Education in Macao – Numbers of Staff and Students for the Academic Year 2010/2011.* Macao: Tertiary Education Services Office.

—(2012a). *Main Responsibilities of the Tertiary Education Services Office.* http://www.gaes.gov.mo/en/contentframe.asp?content=./e_intro2.html (Accessed 20 February 2012).

—(2012b). *Higher Education Institutions in Macao.* http://www.gaes.gov.mo/en/ contentframe.asp?content=./mc_u_link.html (Accessed 20 February 2012).

Gillies, D. (2008). 'Developing governmentality: conduct and education policy'. *Journal of Education Policy,* July 2008, 23 (4): 451–57.

Gordon, C. (1991). 'Governmentality rationality: an introduction'. In G. Burchell,

C. Gordon and P. Miller (eds), *The Foucault Effect: Studies in Governmentality with Two Lectures by and an Interview with Michel Foucault*. London: Harvester Wheatsheaf, pp. 1–52.

Governo de RAEM (Macao Special Administrative Region) (2000). *Relatório das Linhas de Acção Governativa para o Ano Financeiro de 2001*. Macau: Imprensa Official.

—(2001). *Relatório das Linhas de Acção Governativa para o Ano Financeiro de 2002*. Macau: Imprensa Official.

—(2002). *Relatório das Linhas de Acção Governativa para o Ano Financeiro de 2003*. Macau: Imprensa Official.

—(2003). *Relatório das Linhas de Acção Governativa para o Ano Financeiro de 2004*. Macau: Imprensa Official.

—(2004). *Relatório das Linhas de Acção Governativa para o Ano Financeiro de 2005*. Macau: Imprensa Official.

—(2005). *Relatório das Linhas de Acção Governativa para o Ano Financeiro de 2006*. Macau: Imprensa Official.

—(2006). *Law No. 9/2006 – Fundamental Law of Non-tertiary Education System*. http://www.dsej.gov.mo/~webdsej/www/edulaw/law_9_2006/index-e.htm (Accessed 20 February 2012).

—(2006a). *Relatório das Linhas de Acção Governativa para o Ano Financeiro de 2007*. Macau: Imprensa Official.

—(2007). *Relatório das Linhas de Acção Governativa para o Ano Financeiro de 2008*. Macau: Imprensa Official.

—(2008). *Relatório das Linhas de Acção Governativa para o Ano Financeiro de 2009*. Macau: Imprensa Official.

—(2009). *Relatório das Linhas de Acção Governativa para o Ano Financeiro de 2010*. Macau: Imprensa Official.

—(2010). *Relatório das Linhas de Acção Governativa para o Ano Financeiro de 2011*. Macau: Imprensa Official.

Hunt, A. and Wickham, G. (1998). *Foucault and Law: Towards a Sociology of Law as Governance*. London: Pluto Press.

Kivinen, O. and Rinne, R. (1998). 'State, governmentality and education – the Nordic experience'. *British Journal of Sociology of Education*, 19 (1): 39–52.

Macao Daily (2010). 'Wen Jiabao responding to questions in a press conference held in Macao'. 15 November, p. B05.

Macau Millennium College (2012). Home Page. http://www.mmc.edu.mo/info.html (Accessed 20 March 2012).

Miller, P. and Rose, N. (1990). 'Governing economic life', *Economy and Society*, 19 (1): 1–31.

Niesche, R. (2010). 'Discipline through documentation: a form of governmentality for school principals'. *International Journal of Leadership in Education*, 13 (3), July–September: 249–63.

OECD (Organization for Economic Co-operation and Development) (2012).

Programme for International Student Assessment (PISA). http://www.oecd.org/depart
    ment/0,3355,en_2649_35845621_1_1_1_1_1,00.html (Accessed 12 February 2012).

People's Republic of China (1993). *Basic Law of the Macao Special Administrative
    Region of the People's Republic of China.* http://www.umac.mo/basiclaw/english/
    main.html (Accessed 18 March 2012).

Rose, N. and Miller, P. (1992). 'Political power beyond the state: problematics of
    government', *British Journal of Sociology*, 43 (2): 173–205.

Scott, I. (2011). 'Social stability and economic growth', in Newman M. K. Lam and
    I. Scott (eds), *Gaming, Governance and Public Policy in Macao.* Hong Kong: Hong
    Kong University Press, pp. 1–15.

State Council of People's Republic of China (2009). *The Hengqin overall development
    plan to promote close co-operation of Guangdong, Hong Kong and Macau.* http://
    hm.people.com.cn/BIG5/85423/9539554.html (Accessed 4 December 2011).

Tikly, L. (2003). 'Governmentality and the study of education policy in South Africa'.
    Journal of Education Policy, 18 (2): 161–74.

Torres, C. A. (1989). 'The capitalist state and public policy formation – framework for
    a political sociology of educational policy making'. *British Journal of Sociology of
    Education*, 10 (1): 81–102.

UGC (University Grants Committee) (2012). *UGC funded Institutions, Higher
    Education Institutions in Hong Kong.* http://www.ugc.edu.hk/eng/ugc/site/site.htm
    (Accessed 17 March 2012).

UM (University of Macau) (2012). *Charter Revision Task Force.* http://www.umac.mo/
    crtf/why_charter.html (Accessed 20 March 2012).

Va Kio Daily (2009). 'The jurisdiction of Hengqin UM campus'. 28 June.
    http://www.vakiodaily.com/index.php?tn=viewer&ncid=1&dt=2009062
    8&nid=146788 (Accessed 4 December 2011).

Vong, S. K. and Wong, M. W. (2010). 'Made in Macao: how history, politics and
    teachers frame curriculum practice', *Curriculum and Instruction Quarterly*, 13 (4):
    61–109.

Notes

1   The concept of a 'harmonious society' was first proposed by the Chinese
    government under Hu-Wen (Hu Jitao and Wen Jiabao) during the 2005 National
    People's Congress. It stresses the move from economic growth to overall societal
    balance and harmony with the goal of enabling citizens to share the fruits of the
    country's economic and social progress.

5

Japan: Cultural Roots versus Systemic Provision

Shin'ichi Suzuki

In a *Handbook of Japanese Culture and Society*, the editors wrote that 'the social and economic developments that characterize the postwar decades often have prewar roots in the early years of the Showa' (Bestor et al., 2011, p. 2). This chapter develops this line of argument, with an introduction to aspects of the essential demographic context and then two main themes. First comes certain insights into aspects of Japanese culture, historical and contemporary, that have been influential. Second comes a discussion of selected aspects of Japanese education and the socio-cultural pressures that affect them.

Japanese Profile: Demographic, Political and Cultural

Key demographic issues

Japan consists of five main islands and 6,847 small islands, 314 of which are inhabited and some of them form groups that make up a local authority. There are 47 basic local authorities. Okinawa Prefecture, for example, covers 24 islands, of which ten have no people. The total population of Japan in 2012 (on 20 April) was 127,650,000 (male: 62,100,000; female: 65,560,000), of which all but about 5 million are Japanese. The population structure of Japan is ageing as shown in Table 5.1.

Regarding the younger cohort (0–14), only Tokyo exhibits annual growth. It is estimated that the Japanese population will decrease to less than 90,000,000 by 2050.

The population is maldistributed between the urbanized zones and the rest of the country. There are several 'Megalopolis' along the Pacific coast of Honshu,

Table 5.1 Population estimate by age band and sex (1000)

Population as of 1 November 2011 (final estimation)					
Total population			Japanese population		
Both sexes	Male	Female	Both sexes	Male	Female
127, 800	62,179	65,621	126,167	61,442	64,724
Age Group					
0–14	13.7%	12.4%	13.1%	13.8%	12.5%
15–64	65.8%	61.5%	63.3%	65.6%	61.2%
65+	29.4%	40.0%	35.1%	29.8%	40.4%

Calculation based on rounding to the nearest whole number. http://www.stat.go.jp/data/jinsui/.

where around 60 per cent of the total population live. Specifically in 2005, there were about 40.15 million people in the Kanto Region (Tokyo and the six prefectures), about 32 per cent of the total population. Tokyo alone accommodates one-tenth of the total Japanese population: the average population density in Tokyo being about 5,542/km². In 2006, the underpopulated regions accounted for 54.1 per cent of the total space of Japan that is habitable, with only about 10 million people.

Such disparate density and demographical patterns have a historical background. Most of the areas around old urban centres became hinterlands, industrial zones to which younger generations moved. Large-scale internal migrations began in the late 1950s. The Tokyo–Kanagawa industrial belt absorbed population from the then overpopulated countryside. With the expansion of the Japanese economy, networks of diverse job markets extended, absorbing new population into their nodal points. Government policies (the National Comprehensive Development Plan, 1962, and the New Comprehensive Plan for National Development, 1969) accelerated such trends.

Japanese urbanization took several forms: a) towns grew into larger urban zones, embracing agricultural environments; b) old urban areas outgrew their environs to form larger urban zones; c) some firms or factories were attracted to the rural areas and played the role of a core around which new living spaces expanded; d) new towns were built in the rural areas; and 5) rural areas themselves took on urban lifestyles as exurbs. Consequently the agricultural living sphere became complex in its structure as farmers coexisted with industrial and commercial workers (Redfield, 1953, 1965).

These structural shifts gave rise to various issues, one being the decline of demographic fecundity as newcomers tended to have smaller families

(Hashimoto, 2001). Once, Japanese farming communities were more repro-
ductive. Now, more of the younger workers in the urban zones are relatively
poor and do not feel the need to have more children or even to marry.
From the turn of the millennium these former hinterlands became barren in
demographic terms. This situation raises the question of what these impending
demographic and familial changes will mean for the Japan of 2040. Eberstadt
(2011) mentions some dramatic possibilities, including a crisis of ageing, and
looming immigration. According to his analysis it is possible that some fundamental shift in public attitudes could occur, perhaps an ideological or religious
movement, and could sweep Japan. In his imagination, depopulation and a
pervasive gerontocracy could be Japan's lot.

The foundation of national unity

Another key factor is the ideological dynamics since 1945. Japan has a long
and varied history, often influenced by various contacts and communication
with external forces. Buddhism, Confucianism and Christianity have all had an
impact on the endogenous belief systems over the centuries. Today, the Japanese
people are embraced by a large but not always visible envelope of Shintoism
(the state Shinto based on the Tenno Family Shinto worship). The relationship
between democracy and Shintoism is key.

The Japanese political system is democratic in terms of the constitution,
but in practice there are some difficult issues. One example is the principle
of nationality. No Korean or Chinese descendants have the right to vote in
local elections, and still less in a national general election, even though they
have lived in Japan, without violation of any law, for more than two or three
generations. Does nationality supersede universal human rights (Article 97,
Constitution)? This causes volatile situations in terms of marriage and the
nationality of children, and therefore their life prospects when one of the
parents is not Japanese.

According to the culture and the constitution, Tenno is the symbol of
national unity (Article 1, Constitution). Consequently two issues arise in respect
of national and educational unity. First, we have the unbroken line of Tenno's
succession. The constitution does not describe anything about the succession of
Tenno. The details of succession are given by the Tenno House Act. Renewed
in 1947, it requires that only male descendants should succeed to the throne.
Under the old constitution, Tenno was reckoned to be the 'living God'. After
1945, the late Showa Tenno negated publicly his divinity (1946). The current

constitution confirms the equality of the sexes. Tenno is now a human being. There can be no discrimination between boys and girls of the Tenno family. But the Tenno House Act contradicts the constitutional equality of the sexes.

Second, we have the symbols of political unity and of State Shinto. The funeral ceremony of the late Showa Tenno and the succession of Heisei Tenno to the throne were carried out in the traditional form of the Tenno Family. The ceremony was in the fashion of the traditional festivity of the Tenno Family's Shinto and was not visible to the public. The secular government used public money in supporting all the ceremonies concerned. The constitution requires the government to be religion-neutral in its administration (Article 20, Constitution). A large mass of the people visit the Kyuzyo (Imperial Palace) every 1 January to cerebrate the birth of the New Year with Tenno. Tenno with his families greet the people. There are many Shinto-Jinja's (shrines) in Japan, where people come to celebrate the New Year. The festivities are called *Shiho-Hai* (Tenno's worship of the deities in all quarters: east, west, north, south), so Tenno's behaviour on such occasions is religious. Can Tenno be the dual symbol of both politics and religion? What should the Japanese state be?

As to the constitution, people are divided. There are two main groups, one wishing to repeal Article 9, which announces the renunciation of force in settling international disputes, and another wishing to retain it. The US–Japan Peace Treaty, signed in 1948 and renewed in 1960, stirred Japanese society and affected the discussions about Article 9. This schism, together with the issue of Tenno and religion, means there is a residual tension about what form the Japanese state should take.

From Meiji to Taisho

During the era of the 1910s and 1920s, two trends appeared: one current ran towards government-centred state-building and the other towards people-based state-building. Both originate from the late nineteenth century. In 1887 the Society of State Academy was established by state officers, lawyers and professors of law, on the side of the government. They rejected Rousseau's republicanism and supported the idea of state education. This idea was criticized by the group that asserted democracy. The disputes between these two groups represented two fundamental issues of nation-building: a) true Japaneseness; and b) modernization of communities and people. Three key concepts were debated: 'national people', 'national state' and 'Japaneseness'. The *Meiji Tenno* System was a political artifact which tried to embrace all of three concepts. In such a model, the concept of 'family' acted as the emotional foundation on which the notion of a 'Family State' grew as a twin to an 'Empire (Tenno) State'. The Youth Clubs, National Associations of Ex-Soldiers and the Association for Moral-Economic Teachings of Ninomiya Sontku were the agents for such an ideal (Ishida, 1984, 1995). But the contradictions involved culminated in the Taisho Affair of 1921. On the surface it seemed to be a conflict between the Minister of Finance and the Minister of Defence about the annual budget for the cabinet. In reality it was a political fight between parliamentary governance and Japanese military authority. Popular movements for the protection of democracy against militarism developed. Socio-politically these movements were new in the political sense that they became more independent of both the organic Empire and the Family State and standing against any ultra-nationalist approaches (Ishida, 1995). Many people preferred enlightenment to political determinism. When Einstein, John Dewey and others were invited, massive audiences enjoyed their lectures. Young farmers were inspired to run their own lifelong learning colleges in various forms. Social reform movements emerged among poor people, rebelling against unfair manipulation of rice by the merchant. The Japanese Communist Party, the Japan Union of Farmers, the Student Union and the National Society of Levelers were established in 1922 (Irokawa, 1973; Kano, 1973). The Japanese political elite, threatened by theses social movements, took repressive measures. Conservatism reappeared by establishing Dai Nippon Kokusuisha (the Great Japan Union of Nationalists) in 1919 and the Jinja Department of Home Office published a *Historical Treatise on Japanese Polity* in 1921. These movements reflected the main political tensions that occurred in the Meiji era.

From Taisho to Showa

The 1929 international economic crisis reached Japan, and the government could not solve the social and economic issues of unemployment and the deep affluence–poverty divide. Political indecisiveness in solving social issues invited the radical wings of the young military force to revolt against the parliamentary system. On 15 May 1932 militant military officers killed the Prime Minister and others, and on 26 February 1936 1000 soldiers proclaimed martial law. It lasted more than half a year. In the former scheme of things, all military force belonged to Tenno. In this sense, the military revolt against the Cabinet could suggest that Tenno (Showa) himself overthrew his Cabinet. Since the mid-1930s the Japanese Parliament had become a mere shell of democracy. In reality the military bureaucrats controlled the Cabinet. Democracy collapsed. Most educated men and women found themselves on the front line of ideological propaganda and the installation of a conflict-oriented nation.

What happened as a result, in terms of Japanese aggressive expansionism in Asia and the Pacific, is well known, ending in the crushing humiliation of defeat, from which only a very new Japan could emerge.

Ideological Disputes in the Latter Half of the Twentieth Century

Issues of the 1980s

Prime Minister Mr Nakasone initiated the so-called great debates in 1982 through the organs of the Social Meeting on Education and Culture and the Study Group on Peace Issues. The key issues were: a) to amend the 1946 Constitution; b) to authorize the *Yasukini Jinja* as a State Shinto Shrine; c) to reconfirm '*Kimiga-Yo*' as the national anthem and '*Hinomaru*' as the national flag; and d) to rearm Japan. Nakasone established the National Council on Education, which deliberated for three years (1984–87) on the deregulation of state administration, freedom of choice and privatization of public services – but the Council was not successful in realizing what Mr Nakasone intended.

What was stressed in neo-liberal terms was the family as the foundation of social reconstruction. A renewed and strengthened image and meaning of 'family' emerged. Privatization of public services was extensively implemented, and freedom of choice was imposed on Japanese state education.

Issues of the 1990s

During the 1990s the Japanese political situation changed. The Japan Socialist Party approved the Japanese Self-Defence Force to which it had been opposed for more than half a century. Politics entered a phase of uncertainty. Violent right-wing attacks occurred. Everything was related again to the working of the Tenno system, supported by the right and opposed by the left. Eventually, in 1999, the three main political parties supported the Bill of the National Anthem and Flag. Japan, for the first time, legally defined its national anthem and national flag. The political turn to conservative doctrines at the end of the last century resulted in some rudimentary ideological changes. It was partly related to the demise of the USSR, which weakened the appeal of the left.

Conservatism resurfaced in a neo-liberal wave of privatization, freedom of choice and competition. This had the effect of strengthening the Tenno system, but tensions remained.

Culture and the Latent Determinants of National Education

Culture is the basic way of life of a people, and all education is culturally embedded even if the formal dimension is politically delivered (Brock, 2011). The past three-quarters of a century, key elements of which have been discussed above, is the determinant of the conditions of present day Japanese culture. The recent past gives us some latent motifs for individual and collective life. Their power was enduring and still potent at the turn of the millennium. The cultural symbols described below worked as embedded but hidden aesthetic, ethical and religious criteria for Japanese education

State Shintoism

It was urgent for Meiji Japan to build a nation-state. The leaders rebuilt the conventional Tenno regime into a new Tenno system. The strategies were skilfully planned, and national education was the primary strategy for implementing the new idea. The Meiji government arranged to have Tenno's Order on national education issued and this had overwhelming effects upon national education for nearly a century and a half. Owing to the political device of State Shinto, which was introduced and institutionalized by the leading political group of new civic servants, the popular ethos was reoriented to Shintoism through school education (Sato, 1994; Suzuki and Yamaki, 2009).

Western knowledge and three schools on academic hegemony

Before the Meiji revolution, there were principally three schools of academic discipline: Buddhist, Confucian and Kokugaku (Japanese classics). European knowledge and skills were already known. With the urgent tasks of building up Japan's strength as a state against foreign countries and making Japan a new nation, the Meiji government became seriously critical of the three schools. Conventional scholars did not fully understand what spiritual and cultural backgrounds Western knowledge and skills actually possessed. Each of three schools struggled to hold an established status approved by the political authority. The new civic officer group, once educated outside Japan, did not recognize any one of the three schools as the hegemonic scholastic group. Comparing them with Christianity in the European and the American contexts, they found that none of the three could take the part of Christianity whose church had performed its roles in the formation of European polities (Brock, 2010). Thus they placed the Tenno's Family Shinto at the centre of the new 'governmentality' of the Meiji state, not only for administrative preparation for building the new state but for also for nurturing the national family. It was the Japanese application of the 'grammar of modernity' (Suzuki, 2000, 2008, 2011) that included coming to terms with faiths and knowledge from abroad in the interest of interpreting Japaneseness.

Ideological representation: hidden artificial patterns

Regarding Japaneseness, there have been various discourses that were formulated by both Japanese and foreign observers. In 1981 an interdisciplinary consortium was held at the International Christian University (Tokyo). Scholars and students met to discuss the hidden cultural patterns of Japanese society. The late Maruyama Masao addressed the meeting on the *koso*, primordial representation patterns (Maruyama, 1984, 2000). Kato (1984, 2007) compared Japanese attitudes to the foreign cultures with European approaches. Kinoshita, a producer, pointed to the characteristics of the traditional *Noh*-play, and Takeda Kiyoko, the organizer of the consortium, introduced Jung's archetype to search for the hidden pattern of Japanese culture (Takeda, 1984).

According to Kinoshita, Japanese theatre could be built with two-dimensional symbolic space, which is at once 'real' and 'abstract' dialectically. What is abstract exists in the absolute meaning that must represent itself in concrete postures of the actors, the citations and the stages. The actors, *Noh*-masks and *Noh*-dance, which are concrete, produce in an instance such a meaningful space as dramatically indicates what can be universal and immanent in humane life. In *Noh*-play, the Japanese dialogues (the *Noh*-farce) between *Site* (protagonist) and *Waki* (supporter) vindicate that a series of reciprocal phrasal-dialogues could compose complete sentences, without subject words in each utterance, when fully performed. It tells that Japanese as a language has a unique logical form and function as the measure of rational and emotional communication (Kinoshita, 1984).

Such a particular langue-parole-dialogue scheme of Japanese is historical and cultural. It could be formulated as a meta-linguistic pattern of logical dynamic expressions between 'real versus abstract' and 'sensitive versus spiritual'.

Cultural symbols of the Japanese nation-state

There are some profound issues of cultural symbolism which have been institutionalized into daily life. For example, Japanese people enjoy the cherry blossom in spring. *Sakura* symbolizes the coming of spring and beginning of the new public and academic year. *Sakura* is institutionalized in the Japanese social context. Nowadays, the school year opens in April with *Sakura* and it is common for schoolchildren to wear hats and school uniforms with symbolic features of *Sakura*.

Another cultural symbol is that of the good wife and wise mother. The present constitution affirms the equality of the sexes as a fundamental human right. Historically girls were expected to become good wives and a wise mothers throughout their careers and lives. When the Meiji government chose to make Meiji Tenno visible to the mass of the people so that they might correctly identify the new ruler (Taki, 2002; Fujitani, 1996; Suzuki and Yamaki, 2009), Shoken Kotaigo, the Princess of Meiji Tenno, played several roles as the ideal woman for the new age. She appeared in public in European attire as the typical figure of the new women of Meiji Japan. Her books on girls' education, and others edited by her orders, indoctrinated schoolgirls into the traits of traditional femininity. Meiji Tenno and Shoken Kotaigo were taken as the model of man and wife in the new age. Their photos were circulated to schools. Every child and student looked at the photos of them in class every day. The photo kept sending a message of good wife and wise mother to all future husbands and wives (Sato, 1994; Suzuki and Yamaki, 2009). In this way the ideal type of a mature woman became institutionally established (Wakakuwa, 2000, 2001). Women were exhorted to be patriotic and produce male children and train them for the future nation (Muta, 1995, 2000; Takahashi, 1992; Narita, 2000). This of course had a militaristic intention. It also explains how closely interwoven was girls' education with the ideology of the day. Now the basic patterns of family life and family building have changed (Bumpass and Tsuya, 2004).

Literacy is an agent of cultural symbolism through enabling language to play its full part as one of the main dimensions of any culture operating through informal and formal education. Traditionally most learned men could read and write in Chinese. Encountering European learning from the early sixteenth century, some acquired new literate ability in European tongues. The early years of Meiji Japan exhibited a huge amount of translation of foreign books on human, social and natural sciences. At the turn of the twentieth century, many commoners were sufficiently literate to be able to read new books and journals, while the learned men and women could manage one or more foreign tongues. People gradually lost literacy in Chinese. Instead, Japanese people were more acquainted with reading *Kan-Bun* (漢文), the Japanese translations of the Chinese classics.

In the modern age (1870–1930), post-secondary schools for boys (high school: preparation for university) provided students with three kinds of courses in language acquisition: a) English and German, b) English and French, and c) English and English. Entrance examinations to high school required a basic knowledge and skills of *Kan-Bun* and English. On average, learned men could manage *Kanji* and were acquainted with two or three European tongues. It was rare even for well-to-do girls to advance to tertiary education before 1945, but they were literate in Japanese and English when finishing general secondary school. The mass of children of both sexes just acquired basic literacy in the form of the 3Rs. These different grades and forms of literacy, acquired mainly through schooling, made Japanese society almost into two nations.

Education in Present Day Japan

At the threshold of the twenty-first century, Japan was busy reorganizing Japanese society and institutions, in part to address educational issues that had to be resolved. Some of these are legacies from the past.

Educational policy after 1945

The system

Before 1945, the government accepted, in 1927, nine reports and two recommendations submitted by the ad hoc Council on Education. Secondary schooling was diversified and courses adjusted to form the dual system of schooling (Kaigo, 1960). It was divided into two streams: one for the masses, a limited compulsory programme of six years; the other for the selected few leading to access to advanced colleges and universities.

After 1945, the compulsory school system was reorganized into a single-track system. There was no selective examination between primary and secondary stages, perhaps the influence of the American model of schooling. From age three to five/six was a nursery/kindergarten stage, then primary school up to 11/12 followed by secondary up to 17/18 and then tertiary options for those who qualified for them. In 1971, the Central Council on Education (CCE) recommended the diversification of courses for diploma, certificates, degrees and qualifications. Universities were to be reformed as the academic and vocational complex with a hierarchy of top and middle academies and vocationally oriented universities which should correspond to diverse qualifications from certificates to higher degrees (Suzuki, 2005). These proposals were eventually passed in 1987.

School curriculum

The Course of Studies, provided by the *Monbusho* (Ministry of Education) in 1947, was just a set of suggestions for school teachers. They were encouraged to be pragmatic, with child-centred learning introduced in primary schools. After the outbreak of the Korean War in 1950, the programme was changed from one of suggestions to one of legal requirements. The curriculum was organized on subject-centred principles. Between 1955 and 2003, *Monbusho* revised the curriculum for the compulsory stage on 12 occasions. The influence of the industrial and commercial sector was evident, with large corporations prominent, while the initiatives of teachers towards curriculum reform were not always reflected in revisions to the Course of Studies (http:www.nier.go.jp/guideline/index.htm).

Of the recent disputes about the school curriculum, *Ikiru-Chikara* and *Yutori-no-Jikan* were typical of the confusion of curriculum administration. *Monbu-Kagakusho* (the Ministry of Education, Science, Culture and Sport) first introduced the idea of *Ikiru-Chikara* (potentiality for creative life) for curriculum development. It is intended to maximize the potential of every child or young person both for themselves and the well-being and development of their community. A second idea was for *Yutori-no-Jikan* (free hours for children) to be introduced to the Course of Studies. *Yutori* means 'not limited', 'not being confined', or 'not being full of anything'. *Jikan* is time or hour. While the Japanese Course of Studies prescribes the details of lesson hours subject by subject, this initiative was intended to benefit from the natural curiosity and creativity of children in the interests of their respective communities. However, as a result of Japan's experience in the international PISA exercise, *Monbu-Kagakusho* revised the Course of Studies to intensify subject-centred lessons. So the pendulum has swung back, as is evident in a number of other countries for the same reason. Politicians are fixated with international league tables in education and their country's position in them. This is one of the results of globalization, and is not favourable to the natural creativity of children.

The teaching profession

Adopting the principle of university-based teacher training, the Japanese government proposed broader principles and guidelines for universities and colleges intending to provide courses leading to teaching certificates. It was a decisive move to lead to an all-graduate profession that now obtains. As there was no state examination for teachers' qualifications, the government afforded local authorities the power to offer teaching certificates to successful candidates. Universities and colleges were given the right and responsibility of accrediting the graduates registered on their academic and vocational courses. So the quality of Japanese teachers rests on that of the tertiary training institutions, but to serve in any state school teachers had to be assessed and selected by the education committees of the respective local authorities. The testing, selection and appointment of successful candidates was left in the hands of head teachers and local education authorities. Despite all these reforms, the Japanese public frequently complained about the teaching force.

The Central Council for Teacher Education (CCTE) issued a series of recommendations or advice for enhancing the teaching force from 1987 to 1999. What they concerned with were: a) the enhancement of initial training courses; b) continuing in-service training; c) extending partnerships between training institutions and local education committees; and d) the development of internships between universities and schools (CCTE, 1987, 1997, 1998, 1999). Observations and opinions from professional sectors focused on: a) the requirement of higher professional degrees and qualifications (MA or ME degrees); and b) assertions of the importance of academic rigour in all sciences and liberal education (BA or BSc). All these pressures have been a concern in Japanese teacher education for a long time. The Japanese Teachers Union contributed to advancing school education with their own on-the-job training. It has, however, been an unfortunate constraint on the progress of Japanese teacher education provision that the voices of school teachers have not been fully heard in the processes of policy formation on teacher education and training (Suzuki, 1981, 1987, 2004).

Lifelong learning

The National Council on Education (1984–7) proposed to reorganize the whole educational system on the principle of lifelong learning. The technical group of the Council prepared a historical note on energy by which human beings cultivated and developed civilization. The note made it clear that the future lay in the 'knowledge industry', that human civilization should and would be developed not by physical energy but by virtual knowledge with information technologies. Japanese society would need to adapt itself to this reality that was already underway as a key component of globalization.

Accepting the recommendations made by the National Council on Education, *Monbu-Kagakusho* set up the Council on Life-Long Learning (CLL) that submitted its recommendations from 1996 to 1999. The Council indicated that lifelong learning would require reorganization of the existing facilities for non-formal and especially adult education. Japan has a long history in these forms of education, but it became necessary for all local authorities (LA) to reschedule all their programmes to offer inhabitants open-ended learning courses (CLL, 1996). In practice, LAs developed new schemes of public services on libraries and study centres, and restored public or community halls and social education centres (CLL, 1998a, b).

In 1999, the CLL submitted its report titled *How to Utilize Acquired Knowledge and Skills more Broadly*. It stressed the value of reshaping learning to comprehensive schemes in which all people could obtain any qualifications that might be approved higher than diploma. It proposed that the University on Air, the courses provided by higher education institutions and credit-transfer systems outside formal schooling should be reinstitutionalized into an organic learning community. Volunteer activities should also be organized in flexible patterns with new learning communities. This new partnership between learners and public administrations was strongly encouraged (CLL, 1999), but there were logistical problems.

Owing to the existing policy of rationalizing local administration by the amalgamation of small local authorities into larger units, community halls had been closed and social workers' services reduced. Such qualified social workers are still in short supply. The amalgamation policies were combined with local reorganizations which aimed at advancing local industrial readaptations to the changing Japanese economic and demographic structures. The outcomes were not always as expected. The internal network of trade, commerce and production was too fixed to absorb new human resources that came from open approaches to learning conducted by third parties in the partnership scheme with various sectors of local communities. Ironically, the new human resources trained under the progressive idea of the 'knowledge society' did not fit established labour markets. Consequently the lifelong learning policies had to be reassessed.

Key issues in contemporary Japanese education

Japanese education has struggled to adapt to the challenges of globalization despite the high level of expertise in information and communication technology (ICT). Conflicting political ideologies, conventional nation-state schemes, expanding economic markets on a global scale, the phenomenon of ethnic multiplicity through migration and axiological dismay about the cultural canon have all threatened Japanese identity. Mere achievement of high enrolment ratios at compulsory and optional schools have proved to be insufficient for the solution of various problems.

Children and youth service

Japanese children had been conventionally assumed to be in a very secure social environment compared to children in many other countries. In reality, a significant proportion were not safeguarded against various forms of negligence, abuse, indifference and in some cases poverty, famine and ill health. Young couples seemed to be ignorant of the skills of child rearing, and especially the safeguarding of what childhood should be. To this extent Japanese society had become dysfunctional, and so initiatives had to be developed to address the problem.

Early childhood care

The government in the late 1990s paid attention to rebuilding communities in urban and rural areas by offering children more opportunities to participate in community life and to become familiar with natural surroundings (CLL, 1999). In 2009, the newly elected government proposed to reorganize the arrangements for the care and education for all children under five. *Sogo-Kodomo-En* (Comprehensive Child Unit for Care and Education under six) was the core idea of the programme. It was an initiative to unite kindergarten and nursery school and to invite the support of third parties to support services in order to solve the keen shortage of accommodation for children and offer better care. It also intended to support parenting and mothers who wished to work. However, the government was not successful in gaining political agreements in the Parliament. As a result a compromise was agreed in the form of the extension of the existing Approved Child Units system which merely supplemented the shortfall of the dual system of nursery schools and kindergartens. The decision was neither educationally nor psychologically sound, but purely political and bureaucratic.

Earlier, in 2005, the Cabinet Office had carried out an international survey on family awareness. It was a comparative survey of five countries: the USA, South Korea, Sweden, France and Japan. The sample populations were men and women from 20 to 49 years of age. The survey suggested, among other things, that the Japanese decline in family size seemed to be associated with what were regarded as uncertain moral-ethical attitudes to child rearing and insufficient social services and support. Child nutrition in particular seemed to be a problem. It was acknowledged by many local education authorities that there was a need to enrich school meals so as to enable all children to develop physically and mentally. Deficiencies had developed in relation to the extremes of parental overwork or unemployment, helping to create family breakdown at a level to which existing welfare services could not respond adequately. Some parents could not supply their children with sufficient meals and care. The head teachers of primary schools observed that some of their pupils came to school without having had breakfast. This had become an endemic situation and required action. Under government encouragement, local authorities began with rice-centred school meals, as a counter to the situation that had developed with preferences for bread and junk foods. This was in effect an attempt to revert to a more healthy traditional diet in the form of a policy called 'food education into school'. It included new certificates for food teachers (*Eiyo-Kyoshi*; nutrition adviser). The policy would lead to progress in overcoming malnutrition of school children together with social training in behavior, manners and healthy habits (CCE, 2008c). So only a few years ago, in 2008, the Japanese government finally responded to the proposals of the WHO Ottawa Convention of 1986 covering a) school health; b) school meals; and c) provisions for safe schooling (CCE, 2008c).

Career development

At the other end of schooling, many young Japanese had to confront difficulties in their career development. Formal certificates did not always help them. As the number of students enrolled at tertiary institutions increased, the smooth connection between higher education and personal social upgrading had become broken. It became urgent to refashion the whole system of further and higher education.

Japanese industry and commerce was also dissatisfied with school education on which it had traditionally depended to nurture, prepare and supply such human resources as could secure the future of Japanese industry. Under the neo-liberal management strategies, most Japanese firms and companies had stopped offering internal training courses for the workers. Wage rates were growing higher, and more companies looked for cheaper labour from outside Japan.

In response, the government has encouraged local education authorities, school corporations and third parties to remodel the schooling systems in line with the ideas of *Gou-Kou* (Unification of Schools) and school–industry complexes. These take a variety of forms involving sometimes just schools and industries, and sometimes universities and other tertiary institutions as well. There are many permutations arising from different local circumstances. Within the university sector there are not only liaisons among the departments or the faculties within, but also between the state and private universities, as well as between schools, universities and industry at various levels, from local to national. At the time of writing it is not certain if there will emerge a new national scheme for advancing career guidance and new qualifications for children and young persons in a systematic way. If school fees keep increasing, this could hinder the promising connections between the sectors of education from primary to tertiary in the interests of career formation for young people. This is, of course, a problem in which Japan is not alone internationally, as the strong national economies of the twentieth century face increased competition from the BRIC nations: Brazil, Russia, India and China (Brock and Alexiadou, 2013)

The teaching profession

All of the modern Japanese governments have been keen to innovate in both initial teacher education and the continuing professional development of all school teachers. At present all school teachers in service have to satisfy a required credit accumulation in the ten years after initial appointment. The courses for these credits are provided by the professional graduate schools of education or the institutions approved by the minister. It is not free for teachers. As to the course contents of the credit-accumulation, *Monbu-Kagakusho* requires the emphasis to be on *Jitsumu* (practice at school). *Jitsumu* is prescribed by the Course of Studies and the Law of School Education. These cover the genres of a) teaching; b) pupil/student guidance; c) career guidance; d) class/school management; and e) the external management of school. These genres are determined and prescribed by the legal and pseudo-legal orders on teaching services. In contrast to this rather traditional inside-profession approach, the government also favours a neo-liberal non-specialist control of schools. Many local authorities invite head teachers from backgrounds outside the profession. Many such head teachers have no teaching certificates or teaching experience. The government seems to think of schools as production lines with administrative and management principles to match.

The teachers themselves, in such a model, are viewed as artisans crafting the desired outcomes in terms of a) child growth; b) learning; c) social maturity and participation of the adolescent; and d) creation and management of school–community relationships. Teachers are seen as key workers in the aforementioned creation of various forms of liaison between their students and human and natural environments in the interests of sustainable development. Teachers' professional capabilities now should be much wider than the fields prescribed by the laws and orders of school administration. At the same time it is important to maintain the professional independence of the Japanese teaching force so that they may discuss their own professional standards and maintain them. This is at present an ideal rather than a reality.

Literacy and numeracy problems

From about 1990, universities began to complain about the poor academic quality emerging from the school system and especially shortcomings in basic literacy and numeracy. University professors would say that what is even more crucial is students' lack of capability in terms of questioning and reasoning. The situation had arisen because of the gradual decrease of high school cohorts for demographic reasons and the easier entrance examinations and university matriculation in most institutions. The elite universities were unaffected, but the rest accepted lower entry standards. At most private colleges and universities, the board of trustees would prefer to satisfy their financial needs to make both ends meet by allowing lower achievers to enroll.

Historically, most young male farmers of 20 years of age could not solve tests or pass examinations. But in everyday life they had learned the necessary skills and calculations such as the effective usage of artificial fertilizer or the correct amount of manure or fertilizer per square metre in exact quantities. These were acquired through informal education through the learning of good practice. History requires us to ask why formal schooling was not always successful in the early modern stages. Somewhat similar insufficient learning achieved by more students nowadays may indicate the reside left unsolved through modern state schooling. As already mentioned, education is culturally embedded, and it takes time, and sometimes a revolution, as in Bolshevik Russia in the early twentieth century, to create a new education culture for new economic and political times.

From the 1970s onwards, parents attempted to overcome or boost their children's performance in school by supplementing it with *juku* or cramming. While marks increased, many children were deprived of space and time for recreation, a context that is vital for personal development which in turn is vital for economic development individually and collectively (Miyahara, 2006, p. 1). Playing with siblings and friends is in effect an alternative school or education, but *juku* tended to stunt creativity. Children were deprived of time to develop holistically. It was the beginning of a highly controlled life for many of them.

Many Japanese children and young people are suffering from mental, psychological and physiological strains, especially as a result of competitive examinations (Zeng, 1999). They may develop or suffer such conditions as school-phobia, depression, bullying and other anti-social features of behavior such as theft or shoplifting. Such students are said to be *Yoi-Ko*, a conditioning required of them by their parents, in the interest of conformity with expectations ranging from school performance to choice of marriage partners. Many children consider their parental suggestions and choices to be good for them, and work hard for better school records and career goals. In so doing, they may fail to identify their own best interests and aspirations and become alienated. Parental deprivation of genuine childhood can only be overcome by children becoming independent of their parents, emotionally as well as physically (Kasuga, 1997).

There have been a number of governmental initiatives during the first decade of the twenty-first century aimed at alleviating and then overcoming this problem of national proportions. For example:

a) 2002: The 'cultural education initiative' stressed the importance of reviving a holistic view on knowledge and wisdom against the specialization and competition of accelerated globalization and the advancement of information technology.

b) 2003: The 'new human power initiative' stressed the importance of achieving the multidimensional capabilities that identify a mature person.

c) 2005: The 'redesigning compulsory education initiative' redefined national strategies including a new partnership between central and local education authorities.

d) 2008: The 'physical and mental health of children initiative' effects greater and more meaningful collaboration between schools, families and communities.

Whether these policies will succeed in overcoming the difficulties faced by significant numbers of Japanese children and young people is not yet clear. *Juku* is here to stay – a third sector of education. It does not consist only of cramming, but also offers compensatory education, healing and readaptation to the demands of the formal system, the family and traditional cultural traits. Free schools are another alternative, where many children and young persons come for free activities outside the framework of the national curriculum as codified by the state. Their schedules are less demanding and their curricula more diverse.

The Japanese school system is still in conflict with the natural need to fulfil childhood. But it is not alone in the world in that respect in general, only in the specifics of Japanese culture that inform it. It is a curious feature of contemporary Japanese society that while childhood is being constrained, at the other end of the demographic spectrum life is being extended. This again is not unique among the more developed nations of the world, but given Japanese attitudes to age, it places extra pressures there.

Conclusion

Modern Japan has suffered from the consequences of war, both as a perpetrator and as a victim. Aspirations of empire along the lines of those of achieved by major European powers, especially Britain and France, came too late. Their attempted implementation was successfully resisted and then brutally crushed by being the only country to have suffered the atomic bomb. In some ways this massive national change, with its associated pressures on Japanese culture and society, seems to have been operative at the personal level of the individual as well. Education in all its forms, embedded in culture as it is everywhere, has been subject to great stress at all levels.

Demographic changes have not helped, and neither have the many demands of a very sophisticated and competitive economy characteristic of post-1945 Japan. In this regard the influence of temporary occupation by the USA has had mixed results in education, and it is interesting to compare with post-war Germany in this regard (Tanaka, 2005; Shibata, 2003). In such situations, the traits of the traditional society re-emerge and may or may not come into conflict with global trends. In the case of Japan it seems to have been a struggle to marry the needs of internal reform with the pressures of external trends that are now global and highly competitive. As Goodman and Phillips (2003) have asked, 'Can the Japanese change their educational system?'

In this chapter, the writer has attempted to illustrate social, cultural and political traits and contexts within Japan that help to explain why change has proved so difficult, rather than simply describe the education system as a kind of soulless machine as portrayed in a systems diagram. Japanese education may be at some kind of crossroads, but no effort is being spared to negotiate them successfully.

References

Bestor, V. L., Bestor T. and Yamagata, A. (2011). *Routledge Handbook of Japanese Culture and Society*. London: Routledge.

Brock, C. (2010). 'Spatial Dimensions of Christianity and Education in Western European History, with Legacies for the Present'. *Comparative Education*, 46, 3: 289–306.

—(2011). *Education as a Global Concern*. London and New York: Continuum.

Brock, C. and Alexiadou, N. (2013). *Education Around the World: A Comparative Introduction*. London and New York: Bloomsbury.

Bumpass, L. and Tsuya, N. (eds) (2004). *Marriage, Work and Family Life in Comparative Perspective—Japan, Korea and the United States*. Honolulu: University of Hawaii Press, pp. 134–43.

Cabinet Office (2005). *Shoshi-ka ni kansuru kokusai Ishiki-chosa* [*International Survey over the family-Awareness: Report*]. Tokyo: Cabinet Office.

CCE (Central Council on Education) (1998a). *Recommendation* (*Nurturing New Spirit toward the New Millennium*) [Japanese version]. Tokyo: *Monbu-Kagakusho*, 30 June.

—(1998b). *Recommendation* (*Renewing Local Education Administration*) [Japanese version]. Tokyo: *Monbu-Kagakusho*, 1 September.

—(1998c). *Recommendation* (*New liaisons between primary–secondary schools and higher education institutions*) [Japanese version]. Tokyo: *Monbu-Kagakusho*, 6 November.

—(2000). *Report* (*On Smaller Number of Children and Education*) [Japanese version]. Tokyo: *Monbu-Kagakusho*, 1 April.

—(2003). *Recommendation* (*Revised Course of Studies*) [Japanese version]. Tokyo: *Monbu-Kagakusho*, December.

—(2005). *Recommendation* (*Graduate School Education in the New Era*) [Japanese version]. Tokyo: *Monbu-Kagakusho*, 5 September.

—(2008a). *Recommendation* (*On Revised Course of Studies: kindergarten, primary school, secondary school, high school and special education*) [Japanese version]. Tokyo: *Monbu-Kagakusho*, 17 January.

—(2008b). *Recommendation* (*Restructuring Educational Institutions upon the Principles of the New Fundamental Law of Education*) [Japanese version]. Tokyo: *Monbu-Kagakusho*, 10 March.

—(2008c). *Recommendation* (*Measures for Schools to Safeguard Children in Security and Reliance*) [Japanese version]. Tokyo: *Monbu-Kagakusho*, 17 January.

—(2012). *Recommendation* (*On Safety in School*) [Japanese version]. Tokyo: *Monbu-Kagakusho*, 21 March.

CCTE (1987). *Recommendation* (*On Improvement of Teaching Profession*). Tokyo: *Monbu-Kagakusho*, 18 December.

—(1997). *Recommendation* (*New Era and New Teacher Education and Training*) [Japanese version]. Tokyo: *Monbu-Kagakusho*, July.

—(1998). *Recommendation* (*On Initial Teacher Education at the Gradate Schools*) [Japanese version]. Tokyo: *Monbu-Kagakusho*, 29 October.

—(1999). *Recommendation* (*On Creative Liaison between Initial Teacher Education and In-service Training*) [Japanese version]. Tokyo: *Monbu-Kagakusho*, 10 December.

—(2006). *Recommendation* (*On the Future Patterns of Teacher Education*) [Japanese version]. Tokyo: *Monbu-Kagakusho*, 11 July.

CLL (Council for Life-Long Learning) (1996). *Recommendation* (*On Measures for Advancing Life-Long Learning—provisions at local regions*) [Japanese version]. Tokyo: *Monbu-Kagakusho*, 24 April.

—(1997). *Reports* (*On Measures for Total Utilization of Acquired Life-long Learning*) [Japanese version]. Tokyo: *Monbu-Kagakusho*, 31 March.

—(1998a). *Recommendation* (*On the Future of Social Education Administration*) [Japanese version]. Tokyo: *Monbu-Kagakusho*, September.

—(1998b). *Report* (*On Libraries and Information—Urgent New Strategies*) (Japanese version). Tokyo: *Monbu-Kagakusho*, 27 October.

—(1999). *Recommendation* (*Importance of Experiences in Life and Nature for Nurturing Children's Minds—measures for circumstance development in communities*) [Japanese version]. Tokyo: *Monbu-Kagakusho*, 9 June.

—(2000a). *Report* (*Readjustment of Social Education Administration for Enhancing Family Potential for Child Nurturing*) [Japanese version]. Tokyo: *Monbu-Kagakusho*, 28 November.

—(2000b). *Recommendation* (*On Advancing Life-Long Learning and New Information Technology*) [Japanese version]. Tokyo: *Monbu-Kagakusho*, 28 November.

Eberstadt, N. (2011). 'Demography and Japan's Future', in McKinsey and Company (ed.), *Reimagining Japan: the quest for a future that works*. San Francisco: VIZ Media LLC, pp. 82–7.

Fujitani, T. (1996). *Splendid Monarchy, Power and Pageantry in the Modern Japan*, Berkley, CA: University of California Press.

Goodman, R. and Phillips, D. (eds) (2003). *Can the Japanese Change Their Education System?* Wallingford: Symposium Books.

Hashimoto, Y. (2001). '*Toshi eno Minzoku Daiido*' ['Big Migration to Urban Zones—Hypergrowth of Economy and Tokyo'], in Kabayama Koichi et al. (eds), *20 Seiki no Teigi* [*Definitions from the 20th Century*], Vol. 4. Tokyo: Iwanami-Shoten, pp. 219–39.

Irokawa, D. (1973). *Shinpen Meiji Seishin-shi* [*History of Ideas in Meiji Period: a new version*]. Tokyo: Chuou-Koron-Sha, pp. 128ff.

Ishida, T. (1984). *Nihon no Shakai-Kagaku* [*Social Sciences in Japan*]. Tokyo: University of Tokyo Press.

—(1995). 'Sengo Nihon no Kokka-Ishiki' ['State Consciousness after 1945']. In Y. Sakamoto (ed.), *Structural Shifts in World Politics* [Japanese version], Vol. 2. Tokyo: Iwanami-Shoten, pp. 269–333.

Kaigo, M. (ed.) (1960). *Rinji Kyoiku-Kaigi no Kenkyu* [*Studies on the ad hoc Council on Education*]. Tokyo: Tokyo University Press.

Kano, M. (1973). *Taisho-Demokurasi no Teiryu* [*Undercurrents of the Taisho Democracy*]. Tokyo: NHK Books.

Kasuga, K. (1997). *Yoi-ko to iu Yamai* [*Disorders named Good Children*]. Tokyo: Iwanami-Shoten.

Kato, S. (1984). 'Nihon-Shakai-Bunka no Kihonteki Tokucho' ['Fundamental Characteristic of Japanese Society and Culture'], in Takeda Kiyoko (ed.) *Nihon Bunka no Kakureta Kata* [*Latent Patterns of Japanese Culture*]. Tokyo: Iwanami Shoten, pp. 17–46.

—(2007). *Nihon Bunka niokeru Jikan to Kuukan* [*Time and Space in Japanese Culture*]. Tokyo: Iwanami-Shoten.

Kinoshita, J. (1984). 'Fukushiki Mugen Noh wo megutte' ['About so-called Dialogical Imaginary Play of Nho'], in K. Takeda (ed.), *Nihon Bunka no kakureta Kata* [*Latent Patterns of Japanese Culture*] (8th edn, 1990). Tokyo: Iwanami-Shoten, pp. 47–86.

Kinoshita, Z. (1984). 'Fukushiki Mugen Noh o megutte' ['Some Thoughts on Dual Dream of Noh-Play'], in K. Takeda (ed.), *Nihon Bunka no kakureta Kata* [*Latent Patterns of Japanese Culture*] (8th edn). Tokyo: Iwanami-Shoten, pp. 47–86.

Maruyama, M. (1984) 'genkei, Koso, Shitsuyo-teion' [Archetypes, Primordial Base, basso Ostinato), in K. Takeda (ed.), Nihon Bunka no kakureta kata [Latent patterns of Japanese Cultures], (8th edn, 1990). Tokyo: Iwanami-Shoten, pp. 87–152.

Maruyama, M. (2000). 'Shoyo to Zentei' ['Data given and Presuppositions'], in *Nihon Seiji Shiso-Shi* [*History of Japanese Political Thought*], in Masao Maruyama, *Maruyama Maso Kogiroku* [*Lecture Notes by Maruyama Masao*], edited by Iida Taizo et al, Vol. 6. Tokyo: Tokyo University Press, pp. 7–48.

Miyahara, Y. (2006). *Mohitotsun no Gakko--kokoni kodomo no koe ga suru* [*Alternative School where children's voices are alive*]. Tokyo: Shin Hyoron.

Muta, K. (1995). 'Senryaku toshiteno Onna—Meij Taisho no Onna no Gensetsu o megutte' ['Women as Strategy—on Discourses by Women in the Eras of Meiji and Taisho'], in Chizuko Ueno et al. (eds), *Nippon no Feminism* [*Feminism in Japan*], Vol. 3, *Sex-roles*. Tokyo: Iwanami-Shoten, pp. 29–56.

—(2000). 'Ryosai-Kenbo no Ura-Omote' ['Reality of 'Good-wife and Wise-mother'], in Aoki Yasushi et al. (eds.), *Onna no Bunka* [*Women's Culture*]. Tokyo: Iwanami-Shoten, pp. 23–46.

Narita, R. (2000). *'Haha no Kuni no Onna-tachi'* ['Women in Mother-State'],
    in Yamanouchi Yasushi et al. (eds), *Sogo-Sen to Kindaika* [*Total War and
    Modernization*]. Tokyo: Kashiwa-Shobo, pp. 163–84.

Redfield, R. (1953). *The Primitive World and its Transformation*. Ithaca, NY: Cornell
    University Press.

—(1965). *Peasant Society and Culture: an anthropological approach to civilization*.
    Chicago: Chicago University Press.

Sato, H. (ed.) (1994). *Kyoiku* [*Education*], *Zoku Gendaishi Shiryo* [*Second Series of
    Modern History*], Vol. 1. Tokyo: Misuzu-Shobo.

Shibata, M (2003). 'Deconstruction and Reconstruction: a Comparative Analysis
    of the Education Reform in Japan and Germany under the US Military
    Occupation After World War Two', in R. Goodman and D. Phillips (eds),
    op. cit., pp. 43–72.

Suzuki, S. (1969). *'Gendai Kakkoku no Kyoiku-Seido'* ['School Systems in Modern
    States'], in Kenji Matsumoto (ed.), *Gendai Kyoiku-Gaku* [*Modern Education*]. Tokyo:
    Kyodo Shuppan, pp. 203–34.

—(1981). 'Kyoin-Yosei kaikaku no Doko' ['Trends in Teacher Education Reform'], in
    Gakko Kyoiku Kenkyusho Nennpo [*Annual Bulletin of the School Education Research
    Institute*], No. 25. Tokyo: Gakko Kyoiku Kenkyusho, pp. 51–60.

—(1987). *'Nihon ni okeru Chiki-Kyoshikyoiku-Kiko no Kanosei'* ['Possibility of Area
    Training Organization in Japan']. *Educational Research*, 54, 3: 289–99.

—(1989). *'Kyoin no Shishitsukojo Renraku-Kyogikai no Genzyo to Kadai'* ['Local
    Association for Advancement of Teaching: outcomes and tasks']. *Kyoikukatei to
    Kyoshi* [*School Curriculum and Teachers*]: 10–20.

—(2000). 'Educational Partnership between Public and Private Sectors: Some
    Japanese Cases', in *Files of Workshop on Public–Private Partnership in Education*.
    29 May–7 June 2000. Tokyo: Asia Development Bank, pp. 1–9.

—(2002). 'What kind of Geo-bodies and What kinds of Research-Unit for Comparative
    Education?' *Research in the Graduate School of Education* (Tokyo Waseda
    University), 13: 47–55.

—(2004). *'Zenkoku Shiritsudaigaku Kyoshikyoiku-kenkyurenraku-Kyogikai no Rekishi to
    Kadai'* ['National Association of Private Universities for Teacher Education: History
    and Future Tasks—Area Training Organization']. *Kyoshi-Kyoiku Kenkyu* (*Studia
    Institutione*), 17: 1–9.

—(2005). 'Higher Education Administrative Reforms in Japan', in Zhang Xi-mai (ed.),
    Comparison on International Higher Education Administration. Beijing: Higher
    Education Publishing, pp. 149–73.

—(2008). 'Toward Learning beyond Nation-State: where and how?—conflicting
    paradigm of nationalism: Asia and Europe', in M. Pereyra (ed.), *Changing
    Knowledge and Education*. Frankfurt: Peter Lang, pp. 85–103.

—(2010). 'Introduction', 'Afterword', in S. Suzuki and E. Howe (eds), *Asian Perspectives
    on Teacher Education*. London: Routledge, pp. 1–10, 170–6.

—(2011). 'Issues of Dichotomy in Cultural Dialogues; Implications to Comparative Education', in *Proceedings of the 4th World Forum for Comparative Education*, CD edition. Beijing: Beijing Normal University

Suzuki, S. and Yamaki, K. (2009). 'Transforming Popular Consciousness through the Sacralization of the Western School: The Meiji Schoolhouse and Tenno Worship', in Juergen Schriewer (ed.), *Comparativ*. Leipzig: Leibzigerunivetsitaet Verlag, pp. 44–77.

Takahashi, S. (1992). '*Senso to Zyosei*' ['War and Women'], in Senjika Nihon Shakai Kenkyukai [Study Group on Japan in War-times] (eds), *Senjika no Nihon* [*Japan in War-times*]. Kyoto: Kohro-Sha, pp. 247–75.

—(1984). '*Furoito, Yungu, Shiso-shi*' ['Freud, Jung, and History of Ideas'], in K. Takeda (ed.), *Nihon Bunka no kakureta Kata* [*Hidden Patterns in Japanese Culture*]. Tokyo: Iwanami-Shoten, pp. 153–75.

Takeda, K. (1984). '*Furoito, Yunku, Shiso-shi*' ['Freud, Jung, History of Ideas'], in K. Takeda (ed.), *Nihon Bunka no kakureta Kata* [*Latent Patterns of Japanese Culture*] (8th edn, 1990). Tokyo: Iwanami-Shiten, pp. 153–75.

Taki, K. (2002). '*Tnno'no Shozo*' ['The Portrait of Tenno']. *Iwanami-Gendai-Bunnko*, 76.

Tanaka, M. (2005). *The Cross-Cultural Transfer of Educational Concepts and Practices: A Comparative Study*. Didcot: Symposium Books.

Wakakuwa, M. (2000). *Shocho toshiteno Josei-Zo* [*Women's Statures as Symbols*]. Tokyo: Chikuma-Shobo.

—(2001). *Kogo no Shozo* [*Portrait of the Empress*]. Tokyo: Chikuma-Shobo.

Zeng, K. (1999). *Dragon Gate: Competitive Examinations and their Consequences*. London: Cassell.

6

Japan: Internationalisation in Education and the Problem of Introspective Youth

Yuki Imoto

Introduction

For a country such as Japan, internationalization must begin with education. Japan is an island nation, conversing in a language spoken nowhere else on our planet, with few immigrants and foreigners. Japanese universities have thus far failed to attract the best students from abroad. The only other option is a foreign education. Therefore, to internationalize themselves, the Japanese must seek an education overseas. Internationalization must include the elite since they are the ones who will have the most influence on Japan's future. (*Japan Times*, 2009)

In a *Japan Times* article (5 February 2009), Japan experts Dujarric and Honjo problematize the insular state of Japanese education, pointing to the declining number of Japanese students studying at the Ivy league institutions of the USA, in contrast to the growing number of students from neighbouring South Korea. They lament that, 'as the rest of Asia is increasingly engaging the world in the exchange of ideas, Japan remains isolated. Unless the educational, political, and business establishment realizes that Japan must remedy this failure, "Japan passing" will relegate Japan to irrelevancy in the 21st century.'

Indeed, the statistics regarding the 'inward-looking' tendencies of Japanese youth, in contrast to its more 'outward-looking' East Asian neighbours, has been raised as a pressing problem during the first decade of the twenty-first century. This sense of urgency is likewise expressed in a *Washington Post* article:

'I am a grass-eater,' Otani said wistfully, using an in-vogue expression for a person who avoids stress, controls risk and grazes contentedly in home pastures.

Once a voracious consumer of American higher education, Japan is becoming a nation of grass-eaters. Undergraduate enrollment in U.S. universities has fallen 52 percent since 2000; graduate enrollment has dropped 27 percent.

It is a steep, sustained and potentially harmful decline for an export-dependent nation that is losing global market share to its highly competitive Asian neighbors, whose students are stampeding into American schools. (11 April 2010)

Whether its causes are attributed to the inflexibility of the educational and employment system, or the financial barriers of studying abroad, or more broadly and more commonly, to the essential *nature* of the contemporary generation of 'grass-eating' youth who are deemed passive and lacking in motivation to seek the wider world, the 'problem' of insular youth symbolizes the 'problem' of Japan's struggles in the increasingly competitive global era, where neighbouring East Asian countries are making their presence felt.

This chapter introduces and discusses the discourse, or rhetoric, of *uchimuki-shikou* or 'inward-looking' Japanese youth, where the state of such youth has been discussed as a problem hindering the internationalization of Japanese education particularly since around 2010. I use the discourse of *uchimuki-shikou* as a window for understanding how globalization – or the pressures and processes of aligning with global norms and to remain competitive in a world increasingly moving towards economic integration – is expressed and perceived at the national level in Japan through media and policy texts. This process of discourse-making at the national level is never free from politics and the unequal distribution of power. I argue that much of the 'problem' has been constructed around a biased reading of statistics that focuses on the perceived lack of interest among Japanese youth to study at American universities, rather than at foreign universities in general. I further point out the unbalanced focus on the elite segment in the discussions on the internationalization of education.

My foremost interest remains at the level of identifying the rhetorical discourses of globalization in the context of Japanese education, rather than its structural impacts. However, it must be acknowledged that the levels of discourse and reality are interrelated – one having effect on the other in a dialectic process. Much of the chapter will therefore be about explaining the changing socioeconomic contexts of education in Japan. First, I present an overview of the formation of the modern paradigm of Japanese education in the post-war period and the meanings of internationalization (*kokusaika*) in this context. This will be followed by an account of how this paradigm has shifted from the 1990s onwards. I then examine how a discourse of insularity has been constructed by the media and interested agents within this context, which has in turn been picked up in educational policy texts by the government and educational institutions to push forward their political and economic agendas.

From kindaika ('modernization') to kokusaika ('internationalization')

Kindaika and the development of the modern education system

The establishment of the 'modern' education system of Japan can be traced back to the late nineteenth century, as part of the Meiji government's modernization process – referred to as *kindaika* – of importing Western systems and institutions to 'catch up with the West'. Teachers were brought in from Europe and the USA, and 'Western learning' was undertaken with an enthusiasm amounting to fervour. In a context where a culture of schooling and a literate society had already been developing in the previous Tokugawa era (Dore, 1965), modern education soon became the driving tool to develop a Japanese identity through spreading a standardized language and national ideology.

After Japan's defeat in World War Two, education was again identified as the crucial means to bring about social change, this time by the occupying Americans, who placed the elimination of ultra-nationalism and militarism, and the installation of democracy and individualism, as the central themes of reform. The new post-war educational system aimed to correct the elitism of the pre-war system, and its ideology was idealistically egalitarian. Under the 1947 Fundamental Law of Education and School Education Law, a standardized nine-year compulsory education system (which, combined with an additional three years of high school, came to be known as the 6-3-3 system) was introduced, replacing the multi-track, class differentiating routes of the pre-war system.

While the system was radically changed in its structural form under the American occupation, from the 1960s the Japanese government and the business leaders steered the system to become an exam-focused sorting mechanism that would allocate young men and women to appropriate levels and roles in the workplace. *Kindaika* became a key political rhetoric that would drive the nation, as a one bounded mechanism, towards industrial development and economic prosperity. Schooling during the six years of elementary and three years of junior high school was to instill basic skills to establish a literate, productive nation, and Confucian ethical models were endorsed to emphasize discipline, diligence, respect for authority and harmony of the group. The standardized and public nature of education at the compulsory level would lead to high schools (which had reached an enrollment of 82 per cent by 1970 and 94 per cent by 1980) and colleges (attended by 35 per cent of high school graduates in 1975) which were hierarchically ranked. They would award credentials based on a principle of meritocracy – with Tokyo University, whose graduates dominated the powerful positions in government, residing at the top of the pyramid. A strong correlation was formed between the rank of colleges and the size of firm, and between the size of firm and size of remuneration. Graduates of the prestigious national universities, (Tokyo, Kyoto and Hitotsubashi) and private universities (Keio and Waseda) were four or five times more likely to be employed in elite companies, which offered both status and security in the form of lifetime employment (Marshall, 1994).

Success in entrance exams to these elite Japanese institutions thus came to determine a man's chances of attaining class status, and it is in this light that the notorious 'examination hell' developed. As Kariya (1995) argues, the coupling of 'objective' meritocracy based on point-based testing and egalitarianism in the post-war era resulted in the attainment of a mass middle class nation bound by a religious belief in education, despite economic and class inequalities, which gave better chances to some over others. The mass middle class ideology containing the belief that all had the potential ability to succeed and attain the ideal middle-class *salaryman* status and lifestyle exacerbated competition so that, paradoxically, it led to increased inequality of chances through increased demand and growth of the private commercial shadow education industry most famously represented by the institution of *juku* (cram schools).

By the 1970s, criticisms and complaints of the competitive education system had surfaced. School violence, children's psychological problems, bullying and school refusal were raised in the public discourse as social problems caused by the rigid school and examination system. Parents were among those who lamented the competitiveness and psychological strains on their children and themselves. But in spite of such public-level discourse, private interests continued to reproduce competitive educational differentiation and to feed the growing *juku* business. For, as Rohlen points out, when the chips are down most parents want success for their children more than anything else (Rohlen, 1983, p. 108).

From kindaika to kokusaika: the social climate of the 1980s

By the 1980s, the nation had attained a universally recognized high standard of living with its GDP per capita reaching the second highest in the world. In order to live up to and sustain the illusion of the middle-class lifestyle, consumption of goods became a central social preoccupation both as a way of differentiation and identification. 'Internationalization' (*kokusaika*) and 'being international' (*kokusaiteki*) became the buzzwords of this period that affected leisure and lifestyle. Overseas travel became a popular pastime and learning English a boom, with a proliferation of English conversation schools called *eikaiwa* schools which epitomize the commodified form of internationalism (see Seargeant, 2009). The number of students studying abroad, mainly to the USA, began to increase from the early 1980s, although the meritocratic and hierarchized system that linked school to work meant that the elite middle-class route would be better assured to those who attained success in the national entrance examinations to the top Japanese universities. It is not surprising, therefore, that studying abroad has largely been an activity dominated by women, for whom status attainment relied largely on success in the marriage market rather than success in education and employment, and for whom the meaning of becoming 'international' carried less risk and more opportunities than for males who were situated in the centre of the inflexible system (see Schoppa, 2006). Although as Goodman (1990) argues, *kikokushijo* – or 'returnee' children of Japanese expatriates who had received part of their education abroad – attained status as 'international elites' from the 1980s through the establishment of new *kikokushijo* quotas in the entrance examination system, such educational routes remained marginal and particular to certain private universities and high schools that sought to utilize internationalism as a branding strategy.

While interest in and consumption of 'things international' (generally read as American or Western) thus became visible in the 1980s, there was also a growth in the production and consumption of popular and academic writing on discourses of 'Japaneseness' – known as *nihonjinron*. Japan's rapid economic ascendance on the world stage received considerable attention from abroad, as exemplified in Ezra Vogel's 1979 publication *Japan as Number One* in which he described the Japanese-style economy as a model for the USA to emulate. Japan's education system also became a point of fascination and 'attraction' (Rappleye, 2007), with Western educationalists seeking to find and explain answers to Japan's success in the Japanese model of education (e.g. Duke, 1986; White, 1987; Lynn, 1988)[1].

Concurrent with the West's fascination with Japanese organizational culture, the Japanese began to also consume accounts of Japan's 'uniqueness' through *nihonjinron* writings. There was a revived appreciation of the internationally recognized work of the anthropologist Nakane Chie, *Human Relations in the Vertical Society (Tate Shakai no Ningen Kankei)* (1967), in which she characterized the structuring of Japanese society as a vertical relation centred upon the *ie* (the family), and the psychologist Doi Takeo's *The Structure of Dependency (Amae no Kouzou)* (1971) in which he analyzed 'dependency' as the defining cultural feature of Japanese society. Popular writings on 'the Japanese' drew on such models, reinforcing the idea of an 'essential' Japanese psyche and a group-oriented culture. Critics of *nihonjinron* such as Mouer and Sugimoto (1995) and Yoshino Kosaku (1992) argue that the emergence of such cultural nationalism shows that internationalization works in tandem with the strengthening of national identity, in that it leads to an increased awareness of 'Japan' in the context of a wider competitive world, and in particular against the 'West'. The 'outward' force is always accompanied by an 'inward' force – for identity is about the dialogic negotiation of the boundary of inside (*uchi*) and outside (*soto*).

It is thus no mere coincidence that the period when *nihonjinron* discourse and Anglo-American studies on Japan became prevalent is also the period when discourses about 'internationalization' – *kokusaika* – emerged. In the immediate post-war period, Japan had a clear goal of revitalizing the economy and then of catching up with the West. Having secured its position as an economic world power, it was under increasing pressure to establish its identity on the international stage. *Kokusaika*, in this sense, can be considered a political rhetoric that replaced the previous rhetoric of 'modernization' – *kindaika* – in pushing forward national interests. Goodman (1990) indicates how the rhetoric of internationalism is a 'multivocal symbol' that can be used to attain different ends and posits two groups with different ideological motivations – the 'realists' (e.g. businessmen) who see nationalism as an important factor in Japan's economic growth, and the 'idealists' (e.g. some academics – more often Western academics specializing in Japan or marginal Japanese academics) who look towards a global community where people's similarities are more important than their differences (see also Kubota, 2002). Hood (2003) points out that former Prime Minister Nakasone Yasuhiro, the key figure of the 1980s conservative politics, was clearly in the 'realist' camp that sees internationalism as necessarily containing a degree of nationalism.

'Internationalization' became a key rhetoric in educational reforms that Nakasone designed in the 1980s, in creating a new generation of Japanese individuals equipped with 'twenty-first century abilities' to compete on the world scene. Business leaders, who exercised considerable power in directing educational reforms, began to see the need for a new direction towards the nurturing of creativity and the ability to communicate on a par with the other nations, rather than simply relying on Western models and receiving knowledge from the outside passively. 'Individuality' and 'creativity' were key concepts in the formulation of the new 'ideal person' (Cummings, 1999) that would guide the direction of reforms through the subsequent decades. This converged with the concerns over the excessive pressures of the exam-centred system, since creativity and individuality were to be nurtured through a more 'relaxed' curriculum and school environment. The reforms that were subsequently proposed, such as the reduction of the curriculum content, a change from a six to a five-day week, shorter hours and classes where teachers were to be 'guides' rather than authoritative instructors, came to be represented by the slogan of *yutori kyouiku* (meaning 'relaxed education') – a term which paradoxically had first been coined in 1972 by the leftist Teachers's Union in their calls for a return to more humanistic, child-centred learning that had been envisioned as ideals in the American occupation reforms. Due to the 'immobilism' (see Schoppa, 2001) of Japanese politics, however, it was not until the early 2000s that these reforms, originally devised in the Nakasone era, were to be implemented, by which time, as we shall see in the following section, the politico-economic context had taken a considerably different direction.

From Kokusaika to Gurōbaruka?

Japan's 'Lost Decades'

Since the bursting of the economic 'bubble' and the collapse of land and stock market prices in the early 1990s, Japan entered its prolonged and enduring period of economic stagnation. The 1990s came to be known as the 'Lost Decade', marked not only by the economic downturn, but also by a series of events, most notably the Great Hanshin Earthquake and the mass terrorist attack by the religious cult Aum Shinri Kyo in 1995, which generated a wide and definitive sense of crisis across society. As can be inferred from Leheney's observations below, a sense of social malaise came to dominate, in large part through its construction by writers and pundits.

> By mid-1995, the ground had been laid for a wide-ranging pessimism about the country's future. Rather than focusing on specific financial challenges, curricular problems in education, or individual political scandals, Japanese writers and pundits began to discuss the problems as part of a larger social malaise. In some cases, the authors used these concerns to argue for specific political agendas, while in others they served largely to underscore amorphous critiques of postwar Japan. (Leheny, 2006, p. 42)

The Lost Decade brought to the fore pressing problems to be solved, many such problems being framed as pertaining to youth and their moral degradation. Rather than seeing social malaise as a problem of individual psychologies, however, it is important to be aware of the structural factors or the socioeconomic context that has created the need for political changes and reforms. The changes and reforms that have been brought about can largely be attributed to the convergence of severe fiscal problems, an unprecedentedly low birthrate and the emergence of a super-aged society, and the 'global norming' imperative where Japan is induced to become more competitive economically by outsourcing production to other Asian countries and to improve governance by adopting policies from abroad. Under these strains, a restructuring of the employment system has occurred, leading to the discrediting of the stable, egalitarian post-war system, and the dismantling of the 'myth' of a mass middle-class nation.

The economic strain put immense pressure on many Japanese companies, so that, in line with the global norms that placed priority on flexibility and efficiency, a structural shift to a reliance on irregular forms of work such as *arubaito* (part-time work) and *haken* (dispatch work) was implemented (see Fu, 2011). While the older generations were able to protect their stable employment status, the generation that entered the job market after the onset of the recession, the so-called 'Lost Generation', was increasingly barred from the formerly assured route of gaining lifetime employment after their university degree, leading to high rates of youth who were either unemployed or in part-time or irregular jobs. New words such as *parasaito shinguru* ('parasite single' – those who still live at home with their parents even when they are in their late 20s or 30s) and *furiitaa* ('freeters' – those who did not take full-time work, but instead did a succession of part-time jobs), *hikikomori* (shut-ins who withdraw from society) and *niito* (NEETs – those who are not in education, employment or training) were coined from the late 1990s to early 2000s, taking on stigmatized meanings of 'lazy', 'unmotivated' or 'introverted' youth, and raised as social problems. Sociologists such as Genda (2001) and Honda (2006, 2008) are critical of those who put the blame on the victims of this structural squeeze; and as Toivonen and Imoto (2012) point out, this problematization of underemployed youth can be viewed as a 'moral panic' in reaction to the changes and sense of social disintegration, and more significantly, as a concerted process by interested actors in which problems are shifted onto youth, in order to implement policies that often would have other political intentions and consequences.

Crises and change in education

In terms of the education system, too, severe fiscal problems led to the dramatic implementation of neo-liberal ideologies, which had begun to be formulated during the Nakasone era, but had previously been held back by ministry-dominant politics. Efficiency, decentralization and flexibilization became key words, with much that had previously been controlled by the state being off-loaded to the market. The shift of power from state bureaucracy to the business sector also meant a move away from post-war egalitarianism to a multi-track system that would better serve the changing economic structures. Six-year integrated 'elite' secondary schools were introduced, breaking down the post-war 6-3-3 single track system; school choice and ability grouping were also introduced. The changes were incorporated in the revision of the Fundamental Law of Education in 2006, which marked the disintegration of the post-war democratic ideals on which the education system had been established. As described by Roesgaard (2011), this alignment with global norms paralleled the reintroduction of traditionalist moral education, with the revised Fundamental Law of Education encouraging strong notions of patriotism and familialism. She suggests that this strengthening of moral education can be seen as a 'gate-keeping' response to the perceived risks of an increasingly individualized and fragmented society – 'an attempt to retain Japanese national identity and values while also integrating with the world' (Roesgaard, 2011, p. 104; see also Takayama, 2007).

At the levels of compulsory education, a sense of 'crisis' concerning failing academic standards ensued after the *yutori* reforms were implemented in 2002 (Tsuneyoshi, 2004a; Bjork and Tsuneyoshi, 2005). When a relaxed curriculum – which saw a 30 per cent reduction of curricular content – was introduced into public schools in a situation as described above (i.e. within a trend where responsibilities of education by the state were being outsourced to parents, the community and companies), it immediately incited criticism from various groups including the neo-conservatives, who called for a return to 'basics' and to more 'traditional', rigorous styles of education, as well as those on the left, who saw the reforms as leading to social disparity and a widening academic gap.

Fujita pointed out that the *yutori* approach that emphasizes the nurturing of 'creativity' and 'zest for living' is an 'invisible pedagogy' where 'the goals of learning and the criteria for evaluation are not clear to some students and their parents, especially those who do not have rich cultural or linguistic experiences' (Fujita, 2010, p. 29). The result, Kariya claims, was the creation of an 'incentive divide' (2001), where children of education-oriented families gained increasing advantage through taking 'private' routes. The *yutori* reforms were effectively branded as a 'failure' after the publication of the PISA results in 2003 that showed Japan's academic decline in the world rankings, and the ensuing construction of a 'crisis' of academic decline (Tsuneyoshi, 2004a; Willis et al., 2008) led to –or at least *legitimated* (Takayama, 2008) – the revision of the *yutori* curriculum by 2010, with lesson hours being increased by 10 per cent.

Within these ideologically-rooted debates around notions of individualism, ability and equality, the voices of the children themselves have remained muted. These children who experienced the *yutori* compulsory education between 2003 and 2009 (i.e. the current generation of youth born between 1987 and 1996) came to be dubbed the *yutori sedai* (*yutori* generation*)*. The youth who had been exposed to a relaxed education aiming to nurture more individuality in the spirit of *kokusaika* are those who ultimately experienced a 'failed' education system that lacked the rigours and competitiveness of previous eras. Rather than being celebrated for having a 'zest for living', the *yutori* generation has come to be represented in the media as the 'grass-eating', passive generation of youth lacking in motivation to work.

Responses in higher education

In the above context of the post-bubble era, the problematization of youth through labels such as 'freeters' and 'NEETs' can be considered as one discursive consequence of structural changes of employment and education affected by global norms. The resurgence of traditionalist ideologies in educational policy text can be seen as another. The discourses of *gurōbaruka* – the term which has increasingly come to replace *kokusaika* in the media since the late 1990s – can also be discussed as rhetorical manifestations or localized meanings of the structural process of globalization in the Japanese socio-political context. Iwabuchi distinguishes the usage of the term 'global' as follows:

> The usage of 'global' in the media discourse clearly reads as more passive and less confident, signifying the decay and crisis of Japan. As the term 'global standard' exemplifies, Japanese discourses of globalization have most notably revolved around the necessity for Japan to readjust itself to the new US-led global economic order. (Iwabuchi, 2005, p. 104, cited in Burgess et al., 2010, p. 464)

Citing this quote regarding globalization in Japan, Burgess et al. suggest the following conceptual distinction between the meaning of *gurōbaruka* and *kokusaika*:

> *Gurōbaruka* demands passive compliance with external norms which Japan is unable to control, whereas *kokusaika* actively pushes back against perceived threats to Japanese identity. (Burgess et al., 2010, p. 464)

In other words, both *kokusaika* and *gurōbaruka* describe Japanese responses to globalization; but while *kokusaika* (due to the legacy of the Nakasone era) seems to reinforce national boundaries and cultural identities along national lines, *gurōbaruka* (due to the legacy of the post-bubble era) is about responding to outside pressures. It is difficult to make clear distinctions between the two terms in actual linguistic practice, with *kokusaika* and *gurōbaruka* being used interchangeably in policy texts. Yet, when observing education reform, particularly at the level of higher education to which we now turn our gaze, the situation since the turn of the century has increasingly become one of aligning with global norms and of keeping up in the competitive market.

The declining numbers of 18-year-olds has hit hard for the majority of private universities having to find their own ways to survive in an increasingly competitive and commodified educational market. Some 39 per cent of 572 private universities failed to reach their minimum enrolment quota in fiscal 2011 (Aoki, 2012). 'Internationalization' (*kokusaika*), for many of these private universities, has been used both as a rhetorical branding strategy to gain domestic students who are drawn to internationalism (Goodman, 2007) and as 'real' policies of bringing in more international students in the face of a dwindling domestic market, over 90 per cent of them coming from Asian countries. The shift of the supply–demand balance to a situation where universities compete for student enrolment has meant an end to 'examination hell', with the creation of diverse and ambiguous routes to enter private universities. The competition to gain entrance into the top universities such as the University of Tokyo and the domestic status of those universities has not diminished, however, leading to a considerable polarization in academic abilities and in future prospects among university students in Japan.

The government policies that increasingly focus on promoting a small number of universities to become world-leading institutions has also contributed to this polarization. While the government proceeded with the semi-privatization of national universities as part of its neo-liberal reforms in 2004, it sought to create a handful of 'elite' global institutions which would be selected through making universities compete for large amounts of government funding. Such universities would then be required to become a global centre through strengthening international research credentials based on standards set by world university rankings, and offering lectures in English to cater for an international student body (Tsuneyoshi, 2004b; Ishikawa 2009). Ishikawa (2009) argues that modes of 'objectifying academic excellence' are altering the domestic hierarchies and dynamics in Japan which can be seen as 'an emerging hegemony in global higher education' – a process of *gurōbaruka*. An important example of the creation of elite centres of internationalization is the 'Global 30 Project' (*Kokusaika Kyoten Seibi Jigyo*) implemented in 2009, which distributed funding to 13 major universities to drastically increase their intake of foreign students. This had resulted from an earlier 2008 government proposal to increase the number of foreign students in Japan to 300,000 by 2020. The Global 30 Project, as Murata (forthcoming) points out, is based on the practical need for bringing in a skilled foreign labour force to revitalize the Japanese economy, rather than on active intentions to assert Japan's international strength. The context, and thus the meanings and intentions of internationalization strategies, has significantly changed (Ishikawa, 2011).

Gurōbaruka certainly seems to be the prevalent discourse used in the media, with the rhetoric of *kokusaika* becoming the less fashionable term (Burgess et al., 2010, p. 464). Does this mean that there is a decrease in the articulation of national identity and national boundaries? Or have other rhetorical forms emerged to replace the active intentions held in the rhetoric of *kokusaika*? An observation of discourses in the media and policy text seems to point to the emergence of a new rhetorical form – one that better resonates with the climate of the Lost Decades than *kokusaika*. This is the term *uchimuki-shikou* and a discourse that problematizes the inward-looking (*uchimuki-shikou*) nature of youth. The problematic youth who are reluctant or uninterested in going abroad (in contrast to the youth in the era of 1980s *kokusaika*) have become another symbol that stands for the post-bubble 'inward-looking' state of Japanese society.

The Growing 'Problem' of Uchimiki-shikou ('Inward-looking') Youth

A headline in the national newspaper reads:

> Number of students studying abroad dips to 60,000: 59,923 in 2009, a consecutive decrease in the last five years. Affected by the recession and introvertedness (*uchimuki-shikou*). (*Nikkei*, 21 January 2012)

The introverted nature (*uchimuki-shikou*) of youth has become a term commonly used to explain why fewer students are going abroad to study – a 'fact' which has been established through statistics collected by the government and by research institutes and companies. According to reports published by the MEXT, numbers of those studying abroad had increased rapidly from the1980s, hitting a record in 2004 at 82,945, but have been showing a continuous decline since. In 2010, the most popular destination was the USA – 29,264 students (down by 14 per cent from the previous year), followed by China, 16,733 (down by 10 per cent), and the UK, 4,465 (down by 22 per cent).[2]

It is difficult to judge whether the inward-looking tendencies of youth is a 'reality' or not based on these facts (see Furuichi, 2011). It is possible, however, to delineate *how* such perceptions are constructed through statistics and media reporting, and how these play a role in forming realities through policy texts.

How the 'problem' gained currency

In March 2010, the President of Harvard University, Drew Faust, visited Japan. Her expression of concern to higher education specialists that there were fewer Japanese students entering Harvard University, in contrast to the increasing numbers from other Asian countries, was widely reported in the media. The *Nikkei* newspaper reported that the Harvard President had called for a reversal of the current '*uchimuki-shikou*' (inward-looking tendencies) of youth and had urged the Japanese to 'engage more with the outside world'. It also reported that in a meeting with the then Prime Minister Hatoyama, the Harvard President had stressed the need to increase the number of students studying abroad (*Nikkei*, 16 March 2010). The comment made by Drew Faust was soon followed by an article in the *Washington Post* (cited in the introduction of this chapter), where Blaine Harden wrote on the phenomenon that where 'once drawn to U.S. universities, more Japanese students are staying home' (11 April 2010).

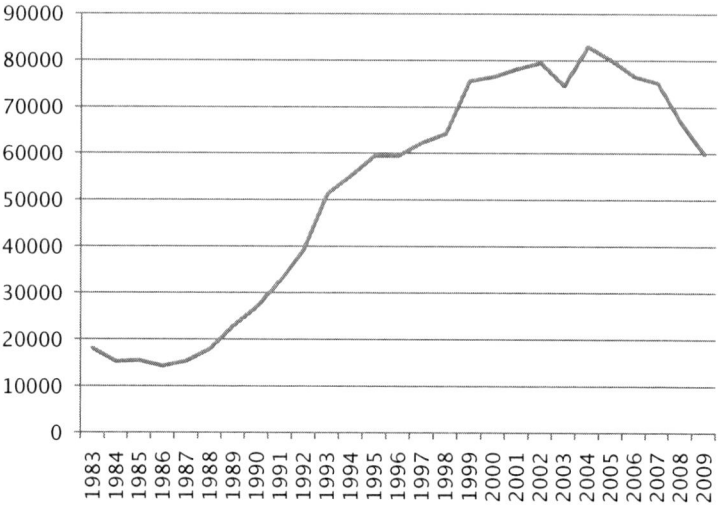

Figure 6.1 The number of Japanese students enrolled in universities abroad, 1983–2009

Source: adapted from http://www.jsps.go.jp/j-tenkairyoku/data/meibo_siryou/sankou08.pdf (28 March 2012).

Furthermore, on 2 November 2010, the American ambassador to Japan gave a speech in which he encouraged educational exchange between USA and Japanese universities, an agenda which was then followed by discussions between President Obama and then Prime Minister Kan during Obama's visit on the 13 November, problematizing the decreasing numbers of Japanese studying in the USA. The conversation led to the Japanese government producing the document *Strengthening the Exchange between Japan and US for further deepening the Japan–USA Alliance* in which Prime Minister Kan 'expressed his concern over the decline of Japanese students who study in the USA and stated his intention to further concentrate and work on this issue'.[3] On the same day, 13 November, at a press conference in the USA, Nobel prize winner Negishi Eiich, who had spent most of his career at Purdue University, called to students and young researchers in Japan to 'take the risks of going abroad', the media reporting of which amplified the ringing rhetoric of *uchimuki-shikou*.

It was through the consciousness-raising by these American individuals and institutions that the Japanese media picked up the problem, establishing a widespread acknowledgement that Japanese youth were *uchimuki-shikou*, as indicated in the sudden rise in the usage of this term from 2010 in national newspapers such as the *Nikkei* shown in Figure 6.2 below.

How the discourse was appropriated

Following this media coverage, the MEXT[4] and other governmental bodies began to use the term *uchimuki-shikou* in various policy proposals and discussions concerning the internationalization of education in Japan. A *Nikkei* article reported:

> In order to solve the issue of inward-looking youth such as the decreasing number of students studying abroad, the MEXT has set up a committee to discuss how to strengthen English education. It will reconsider the goals for junior and senior high school regarding the attainment of English abilities and plans to draw suggestions for pedagogical improvement by the summer next year. (29 November 2010)

The term *uchimuki-shikou* became the key 'problem' in which to frame advisory committee reports, such as those published by the *Sangaku Jinzai Ikusei Partnership Gurōbaru Jinzai Ikusei Iin-kai* (the Industry–Academic Partnership for Human Resource Development, Global Human Resource Development Committee) jointly held by METI[5] and MEXT in October 2010; and the

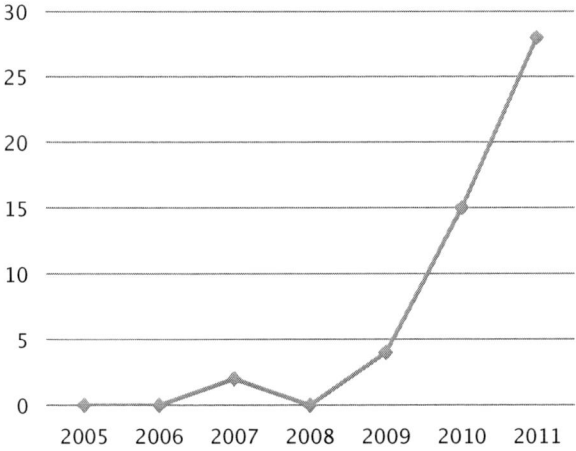

Figure 6.2 Number of articles in the *Nikkei* that reference the term '*uchimuki-shikou*' ('inward-looking') in connection with '*wakamono*' (youth), 2005–11

Keidanren's[6] *Gurōbaru Jinzai no Ikusei ni Muketa Teigen* (*Proposal towards the Development of Global Human Resources*) published in June 2011.

The discourse was also taken up in December 2010 by the Working Committee for Global Human Resource Development (*Gurōbaru Jinzai Ikusei Kentou Iinkai*), comprised of key persons in the Japanese business, politics and international development sectors. Calling for changes in the recruitment system, and for more action on the part of companies to send employees abroad, the report begins by setting out the following problem:

> The background to the problem
> (1) The uchimuki-shikou of youth
> The uchimuki-shikou of Japanese society, in particular of its youth, is being repeatedly mentioned. For example, the decrease in the number of students studying abroad, in contrast to the trends in China and Korea, has been reported. The remarks by the President of Harvard that there was only one Japanese student entering the undergraduate program shocked the nation, but it is symbolic of the current trend. There are also research results that indicate that the number of youths particularly in their 20s traveling abroad are decreasing. We cannot simply lament on the situation. The diminishment of the 'hungry spirit' and 'challenge spirit' can, in the broad sense, be seen as the negative result of our affluence. However, companies, universities and society as a whole must think of ways to deal with the crisis. Some Western countries that have experienced similar problems have found ways of dealing with these issues.[4]

In this way, the series of committee reports on 'Global Human Resource Development' from 2010 each began by setting out the problem: the *uchimuki-shikou* of youth, which was to be solved through the implementation of reforms that would 'open up' and 'align' the Japanese system with the outside world (largely referring to the US).

The advisory reports consequently fed into the 'New Growth Strategy', first set up by the Kan Cabinet in late 2009 and formulated through 2010 and 2011. Among the Cabinet's strategies for promoting innovation was the 'cultivation of global talents', which would involve sending 300,000 Japanese students abroad by 2020. This goal was to be achieved through the policy implementation of the 'Reinventing Japan Project ('*Daigaku no Sekai Tenkairyoku Kyouka Jigyou*') aimed at the leading Japanese universities, from the fall of 2011. While the primary intentions of the Global 30 Project had been to accept more foreign students in Japan, the Reinventing Japan Project directed its interests towards the reversal of the *uchimuki-shikou* tendencies of Japanese students and to thus actively reach out to the world. Specifically, initiatives bidding for funds from the 2.2 billion budget for the first fiscal year would focus on forming collaborative educational programmes such as double degrees, credit transfers and short-term exchanges.[5]

The Reinventing Project comprises two categories: the first can be seen as a direct culmination of then Prime Minister Hatoyama's proposal called CAMPUS (Collective Action for Mobility Programme of University Students) Asia in 2009, in which he called for integration and educational mobility between China, Korea and Japan,. The second category culminates from the growing concerns over the 40 per cent decline in Japanese students enrolling in US universities – which instigated the nationwide concern about *uchimuki-shikou* youth – and provides funding, particularly for alliances with US universities.

The *uchimuki-shikou* discourse has not only been appropriated by state-level actors but also by leading educational institutions as they formulate policies that appeal to their funding bodies as well as the general public. A notable case was the announcement made by the University of Tokyo (commonly referred to as 'Todai'), in January 2012, of their proposed policy to shift undergraduate enrolment from April to the fall in line with the norm of the leading Western universities. Todai argued that fall enrolment would lubricate the flow of foreign students entering Japanese universities, as well as the flow of Japanese students and researchers studying abroad. Not surprisingly, one of the key words employed to explain this reform plan, which would trigger reform across other major universities as well as affecting the recruitment system of companies in Japan, was that there is a need to change the *uchimuki-shikou* of youth. The President of Todai suggested that students need to be 'toughened-up' by going to study abroad, and that flexibilizing the semester system would be a symbolic event that marks Todai and Japan's increased commitment in global awareness, openness and competitiveness. (*Nikkei*, 6 February 2012)

Juku and major educational companies such as Bennesse have also launched new business initiatives, offering ways of breaking through the *uchimuki-shikou* tendencies. From April 2012, Bennesse initiated a new educational service to support students who are thinking of applying simultaneously to undergraduate programmes in Japan and abroad. These courses are to be introduced at major *juku* in the Tokyo area owned by Bennesse which prepares clients to enter the top universities or high schools. In its promotion of the new initiative, Bennesse actively used the rhetoric of *uchimuki-shikou,* alerting that the number of Japanese students pursuing studies in the US had declined by 15 per cent in 2010 compared to the previous year.

As I have illustrated above, the discourse of *uchimuki-shikou* was triggered by American commentary, disseminated through the media and appropriated in policy texts and business initiatives, resonating with the general aura of 'malaise' and the 'problems' pertaining to youth that had emerged in the 'Lost Decades'. Rather than a reflection of realities, *uchimuki-shikou* is better understood as a rhetoric constructed and circulated by various actors with interests in promoting Japanese students to the outside world, while being situated in the larger discursive paradigm of *gurōbaruka*. We should further note that this process of problematizing youth, and of dubbing them as 'insular', is nothing new. Going beyond the specific discursive context of *gurōbaruka*, we find certain continued themes in Japan's long 'youth problem pedigree' (Toivonen and Imoto, 2012, p. 21), where old, highly familiar narratives reappear in only slightly revised shapes, prompted by a new context as well as alliances of interested actors.[9]

Conclusions: Diversification Beyond the Uchi/Soto (Inside/Outside) Boundary

While introducing the reader to the key debates and scholarly discussions surrounding the internationalization of Japanese education, I have considered, through the rhetoric of *uchimuki-shikou*, how discourses pertaining to youth are created and how they impact educational policies. By framing an agenda as a 'problem' of youth that needs to be solved, internationalization policies take concrete form. Such discourses also tend to shift the problem from elsewhere onto young people and their intrinsic nature. In addition to the issue of individual financial circumstances, one needs to consider the following factors that have largely been ignored in media representations that depict Japanese youth as being reluctant to go abroad.

First, the discourse of *uchimuki-shikou* relies heavily on the American perspective when pointing to the declining number of students studying abroad. Although the number of students going to the US has seen a sharp decline since 2000, the numbers going to neighbouring Asian countries show more varied and subtle trends (Table 6.1). *Uchimuki-shikou*, though framed as a problem of Japanese society and youth, is based upon a problem for the USA educational market, and USA–Japan relations. Second, there is generally a lack of mention of the decreasing population of the youth cohort in question (Figure 6.3). When considering the overall ratio of young people studying abroad, the

Table 6.1 The number of Japanese students going to study abroad, by country

	2000	2004	2008	Decrease between 2004 and 2008
China	13,806	19,059	16,733	△2326
Korea	613	914	1062	▽148
Taiwan	–	1879	2182	▽303
United States	46,497	42,215	29,264	△12,951

Adapted from http://www.kantei.go.jp/jp/singi/global/dai2/siryou4.pdf (home page of Gurobaru Jinzai Ikusei Suishin Kaigi of the Prime Minister's Cabinet). Accessed on 28 March 2012.

change in numbers is much less dramatic (see Furuichi, 2011). Third, there is lack of mention of the increasing diversity of Japan *within* Japan (see Graburn et al., 2010) or 'internal internationalization' (*uchinaru kokusaika*) (Tsuneyoshi, 2005), which means that an inward-looking tendency does not necessarily equate to a disinterest in things 'international'.

The third issue mentioned above, of diversity within the borders of Japan, links to the issue of the lack of attention given to the disparity between the elite universities and the majority lower-tier universities in media and policy texts. Regional universities and the smaller private universities that are struggling

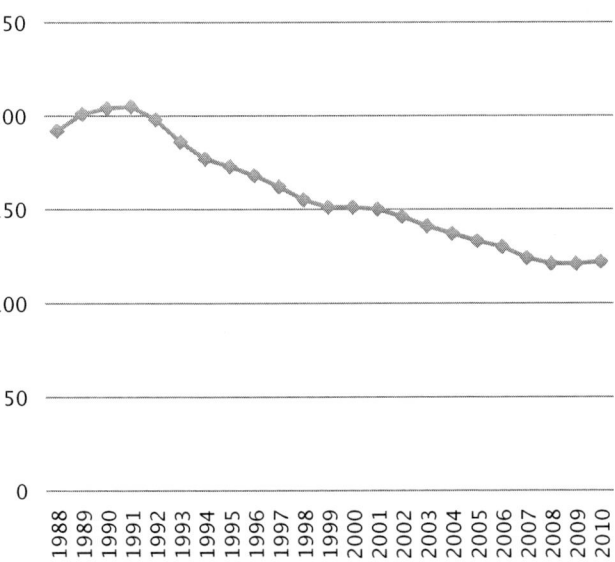

Figure 6.3 The number of 18-year-olds in Japan x 10,000 (1988–2010)

Source: http://www.kantei.go.jp/jp/singi/global/dai2/siryou4.pdf (24 March 2012).

to maintain student enrolment are more actively setting up international exchange programmes, utilizing the rhetoric of *kokusaika*. For example, Akita International University, a regional public university, sends 99 per cent of its students on exchange programmes abroad, while Miyazaki International University, a small private regional university, sends out 31 per cent. Elite national universities, on the other hand, have much fewer numbers of students going abroad – a meagre 0.4 per cent for the case for Todai, compared to the national average of 2 per cent (*Asahi*, 23 December 2011, 28 January 2012). The problem of *uchimuki-shikou* thus seems to mainly apply to the elite universities and pays scant attention to the recent initiatives among smaller universities aggressively moving towards globalization strategies.

The recent focus among scholars of Japanese education has been at the level of higher education where the effects of neo-liberal reforms are first felt and alignment to global standards is most visible, since universities are the 'node' that links human resources from school to work. However, the more nuanced variations of internationalization are perhaps seen at the lower, compulsory levels of education, particularly in the debates surrounding migrant education. One notes an increasing disparity between externally oriented elite 'international' education (Imoto, 2009) and the much less visible internal 'international' education for minorities and immigrant children (Tsuneyoshi, 2005). This suggests that the meanings and uses of internationalization is contingent on *where* (which part of the educational system: compulsory or non-compulsory, public or private, urban or regional) one looks. Discourses such as *uchimuki-shikou* and *gurōbaruka* in the context of Japanese higher education highlights certain dimensions of education (i.e. the dimensions that are most directly linked to the business sector) over others, as well as reinforcing the boundary of 'Japan' through the *uchi/soto* (inside/outside) metaphor.

In sum, the rhetoric of *uchimuki-shikou* allows actors to promote Japan's internationalization, but the term also masks the increasing diversity within Japanese education by reinforcing the dichotomy of *uchi/soto* (inside/outside), and tends to foreground the elite institutions. It remains to be seen whether the impacts of the Reinventing Japan Project and similar strategies outlined since 2010 will lead to the 'problem' of *uchimuki-shikou* being solved or dissolved. It also remains to be seen whether the discursive shifts since the 3-11 triple disasters will open up new frames of discourse pertaining to Japanese youth and education, which institutions and governments may appropriate and mobilize to deal with the increasingly austere national finance, pressures of globalization and of Japan's shifting position vis-à-vis the USA and the neighbouring East Asian nations.

Acknowledgements

The author would like to thank Tuukka Toivonen for helpful comments and suggestions upon reading drafts of this chapter.

References

Aoki, M. (2012). 'Reform means the world for Todai'. *Japan Times*, 18 February.

Asahi (23 December 2011). '*Ryuugaku suru gakusei 2% Daikibo kou hodo teiritsu: Asahi shimbunsha Kawai juku chousa*' ['Students studying abroad 2%, larger universities have lower rates: survey by Asashi Newspaper and Kawai Juku'].

—(28 January 2012). '*Kokusaika e no jinarashi gakunaikaikaku shidou: Todai aki nyuugaku no yukue*' ['Setting the ground for internationalization, the start of internal reform: the path of Todai's fall enrollment'].

Bjork, C. and Tsuneyoshi, R. (2005). 'Education in Japan: competing visions for the future'. *Phi Delta Kappa*, 86.

Burgess, C. (2004). 'Maintaining identities: discourse of homogeneity in a rapidly globalizing Japan'. *Electronic Journal of Contemporary Japanese Studies*.

—(2007). 'Multicultural Japan? Discourse and the "myth" of homogeneity'. Japan Focus, 24 March.

Burgess, C., Gibson, I., Klaphake, J. and Selzer, M. (2010). 'The "Global 30" Project and Japanese higher education reform: an example of a "closing in" or an "opening up"?' *Globalisation, Societies and Education*, 8 (4): 461–75.

Cummings, W. (1999). 'The institutions of education: compare, compare, compare!' *Comparative Education Review*, 43 (4): 413–37.

Doi, T. (1971). *Amae no Kouzou* [*The Structure of Dependency*]. Tokyo: Kondansha.

Dore, R. P. (1965). *Education in Tokugawa Japan*. Berkeley, CA: University of California Press.

Dujarric, R. and Honjo, Y. A. (2009). 'Why can't Japanese kids get into Harvard?' *Japan Times*, 5 February.

Duke, B. (1986). *The Japanese School: Lessons for Industrial America*. London: Praeger.

Fu, H. (2011). *An Emerging Non-Regular Labour Force in Japan: The Dignity of Dispatched Workers*. London and New York: Routledge.

Fujita, H. (2010). 'Whither Japanese schooling? Educational reforms and their impact on ability formation and educational opportunity'. In J. A. Gordon, H. Fujita, T. Kariya and G. LeTendre (eds), *Challenges to Japanese Education: Economics, Reform, and Human Rights*. New York and London: Teachers College Press, pp. 17–53.

Furuichi, N. (2011). *Zetsubo no Kuni no Koufuku na Wakamono tachi* [*The Happy Youth in a Nation of Despair*]. Tokyo: Kodansha.

Genda, Y. (2001). *Shigoto no Naka no Aimai na Fuan*. Tokyo: Chuo Koron. (Translated by Jean Connell Hoffas and published in 2005 as *A Nagging Sense of Job Insecurity: The New Reality Facing Japanese Youth*. Tokyo: International House of Japan.)

Goodman, R. (1990). Japan's 'International Youth': The Emergence of a New Class of Schoolchildren. Oxford: Clarendon Press.

—(2007). 'The concept of kokusaika and Japanese educational reform'. *Globalisation, Societies and Education*, 5 (1): 71–87.

Graburn, N., Ertl, J. and Tierney, R. K. (2010). Multiculturalism in the New Japan: Crossing the Boundaries Within. New York and Oxford: Bergahn Books.

Harden, Blaine (2010). 'Once drawn to U.S. universities, more Japanese students are staying home'. *Washington Post*, 11 April.

Hood, C. (2003). *Japanese Educational Reform*. London and New York: Routledge.

Honda, Y. (2008). *Kishimu Shakai: Kyouiku, Shigoto, Wakamono no Genzai* [*The Creaking Society: The Current Reality of Education, Work and Youth*]. *Tokyo*: Soufusha.

Honda, Y., Naito, A. and Goto, K.. (2006). *'Niito'tte Iu na!* [*Don't Your Dare Use the Word 'Niito'!*]. Tokyo: Kobunsha.

Imoto, Y. (2009). *The production and consumption of "international preschools" in Japan: a study of the organization of diversity*. Unpublished thesis submitted to the University of Oxford.

Ishikawa, M (2009). 'University rankings, global models and emerging hegemony: critical analysis from Japan'. *Journal of Studies in International Education*, 13 (2): 159–73.

—(2011). 'Redefining internationalization in higher education: Global 30 and the making of global universities in Japan', in D. B. Willis and J. Rappleye (eds), *Reimagining Japanese Education: Borders, Transfers, Circulations and the Comparative*. Oxford: Symposium Books.

Kariya, T. (1995). *Taishuu Shakai no Yukue: Gakureki-shugi to Byoudou-shinwa no Sengoshi* [*The Mass Education Society: A Postwar History of Meritocracy and the Myth of Egalitarianism*]. Tokyo: Chuo Koron.

—(2001). *Kaisouka Nihon to Kyouiku Kiki: Fubyoudou Saiseisan kara Iyoku Kakusa Shakai e* [*Stratified Japan and Educational Crisis: From the Reproduction of Inequality to a Society of Incentive Divide*]. Tokyo: Yushindo Kobunsha.

Kubota, R. (2002). 'The impact of globalization on language teaching in Japan'. In D. Block and D. Cameron (eds), *Globalization and Language Teaching*. London and New York: Routledge, pp. 13–28.

Leheney, D. (2006). *Think Global, Fear Local: Sex, Violence, and Anxiety in Contemporary Japan*. Ithaca, NY and London: Cornell University Press.

Lynn, R. (1988). *Educational Achievement in Japan: Lessons for the West*. Armonk, NY: M. E. Sharpe.

Marshall, B. (1994). *Learning to be modern: Japanese political discourse on education*. Boulder, CO and Oxford: Westview Press.

Mouer, R, and Sugimoto Y. (1995). 'Nihonjinron at the end of the twentieth century:

a multicultural perspective', in J. P. Arnason and Y. Sugimoto (eds), *Japanese Encounters with Postmodernity*. London and New York: Kegan Paul International, pp. 237–69.

Murata, A. (forthcoming). 'Stuck in between: English language environments for international students and skilled foreign workers in Japan', in S. Horiguchi, Y. Imoto and G. Poole (eds), *Foreign Language Education in Japan: Dialogues in Ethnographic Approaches*.

Nakane, C. (1967). *Tateshakai no Ningenkankei* [*Human Relations in a Vertical Society*]. Tokyo: Kondansha.

Nikkei Shimbun (16 March 2010). '*Nihonjin ryugakusei genshou ni kenen: Harvard gakucho "ichinensei ha hitori"*' ['Worries over the decrease of Japanese students abroad: President of Harvard says "only one in the sophomore year"'].

—(28 November 2010). '*Ryuugaku mashi nado mezasu*' ['Aiming for increased study abroad'].

—(12 January 2012). '*Kaigai ryuugaku 6 man-nin ware, 09 nen 59,923, 5 nen renzoku-gen "fukyou ya uchimuki-shikou" de*' ['Number of students studying abroad dips to 60,000: 59,923 in 2009, a consecutive decrease in the last five years. Affected by the recession and introvertedness'].

—(6 February 2012). '*Todai ga Aki nyuugaku ikou e*' ['Todai is moving to fall enrollment'].

Parmenter, L. (2000). 'Internationalization in Japanese Education: current issues and future prospects'. In N. P. Stromquist and K. Monkman (eds), Globalization and education: integration and contestation across cultures. Oxford: Rowman & Littlefield, pp. 237–54.

Rappleye, J. (2007). *Exploring Cross-national Attraction in Education: Some Historical Comparisons of American and Chinese Attraction to Japanese Education*. Didcot: Symposium Books.

Roesgaard, M. (2011). '"The ideal citizen", globalization, and the Japanese response: risk, gate-keeping, and moral education in Japan', in D. B. Willis and J. Rappleye (eds), *Reimagining Japanese Education: Borders, Transfers, Circulations, and the Comparative*. Oxford: Symposium Books, pp. 85–106.

Rohlen, T. (1983). *Japan's High Schools*. Berkeley, CA: University of California Press.

Seargeant, P. (2009). *The Idea of English in Japan: Ideology and the Evolution of a Global Language*. Bristol, New York and Ontario: Multilingual Matters.

Schoppa, L. (2001). *Education Reform in Japan: A Case of Immobilist Politics*. London and New York: Routledge.

—(2006). *Race for the Exits: The Unraveling of Japan's System of Social Protection*. New York: Cornell University Press.

Takayama, K. (2007). 'Japan's Ministry of Education becoming the right: neo-liberal restructuring and the Ministry's struggle for political legitimacy'. *Globalisation, Societies and Education*, 6 (2): 131–46.

—(2008). 'The politics of international league tables: PISA in Japan's achievement crisis debate'. *Comparative Education*, 44 (4): 387–407.

—(2011). 'Reconceptualizing the politics of Japanese education, reimagining comparative studies of Japanese education', in D. B. Willis and J. Rappleye [eds], *Reimagining Japanese Education: Borders, Transfers, Circulations, and the Comparative*. Oxford: Symposium Books, pp. 247–80.

Toivonen, T. and Imoto. Y. (2012). 'Making sense of youth problems', in R. Goodman, Y. Imoto and T. Toivonen (eds), *A Sociology of Japanese Youth: From Returnees to NEETs*. London and Oxford: Routledge, pp. 1–19.

Tsuneyoshi, R. (2004a). 'The new Japanese educational reforms and the achievement "crisis" debate'. *Educational Policy*, 18 (2): 364–94.

—(2004b). 'The 'new' foreigners and the social reconstruction of difference: the cultural diversification of Japanese education'. *Comparative Education*, 40 (1): 55–81.

—(2005). '*Kokusaika to Kyouiku: "uchinaru kokusaika" no shiten to nihon no kyouiku*' ['Internationalization and education: the perspective of 'internal internationalization' and Japanese education']. *Kakei Keizai Kenkyu*, Summer, 67: 40–49.

Vogel, E. (1979). *Japan as Number One: Lessons for America*. Cambridge, MA: Harvard University Press.

White, M. (1987). *The Japanese Educational Challenge: A Commitment to Children*. New York: Free Press.

Willis, D. B., Yamamura, S. and Rappleye. J. (2008). 'Frontiers of education: Japan as "Global Model" or "Nation At Risk"?' *International Review of Education*. 54 (3–4): 493–515.

Yoshino, K. (1992), *Cultural Nationalism in Contemporary Japan*. London and New York: Routledge.

Notes

1. Takayama (2011) argues that Anglo-American social science literature on Japanese education has been dominated by an 'Orientalist' discourse of Japanese uniqueness that sees the Japanese case as an 'exception', producing a static and bounded image.

2. http://www.mext.go.jp/b_menu/houdou/22/12/1300642.htm. MEXT Homepage. (Accessed 25 March 2012.)

3. http://www.mofa.go.jp/mofaj/area/usa/visit/president_1011/pdf/exchange_en.pdf. MOFA Homepage. (Accessed 18 March 2012.)

4. MEXT: Ministry of Education, Culture, Sports, Science and Technology.

5. METI: Ministry of Economy, Trade and Industry.

6. Keidanren: Japan Business Federation.

7. http://www.jsps.go.jp/j-tenkairyoku/data/meibo_siryou/sankou07.pdf. JSPS Homepage. (Accessed 20 March 2012.)

8. http://www.jsps.go.jp/j-tenkairyoku/data/meibo_siryou/sankou06.pdf. JSPS Homepage. (Accessed 20 March 2012.)

9. Criticisms of youth as 'inward-looking' have a long history in Japan. Examples include the *capsule ningen* discourse in the late 1960s (see Furuichi, 2011), which foreshadowed the *otaku* debate in the 1990s, which overlapped with the problematization of *hikikomori* in the 2000s. In such cases it was said that affluence and the influence of new technologies were turning youth into passive and withdrawn creatures.

7

Japan: A Silent End to a Silent Revolution? Post-war Changes in Resource Allocation

Takehiko Kariya

Introduction

Public education is financed through public resources: national, sub-national and/or local tax revenues. Public educators rarely doubt this fact, but more often simply give little thought to issues of finance. Without knowing how public funding is allocated or what ideas underpin existing modes of resource allocation, educators can continue teaching and students continue learning. Public education is, in this sense, so highly institutionalized in terms of finance that educators as well as learners take existing patterns for granted, almost never stopping to consider the ways that allocation influences and impacts on the day-to-day educational process unfolding in classrooms. Yet, there is a clear, identifiable relationship between financial allocation and education practice. As such, a deconstruction of the institutionalized 'taken-for-grant-edness' surrounding resource allocation and delivery schemes is necessary as a means to reveal hidden principles that implicitly shape teaching and learning.

This chapter examines the case of Japanese compulsory education: how public funding is allocated and the resulting resource distribution. What principles regulate this allocation process? What ideas and ideals underpinned these principles when the funding allocation system was first established? How are educational teaching and learning practices influenced by these systems of resource allocation and underpinning principles? While Japanese education is often regarded as an exemplar of egalitarianism (Kariya, 2010), the ways in which public funding allocation intersect with this egalitarianism has been largely unexplored to date. Interestingly, this is true not only in scholarly work outside of Japan but also of work within Japan. This research void is particularly evident when the question of connections between resource allocation and classroom practice is posed. Thus, in addressing these questions this chapter seeks to describe the historically contingent linkages between the public funding allocation system and classroom practices in the Japanese articulation of the egalitarian educational ideal in the post-World War Two period.

In the first section, the Japanese approach to public funding allocation and its associated mechanisms are explained in terms of a Weberian 'ideal type' model. To make the divergent logic that underpins the Japanese model explicit, a comparison is made with the United States. The third section consists of a brief history of the formation and establishment of the Japanese scheme. It devotes specific attention to what intentions the Ministry of Education planners had in the 1950s and how their initial policy objectives changed in subsequent decades, revealing that Japan's public funding scheme to education was actually a compromise solution forged in the immediate post-war context of limited financial resources. In the fourth section, a statistical analysis focusing on changes in actual distribution of public resources to prefectures over time examines the unintended results for egalitarian education brought about by this allocation scheme. It shows that, contrary to the intentions of Ministry planners, the system worked to produce a highly progressive inter-prefectural resource distribution, fostering more equal conditions in education nationally, as well as a somewhat more equal distribution of students' academic achievement. The fifth section examines the second unintended result that this scheme produced: a highly collectivist socialization among Japanese youth, a characteristic most frequently described as cultural derivative. The argument put forth in this section challenges this cultural explanation, pointing to how this collective socialization can be seen as a by-product of the prevailing education funding system. In conclusion, the theoretical significance of this perspective is highlighted, before turning to examine policy changes over the past decade pushed through under the name of 'decentralization'; changes that are undermining the entire post-war system: a silent end to a silent revolution, but also to Japan's egalitarian model.

Japan's Educational Resource Allocation Scheme: Basic Mechanisms

The basic structure of Japan's current public funding allocation scheme to compulsory education was established in 1958. Since its establishment, a pair of legal mandates that constitute the core of the public educational funding scheme have operated hand in hand. One is the State Subsidies Law for Compulsory Education enacted in 1952. The other is the Class Size and School Staff Standards Act passed in 1958. The State Subsidies Law for Compulsory Education ('State Subsidies Law' hereafter) required the national government to pay one half of teachers' salaries and other allowances in public elementary and junior high schools nationwide. The other half would be paid by each of Japan's 47 sub-national jurisdictions (43 prefectures plus four other administrative units, but hereafter all 47 jurisdictions shall be referred to as 'prefectures' for convenience).[1] The Class Size and School Staff Standards Act ('Class Size Standards Act' hereafter), on the other hand, mandated that each prefecture should calculate the total number of teaching staff theoretically needed in each prefecture according to a specific formula laid out in regulations pertaining to the Act.

These two acts worked together the following way. The Class Size Standards Act, when first established, set the maximum size of classroom at 50 students nationwide (although there were a few exceptions as discussed later). This Class Size Standards Act also functioned as the primary means of formulating theoretical calculations of necessary human resources and total cost because it laid out nationally standardized pay scales for teachers.[2] Once this human resource cost was calculated, the national government, bound by the State Subsidies Law, would pay one half of this total cost, with prefectures providing matching funds covering the other half. Put another way, prefectures would calculate the number of necessary teachers by combining the needs of individual schools calculated according to the nationally mandated class size of 50 students (this school-level calculation is described in detail below). This total number when calculated according to nationally standardized pay scales became the basis for the national government to allocate funds (one half of the total projected prefectural educational allocation).

One main goal of establishing this scheme was to standardize the quality and quantity of education by nationally standardizing and subsidizing human resources costs associated with compulsory education run by local communities. This goal reflected concern with the wide disparities in local public financial resources across prefectures brought about by the costs of compulsory education. In this sense, the highly centralized system of financing teachers' salaries on the one hand, while setting the maximum class size on the other, was an integral part of egalitarian education in Japan, which aimed to achieve uniformity in educational provision nationally, but particularly at the compulsory level.

A unique feature of this public funding system derives from the way in which the theoretically needed number of teachers is calculated by the application of the Class Size Standards Act.[3] To understand how it works, it is useful to describe this mechanism by means of an 'ideal type'. By using a simple example of an elementary school where usually one classroom teacher teaches the class, the theoretically required number of teaching staff can be calculated in the following way. When the maximum class size is set at 50 students and when there are 51 students in a single year cohort (grade level) in the school, the class is divided into two: two teachers are required to be employed to teach these two classrooms because the number exceeds 50. In this case, in one classroom one teacher teaches 26 students and in the other classroom the second teacher teaches 25 students. However, in the case where 101 pupils were enrolled in a specific grade, only three teachers would be required: teaching classrooms of 34, 34 and 33 students each. If one student left the school before the school year began, the rest of the 100 students could be divided into two classrooms, which theoretically would only need to employ two, not three, teachers.

Once the number of teaching staff for each individual cohort (grade level) is determined according to this formula, the total number for the entire school can be calculated by totalling the teachers required to instruct the six year grade groups in that particular elementary school. In reality, more complex formula are used to calculate the total number of teaching staff in a school because the number of administrators (e.g. principals and vice principals) and the number of specialized subject teachers (art, music, physical education, etc.) are also taken into consideration, but the basic mechanism in calculating the necessary number of teaching staff in each school can be understood as outlined above.

Once the number of teaching staff in each school is calculated, the total number of teachers needed in each city or town, prefecture and, indeed, the whole country can be determined by totalling these figures. The human resource costs for total teaching staff can also be produced by applying the national standardized pay scale for teachers. Last, the necessary outlays (subsidies) by the central government to each prefecture can then also be calculated according to the State Subsidies Law, as mentioned above.

The uniqueness of this funding allocation system derives from the fact that it is both the total number of students in one school and also the mandated cut-off for maximum class size that combine to determine the total human recourses cost for teaching staff in the school. This uniqueness is even clearer if we compare it with the allocation scheme most familiar in the West: the 'per-capita principle'.

In a per-capita (student) funding scheme, education budgets are primarily determined based on the overall number of students in a 'unit cost' formula. Once the per-student cost is determined, the total cost of education is produced by a simple calculation that multiplies the mandated per-student cost by the total number of students. Of course, this theoretical figure is, as in the Japanese case, subject to minor adjustments to compensate for specific situations in school districts, but overall it is the per-capita formulation that prevails.

In the USA, for example, a principle of 'pupil hours' has been used to calculate the per-capita cost. Pupil hours are defined as the number of hours a teacher teaches multiplied by the number of pupils who receive instruction. For example, if a teacher teaches 40 students for three hours a day, it results in 120 pupil hours. In this formula, a teaching load in which a teacher instructs 30 students for four hours a day is equivalent to that of a teacher who teaches 40 students for three hours a week (i.e. 120 pupil hours). If he or she teaches for five hours a week, both scenarios produce 600 pupil hours per week.

Interestingly, this principle was once admired as an ideal method by a high ranking official in the Ministry of Education in Japan, Satō Mikitarō, who was instrumental in establishing the Class Size Standards Act. Satō's explanation of how it worked can be summarized as an 'ideal type' as follows (Satō, 1975):[4]

> (I)n America, pupil hours are usually set at a maximum of 150 hours per day, but ideally at 120 hours. Accordingly if a class size is set at 30 students, teachers are expected to teach between 4 and 5 hours a day. Once these values are determined, the number of classes a day students learn can be factored in to produce the number of teachers theoretically needed. For example, if class size is set at 30 students and students are expected to learn for 30 hours a week, the pupil hours of a single classroom produces 900 pupil hours, which determines that in total 6 teachers are needed per week – dividing 900 pupil hours by 150 pupil hours as a unit of a day. It also produces a teacher–pupil ratio of 30. I assume that this idea of pupil hours is behind the reason why 'pupil teacher ratio' is used as a method of calculating the necessitated number of teachers. (Satō, 1965, pp. 74–5)

As explained above, the use of 'pupil hours' as the base unit in the formula to calculate the necessary number of teaching staff in a school produces the needed human resources cost. One basic idea underlying this scheme is the notion that the unit cost should be directly responsive to any increase or decrease in the number of students in a teaching unit. When a teacher teaches even one additional student in a class, it is automatically reflected in his or her teaching load by increasing his or her pupil hours. It also automatically adjusts the necessary number of teaching staff as well as the human resource cost for the entire school.[5]

In practice, there are some more detailed techniques in formula used to make the scheme flexible, but it is clear that a principal idea behind this is its individualistic character; namely, the idea that even one additional student (one unit increase) changes the teaching load. This idea both reflects and approximates the extra work created by an additional student in contexts where teaching and learning are individualized to each student. That is, one additional student is naturally recognized as a contributor to an increased teaching load and a factor in human resource allocation.

By contrast, the Japanese scheme is much less responsive to fluctuations in the number of students. When the maximum number of students in a classroom is set at 50, for example, a cohort having 51 to 100 in a school needs two teachers, with each teacher teaching between 25 to 50 students in each classroom. Pupil hours, if calculated, could hypothetically differ by as much as double in such a scheme: the difference between a classroom with 25 students and one having 50 students where instructional hours per week is constant. Until the threshold of one student more than the maximum mandated class size is reached, the incremental increase of students is not reflected in the number of teaching staff. As a result it, it also remains unreflected in the human resources allocation for teaching.

It is noteworthy that when the Japanese method of resources allocation was being planned after World War Two, individualistic American-style teaching practices were being introduced by the occupation authorities, in particular by CIE (the Civil Information and Education Section) (Shibata, 2008). This is perhaps one reason that the Ministry officer quoted above referred admiringly to the pupil hours method as an ideal, one thought to fit better with such newly introduced individualistic pedagogies than the Japanese scheme that was being planned. This issue will be returned to later, but at this point we note that Satō's explanations of the American methods is evidence that Japanese planners of the post-war system were clearly aware of the distinctive principles underpinning these two divergent allocation schemes. They were also cognizant of the connection between the American allocation scheme and its closer compatibility with the individualized pedagogies adopted in post-war Japan as opposed to the 'maximum class size scheme' they themselves were in the process of planning. So why then was the Japanese scheme adopted while the American model remained merely the 'ideal'?

Historical Background: Origins of the Japanese Scheme

Examining the conception of 'the maximum class-size scheme', we find that the system was not initially planned; it emerged from a compromise under scarce financial resources after the World War Two. The war had devastated Japan, of course its economy and industry but also the physical and personnel conditions surrounding education. Facing severe budget shortages, neither the national nor local governments had resources to employ enough teachers to staff the newly enlarged compulsory system: the occupation-era reforms had added three more years by making junior high school compulsory. This lack of resources, both material and personnel, inevitably resulted in enormous classes that often exceeded 50 students in one classroom. The *average* number of students in one classroom across Japan in 1948 was more than 45. Faced with the enrolment in elementary school of the post-war 'baby-boom' generation this number stayed high throughout the decade, fluctuating between 42 and 44 as late as 1960 (MEXT, each year).

Another emergent question in education policy following the war was how to mitigate regional disparities. These inequalities were the result of the pre-war education system that placed the financial burden of budgetary support to compulsory education on local communities. Looking back, one finds yawning disparities in education budgets among prefectures in the pre-war system; differences that were concretely reflected in average teachers' salaries as evident in the proportion of certified to non-certified teachers. Figure 7.1 illustrates this clear correlation between an index of general public financial resources per capita and education expenditures per capita (pupil) in elementary school education among 47 prefectures in 1928 (Abe, 1933).[6] It shows a positive correlation: the wealthier a prefecture in its overall local budget (adjusted by its population), the greater the education expenditure per student. Another positive correlation can be found between education expenditures per capita on the one hand, and the average teacher's salaries and the share of fully certified teachers in prefectures on the other hand, although this data and relevant figures are omitted here due to limited space.[7]

The more a prefecture spent per student for elementary school education, the higher the teacher's salaries and the higher proportion of teachers having full teaching certificates (*Seikyōin*, in Japanese). Educational conditions in elementary school in the pre-war period thus differed greatly among prefectures, depending upon the resources available for public finance. High ranking officials in the Ministry of Education who had worked for the Ministry both in the pre- and post-war periods frequently mentioned that unequal conditions

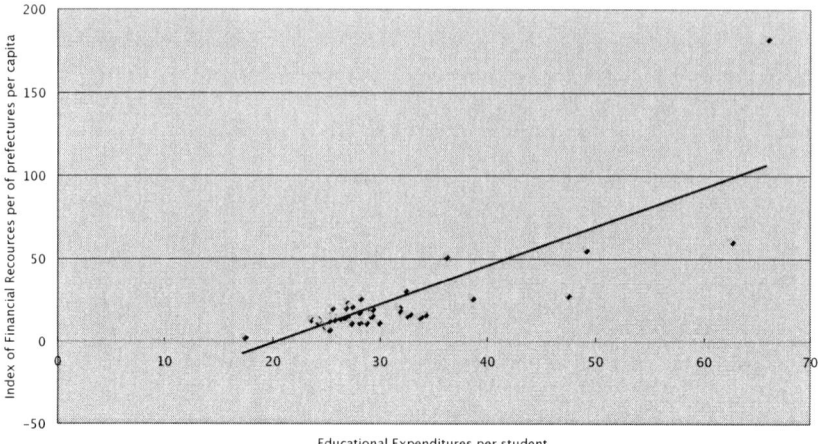

Figure 7.1 Correlation between Index of Prefectual Financial Resources and Educational Expenditure per student in Elementary School among 47 prefectures in 1928 (in JY)

and imbalances in funding for compulsory education among different regions was a serious issue that post-war education reforms were aimed to rectify (Naitō, 1950; Amagi, 2002) .

The Fundamental Law of Education (1947) established right after the war provided the legal mandate to rectify these huge disparities, stating in Article 3: 'Citizens shall all be given equal opportunities to receive education according to their abilities, and shall not be subject to discrimination in education on account of race, creed, sex, social status, economic position, or family origin.' Rebuilding compulsory education on a more equal foundation thus became an urgent policy goal for the Ministry of Education. 'Democratization' of Japanese education, the main goal of the occupation reforms, almost without exception meant 'Americanization' in the various aspects of the system: '6-3-3 school system', decentralization of education administration and guaranteeing equal opportunity of education among others (Naitō 1950). Another policy focus became American-style pedagogies, founded on the premise of child-centred ideas emphasizing experiential education. These were to be introduced, encouraged, and supported in Japanese schools as a means to nurture more individualistic and independent citizens for the newly democratic society.

However, facing an acute lack of resources, the government's attempt to construct the American education model became gradually diluted. More 'realistic' policies were instead adopted and implemented and the 'Japanization' of the post-war education system gained momentum through the 1950s and into the 1960s. The recovery of Japan's independence in 1951 accelerated this trend, gradually removing American influences on education policies enforced by the CIE. Those years roughly coincided with the period in which the Japanese funding allocation scheme described above began to be planned and enacted.

In the processes of planning the scheme, the Ministry of Education had initially sought for a per-head scheme of education funding following the American model. Naitō Takasaburō, a then high ranking Ministry of Education official, recalled with regret the infeasibility of adopting the American type per-head scheme:

> The unit cost for compulsory education should be calculated solely based on the number of students, and should not include numbers of classrooms and schools, with specific compensations for small sized schools and local communities with low population densities. Under the [severe] circumstances facing our compulsory education system, however, we had no other choice except to accept this three part scheme that calculates numbers of students, classrooms, and schools to produce our unit cost. (Naitō, 1950, p. 190)

Naitō follows Saito in arguing that the per-head scheme would have been the most rational model to produce unit cost calculations. The gap between the Ministry of Education officials' initial intention and the implementation of the three-part formula highlights how the funding allocation system was a compromise solution made in the context of scarce resources.

When the Japanese scheme was first established, the maximum class size was set at 50 students. During the first several years, exceptions were made to allow more than 50 students in one classroom in prefectures whose educational budget was too limited to employ additional teachers. Given the number of already established schools, enrolled students and employed teachers under the limited budget, this three-part calculation scheme actually functioned as a compromise that passively accepted the status quo of poor educational conditions and insufficient local budgetary resources. Satō Mikitarō, the aforementioned planner of the Class Size Standard Act, in retrospect openly admitted that this scheme inevitably produced large class sizes. A classroom with 50-plus students in elementary school was obviously too large for a teacher to respond to individual learning needs. Clearly these classrooms could not provide an environment supportive of child-centred pedagogies, thus providing little motivation for teachers to develop these approaches.

Satō provided further reflections on the differences between the Japanese scheme and those elsewhere:

> In other countries, the method of calculating the number of teachers necessary was solely and directly produced by the number of students enrolled. The idea underpinning this was that each teacher's teaching load should be appropriately and evenly shared in consideration of the number of students each teacher teaches as a unit. Such a scheme is not appropriate in our current system, where we fix the class size and teach the same year group of students in the same classroom. (Satō, 1975, p. 77)

Satō also highlights inflexibility as one consequence of the system and thus a weakness of the Japanese system: 'it ignores the number of students, large or small, in one class room [as long as the number is under the maximum class size set by the Act]' (Satō, 1975, pp. 72–3)

This emergence of this compromise unsurprisingly coincided with the attenuation of the American model of child-centred pedagogy. In 1958, the exact year the Class Size Standard Act was passed, the national curriculum was revised. This revision revealed the conclusion of the 'Americanization' of pedagogies, instead emphasizing the importance of learning facts through more rigorous means. As a result, not only the class size but the content of curricula subsequently became more standardized under the control of the Ministry. Thus, uniformity in learning across Japanese classrooms and schools increased under the centralization of educational administration. This move was often regarded as the recovery of the Ministry of Education's power to control local education authorities as well as local schools under the banner of standardization aimed at achieving 'equal opportunity of education' (Kariya, 2009).

Two Unintended Results of the Japanese Approach

A silent revolution

To improve teaching conditions through a reduction in class size, the mandated ceiling of students per class within the Class Size Standard Act has been amended numerous times over the past five decades. The government reduced the maximum class size from 50 to 45 in 1968, then again to 40 in 1980. In 2011 it was further reduced to 35 (Kariya, 2009). This reduction, in particular the first shift to 45 students during the mid-1960s, was implemented at a time when the total number of school-age children was in rapid decline. These periodic declines were caused by graduation out of compulsory education of the first generation of 'baby boomers' – those born in the years immediately after the end of World War Two. In other words, the means of reducing the class size was not only implemented by increasing the national education expenditures, but also by taking advantage of demographic changes in the school-age cohort children by retaining existing teachers so as to minimize additional budgetary allocation. When the large number of post-war baby boomers first enrolled in elementary education during the1950s (over 2 million in each year cohort), a large number of teachers were hired. After this baby boom generation passed through elementary school, it would have produced enormous redundancies in teaching staff if the existing class size ceiling had been kept in force. In place of dismissing teachers, however, the government reduced the maximum class size in order to improve teaching conditions with as little additional public expenditure as possible. This approach also served to avoid potential political conflicts that would have emerged from a massive dismissal of public school teachers, who were unionized into one of the most powerful and politically active labour unions in the entire post-war period – the Japanese Teachers Union (*Nihon Kyōshokuin Kumiai*).

Once the government adjusted the maximum class-size ceiling, everything else changed with it: the necessary numbers of teaching staff and the human resource outlay. At the same time, these changes also altered the relative distribution of public funding for compulsory education nationwide (that is, amongst Japan's 47 prefectures) because prefectures varied in school size, classroom sizes, school-aged population and age composition of teachers.

We have already seen how pubic funding in the pre-war period was unequally distributed among prefectures: the wealthier a prefecture, the greater the expenditure for compulsory education per pupil. How did the post-war funding scheme alter such inequalities? We can test this by looking into correlations between financial resources and education expenditure per pupil across individual prefectures at various points in the post-war period.

Figures 7.2 to 7.4 indicate correlation coefficients between the index of general financial resources (not only education but all aspects of local government finance) and education expenditures per student among prefectures in 1955, 1965 and 1975 respectively.[8] The lines drawn in the figures are regression lines. In 1955, we find a positive correlation between prefectures' general financial resources and education expenditures per student: the greater the financial resources of the prefecture, the greater the expenditure per student for compulsory education. The unequal distribution of education funding among prefectures of the pre-war period had clearly carried through into the early post-war period. The 1965 data, however, suggests that this positive correlation had virtually disappeared: the line becomes almost flat. In 1975, there is a definite negative correlation, illuminating a 'progressive' way of funding

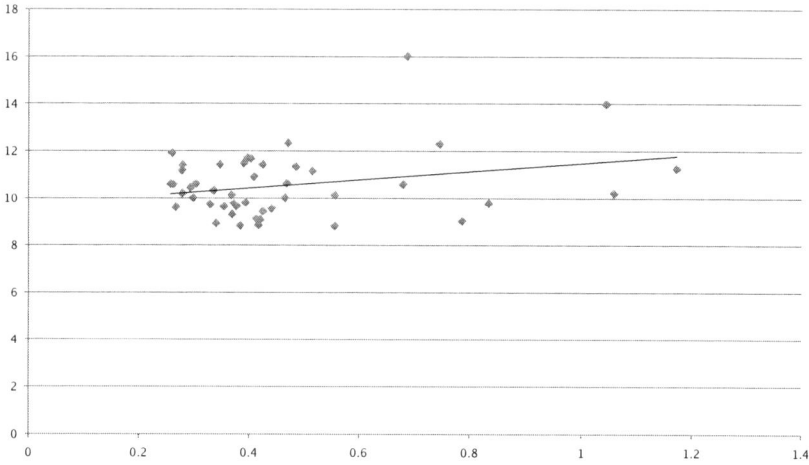

Figure 7.2 Correlation between Index of Prefectual Financial Resources (X axis) and Educational Expenditure per student for Elementary School (Y axis) among 46 prefectures [not including Okinawa] in 1955 (in thousand JY)

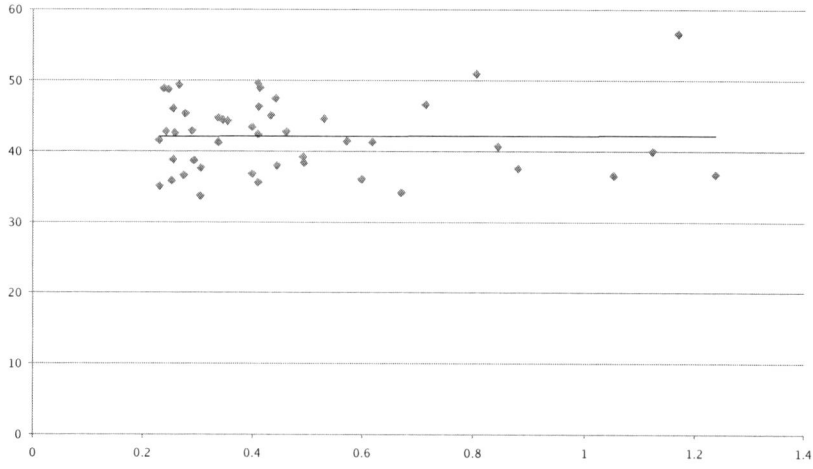

Figure 7.3 Correlation between Index of Prefectual Financial Resources (X axis) and Educational Expenditure per student for Elementary School (Y axis) among 46 prefectures [not including Okinawa] in 1965 (in thousand JY)

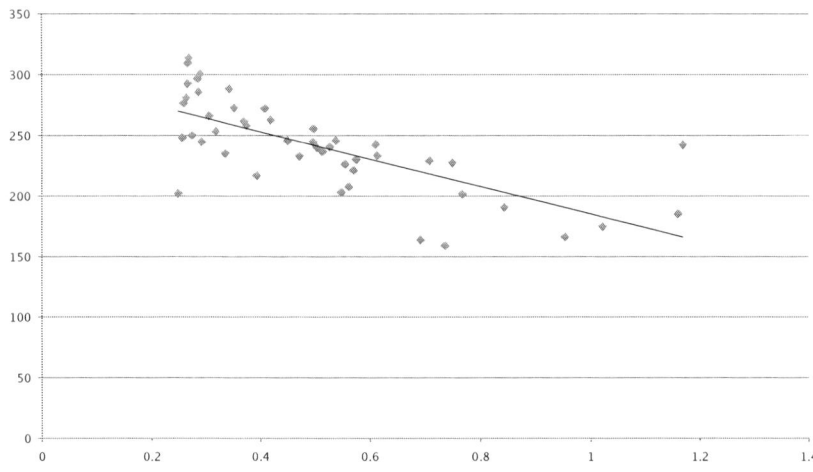

Figure 7.4 Correlation between Index of Prefectual Financial Resources (X axis) and Educational Expenditure per student for Elementary School (Y axis) among 47 prefectures [including Okinawa] in 1975 (in thousand JY)

distribution in which financially *poorer* prefectures tend to spend *more* on education expenditures per student. Space does not permit a more detailed look at other years, but a similar overall trend towards a negative correlation – progressive funding – continues up to the present, although the correlation becomes weaker (Kariya, 2009).

This reversal occurred because of divergent demographic trends across different prefectures. At the time the school-aged population first dipped during the 1960s and early 1970s, in prefectures where both population and population density were low, the number of schools with smaller class sizes increased. The mechanism worked in the following way. In high-population, high-density districts, a school with six grades would most likely enrol 50 students per class, per grade. As such, it would need, here hypothesizing a single classroom per grade, six classroom teachers for 300 students in the school. In low-population, low-density districts, however, a school with six grades would be unlikely to enrol 50 students per class, per grade. Hypothesizing that only 25 students per class, per grade were enrolled, that school would still need the same six classroom teachers for 150 students. The crucial point is that the number of teachers is exactly the same as the human resource outlays, but the number of students is one-half. In effect, the human resource cost is, in this illustrative scenario, twice as high in relation to student numbers in the low-population, low-density district when compared to the high-population, high density district. Extending the logic, for prefectures that experienced larger declines in school-age population producing smaller class sizes and schools, educational expenditures tended to rise. Prefectures with already small and/or further declining age populations were also most likely to be those with already limited financial resources. This is how the Japanese allocation scheme moved, over time, in a progressive direction.

In this way, the long-standing unequal distribution of education funding existing since the pre-war period was resolved and egalitarian education, at least in terms of finance, was achieved. So drastic was such a transformation that one might even call it a revolution in educational finance. Importantly, this egalitarian system was achieved without any drastic policy changes with the sole exception of an incremental reduction in maximum class size, which applied to all the prefectures, whether strong or weak financially.

The significance of this can be grasped with a hypothetical comparison: what policies would have been implemented if a per-head method of resources allocation had been adapted in Japan? In such a scenario, the driving principle of resource allocation policy would need to be explicitly shifted from regressive to progressive. Any such move would have ignited intense political and ideological debates, as education reforms worldwide show us. In order for the national government to invest 'progressively' – more per-capita expenditures to poorer prefectures – it would have had to forge an extremely difficult political consensus around a revision to the formula of calculation for the human resourse costs. In other words, if the standardized unit of 'pupil hours' was set at the same nationally, the methods for allocating funding themselves would necessarily need to be *actively* amended in a progressive way to produce the same egalitarian results – no small feat politically.

Historical research on relevant policy documents in the Japanese Ministry of Education confirms that these intense political debates and/or drastic shifts in fundamental principles in policy did not occur. That is, the revolutionary transformation was achieved from a regressive to a progressive position without intensive policy discussions or any new legislation to change its principle of resources allocation. As we saw, the planners who created this system saw the system as a compromise necessary in the context of scarce resources in the immediate post-war period. They did not predict, let alone expect, that such a great egalitarian shift would later emerge.[9] This transformation was, in this sense, an unintended result. This radical yet great egalitarian shift was thus, in fact, an unintentional *silent revolution*, in which no critical, and thus high-profile and politically contentious, policy changes were necessary.

Collectivist socialization

Under this Japanese resources allocation scheme, the classroom emerges as the most important unit for teaching and learning. Each year, students are assigned into a specific classroom (*Gakkyū* in Japanese) and the membership of the classroom is fixed for at least one or two years. Students are usually taught almost all their subject classes by a single classroom teacher who is assigned for the same period as his/her students to that specific classroom. As discussed above, during the post-war period the average size of the class shifted gradually from nearly 50 students in the 1950s to 30 students in the early 1990s, figures which were among the highest of any advanced country (OECD, 2011). As Satō recognized at the beginning of establishing the system, such large class sizes did not fit well with child-centred teaching of the American mould.

Faced with this contradiction on a daily basis, Japanese teachers thus developed their own teaching methods better suited to learning environments of 40 to 50 students and its very different group dynamics. For example, group activities (*Han Katsudō* or *Han Gakushū* in Japanese) are often utilized by Japanese teachers to organize students' learning by encouraging collaboration and group work among peer students in the same classroom. Japanese teachers also developed effective ways of asking questions to large-sized classes to encourage not only the students questioned but the rest of students in the class to also learn from the exchange. As Stigler and Hiebert (1999) recorded, Japanese teachers, in comparison with their American counterparts, successfully organized their teaching to fit this larger class sizes, skilfully emphasizing students' understanding and thinking even while producing higher results in students' learning in mathematics vis-à-vis their American peers. Numerous books have been published by experienced Japanese teachers explaining the 'know-how' of good teaching methods in the context of large class sizes by harnessing the power of the group dynamic (e.g. Kubo, 2005). Long-term teaching situations in larger class size settings inevitably provided the necessity and opportunity for Japanese teachers to develop these techniques.

Moreover, since Japanese elementary and middle schools' 'content' covers a wider range of daily life issues – hygiene, serving and eating lunch together, daily cleaning of classrooms, participation in school trips and sports day events – and such activities are organized as classroom units, the class becomes a socialization community that extends beyond traditional academic lessons into all aspects of students' school lives (Yanagi, 2005). In other words, it is in the context of these group dynamics that students learn not only academic subject matters but other daily life relevant knowledge as well, in addition to the social and communication skills to act as a member of a group in effective and collaborative ways. Some Japanese educators even use the metaphor of 'the classroom as a kingdom' (*gakkyū ōkoku* in Japanese) to describe both the dominant position of the classroom as an organizational unit, but also the relative independence the class group has from other class groups (Yanagi, 2005).

Socialization in such an organizational context clearly catalyzes and creates 'collectivist' attitudes and behaviours among Japanese students. One can thus make a case that the collectivist socialization among Japanese children is a by-product of the Japanese resources allocation scheme, which reinforces the significance of classroom (the group) as the most important unit of teaching and learning. The mechanisms at work in Japan are thus divergent from systems employing individualized pedagogies, which require but are also made possible by more individualistic ways of resources allocation such as the per-head method prevailing in the US and other Western countries.

Conclusion: A Silent End to a Silent Revolution?

The Japanese approach to public funding allocation to compulsory education was established as a compromise under severe financial constraints in the immediate post-war period. The planners of the system at the Ministry of Education explicitly recognized and admitted that the scheme was not ideal, but had few other viable options at the time. They were aware of the 'lack of fit' with pedagogies newly introduced by the CIE: the scheme was neither flexible enough to respond to incremental changes in the number of students, nor sensitive enough to individual students with classrooms that averaged over 40 students per unit. In contrast to the individually focused per-capita (student) American scheme that complemented child-centred pedagogy, the Japanese model brought about a group-based teaching style; one much less personalized to individual learners' identities and needs.

Unintentionally, this scheme resulted in a highly progressive resources distribution among prefectures. It also created the foundations for collectivist socialization among students. These two unintended results in combination were perhaps the key driving factors leading to Japan's egalitarian education. Although it is difficult to empirically isolate the impact of this scheme of equalization on actual educational achievement, my earlier work made an attempt (Kariya, 2009). That work utilized regression analyses to estimate the effects of the general financial resources of prefectures on the average test scores of national standardized tests among prefectures by comparing testing outcomes for the years 1962 and 2007. It found that while prefectures' financial resources had a large and statistically significant effect on the average scores of Japanese language and mathematics test scores in 1962, its effect had become smaller (even insignificant for mathematics) by 2007. This suggests that the wealth of a prefecture loses its significance over time in explaining discrepancies in student academic achievements among prefectures. In other words, by 2007 the wealth of the prefecture in which a student was educated did not show significant effects on his/her achievement – a vastly different result from 1962 when the public funding was not yet progressively distributed.

Admittedly, it is again difficult to conclude with certainty that this shift is caused solely by the very 'egalitarian shift' in resources allocation given that so many other aspects of society were also changing over this same period. Nonetheless, it is certain that it would have been far more difficult, if not impossible, for such 'egalitarian' results in student achievement to arise if the regressive, pre-war resources allocation system had remained unchanged. One could even hypothesize that collectivist socialization among students might have supported this egalitarian trend by increasing uniformity and encouraging collaborations for learning among peer students in large classes, although we have no clear evidence to suggest this type of correlation at this time.

From these discussions, we can conceptualize Japanese educational egalitarianism as 'zone-based equality' (*Men no Byōdō* in Japanese). By this, I mean an egalitarian idea underpinning Japanese education funding that seeks to equalize resources allocated among different geographical administrative units such as prefectures, cities, school districts and schools. This stands in sharp contrast to the Western idea of individual-based equality that seeks to equalize resources among individuals as units, an approach evident in the per-student scheme prevalent in the West. In the West, it appears that an individualistic approach initially accepts individual differences in abilities (e.g. IQ) and attributes (e.g. cultural and social capital accumulated in and transmitted from family). These are thought to combine to produce differences in academic achievement. As a result, individually appropriate but differentiated approaches are taken to equalize outcomes of academic achievement among students. Ability tracking, individualized learning and instruction are clear examples of this approach.

By contrast, a zone-based equality approach attempts to prevent, as far as possible, differences among individuals within the same 'zone'. It provides equal, but not individually differentiated, educational conditions on a basis of collective units such as prefectures, cities, school districts, schools and class-rooms. Forging uniformity in the educational conditions based on collective units not only prevents individuals' differences in ability and attributes from becoming visible, but also regards it as a necessary condition to attain equality in education. The Japanese scheme of resource allocation and the group-based teaching methods subsequently invented as a result fit well with this concept of zone-based equality. The end result is a highly progressive approach to resource allocation as well as a collaborative, though less individualistic, collectivistic learning environment.

Despite its great egalitarian achievement, however, the Japanese scheme is currently being undermined. The centralized education system success-fully distributed resources and budget allocations equally to different regions. Supporting this were several other national mechanisms pushing for egali-tarianism and uniformity: a national curriculum, nationally inspected school textbooks, a nationally controlled teacher training and certificate system, and even nationally monitored physical school conditions and environmental regulations. This system has, however, been increasingly criticized as overcen-tralized, depriving local school districts and schools of self-governance. Not only educators but liberal political scientists and economists levelled harsh critiques at the dominance and control by the Ministry over local schools. Supported by long-standing antagonism against Ministry dominance, the decentralization of central government power, particularly fiscal decentralization, has been on the national policy agenda since Prime Minister Koizumi's structural reform plans of 2004 (Kariya and Rappleye, 2010).

In that year, the Japanese government decided on a plan to transfer tax-collecting authority worth ¥3 trillion (approximately US$9.1 billion) to local governments and cut the same amount of subsidies to offset the revenue loss. Out of the ¥3 trillion, about ¥0.85 trillion subsidies for teachers' salaries from the Ministry was targeted for transfer. In December 2005, the government decided to transfer this amount to local governments by reducing the central government's contribution to teacher salaries from 50 per cent to 33 per cent and by revising the State Subsidies Act. The government is still in the midst of discussing the possibility of a complete abolition of the national teacher salary subsidy system in order to transfer even more money (via tax-collection authority) from the central to local governments. There have even been further proposals to abolish the Class Size Standards Act as well. Driving this reform push are high levels of national and local government debt and the subsequent search for bold budget-cutting approaches. As such, the present subsidy system that did so much to foster egalitarianism for compulsory education is in danger of coming to an abrupt end (Kariya, 2010).

If the current system were indeed abolished under the banner of 'decentralization', each local government would be given more discretion to decide how much should be paid for compulsory education. Increasing demands for more individualized, child-centred learning in schools have accelerated the criticism against the uniformity of education, allegedly a negative consequences of this centralized system. However, few in Japan realize that Ministry control and regulations over education on the one hand, and the centralized system of subsidies for education on the other hand, are not necessarily one and the same.

Looking closely at the relations between these two components of the current system we find, strictly speaking, that the State Subsidies Law has nothing to do with other aspects of the Ministry's administrative control over education. Nonetheless, advocates of decentralization of education tend to regard national subsidies as a prime source of power through which the central government controls many other aspects of local education. Paradoxically, unless administrative decentralization is enacted, even if the national subsidies scheme is decentralized, centralized control over national curricula or other regulations may be left just as they are. In the worst-case scenario, decentralization will just increase the 'freedom' of struggling local government to reduce compulsory education budgets, but other central Ministry controls over local education would remain in place (Kariya, 2010).[10] It is ironic then that reasonable demands for decentralizing education administrations as well as for individualizing students' learning could come together in such a way as to undermine the egalitarian system of education resourses allocation that has achieved equal educational conditions in Japan throughout the post-war period. The silent Japan egalitarian revolution may well have a silent ending, if the majority of Japanese people continue to ignore its significance and contribution to an equal and just society.

References

Abe, S. (1933). *Kyōiku Kaikaku Ron [Essays on Education Reforms]*. Tokyo: Iwanami Shoten. (Reprint was published in 1971 by Meiji Tosho.)

Amagi, I. (2002) *The Oral History: Amagi Isao*. Tokyo: National Graduate Institute for Policy Studies.

Burke, Arvid J. (1951). *Financing public schools in the United States*. New York: Harper.

Callahan, R. (1962). *Education and the cult of efficiency: a study of the social forces that have shaped the administration of the public schools*. Chicago: University of Chicago Press.

Kariya, T. (2009). *Kyōiku to Byōdō [Education and Equality]*. Tokyo: Chuo Koron Shinsha.

—(2010). 'The End of Egalitarian Education in Japan?: The Effect of Policy Changes in Resource Distribution on Compulsory Education'. In June A. Gordon, Hidenori Fujita, Takehiko Kariya, and Gerald K. LeTendre (eds), *Challenges to Japanese Education: Economics, Reform, and Human Rights*. New York: Teachers College Press, pp. 54–66.

Kariya, T. and Rappleye, J. (2010). 'The Twisted, Unintended Impacts of Globalization on Japanese Education', in *Research in Sociology of Education 17: Globalization, Demographic Change, and Educational Challenges in East Asia*. Bingley: Emerald Group Publishing Limited, pp. 17–63.

Kida, H. (ed.) (1987). *Shōgen Sengo no Kyōiku Seisaku [Testimony on the Postwar Education Policies]*. Tokyo: Daiichi Hoki.

Kubo, I. (2005). *Issei Jugyo no Fukken [The Return of Classroom-based Teaching]*. Tokyo: Kodomo no Mirai-sha.

MEXT (Ministry of Education) (1948–65). *Gakkō Kihon Chōsa [Basic Statistics on School Education]*. Tokyo: MEXT.

Naitō, T. (1950). *Kyōiku Zaisei [Education Finance]*. Tokyo: Seibundō-shinkōsha.

Newson, N. Willian and Pollack, Richard S. (1939). 'Computing Teacher Load: Analysis and Comparison of Various Methods'. *School Review*, 47, 8: 586–96.

OECD (Organization for Economic Co-operation and Development) (2011). *Education at a Glance. 2011 OECD Indicators*. Paris: OECD.

Satō, M. (1975). *Gakkyū kibo to Kyōshokuin Teisū [The Class-size and the Number of Teachers Quota]*. Tokyo: Daiichi Hōki. (Reprint was published in 2002 by Nihon Tosho Center.)

Shibata, M. (2008). *Japan and Germany under the U.S. Occupation: A Comparative Analysis of Post-War Education Reform*. Lanham, MD: Lexington Books.

Stigler, J. W. and Hiebert, J. (1999). *The Teaching Gap*. New York: Free Press.

Theisen, W. W. (1938). 'Financial Reporting'. *Review of Educational Research*, 8, 2 (April): 154–62.

Yanagi, H. (2005). *Gakkyū no Rekishi [A History of Classroom]*. Tokyo: Kodansha.

Notes

1. As discussed in conclusion, the national government proportional outlay has recently been reduced from one half to one third under the decentralization reforms implemented in 2006.

2. As explained in detail later, beginning in 2006 when the State Subsidies Act was amended, the current system no longer requires that each prefecture must use this scale for actual payment. Before 2006, the national pay scales used for teachers in a small number of nationally run schools (most were schools affiliated to national universities) were used as the de facto standards to calculate teachers' salaries in the prefectures in which they were located.

3. I utilize the term 'theoretically' here to suggest that the figure calculated is what is possible, but it does not always reflect the actual number of teachers employed for various reasons.

4. I surveyed the existing American literature and found historical documents from the 1930s when American educational administrators began debating this very same issue (Theisen, 1938; Newson and Pollack, 1939; Burke, 1951; Callahan, 1962). Strikingly similar discussions are found in those documents and debates, therefore I am assuming that Japanese education administrators referred to them in order to plan their allocation scheme.

5. In reality, more complicated formula are used to compensate varied and specific conditions in each school (Newson and Pollack, 1939; Callahan, 1962), yet the broad contours described here are accurate.

6. Abe, a former top rank Ministry of Education official, described disparities in educational funding in the pre-war period through quantification and statistics. I utilize those descriptive statistics here, but extend the analysis through original calculations of correlation coefficients. For further details, see Kariya (2009).

7. For those who can read Japanese, these figures can be found in Kariya (2009), in particular pages 62–3.

8. The index of general financial resources are calculated as a ratio between the total amount of expenditures a prefecture has for all social services and the total revenue the prefecture has from their local tax revenues. When expenditure exceeds the revenue, the local government was subsidized by the national government in the form of 'the tax revenue allocated to local governments'.

9. According to Kida (1987), a former Vice Minister of Education, several high ranking officials in the Ministry of Education predicted that it would be possible to reduce the maximum class from 50 to 45 students after the first generations of 'baby boomers' graduated from elementary and junior high schools by retaining teachers who would have otherwise been redundant. Yet there is no evidence that they foresaw that the scheme would produce the progressive resources distribution that emerged in the 1970s.

10. In other advanced countries, such as the UK, education policies combined neo-liberals' financial decentralization and neo-conservatives' nationalistic curriculum reforms. Insofar as financial decentralization reduces budgets but does not increase local control and discretion over content in schools, this worst-case scenario emerges.

8

Mongolia: From Nomadic to Communistic to Liberal

Enkhzul Dambajantsan

Country Background

Mongolia is best known to the world for Genghis Khan, the traditional nomadic life, and recently for the mining boom and a fast-growing economy. The country has an enormous area (1.5 million square kilometres) and a sparse population of only 2.9 million (as of 31 December 2011). Given the relatively small population, education has been and is still the key to the country's growth and development. Education, therefore, has traditionally been valued highly. Its importance is increasing further as we all move towards a global, knowledge-based economy.

The country has a rich history, tracing its origin to the first powerful empire established on Mongolian territory in the fourth century BC. Among all the empires, the strongest was the Mongol Empire led by Genghis Khan in the thirteenth century, which controlled half of the known world. By the seventeenth century, Mongolia's power had weakened, and taking advantage of this weakness, Manchurians established control in Mongolia in 1691 which lasted for over two centuries.

In 1911, Mongolia declared its independence, which was challenged, but with persistent efforts, the country gained de facto independence in 1921. The new Soviet Union provided support for Mongolia in declaring its independence, due to which Soviet influence increased in the following years and Mongolia adopted communism for more than half a century. In the early 1990s, the Soviet Union was collapsing, and so was the communist system in Mongolia. Following peaceful demonstrations and hunger strikes, the democratic revolution occurred in 1990, with the adoption of democracy and a free-market economy.

The education system of Mongolia has been through a long and varied journey: from traditional education to communist to a liberal system. Especially during the last 20 years since the transition to democracy, it has experienced extensive reforms, successes and challenges. This chapter provides an overview of the Mongolian education system, together with a critical assessment of the key attributes defining the system.

Traditional Education

The importance of education is deeply established in Mongolian tradition, as reflected in numerous Mongolian proverbs such as 'Adorn yourself with knowledge but not ornaments' (*'Edeer biyee chimeheer erdmeer biyee chim'*) and 'Richest is the Man with Knowledge' (*'Erdem bileg erkhem bayan'*). Mongolian traditional life is nomadic, and being constantly on the move made it difficult to establish formal education. Therefore, education had traditionally been provided informally, mostly by the elders to the younger generation. It came in many forms, including, but not limited to, apprenticeship, lectures, proverbs and even through games and entertainment. For example, an old man will throat-sing and tell a story with a traditional musical instrument, which teaches literature to the younger generations, providing them with the same knowledge they would have obtained if taught in a classroom in a formal education system. When a child misbehaves, the elders speak calmly in proverbs instead of directly lecturing or scolding, through which youngsters are provided with moral education, logic and reasoning. Adults play with children using available resources such as ankle bones of animals, by creating various shapes of animals and plants, and then explaining to the children their structure and roles.

Mongolians devised many traditional intellectual games that helped develop the thinking of children, as well as musical instruments through which artistic education was provided. Traditional medical education was passed on from one generation to another, enabling the local community to provide medical aid to each other, such as prescribing medical plants, bandaging wounds, repairing fractured bone, massaging and other methods.

In Mongolian traditional education, knowledge and skills related to animal husbandry has been very crucial, as their lives and livelihoods depended heavily on livestock. From a very young age, children are still taught about the five kinds of domestic animals Mongolians tend. As a result, they understand the nature, characteristics and benefits of each type of animal, learn to identify them by their colour patterns, and obtain the skills necessary to herd, tend and raise the animals. Such knowledge enables the young people to carry on livestock herding on their own as it is then passed from generation to generation.

As religion spread out into the country by the end of seventeenth century, it became a common practice for families to have their son(s) apprenticed to a monk in a monastery so as to learn Buddhist philosophy. In return for the provision of such religious education, parents usually gave livestock, gold, silver and other presents to the monk teaching the children, which equates to a tuition fee in the modern system. This religious education persisted alongside the traditional education until the independence revolution, which completely changed the picture of the Mongolian educational system.

General Education

Following the independence revolution in 1921 and subsequent adoption of communism, various objectives and efforts to reform the country took place, the first of which was a mass literacy campaign. All school-aged children were enrolled into schools and provided with free education at all levels. Illiterate adults were divided into groups that met frequently in a home of a group member and were taught literacy by a group leader. These efforts certainly paid off and by the 1960s, the country announced that the target of universal literacy had been achieved. Given that there was a literacy rate of a mere 2.1 per cent in 1921, this was a success story compared with others in East Asia at the time (NSO, 2011). Since then the literacy rate has remained steady, and is now 98 per cent for the total population and 99 per cent for the population in the city (NSO, 2011).

A second real advance was the introduction of compulsory education, taking up the Soviet model, consisting of primary and lower secondary schooling, each of four years duration, followed by a two-year non-compulsory upper secondary education with technical, vocational or general focus. Due to budget constraints, only the top 70 per cent of a particular age cohort by their achievement was admitted to upper secondary education and the students who could not make their way to the top 70 per cent usually chose either vocational or technical education. The Soviet model of general education of the day was well known for the rigour of the programme. It had high academic concentration and was regarded as 'intellectually demanding' and of 'good quality'. Despite the rigour of the programme, qualifications of graduates with ten years of schooling were not usually accepted by foreign higher educational institutions. Consequently such students had to study one to two years in a university in order to study abroad. In order to increase international recognition of qualifications obtained in Mongolia, and to align educational provision with international standards, the country has recently adopted a 12-year general education system. The new system consists of five years of primary and four years of lower secondary schooling, followed by three years' non-compulsory upper secondary education with general or vocational focus. Table 8.1 illustrates the new educational structure.

The new 12-year education system offers Cambridge programmes developed by the University of Cambridge International Examinations. The programmes are offered in a bilingual context. Courses such as Mongolian language and literature are taught in Mongolian, whereas other courses such as mathematics, biology, and physics are taught in English. The graduates are provided with two certificates, a Mongolian and an International Certificate, making their qualifications acceptable at international level. The country has only begun piloting this programme in three schools, and upon the successful completion of the pilot, the new programme will be adopted in all schools. Yo. Otgonbayar, the Minister of Education, mentioned in his recent interview in the *Daily news* (*Odryn sonin*) that:

> Delegates from Cambridge International Examinations stated that 'Mongolian standards for some courses are above the international standards. We will keep those standards and will only work on the standards that are below the international. When introducing new standards, local teachers tend to be reluctant. However, in Mongolia the situation is different in that the teachers are positive and willing to adopt the new standards, which gives us a motivation and hope.

Although the adoption of the new standards is welcomed by many, its successful implementation requires adjustment to local contexts and the development of adequate learning and teaching resources and other transitional arrangements. As a result, the quality of general education varies from urban to rural contexts and from public to private schools. In the public perception, the most established public schools provide the best quality education. There is also a belief that rural schools are usually behind on the curriculum (Steiner-Khamsi et al., 2003), lack adequate resources and are of relatively low quality. Due to public scepticism regarding the quality of education, formal schooling is often supplemented by private tutorials and courses, when parents can afford this so-called 'shadow system'. Many parents are concerned with their children's knowledge of

Table 8.1 The structure of Mongolia's education system*

| Age (norm) | | | | | | | | | | | | | | | Years required for completion (norm) | | | | | | | | |
3	4	5	6	7	8	9	10	11	12	13	14	15	16	17	1	2	3	4	1	2	1	2	3+
Pre-school education			Primary education					Lower secondary education				Upper secondary education			University degree programmes				Masters degree programmes		Doctorate		
			Compulsory education																				
												Upper secondary education with vocational track			Colleges (up to four years)								
															Vocational schools								

*As amended by the Parliament on 9 May 2012.

foreign languages, mathematics, arts and other high-demand courses. Most of all they are concerned about preparation for the university admission examination. Therefore it is not uncommon for parents to hire private teachers for their children or send them to private courses (Batjargal et al., 2005; Steiner-Khamsi et al., 2003), in effect making the 'shadow' provision an integral part of the general education system.

There are improvements in teaching methodology as the country sees a shift from teacher-centred to learner-centred approaches. In the former education system, the teachers employed an authoritarian approach in that they lectured with little questioning or participation on the students' side. They had considerable power and were rough with students who misbehaved or who failed to put in the necessary effort to study. Fear of the teacher was believed to have produced good results in the communist era, but such an authoritarian approach has nearly disappeared. Nonetheless there remains a custom for children to have respect for their teachers and be more patient with criticism. More and more teachers have recognized this need and are improving their pedagogy to enable students to undertake independent learning and develop their creativity and critical thinking (Gundenbal and Salmon, 2011).

Access to general education is improving with the support from government by policy. The number of schools has increased steadily, supplemented by the establishment of private schools (see Table 8.2). In addition, pre-higher education is provided free of charge and so are the basic educational resources including books. Students are even provided with free lunches, and those from disadvantaged backgrounds are also supported with allowances from government for learning facilities. From these endeavours, it seems that anyone should be able to afford to go to school. However, in reality there are still some problems that mostly relate to children from disadvantaged backgrounds.

In search of better employment and educational opportunities, many families who are finding their lives difficult in the countryside are migrating to towns and cities. One-third of the families participating in a research project reported moving to urban areas solely for better quality education for their children (Mongolian National University, 2005). With this urbanization, the schools in urban areas have reached the limits of their capacity and they have no choice but to reject additional student enrolment. Many schools are overcrowded, running classes in three shifts, in each of which there are 36 students on average in each class (Steiner-Khamsi et al., 2003). In turn, some schools in rural areas are facing the risk of closure as more students transfer to city schools. Such transfer to urban schools means a reduction in funding for rural schools as the

Table 8.2 Main indicators of Mongolian education system

Main indicators	2004–2005	2005–2006	2006–2007	2007–2008	2008–2009	2009–2010	2010–2011	2011–2012
Number of schools	710	724	742	754	748	755	751	752
– State	584	585	590	597	594	605	609	614
– Private	126	139	152	157	154	150	142	138
Number of students in general education	557346	556876	542505	537546	532058	522066	512213	505409
– Female	285761	285128	276704	273271	269175	262576	257302	253456
– Male	271585	271748	265801	264275	262883	259490	254911	251953
Number of higher education institutions	184	180	170	162	154	146	113	101
– state-owned	49	49	48	47	48	42	16	15
– private	129	125	116	109	101	99	92	81
– branches of foreign institutions	6	6	6	6	5	5	5	5
Students in higher education	123824	138019	142411	150326	161111	164773	170126	172298
– female	76049	83871	86183	91720	97796	99472	101455	101557
– male	47775	54148	56228	58606	63315	65301	68671	71241
Number of graduates	22397	23628	25938	29599	33007	34211	35847	–
– Female	14524	15424	16932	19427	21046	22138	22888	–
– Employed	7924	7606	9562	10496	13038	13906	12975	–

Source: Ministry of Education, Science and Culture, 2012.

government funding to a school is dependent upon the number of students. If a local school closes, children would have to go to school in the nearest *soum* (an administrative unit in Mongolia), presenting even more challenges in terms of access to education (Mongolian National University, 2005).

There are hidden costs of schooling. For example, students are expected to buy supplementary books or attend after-school courses, usually offered by their own teachers (Batjargal et al., 2005). They have to contribute to school maintenance fees, class funds and other costs. Some children have to support their families by working at a young age or taking time off from school in order to help their families with tending the herds during the severe and cold winter (Mongolian National University, 2005). When such opportunity costs and other lost opportunities are considered, the cost of attending schools has become expensive. It presents real challenges to the living standards of children from disadvantaged backgrounds, as a result of which considerable numbers of children sacrifice their future by dropping out.

The disabled seem to be the most marginalized group in terms of access to education. There are several special schools for disabled children, but in general there are many constraints: poor infrastructure, specifically lack of wheelchair access in many educational institutions and in public places, including public transportation; a lack of support in the classroom environment; and lack of sufficient professional preparation of teachers in ordinary schools to assist students with disabilities.

Despite such constraints, the general education system in Mongolia is believed to be changing for the better, by adopting the same standards as the Cambridge International Examinations and applying efforts to improve pedagogical quality and increase access to education. Although these efforts are certainly contributing to improvement, many of the existing problems are directly linked to broader socioeconomic issues. This requires the prior resolution of basic socioeconomic problems in order to ensure that everyone is provided with fair and equal access to good quality education that meets international standards.

Introduction to Higher Education

As in general education, the Soviet model was adopted in the higher education sector. The Mongolian National University, the first higher education institution of Mongolia, was established in 1942, and up to the democratic revolution of 1990 the number of higher educational institutions had increased to 26 (Nyamkhuu et al., 2004). Higher education was fully funded by the government, and in addition students were provided with living allowances and the opportunities to study in republics in the Soviet Union. Students had much social involvement; for example, during the summer, students would work as a group for the duration of one month, mostly helping in harvesting. This is believed to have many positive influences for the students, including the learning of a work ethic, cooperation skills and responsibilities from such collaborative endeavours. These are some of the attributes of the former higher education system that are now coming to be seen to be missed in the early twenty-first century.

After the collapse of the communist system, the country faced many economic and social problems, such as a high unemployment rate, scarcity of goods and services, hyperinflation, low wages and government funding constraints. The education system encountered difficulties such as the poor quality of teaching and resources, poor access to education and an increasing drop-out rate. Government was no longer able to provide free higher education and decided to reform the sector by enabling legal conditions to reduce government involvement in the management of tertiary education (Nyamkhuu et al., 2004). Thus, an Education Law was passed in 1991 enabling the privatization of state-owned institutions, the establishment of private institutions and introduction of tuition fees.

In 2003, the government of Mongolia listed 11 institutions for privatization and 16 for restructuring, along with the list of institutions that were excluded from privatization including national universities, schools, kindergartens, science academies and the national theatres. The excluded institutions included universities such as the National Pedagogical University and the Medical University. Following the passage of an Education Law in 1991, private institutions increased in number as fast as the 'mushrooms after the rain', as it is metaphorically described in Mongolia. Higher education has expanded enormously – from having no private but only 26 state-owned institutions to having 185 institutions out of which 136 were private when the expansion reached its peak in the academic year of 2002–3 (MECS, 2012a), although the expansion slowed down in the following years (see Table 8.2).

The expansion of private higher education did not have a significant impact on improving the access to the tertiary sector as the private institutions were mainly located in urban areas. Students in urban areas have better chances to get admission to the leading institutions due to their better quality education received in secondary schools and better preparation for admission examinations. This can be evidenced by the finding that 71 per cent of students in higher educational institutions were from larger cities or towns (World Bank, 2010).

Tuition fees, along with government subsidies and income from operations and donations, constitute the main sources of income for universities, which in turn becomes another factor that hinders rural student participation in higher education. In the last few years, tuition fees more than doubled, causing an even greater financial burden. This was especially so for the families in rural areas as evidenced by a research outcome that shows that 70 per cent of the loans that herders take from banks are for tuition fees (World Bank, 2010). Official statistics suggest that tuition costs in university/college revenue has increased from 20 per cent to 80 per cent between 1993 and 2000, and that the cost of higher education in Mongolia is now borne more by individuals than by the state (Altantsetseg, 2002).

As compensation for introducing tuition fees, a 'State Training Fund' was established in 1992 with the purpose of providing tuition grants and loans to students from disadvantaged backgrounds. This included those from herder families, from families with more than two children studying at higher education institutions, and those whose parent/s work in the public service sector. This initiative has benefited many, but occasionally its effectiveness has been questioned. The children targeted to benefit from tuition exemption or waivers are disadvantaged from their early years of schooling onwards and by the time they enter university, they are already behind their peers in terms of preparations for advanced study. Despite these challenges, it should be emphasized that access to higher education has expanded, having over half of a particular age cohort pursue higher education compared to only 14 per cent in 1991 when the country transitioned to a market economy (World Bank, 2010).

In the Soviet model, higher education was closely controlled by the government and a quota was placed on the number of admissions for all subjects. Students chose their area of study by the order of their ranking in general admission examinations. Once the quota was filled, the remaining students had to choose any subject available. Vocational and technical education had been in high demand, and all professions and occupations were considered as equal in terms of social importance. After completion of higher education, the graduates were allotted to employment in different organizations. There was no competition but a guarantee of employment as long as the student passed the course. However, this picture has shifted quite substantially in modern times. Social equality existing in the communist system is no longer in place and professions are assigned different importance in the strata of social status. It has almost become an expectation from parents and society that a person has to obtain a university degree. In order to fulfil this expectation, many young people who could not get admission to their desired courses in their desired universities take admission in smaller and less competitive institutions, instead of obtaining technical or vocational qualifications. This choice is made easier with the wide selection of higher education institutions and programmes now available, but is detrimental to the achievement of internationally recognized standards.

Parents, family members, relatives and even friends have significant influence not only on a person's decision to pursue higher education, but also on the choice of what to study. A large number of students choose their profession based on their parents' suggestions or pressure, rather than pursuing their own interests. There are a number of 'hot' subjects to study, such as business, finance, management and law, which is evidenced by the fact that in the academic year of 2010–11, 36 per cent of the students and 40 per cent of the graduates were in the business, law or management fields (see Table 8.3).

Although there certainly is demand in these sectors, the demands in other sectors, especially those that require technical and vocational qualifications, are not being met. The country is facing a shortage of qualified personnel in

Table 8.3 Students and graduates, by profession, in 2010–11

Discipline	Students		Graduates	
	Total	**out of which, female**	**Total**	**out of which, female**
Education	22,381	18,050	5775	4716
Art & humanities	14,807	10,702	3174	2339
Social science, business & law	61,050	38,966	14,544	9400
– business management	36,514	23,927	8383	5608
Natural science	11,955	4807	2126	912
Technology, production & construction	32,613	10,474	4178	1662
Agriculture	5286	2988	791	492
Health & social welfare	15,973	12,548	3135	2614
Services	8045	2633	2124	753
Other	688	389	-	-
Total	172,798	101,557	35,847	22,888

Source: Ministry of Education, Science and Culture, 2012.

sectors such as mining, construction, technology, logistics and communication, although only 23 per cent of the students are studying in these sectors (World Bank, 2010). In order to fill this supply deficiency, local employers have to hire migrant workers, mainly from China. Due to this mismatch between labour supply and demand, only 36 per cent of the university graduates compared to 60 per cent of the vocational and technical school graduates find employment within six months of graduation (World Bank, 2010; also see Table 8.2).

There is a fierce competition for employment, especially where there are too many graduates in the same sector. As the government offers many programmes, scholarships, grants and loans to Mongolian nationals to study at leading foreign institutions in order to promote the development of the young generation, this competition is further intensified by those who graduated abroad. Therefore, some of those who lost in the competition seem eventually to take up occupations unrelated to what they learned at university. It is not uncommon that people with a university degree end up doing jobs that do not normally require a degree or professional qualification such as shop attendant, receptionist and clerical assistant. The reason for this mismatch between the supply and demand in the labour market can be explained by the following factors: a) different levels of importance ascribed to different occupations; b) a lack of any comprehensive research to identify the market needs to help parents and students make an informed decision; and c) the qualifications of graduates not conforming to the expectations of employers.

To tackle the mismatch between labour supply and demand, the government is pursuing a policy to support and restrict enrolment by professions. As set out in the 'Master Plan to Develop Education of Mongolia in 2006–2015' (MECS, 2006), the percentage of enrolment in technical education and vocational training is to be increased by 56.1 per cent. The enrolment of students in engineering, technology, natural sciences and agriculture will be increased from 29.1 per cent to 45 per cent, whereas enrolment in social science and humanities and law will be reduced to 10 per cent from 18.5 per cent, and to 4 per cent from 5.8 per cent, respectively. Government is further supporting the implementation of its policy by introducing strategies such as increased financial support to students studying in these areas and the retraining of lecturers in those fields.

There are a number of good quality universities and higher education institutions. These are usually the state-owned, or formerly state-owned, universities. They are considered as having better quality as they at least have more educational facilities and resources and can attract better-qualified personnel. However, higher education quality is often compromised at small private institutions by the lack of proper teaching and learning resources and inadequate numbers of full-time teaching staff (World Bank, 2010). For marketing purposes, some institutions offer joint degree courses, giving the graduates the flexibility to switch between professions. Here again, quality has been sacrificed, as the curriculum has to accommodate courses for two different disciplines rather than focusing on one, although the disciplines may be related. On observation, their curriculum tends to cover many basic professional courses at the expense of advanced courses, with some courses overlapping in content. However, it should be noted that these faults do not exist in all private institutions and there are a number of very good quality private institutions well regarded by the Mongolian public.

In order to strengthen the existing higher education system and improve its quality, the Mongolian government consolidated 42 state-owned universities into 16 in the academic year of 2010–11. This envisages stronger and better-managed universities with concentrated educational resources. Within the implementation of this plan, the government has planned to build some new university campuses. By establishing a campus culture the government hopes to create conditions for students to enjoy more extra-curricular and social activities. These reform initiatives require much investment, and the government has been generous with its spending in the sector. Government expenditure on education is approximately 20 per cent of the state budget, which equals 7.5 per cent of GDP (Gundenbal and Salmon, 2011). As the Mongolian economy gets stronger with an expected annual GDP increase at constant two-digit levels, the educational problems associated with funding are expected to lessen as more opportunities will be created in the tertiary sector.

In addition, Mongolian higher education is distinctive in three particular ways: the Soviet science model; the pay structure; and the gender imbalance.

The Soviet science model

Following the Soviet science model, Mongolia separated research from teaching and established institutes solely for academic specialization and research. This research versus teaching dilemma faces academics in other countries but is usually less of a problem due to the fact that lecturers have traditionally been more oriented toward teaching than research. However, it should be noted that they were never separated, as their research record was much appreciated and academics conducted research at least for their own interest. In fact the creation of league tables for universities in many other countries in recent years, plus the obsession of governments with world university rankings is in a curious way bringing their higher education profiles more in line with that in Mongolia.

Pay structure

In many institutions, lecturers are paid by the hours they teach, meaning that the more hours they teach, the higher the pay they receive. Thus, it is economically wise for lecturers to spend more time teaching and less time on research, due to research lacking a proper reward structure. In addition to lengthy hours of teaching, lecturers have administrational duties, such as sitting on committees (e.g. the admission committee), mentoring students and revising degree programmes. The pay structure needs to be revised so as to accurately reward the lecturer for each of his/her duties, including teaching, research and administration/service, but probably with a shift towards research in line with international norms.

Gender imbalance

There is an increasing gender imbalance among university students in Mongolia. Although there is more gender equality in general education, in higher education female students have a dominance of 60 per cent, which further increases to 65 per cent by the time of the graduation (see Table 8.2). As the number of educated females increase, the social and occupational role of male and female seems to be shifting. In this regard Mongolia is ahead of another international trend, that of relative female success at school and university as compared to male performance. In the case of Mongolia, it may be that the traditional herding economy in the past was disadvantageous to males in terms of participation in formal education.

In summary, the Mongolian higher education system features a shift from a centrally planned, free and equal higher education system to a fee-paying, liberal system, bringing with it its own advantages and challenges. Another feature is the rapid expansion in the sector after the democratic revolution, making it possible for every upper secondary school graduate to obtain higher education as the social expectations pushed those young people to obtain higher education over vocational or technical education. In order to tackle the challenges that arose amidst the transition to a liberal higher education system, universities and their resources are being consolidated, certain subjects are being prioritized and the government is spending more.

Conclusion

Due to Mongolia having a long, well-established and highly valued tradition of informal education, the formal education system was only established a hundred years ago. This formal education system adopted the former Soviet model due to the coincidence of independence. Key features of the Soviet model included central planning and monitoring, heavy academic concentration and free education with fair and equal access. One of the key successes of the introduction of formal education was the achievement of a universal literacy target within four decades from only 2.1 per cent in 1921 to near 100 per cent in 1990.

After the collapse of the communist system in Mongolia, the country liberalized the education system which has presented some challenges, such as poor access, low quality and the lack of proper educational resources, most of which were related to broader socioeconomic issues. The government has been very persistent in tackling the above-mentioned issues and developing the education sector in line with international standards. Recent achievements include the transition to a 12-year general education system with the high standards of the Cambridge International Examination Awards. Meeting these standards is driving the development of better teaching and learning resources, the integration of Mongolian universities witnin international standards of quality assurance, and improved support for students at all levels.

The rapid economic growth of the country is certainly going to accelerate the outcomes of these initiatives; thus expectations are raised that everyone shall be provided with fair and equal access to quality education at all levels that align with international standards.

References

Altantsetseg, S. (2002). *Financing of State Universities in Mongolia: Constraints and Opportunities*. Hungary: Open Society Foundation.

Asian Development Bank (2012). *Sector Assessment (Summary): Education*. http://www2.adb.org/Documents/RRPs/MON/43007/43007-023-mon-ssa.pdf (Accessed 20 March 2012).

Batjargal, A., Enkhtuya, N., Bolormaa, Ts., Tumendelger, S. and Alison, D. (2005). *Tulburtei davtlaga, damjaa [Private Tutorials and Courses]*. Ulaanbaatar: Mongolian Education Alliance.

Dairii, A. and Suruga, T. (2006). 'Economic Returns to Schooling in Transition: A Case of Mongolia'. *GSICS Working paper series*, 9. Kobe: Kobe University.

Gantsog, Ts. and Altantsetseg, S. (2002). *Cost of Socio-Economic Reform: Problems to Ensure Human Development in Mongolia*. Presented at International Symposium of the Human Well-Being Society of Chubugakuin University, Japan, December 2002.

—(2003). *Globalisation, WTO and Mongolian Higher Education*. Presented at Indiana University, Bloomington, USA, November 2003.

Gundenbal, Ts. and Salmon, A. (2011). *The Mongolian Education Sector: The Role of International Volunteers*. Ulaanbaatar: VSO.

Hall, D. and Thomas, H. (1999). 'Higher education reform in a transitional economy: a case study from the School of Economic Studies in Mongolia'. *Higher Education*, 38: 441–60

MECS (Ministry of Education, Culture and Science) (2006). *Master Plan to Develop Education of Mongolia in 2006–2015*. Ulaanbaatar: Ministry of Education, Culture and Science.

—(2010). *Deed bolovsrolyn shinechlelyn zuraglal 2010–2021* [*Roadmap for Higher Education Reform 2010–2021*]. http://www.mecs.gov.mn/article-398-435.mw (Accessed 20 March 2012).

—(2012a). *Deed bolovsrolyn salbaryn negdsen uzuulelt* [*Indicators of Higher Education Sector*]. http://www.mecs.gov.mn/data/statistik/db/2011_2012/MB1.pdf (Accessed 20 March 2012).

—(2012b). *Baga dund bolovsrolyn salbaryn negdsen uzuulelt* [*Indicators of Primary and Secondary Education Sector*]. http://www.mecs.gov.mn/data/statistik/bdb/2010_2011/BDB1.pdf (Accessed 20 March 2012).

Mongolian National University, Childhood Poverty Research and Policy Centre (2005). *Shiljikh hudulguun huuhdyn amidrald* [*Impacts of Migration on Children's Lives*]. Ulaanbaatar: Save the Children Fund, UK.

NSO (National Statistical Office) (2011). *Khun am, oron suutsny 2010 ony ulsyn toollogyn negdsen dun, sedevchilsen sudalgaanuud* [*Consolidated Results of Population Census 2010*]. http://www.nso.mn/v3/files/Monographs.pdf (Accessed 20 March 2012).

Nyamkhuu, Ts., Sunjidmaa, J. and Narantsetseg, P. (2004). *Bolovsrolyn salbaryn uuchlult, shinechlelt, huvichlal* [*Changes, Reforms and Privatization of Education Sector*]. Ulaanbaatar: Open Society Forum.

Otgonbayar,Yo. (2011). 'Bid ireh onoos elseltyn yeronhy shalgaltyn togtoltsoog oorchilno' ['General admission test system will be revised from next year']. *Odryn sonin*. http://www.mecs.gov.mn/article-236-470.mw (Accessed 20 March 2012).

Otgonjargal, O. (2004). *Higher Education Financial Reform in Mongolia: Introduction of Cost-sharing and its Reasons, Process and Consequences*. New York: Columbia University.

Robinson, B. (1995). 'Mongolia in transition: a role for distance education'. *Open Learning*, 10: 3–14.

Robinson, C. D. W. and Otgonbayar, Ch. (2003). *Surch Amidarya: Learning for Life Non-formal Basic Distance Education in Mongolia /Impact Evaluation*. Ulaanbaatar: UNESCO.

Save the Children, UK (2009). *Yerunkhii bolovsrolyn surguulid suraltsagchdyn biye makhbodid khaldakh, khuulid zaagaagui tulbur huraamj avakh, yalgavarlan gaduurkhaltyn baidal* [*Research on Physical Abuse and Unlawful Charges and Payments and State of Discrimination*]. http://www.mongoleducation.mn/modules. php?ss=4&id=435 (Accessed 20 March 2012).

Steiner-Khamsi, G. and Stolpe, I. (2004). 'Decentralization and recentralization reform in Mongolia: tracing the swing of the pendulum'. *Comparative Education*, 40, 1: 29–53.

Steiner-Khamsi, G., Stolpe, I. and Tumendelger, S. (2003). '*Bolovsrolyn tolookh nuudel*' ['School-Related Migration in Mongolia']. *Mongolian Journal of Social Sciences*, 45, 4: 82 –112.

Weidman, J. C. and Yeager, J. L. (1999). 'Mongolian higher education in transition'. *International Higher Education*, 15: 22–23.

World Bank (2010). *Mongolia Policy Note. Tertiary Education in Mongolia: Meeting the Challenges of the Global Economy*, Human development sector unit, World Bank.

9

North Korea: An Overview

Jeong-ah Cho, Huang-kue Lee and Ki-Seok Kim

Introduction

'They have no alternative form of reality.'[1] Scott Altran, a psychologist at the University of Michigan, was speaking of the reasons behind the public displays of grief on the part of North Koreans on hearing of the death of Kim Jong Il in December 2011. For an outside observer, in the context of a leader who has been held responsible for the deaths by starvation and human rights violations of hundreds of thousands of his subjects, these displays of deep sorrow and grief do indeed point to a people who possess no such alternative view of reality. What, then, constitutes their 'form of reality'? How has this form of reality been created? Why has it been formed in this way? One way to understand this question is to acquire an understanding of the education system that has socialized and formatted North Koreans in the way that it has. This chapter provides an introduction to the North Korean education system, its developmental path, current trends and future trajectory.

A Brief History of North Korea

North Korea (the Democratic People's Republic of Korea, DPRK) is located in the north of the Korean Peninsula. According to the census undertaken in 2008, the population of North Korea stands at approximately 24 million (Central Bureau of Statistics Pyongyang, 2009). The Korean Peninsula was initially divided into Soviet and US zones of occupation along the 38th parallel after the Japanese surrender in 1945. The Demilitarized Zone, created after the ceasefire which ended the Korean War in 1953, then became the de facto national borders of the North and South Korean states.

Until the end of the 1960s, North Korea successfully adhered to an independent economic policy. Following a freeze in support from the Soviet Union and external events such as the Vietnam War and the Cuban missile crisis, the North decided to pursue policies more focused on national defence and security. These efforts resulted in economic difficulties and resource shortages, and as a result, by the late 1970s, the country defaulted on external debts, and slipped into long-term economic stagnation.

The 1990s saw a series of changes that threatened to rock the foundations of the North Korean state. The collapse of communism saw North Korea deprived of heavily subsidized material support from allied socialist countries such as raw materials, electric power and, most critically, food. The collapse of the Eastern Bloc was the harbinger of inexorable international isolation as well. The death of the founder, President Kim Il Sung, in July 1994 was a storm initially weathered successfully by his late son Kim Jong Il. The country was then rocked, however, by a series of devastating natural disasters including floods and crop failures over several harvests. Already deprived of key markets and subsidized raw materials, national industries began to collapse, and with them the food distribution system. Deaths from resultant starvation increased drastically. According to estimates by scholars and researchers, between 300,000 and 1,000,000 died of starvation during the famine of the mid and late 1990s, a period referred to as the the 'Arduous March'.[2]

These combined challenges exposed the unique power structure and ideology of North Korea to severe stresses. The state, unable to guarantee the distribution of resources, and with it, basic food supplies, let alone other elements of social security including health care and education, was essentially forced to turn a blind eye as its citizens looked to their own individual survival. When they inevitably did so, they did in the form of limited involvement in private enterprise and cooperative markets. This created a potential fracture in the covenant between the state and the subject. The late 1990s saw gradual improvements in the economic situation. However, the basic social security systems and the centralized distribution system failed to return to previous levels of control.

The Education System

Educational goals

The goal of education in North Korea is to train a 'Communistic Person' whose duty, in turn, is to maintain the socialist system. According to article 43 of the

'Socialist Constitution' the goal of education is defined thus: '[T]hrough the thorough implementation of the fundamental principles of socialist pedagogy in education, the country is to nurture future generations of strong revolutionaries, able to fight as champions of society and the people; in short, a new breed of communist, equipped with 'Intelligence, Morals, Integrity and Physical Strength'.' Other seminal treatises regarding education consistently support this and similar goals, such as the 'Theses on Socialist Education',[3] proclaimed by the founder Kim Il Sung in 1977, and also Article 29 of the Education Act.[4]

The following four points form the core of educational theory and practice. First, both the nature of the party and the essence of the working class should be realized through education. The 'Monolithic Ideological System' of the party is therefore considered a core element of this. Second, and importantly, the notion of *Juche* ('self-reliance') should be firmly established in education, which means in practical terms that students should be trained to inform themselves of their country's history and the history of the Korean people. Third, education and revolutionary practices should be combined. Revolutionary practices mean not only political practices but also the daily activities of communistic social life. Therefore, polytechnic education works as a key principle in socialist education, reflecting the combination of education and worker. Fourth, the nation alone is responsible for all aspects of education and therefore is the sole source of direction and leadership in educational policy.

The school system

Compulsory education lasts for 11 years in North Korea, consisting of one year of kindergarten,[5] four years of primary (*So-hak-gyo*) and six years of secondary school (*Jung-hak-gyo*). Higher education lasts from between four and five and a half years. All educational institutes are established and operated by the government, and there are no private educational institutes.

Since its establishment, North Korea has made the continued expansion of compulsory education, and with it educational opportunity, a key policy goal. A compulsory four-year period of primary education was initiated in 1956. The duration of compulsory education continued to grow, and by 1975 the current 11 years of fully supported compulsory education had been achieved nationwide. Fully supported here refers to the fact that all tuition fees, textbooks, school uniforms and stationary were supplied by the government. Both this and the fact that North Korea was the first Asian country to implement an 11-year government-funded system of compulsory education are often held up as key evidence of the superiority of the North Korean political system. However, following the economic crisis of the 1990s, basic school necessities, such as textbooks, are no longer supplied free. Therefore, at present, the original meaning of a fully supported compulsory education system has been largely lost.

In the primary, secondary and higher education systems, elite and selective educational institutes exist. One such institute is Pyeongyang Middle School No. 1 (*Jei Il Jung-hak-gyo*), which trains those gifted in the sciences. There are 200 similar middle schools designated as 'No. 1' at the national, provincial and city level. Foreign Education Institutes are specialist secondary schools run for students with aptitudes for foreign languages. Specialist arts and sports education institutes also exist. In addition, there are Revolutionary Education Institutes such as Mangyeongdae Revolutionary Education Institute, which provide a privileged education for the children of senior officials and the families of those killed in war or revolutionary activities.

In the higher education system, there are several categories of institutions. There are only four general universities[6] that offer a broad range of majors and programmes. All other tertiary institutions are relatively specialized universities and technical colleges, which provide education and training aimed at particular fields of employment, for example medicine, engineering and primary and secondary education teacher training. Course durations vary accordingly. The efficiency of the universities is arguably limited, with relatively low numbers of students of around 1,000 per university. Technical colleges are training technicians on courses of relatively short duration.

Aside from the regular education system, part-time higher education specialized vocational institutes for adult learners also exist, and are known as the 'Working and Studying System'. Such institutions account for a third of all universities/colleges, and are able to award degrees in the same way as other universities. These colleges are affiliated to factories and agricultural farms, or to the evening vocational programmes in fields such as telecommunications run by general universities. In addition, there are also vocational training institutes offering six-month to one-year courses, which produce qualified workers and technicians in different specialties and which are open to direct entry by high school graduates.

In 2009, the total number of educational institutes stood at 4,800 primary schools, 4,600 middle schools and 480 universities (technical colleges included),[7] while the number of students was 1.52 million primary school students, 2.47 million middle school students and 438,000 university students attending courses lasting from four to five and a half years (Central Bureau of Statistics Pyongyang, 2009). These figures are estimates only, since basic statistics on enrolment rates, advancement rates and educational budget are not released by North Korea. According to data analysis from the 2009 population, the enrolment rate of primary and middle schools was recorded at 99.98 per cent.

However, the rate of advancement after graduation from middle school appears to be low. The rate of advancement to four-year university courses after graduation from middle school is 12 per cent, while the rate of advancement to higher education institutes, including universities, colleges and vocational training institutes, is approximately 27 per cent. More than 70 per cent of students move directly into either the military or the workforce. If male students do not enter higher education institutes directly after secondary school, they

Table 9.1 Systems of schooling

Age	Level	School					
16+	Higher education	Graduate School (3–4 years)					Adult education
		University (4–5.5 Years)	Technical College (2–3 years)	Factory College	Vocational Training Institutes		
15	Secondary education	Compulsory Education	Middle School (*Jung-hak-gyo*) (6 years)				
14							
13							
12							
11							
10							
9	Primary education		Elementary School (*So-hak-gyo*) (4 years)				
8							
7							
6							
5	Pre-school		Kindergarten (2 years)		Upper Class (1 year)		
4					Lower Class (1 year)		

go on to undertake their ten years' compulsory military service, after which they are sent either to continue their studies in higher education or join the workforce.

Educational administration

The educational administration system of North Korea consists of a dual structure, one parallel in nature. On the one hand, a conventional, vertical administrative structure exists, from the national, city and district levels down to the individual front-line institute level. This work is conducted by professional administrators and technocrats. Operating alongside this is a highly politicized party structure whose purpose is to provide a form of political monitoring, operating as educational commissars.

Major education policies are determined in the plenary meetings of the Central Committee of the Worker's Party of Korea (WPK). The Education Department under the Central Committee of the party is in charge of education. As its sub-organization, the Education Department is rooted in the local party, the Party Committee of School in individual schools. Amendments to constitutional articles related to education, the creation of and amendments to education-related laws, the establishment of basic principles in education policy, reporting, consideration and approval of the national education budget and its formal execution are all matters taken up by the Supreme People's Assembly.

The execution of education policy is supervised by the Education Committee of the Cabinet which is an administrative body. Under the auspices of the Education Committee, there exist ministries for both common education and higher education. The Ministry of Common Education is in charge of kindergarten, elementary school, middle school and university education, while the Ministry of Higher Education is in charge of general university education. The Ministry of Common Education hands down educational directives to the education office of the People's Committee located in each province; the education office of the People's Committee then delivers these directives to the People's Education Section located at the city and district level.[8] The directives are then delivered to each individual school and implemented within each institution. General administration and educational administration are integrated. This educational administration system is therefore characterized by both a highly centralized and top-down approach, with a parallel political structure providing ideological oversight. No autonomy at the institutional level exists and all feedback is collected through the WPK and its administrative organization.

The administration system of individual schools follows the same dual organizational structure. The administrative organization consists of a conventional hierarchical structure of school principals and deputy principals, followed by their section and accounting staff. In the parallel organizational structure overseen by the party, the schools' party committees contain bodies concerned with social-political activities such as a teacher's social groups, and student's social groups. The chairman of the party's committee is responsible for all matters relating to political and ideological guidance for both teachers and students, whereas the principal of the school is in charge of purely administrative matters such as management and operations and the financial affairs of the school.

Curriculum

Characteristics of the curriculum

Curriculum is defined here as a general plan in education, which indicates when, where and how to implement learning activities and goals (Education Research Institute of Seoul National University, 1994). The school curriculum in all societies reflects characteristics of that society, reflecting the idealized image of man which the society seeks, and presents a methodology to realize that ideal. The curriculum in North Korea reflects the unique characteristics of North Korean society in the following ways.

State control

The basic educational system, its policies, direction, contents and methodologies to be used, are all determined and delivered at the national level, under the overall control of the party. Thus both the everyday operational processes as well as educational outcomes are strictly controlled. The contents of the curriculum at all levels, production and distribution of textbooks are all controlled at the national level. This control is layered as well. For example, with regard to the curriculum of majors at university, any changes must be made at the institutional level and then submitted to the Education Committee for approval. The Education Committee is free to make directions regarding how content is delivered, distributing such directives to each educational institute to ensure uniformity in both the content and methodologies used throughout the system.

Furthermore, the operation of the curriculum is both highly centralized and standardized. In the process of selecting, organizing and delivering the knowledge to be taught in school, both the autonomy and freedom of choice of the individual schools, teachers as well as the learners themselves is heavily restricted. All schools must teach subjects according to predetermined methodology and schedule, with no room whatsoever for individual discretion by the school or individual teacher. Teachers are required by law to put forward teaching proposals but these must adhere rigidly to the curriculum and class directions established at the national level, while schools review these collectively. Aside from this, all matters relating to the progression of students through the education system are managed by the national test system. In this way, the attainment of both educational qualifications and, by implication, education opportunities, are centrally controlled.

The demonstrative linkage between education and politics

There is an inevitable linkage between public education and politics in all societies. Some primary functions are that it regenerates the value systems and dominant ideologies as well as the knowledge and technology base which are central agents in maintaining and developing society. However, many countries are reluctant to focus on the overt political dimensions of education, preferring a position of political objectivity.

In dramatic contrast, North Korea emphasizes the political features and functions of education, maintaining that the ideological functions of education are as important as the function of transmitting knowledge. From the establishment of the North Korean state until the present, education has served as the key means by which the evolving political objectives of the state have been achieved. Shortly after foundation, the primary goal of education was socialistic nation building, creating a national consensus and the political integration of the population into a socialist body politic. Having established a socialist system, the goals then shifted to the need to strengthen the 'ideological fortress of communism' (Kim Il Sung, 1997), widely interpreted as meaning the consolidation of the nascent socialist state through political education of the population. The 1950s and 1960s saw political infighting and purges within the WPK. This instability culminated in the creation of the leadership cult of Kim Il Sung. Accordingly, the education system was seen as a vital tool, establishing, justifying and perpetuating this system of government in which power is transferred from father to son. This system managed to survive amid the chaos of the 1990s famine.

These political functions and their critical role have been clearly reflected in the Education Law and a variety of educational directions. The 'Theses on

Socialist Education' argues that the 'political and ideological discipline occupies the most important position in socialist education' (Kim Il Sung, 1997) and that the inculcation of the *Juche* ideology, the central ideology of North Korea, is the singularly most important function of education. Aside from *Juche*, the core subjects of political education include party policy making, the revolutionary tradition, working class consciousness, collectiveness, the ethics of work, and patriotism for the proletariat, among others.

Polytechnic education

The 'combination of education and revolutionary practices' in North Korean education means the transmission of knowledge through socialist educational methodologies. This is commonly seen in the curriculum of socialist countries including the Soviet Union; and finds its theoretical basis in the political philosophies of both Marx and Lenin. They envisioned 'polytechnic education' as a means of achieving what they termed the 'Whole Man', which entailed the full realization of man's potential. After the revolution, the Soviet Union introduced the idea of polytechnic education, implementing educational reforms to create a system which was then copied by North Korea through educational exchanges with the Soviet Union. Instead of the term 'polytechnic education', the North described its variant as a 'combination of education and revolutionary practices' in an effort to link education more closely to the demands of daily life. Accordingly, it became easier to educate students with skills, knowledge and qualifications highly relevant to the practical demands of work and life in the newly formed socialist society (Nam, 1991).

Another aspect of North Korean polytechnic education is its view of labour as an educational resource. The theoretical aspects of education are combined with practical work- related activities within the curriculum; time being allotted for such activities within the regular schedule. These work-related activities are designed to not only help students develop positive attitudes to work, and understand the importance and value of work, but also to cultivate key work-related technical skills required of future workers.

However, in terms of the practical aims of developing work-related and technical skills, polytechnic education has largely failed due to the poor economic situation and the primitive nature of actual field conditions in North Korea. Instead, work-related activities in schools have been largely used to provide a pool of cheap labour, and so have lost much of their educational meaning.

Primary school education

North Korean children are eligible to enter the primary school from the age of six. The new semester begins on 1 April every year. Thirteen subjects in total are covered in the four years of primary schooling and are characterized by a relatively rigid division between subjects.

The primary curriculum is divided into the following broad subject groupings: political ideology, language, natural sciences and mathematics, computer technology, art, music, physical education and hygiene.

An analysis of time devoted to each subject may indicate their relative importance within the curriculum. In this respect, a full 17 per cent of total class time is devoted to the subject political ideology, which includes the following subjects among others: 'The Childhood of the Great Leader Kim Il Sung', 'The Childhood of Respected Leader, Kim Jong Il', 'The Childhood of Heroine Kim Jong'[9] and 'Socialist Morals'.

English and computer technology are relatively new, introduced first in September 2008, and are taught from the 3rd Grade onwards. Computer education, although heavily prioritized, has not been fully implemented due to equipment and material shortages. The sciences and computer technology are seen by the ruling elite as critical elements of the national development strategy, which aims to use cutting-edge scientific and technological applications to address ongoing economic difficulties.

Table 9.2 Primary school curriculum

Subject	Class hour per week			
	Year 1	Year 2	Year 3	Year 4
The Childhood of the Great Leader Kim Il Sung	1	1	1	2
The Childhood of 'Respected Leader, Kim Jong Il	1	1	1	2
The Childhood of Heroine Kim Jong Sook				1
Socialist Morals	2	2	1	1
Korean	6	6	7	8
English			1	1
Mathematics	6	6	6	6
Natural Sciences	2	2	2	2
Hygiene				1
Music	2	2	2	2
Physical Education	2	2	2	2
Art	2	2	1	1
Computer Technology			1	1

Source: Education Center for Unification (2011).

Approximately 20 per cent of total class time is devoted to art, music and physical education. In addition to this, compulsory small group after-school programmes in art, music and physical education mean that these subjects occupy an important place within the curriculum. By the end of primary school, every student is able to play at least one musical instrument, most commonly the accordion, harmonica, guitar or recorder.

Of much greater importance, however, are the extra-curricular activities undertaken under the auspices of the Young Pioneers youth organization (*So-nyeon-dan*), in which political and ideological indoctrination takes place. Although theoretically all students join from Grade 2, early entry on politically significant dates is reserved as a special honour for privileged or high-potential candidates. Members of the Young Pioneers participate in regular political education sessions as well as major national events. Social activities include small-scale horticulture, raising rabbits for food and pelts, and recycling.

Secondary school education

A total of 23 subjects are covered in secondary school. Again, distinction between disciplines is rigid and the curriculum is highly prescribed. In the subject of political ideology, as in primary school, the primary focus is on studying the life works and examples set by important revolutionary leaders and role models. In fact, subjects such as the 'Great Leader Kim Il Sung's Revolutionary Activities' and 'Respected Leader Kim Jong Il's Revolutionary History' essentially replace the teaching of contemporary history altogether. In addition to this, 'Current Party Policy' is also taught. Approximately 10 per cent of class hours in secondary school is devoted to this subject.

Korean language and literature, Chinese character, foreign languages, history, geography, mathematics, physics, chemistry and biology are taught, as well as 'Socialist Morals and Law'. English and Russian had, until 2000, been optional by school and class; since that date, however, the proportion devoted to English has been gradually increased.

Practical activities take place over one week and the curriculum varies depending on both the gender of the students and the major industry of the region. Much of the activities aimed at male students focus on content material related to engineering and machines and technology, while female students focus on subjects related to home economics such as needlework and cooking. In terms of class time per subject, mathematics and physics alone account for 20 per cent, and, overall, the natural sciences account for 40 per cent of total class hours. Language, history and geography account for less than 40 per cent.

All students participate in the Labour Mobilization activity, which is an integral part of the school curriculum. During the farming season, all middle school students engage in agricultural support work: students in the younger grades work for four weeks annually while older students serve for eight weeks.

After the 5th Grade of secondary school, students finish their service in the Young Pioneers and then join the older youth group, the Youth Coalition of Kim Il Sung Socialism. They also become members of the Red Youth Guard.

Table 9.3 Secondary school curriculum

Subject	Class hour per week					
	Year 1	Year 2	Year 3	Year 4	Year 5	Year 6
Great Leader Kim Il Sung's Revolutionary Activities	1	1	1			
Great Leader Kim Il Sung's Revolutionary History				2	2	2
Respected Leader Kim Jong Il's Revolutionary Activities	1	1	1			
Respected Leader Kim Jong Il's Revolutionary History				2	2	2
Heroine Kim Jong Sook's Revolutionary History				1		
Socialist Morals and Law	1	1	1	1	1	1
Current Party Policy				1week	1week	1week
Korean	5	5	4			
Literature				4	3	2
Chinese character	2	2	1	1	1	1
Foreign languages	4	3	3	3	3	3
History	1	1	2	2	2	2
Geography	2	2	2	2	2	
Mathematics	7	7	6	6	6	6
Physics		2	3	4	4	4
Chemistry			2	3	3	4
Biology		2	2	2	3	3
Physical education	2	2	2	1	1	1
Music	1	1	1	1	1	1
Art	1	1	1			
Design				1	1	
Computer technology				2	2	2
Practical activities	1week	1week	1week	1week	1week	1week

Source: Education Center for Unification (2011).

All female and male students receive basic military training in training camps as well as within the school itself. In middle school, students receive six hours' military training a week, for a total of 240 hours a year, as well as a field exercise of 15 days duration a year. The political and social activities undertaken after school in the various party affiliated youth organizations are considered critical elements of socialization for North Korean students.

Higher education

Universities and colleges place a great emphasis on fields that train experts needed in the manufacturing, agriculture and fisheries industries. Every college was established in connection with a related industry and aims at nurturing the human resources suitable for the practical tasks of each industry through educational courses closely related to that industry.

In North Korea, a capitalistic labour market does not exist and the government alone plans the graduate students' workplaces and deploys them accordingly. This system may bring certain advantages in terms of the close ties it engenders between higher education and related industries. However, workers trained under this system suffer from a general inability to innovate, create new technologies or provide the necessary leadership when it comes to the demands of industrial restructuring in the context of rapidly evolving technological change. In light of these weaknesses, North Korea has recently been attempting to copy the reforms China undertook in its own university system by creating tentative links across disciplines and subject areas.

University courses are categorized into the following broad fields of study: politics and ideology, general subjects, general foundation, major foundation, major subjects.[10] In general, political and ideological subjects take up around 25 per cent of university capacity, general subjects account for 10 to 15 per cent, general foundation subjects account for 10 to 40 per cent, major foundation subjects account for 10 to 40 per cent, and major account for 10 to 15 per cent. In communist countries, foundation courses are highly important as opposed to majors. Depending on the university and major, practical training accounts for 20 to 30 per cent of total class hours, which is a relatively high proportion. This state of affairs exists due to the utilitarian aim of deploying trained experts into actual work as soon as possible.

Approximately 30 to 50 subjects need to be completed before graduation, and due to the recent introduction of an elective system, students may now select a limited number of electives. Moreover, students must also complete more than one foreign language subject such as English or Russian, and some universities and departments have begun initiating second-language education. In addition to this, except for some universities such as Kim Chaek University and Pyongyang Computer Technology University, most university courses include a 12-week work experience programme. Finally, every university student undertakes 26 weeks of military training during their sophomore year at the Gyododae, a paramilitary organization.

To improve the quality of higher education, universities have attempted a number of reforms since 2000. These reforms are as follows. First, they have attempted to merge university departments where possible, necessitating the streamlining of curriculum. Second, they have attempted to speed up the training of productive workers by shortening the overall educational period. Many courses which were formerly of five to six years in length are now from four to four and a half years. In addition, those university graduates who wanted to continue their education at graduate schools first needed to work for a designated period in a related field of work. However, in 2002, four universities, including Kim Il Sung University, started to offer articulated courses enabling students to enter graduate schools immediately after graduation. Third, mainly among major universities, new credit and elective systems are being introduced. North Korean university courses automatically assigned subjects for each academic year. However, recently the number of compulsory subjects has begun to be reduced and electives are being increased so that students may now have some choice as to the subjects they can study. Some major universities are also changing to a partial credit system. Attention is also being paid to improving teaching methods. Formerly characterized by teacher-centred, lecture-based and rote-learning approaches, recently educational methods aimed at 'cultivating the ability to reason' are being emphasized and the development of alternative teaching methodologies is being encouraged. As part of a general 'modernization' of education, the development and utilization of various educational media is increasing. In universities, electronic media such as electronic books and video data, as well as computer assisted simulation and design, computer mediated instruction, computer assisted instruction and distance education through computer communication networks are also being introduced.

Current Trends

Economy and education in crisis

Since the 1990s, North Korea has faced a series of rolling crises at every level of its society, namely the collapse of allied socialist countries, increasing isolation from international society, the death of Kim Il Sung, natural disasters and the resultant severe economic downturn. The environmental disasters of the mid-1990s struck directly at the heart of the educational infrastructure itself. In 1995, 4210 kindergartens and 2290 primary and secondary schools (a quarter of all primary and secondary schools) were destroyed and approximately 350,00 textbooks (about 3,000 tons) were swept away in floods (UNICEF, 2003).

Apart from the physical damage to the educational infrastructure, teachers, deprived of their rations due to food shortages, needed to find alternative means of physical survival. Classes could not be held on a regular basis, leading to a collapse in both the quality of educational output as well as the more intangible issue of the teacher's authority and social standing. Since most students were facing starvation and needed to work in order to survive in the face of a non-existent food distribution system, attendance rates in all institutions dramatically declined.

By the 2000s, school facilities were finally restored and teachers had largely returned to schools, with a concomitant increase in attendance rates. However, due to the duration of the crisis, actual average academic abilities among students were much lower than before the economic crisis.

The introduction of 'utilitarianism' in education

In the 2000s, after the economy had overcome the worst of the crisis, efforts to restore the education system accelerated. Moreover, as part of a general national development strategy, educational policies aimed at producing outstanding individuals in the fields of science and technology have been undertaken with great vigour. In early 1998, North Korea announced that it would officially declare the end of the 'Arduous March' period and proclaimed the creation of a 'Powerful country based on the *Juche* ideology' as an immediate revolutionary goal. Science and technology have become one of the three pillars of the state, taking a place alongside ideology and the military. This is a strategy aimed at addressing both internal and external crisis by enhancing military power and developing the country by overcoming financial difficulties through the exploitation of science and technology. Based on this development strategy, training competent human resources in the science and technology fields has become increasingly emphasized. 'Training competent people who can take part in building a powerful country through a revolution in education' is now a key revolutionary responsibility of the educational system.[11]

In the 2000s, reflecting the weight of this responsibility, educational reforms focusing on enhancing efficiency and excellence have been undertaken. In most societies, a key issue of education policy has been achieving a balance between equality and excellence. As a socialist state, expanding educational opportunities and realizing equality in education have also been key goals for North Korea. However, in order to efficiently train competent and able workers with the limited resources and budgets available in the aftermath of the 'Arduous March', some compromises regarding the aims of egalitarianism were needed. Educational policies after 2000 have therefore focused on selecting those individuals who show promise and concentrating support and resources on them rather than improving the overall educational conditions or equally distributing educational resources. North Korea argues that training many highly competent people in a short period is a way of accomplishing utilitarianism in education in its truest form.

The main focus of educational reforms is to enhance science and technology education, especially in the field of information technology (IT) and also putting every effort into nurturing competency in this field. Computer education in secondary education, starting sporadically in the early 1990s, was aimed at training talented human resources in the fields of science and technology and became a regular course in 1998. It achieved a still higher profile when the early educational system which began training children with special abilities in computer science was established from the late 1990s to the early 2000s. In higher education, the creation of additional departments related to advanced science and technology fields such as IT and BT (Blue Tooth technology) has been a prominent development. By 2003, 77 universities were involved in the education and training of information technology experts.[12]

Second, there has been considerable attention paid to identifying and fostering students of high potential. From 1998, elite middle schools have been established in each province, city and district. This system is designed to streamline the progression of top students to universities by ranking middle schools in order from the elite Pyongyang No.1 Middle School to the provincial, city and district area No.1 schools, followed by general middle schools at the bottom.[13] Furthermore, the system for selecting children with special aptitudes in computer science was strengthened. In middle schools, the best students are selected among every student in the country through national mathematics and computer science contests and are then placed in classes for high-potential students, Geumsung No. 1 and No. 2 Middle Schools. Testing and evaluation continues to further narrow the pool of students with special abilities in computer science. In addition to this, major universities have also created 'honours classes' in their natural science departments, with different curricula, greater flexibility and rather wide latitude in the selection of electives for such students compared to those on general courses.

Lastly, international exchanges have been attempted, albeit on a limited scale. Although most foreign study programmes are in China and former East European bloc countries, the number studying in North America has been growing recently. In both 2007 and 2011, North Korean professors of natural science, engineering, business and management universities have participated in training programmes at Syracuse University in the USA and the University of British Columbia in Canada for three-month and six-month periods, respectively.

Increasing educational responsibilities for parents and a widening educational gap

Part of North Korea's survival strategy during the 'Arduous March' was the concentration of extremely scarce educational resources on students with special aptitudes and this led to a dramatic reduction in support for schools in general. Parents were also forced to bear quite a large proportion of educational expenses such as textbooks, school supplies, hardware such as desks and chairs, and school maintenance expenses, which were provided by the state before the crisis. To some extent, these changes have continued into the present, even though the worst of the crisis had passed.

Moreover, with increased parental involvement in education, private education, albeit limited in form, has emerged and with it a widening educational gap. Before the 1990s, private education consisted mainly of 'private lessons' and was strictly confined to music, art and physical education. Separate private educational institutes other than public schools simply did not exist. Private education emerged during the recent financial crisis and during the resultant early experimentation with marketization. Some scholars have argued that increased competition to enter the best secondary schools and universities is leading to the birth of a nascent private education market (Cho, 2007). In the late 1990s, when the secondary education system changed to a ranked system, a huge deviation occurred in levels of national support according to students' academic abilities and potential to enter university. Students attending general middle schools had increasingly limited opportunities to take university entrance examinations, and in the early 2000s, competition to enter universities became fiercer as academic ability became an important element in selecting future leaders. In order to enter the No.1 middle schools and universities, parents with financial means hired private teachers to teach entrance examination subjects such as mathematics, science and foreign languages and this led to an expansion in private education. After the economic crisis, teachers could not maintain their living standards on their school salaries alone, and so began offering private lessons. This is one of the structural factors contributing to the birth of private education.

While private education remains very limited, emerging private education and growing parental or personal responsibilities in education signal important changes in the way North Koreans understand education. In the past, education was seen as a national goal to cultivate the people. The recent emergence and expansion of private education indicates that education has come to be seen as belonging, at least partially, to the private domain. Policies emphasizing efficiency and excellence in education, growing personal responsibilities for the costs of education, and an emerging private education market have all contributed to enlarging the educational gaps within North Korean society.

Conclusion

Education in North Korea has undergone a number of metamorphoses since the formation of the North Korean state. Clearly, utilitarianism appears to be the dominant force at present, with the North Korean authorities eager to achieve an 'immediate leap' through pursuing excellence in education and training highly competent workers in the science and technology fields. Utilitarianism in education operates on a pendulum, influenced heavily by external factors. When social cohesion is a priority, social engineering aims come to the fore. In times of crisis, however, education takes on a strongly utilitarian aspect. It is clearly understood by the North Korean authorities that all the above-mentioned reforms aimed at improving the quality and efficiency of university education will not yield the kinds of economic results North Korea needs if not carried out on a long-term basis. At a deeper level, it is also understood that developing creativity and comprehensive problem-solving abilities in students by reforming courses and educational methods, and reorganizing school administrative management systems, are very much needed as well. This presents a dilemma for the North Korean authorities.

These perceived needs will lead to a continued reduction in time, resources and attention devoted to political and ideological education, which, if allowed to continue on a long-term basis, may have profound social or political effects. On the other hand, continued restrictions in accessing the latest global innovations and technology are also an obstacle to the development of North Korean education. Direct contact with the Western world is extremely limited and internet access to the outside world is blocked. As mentioned above, and to partially overcome these limitations, visits to advanced countries or short-term periods of overseas study are recent, albeit extremely limited, innovations. Closed and inflexible political and social structures remain the primary obstacles in developing education. Therefore, restricting changes in education to the policy level without opening the society and embracing greater democratization cannot improve education, nor can it lead to economic development if that economic development is dependent upon improvements in education.

The two main current tasks of education are somewhat contradictory. On the one hand, education is viewed as a way of creating sound ideological conditions for a smooth transition of power for the new successor, Kim Jong Un. On the other hand, education must also try to resolve the social problems created by an overly utilitarian policy in education. The ranking of middle schools, diverting limited resources mainly to special education for talented children and away from general public education, and engaging with the increasing gap in academic abilities deepened by the expansion of private education are currently pressing issues. These problems have profound implications for national development in the long term. North Korea could once boast of a 100 per cent literacy rate, which came from an equality-oriented education policy that widened educational opportunities and promoted free compulsory education. When general education is weakened, it also increases the burden of special education for gifted children, concentrating attention as it does on an ever smaller number of elite students to achieve society's intended goals.

In conclusion, achieving social development through improvements in educational quality requires engaging with international society through democratization of political structures and greater openness in North Korean society. It also requires the pursuit of educational excellence based on a strong public education system and securing scarce resources through educational collaboration with the outside world. Undertaking such moves, however, are essentially matters of political and ideological consideration and are therefore outside the realm of conventional educational policy.

References

Beobryul chulpansa (2004). 'Kyoyukbeob (Education Act)', *Choseon Minjujueui Inmin Gonghwaguk Beobryungjib* (DPRK Law), Pyongyang: Beobryul chulpansa (Law Press.

Central Bureau of Statistics Pyongyang (2009). *DPR Korea 2008 Population Census*.

Cho, J. (2007). 'Utilitarianism in Education and Uneven Development of Education in North Korea in 2000s'. *Korean Journal of Sociology of Education*, 17 (4).

Education Center for Unification (2011). *Understanding North Korea 2011*. Seoul: Ministry of Unification, pp. 204–5.

Education Research Institute of Seoul National University (1994). *Terminology for Pedagogy*. Seoul: Hawoo.

The Hankyoreh. 23 November 2010.

Joseon Central Telecommunication (2004). *Joseon Central Annual Report 2004*. Pyeongyang: Joseon Central Telecommunication.

Kim Il Sung (1977). 'Theses on Socialist Education', in *Kim Il Sung Selections 7*. Pyongyang: Worker's Party of Korea Publication.

Lee, Hyang-kue (ed.) (2011). *The North Korean Education for 60 Years: its Formation, Development and Prospect*. Seoul: Kyoyukkwahaksa.

Lee, Seok (2004). *Famine in North Korea during 1994~2000: Occurrence, Striking and Features*. Seoul: Korea Institute for National Unification.

Ministry of Education (2004). *The Development of Education: National Report of the Democratic People's Republic of Korea*. Paris: UNESCO.

Nam, J. W. (1991). *Socialist Pedagogy*. Pyongyang: Educational Books Publication.

Nodong Sinmun (New Year's Joint Editorial) (1 January 2008).

Statistics Korea (2012), *2012 Bukhan ei juyo tonggye jipyo* (The Handbook on Major Statistics of North Korea), Daejeon: Statistics Korea.

Time. 27 December 2011.

UNICEF (2003). *Analysis of the situation of children and women in DPRK*. New York: UNICEF.

Notes

1 'The Great North Korean Crying Game'. *Time*, 27 December 2011.

2 According to population estimates taken from Statistics Korea, deaths caused by the economic difficulties and famine in North Korea between 1996 and 2000 were 336,000 (*The Hankyoreh*, 23 November 2010). S. Lee estimated the death toll caused by famine in North Korea during 1994–2000 at 630,000 to 1.12 million (Lee, 2004).

3 The 'Theses on Socialist Education' built on this framework with elaborated

objectives, principles, content and methods of education, suggesting the need for further creativity and independence, and emphasizing the 'social function of education in that those educated through communist revolutionary training should work for the advancement of the socialist system and fulfill their revolutionary duties to the working class' (Kim Il Sung, 1977).

4   Article 29, of the Education Act admonishes thus: 'educational institutes are required [to] teach healthy ideas, moral integrity, and deep knowledge to their students, to provide political and ideological education to develop physical strength and profound emotions, to provide in depth training in science and technology, and combine these through physical education and liberal arts education'.

5   Kindergarten is two years; however, the first year of it is non-compulsory.

6   Four general universities are Kim Il Sung University, Kim Chaek University, Koryo Sungkyunkwan University and Wonsan Agriculture University.

7   http://kosis.kr//bukhan/ (Accessed 1 December 2011). According to the latest official documents, in 2004, 4948 primary schools and 4,825 secondary schools were in operation nationally (Ministry of Education, 2004).

8   Administratively, the entire country is divided into nine provinces and the capital city of Pyongyang. Provinces are further divided into cities (*Shi*) and districts (*Gun*).

9   Kim Jong Sook, Kim Il Sung's first wife and Kim Jong Il's mother, was known as a female resistance worker, fighting against the Japanese army. She died in 1949.

10   General subjects, such as foreign languages and physical education, are compulsory for all students regardless of their major. General foundation courses for science students consist of mathematics and physics. The major courses are comprised of the major foundation subjects and the specific major subjects. For example, in the case of students taking ICT as their majors at Kim Chaek University, the general foundation course consists of mathematics, physics, basic computer technology and circuitry analysis. The major foundation subjects are signal processing, principles of communication and database design. Finally, the major subjects consist of code division multiple access, satellite communication and optical communication systems.

11   New Year's Joint Editorial in 2008.

12   Joseon Central Telecommunication (2004).

13   As part of the Gifted Education System in secondary education, Pyeongyang Middle School No. 1 was established in accordance with Kim Jong Il's direction in 1984. Next year, 12 No. 1 middle schools were built in each province (*do*) to adopt the system.

South Korea: Education in a Multicultural Society

Jiyeon Hong

Introduction

One of the common misconceptions of South Korea is that it is comprised of a single ethnic population. On the contrary, South Korea has rapidly become a multi-ethnic nation in the past two decades. The main causes for the population shift are primarily attributed to the increase in international marriages, the influx of foreign immigrant workers, and North Korean defectors (Lee, 2011). It is the children of these demographic groups who are transforming the country's present culture through the creation of a multicultural society. Korea is now more diverse than ever. This diversity has resulted in significant implications for public education, particularly early childhood education, as these children from different cultures have begun entering the national school system. Consequently, there is a need for educational policies to address the implications. The government acknowledges the gravity and urgency of the issues involved in accommodating multicultural families in public institutions, and has made such considerations a national priority. It has, in fact, taken steps to initiate new policies.

To properly examine the strategic planning of educational policies as it relates to children from different cultures, the inevitable questions that require attention are: (a) Who are the families with different cultures and what is their current situation? (b) What kind of educational policies have already been introduced with these groups in mind? (c) What kinds of educational policies still need to be implemented to best serve the needs of such children and their families? Initial investigation of these three questions has led to the conclusion that the strategies for educational policy-making and implementation need to be understood on four levels: the personal, parental, societal and political.

A century ago, Korea was dubbed the *hermit nation* (Griffis, 1882). Since then it has transformed itself from an unknown, isolated country into a diverse, multicultural society. In the last two decades, the population of foreign immigrants, in particular, has increased exponentially as they have made South Korea their new home and begun to raise their own families, some with successive generations.

This phenomenon has produced some educational issues. First, unlike native Koreans, the children of immigrant families do not enter the educational system during their early childhood years due to the parents' unfamiliarity with the Korean language. Second, immigrant parents are unable to take advantage of their local schools' resources because they are unfamiliar and uninformed about the Korean educational system. These two issues are resulting in relatively poor academic performance among immigrant children, which in turn affects the educational system as a whole. It is thus necessary to address two key questions as South Korea continues to develop into a multicultural society: (a) What is the current state of immigrant children including any problems they may face during their early childhood years? (b) Is it possible to either mitigate or eliminate such problems and, if so, what is a feasible approach? In order to answer these questions, the rest of the chapter discusses three key three inter-related aspects: the demographics of these immigrant families and their current situation; the substantial problems of multicultural families as they relate to early childhood education; and a possible approach to education policy in order to mitigate existing problems.

General Structure of Korean Education

On the surface there is little that is unique about the present structure of the school system of Korea. Under the Japanese occupation (1909–45), formal schooling consisted of six years of primary school, five years of secondary school and four years of higher education. Under the US military government that took power in 1945, this 6-5-4 pattern was altered to 6-6-4, common in the United States.

The Education Law of 1959 specified that primary education should be compulsory, and divided secondary education into a four-year middle school and a high school of two or three years' duration. With the advent of the Korean

War (1950–3), these plans were abandoned, and the present 6-3-3-4 pattern was adopted. Such a structure is clearly much like that found in most countries today.

From the 1980s, junior vocational colleges had evolved, trade schools at both the middle-school and high-school levels had been retained, lower civic schools had been phased out, and the former high-school-level teacher-training schools, the normal schools, had been incorporated into the system of junior teachers' colleges within the overall structure of education. There are now three types of high school: a) offering a general college-preparatory curriculum; b) offering vocational specialization (agriculture, fishery, commercial, technical); and c) combining both general and vocational schools including those for the deaf, blind, mentally handicapped and other kinds of severe disability.

From 1985, the mandatory introduction of middle schools was conducted in some provinces, and the whole nation adopted this mandate of the middle school in 2004. At the same time the significance of early education continued to be highlighted, and great progress has been made over at least two decades. South Korea has had outstanding success in the international PISA surveys in the early twentieth century. This has been boosted by a massive involvement of increasing numbers of children in additional private tutoring, the so-called 'shadow system' of education common in other East Asian states (Bray, 2009). The country has also been very successful at higher education level in terms of seeing some leading universities break into the top 100 elite according to international rankings. All this is of course not unrelated to the economic success of South Korea in a number of mainly technological industries. The country is also a global leader in ICT in that the proportion of the population with access to broadband is very high indeed.

However, despite all this success, understanding the needs of early childhood education is a challenging task because of the diversity of the field. Whereas the infant care act was enacted in 1991 and regulated by the Ministry of Health and Welfare, the Early Childhood Education Act was not passed until 2005, and regulated by the Ministry of Education. Furthermore, early childhood education in South Korea has two different sectors, private and public, both of which are regulated by the Ministry of Education. Currently 43.4 per cent of the three–seven year cohort children are enrolled in early childhood education provision.

On a national level, in early childhood education significant and successful efforts have been made to develop and distribute standard curricula. The focus of early childhood education has become diverse in terms of content. For instance, the area of cognitive science and mathematics was a main topic in

Table 10.1 Current enrolment number in the early childhood education system

years	total number of children	total number of enrolment	3 years old	4 years old	5 years old	6 years old	7 years old
2005	1,803,469	541,603	74,824	176,963	287,000	2728	88
2006	1,560,067	545,812	77,669	170,652	292,870	4585	36
2007	1,533,866	541,550	93,005	170,726	271,326	6461	32
2008	1,374,161	537,822	99,499	184,176	246,871	7240	34
2009	1,366,483	537,361	100,406	185,195	251,067	646	47
2010	1,310,030	538,587	111,482	181,441	244,654	917	93
2011	1,301,808	564,834	133,986	196,602	233,724	412	110

Source: Korean Education Development Institute (2011).

the 1980s, then the focus moved to social and emotional aspects in the 1990s, and on to language and curriculum and teacher education in the 2000s. One of the emerging issues is the inclusion of free kindergarten education for all young children. Another is more interdisciplinary policies related to the health, nutrition and safety of all young children whatever their culture. In a continually evolving educational system, the policies that provide a better future for young children must be inclusive of children from non-Korean and indeed any cultural family background. Education is culturally embedded but the formal dimension is necessarily politically delivered (Brock, 2011). The challenge is to achieve some kind of correspondence between the two. This is especially difficult in an increasingly multicultural context.

Current State of the Multicultural Family and Children in Korea

For the purposes of this paper, the term 'multicultural family' means a 'non-Korean family'. The composition of such multicultural families in Korea can be defined by three population groups: a) from international marriages; b) from immigrant workers; and (c) North Korean defectors. The first group is characterized by families resulting from an international marriage between a Korean male and a foreign female or between a foreign male and a Korean female. The second group is comprised of families in which the parents are foreigners who are temporarily working in Korea. These couples may have married in Korea or in their own countries before formally immigrating. The final group consists of North Korean families and children who were born in either North or South Korea. While each group is considered a multicultural family, the social, economic and political dissimilarities among the groups are too divergent to be ignored, even if their language and skin colour are identical to those of ethnic South Koreans. It is important to note that all statistics in this paper include only the data of international marriages and immigrant worker groups since no official records exist for North Korean defectors.

The data in Figure 10.1 and Table 10.2, based on the Ministry of Public Administration and Security census from 1 February 2011 to 30 May 2011, indicate that the foreign immigrant population by international marriage has been increasing in recent years. In 2010, the total number of international marriages was 34,235, which is 900 cases more than the total number of international marriages in 2009. Between 2002 and 2010, the total number of international marriages has nearly doubled. This phenomenon of international marriages is a direct result of the exodus of young Korean adults from the agriculture industry, which has dramatically altered the face of agricultural communities. The agricultural sector now primarily consists of older males as younger Korean men have found opportunities outside of the agrarian field. Moreover, Korean females tend to avoid marrying Korean males involved in agriculture. These two factors have led to the increased prevalence of older Korean males seeking those foreign wives who may be more amenable to a rural life.

The numbers shown in Figure 10.1 and Table 10.2 demonstrate that Korean males are more inclined to have foreign wives than Korean females marrying foreign husbands. In fact, the number of Korean males married to foreign

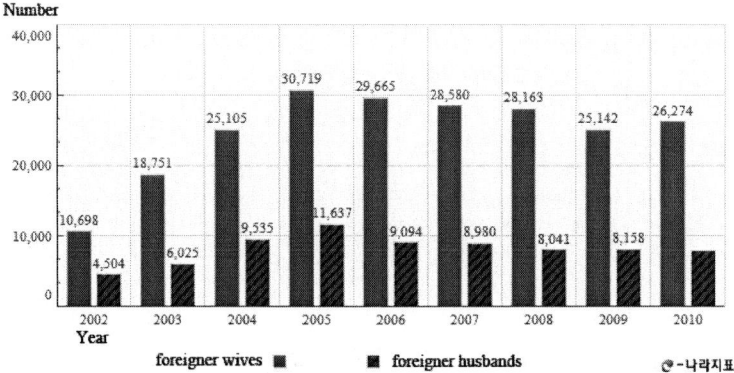

Figure 10.1 Number of international marriages from 2002 to 2010

Source: Vital Statistics 2011, the Ministry of Public Administration and Security, Statistics Korea.

females was 26,274 in 2010. In contrast, the number of Korean females married to foreign males was only 7961 in the same year. The figures show that the majority of these foreign wives originated from several Asian countries. China and Vietnam were the top sources (at 26.6 per cent or 9,623 marriages) while the Philippines (7.3 per cent, 1906), Cambodia (4.6 per cent, 1205) and Japan (4.5 per cent, 1193) rounded out the top five nations. Careful examination of these tables clearly illustrates that international marriages are increasing in Korea, which in turn has led to a growth in the number of children having a multicultural milieu in which to experience their early years, the period when children learn an immense amount through the informal mode of education

According to the Korean Ministry of Public Administration and Security, the total number of immigrants in Korea that includes naturalized immigrants was 1,265,006 persons, which represented 2.5 per cent of the entire Korean

Table 10.2 Number of international marriages by nationality from 2003 to 2010

	2003	2004	2005	2006	2007	2008	2009	2010
total number of International Marriage	24,776	34,640	42,356	38,759	37,560	36,204	33,300	34,235
Korean Male+ Foreign Female	18,751	25,105	30,719	29,665	28,580	28,163	25,142	26,274
China	13,347	18,489	20,582	14,566	14,484	13,203	11,364	9623
Vietnam	1402	2461	5822	10,128	6610	8282	7249	9623
Philline	928	947	980	1,117	1497	1857	1643	1906
Japan	844	809	883	1,045	1206	1162	1140	1193
Cambodia	19	72	157	394	1804	659	851	1205
Thailand	345	324	266	271	524	633	496	438
USA	322	341	285	331	376	344	416	428
Mongol	320	504	561	594	745	521	386	326
etc.	1224	1158	1183	1219	1334	1502	1597	1532
Korean Female+ Foreign Male	6,025	9,535	11,637	9,094	8,980	8,041	8,158	7,961
Japan	2250	3118	3423	3412	3349	2743	2422	2293
China	1190	3618	5037	2589	2486	2101	2617	2090
USA	1222	1332	1392	1443	1334	1347	1312	1516
Canada	219	227	283	307	374	371	332	403
Australia	109	132	101	137	158	164	159	178
U.K.	88	120	104	136	125	144	166	194
German	94	109	85	126	98	115	110	135
Parkistan	130	100	219	150	134	117	104	102
etc.	723	779	993	794	922	939	936	1050

Source: Vital Statistics (2011), the Ministry of Public Administration and Security, Statistics Korea.

population on 23 June 2011. Table 10.3 (Vital Statistics, 2011) states that the number of multicultural children was 151,154, constituting 11.9 per cent of the foreign population of Korea.

More significantly, the population of children 12 years of age and younger was 86.80 per cent in June 2011. Hence the current prevalence of international marriages and the ensuing number of multicultural children draws specific attention to the educational policies and needs related to this growing demographic, and ultimately to any underlying issues that may or may not be readily visible or understood.

Previously, educational policy had focused on issues related to child care and other concerns of upbringing. Multicultural concerns were not given any priority or significance until 2006 when the Korean government gave attention to immigrants and their children. This movement was not involuntary or arbitrary, as the government realized the growing influence these people had on society as a whole. More importantly, Korean officials understood the necessity of providing resources for all people in this increasingly global and international era.

In 2006, 17 different government bodies that included the President and the Prime Minister convened to discuss the 'Cardinal Direction and Propulsive System of Foreigners Policy' for the first time in Korea. This gathering led to enactment of various pieces of legislation. For example, in 2007 the Ministry of Justice passed the Act on the Treatment of Foreigners in Korea (Korean Legislations, 2007). The following year, the Ministry of Health and Welfare adopted the Law of Support for Multicultural Families Act. These two pieces of government legislation became the catalyst for widespread support for multicultural families and children in Korea. In 2008, the *Customized Support Steps according to the Stages of the Life Cycle of the Multicultural Family* was released. This indicates that required needs are varied in terms of the stages of the life cycle, and phased support should be provided. The development and growth of multicultural family support centres was initiated, resulting in the creation of 201 such centres by December 2011. The *Guidebook for Living in Korea for*

Table 10.3 The age population rate of multicultural children

Age	under 6	7~12	13~15	16~18	total
Population	93,537	37,590	12,392	7,635	151,154
Rate	61.90%	24.90%	8.20%	5.10%	100%

Source: Vital Statistics (2011), the Ministry of Public Administration and Security, Statistics, Korea.

Foreigners is now published in nine different languages including Korean. The main goals of all these efforts include the early acclimatization of immigrants to Korea; the provision of necessary resources for sustainability; the nurture and growth of their children; and the acceptance and greater understanding of this new subset of 'multicultural Koreans'. Despite these well-meaning efforts, there still remain issues within Korea's educational infrastructure that need to be addressed as it pertains to multicultural children growing up in South Korea.

Issues related to Early Childhood Education

Before delving into the issues of early childhood education in Korea, it is necessary to define what multicultural education means or represents. Multicultural education in Korea takes shape in two distinct modalities: first, to teach native Koreans the aspects of living in a nation with multicultural families; second, to educate multicultural families how to incorporate themselves into the Korean society in the most beneficial and unencumbered manner (Cheon, 2007). A full-scale movement on education policies for multicultural children has been led by the Ministry of Education, Science and Technology (herein after referred to as MEST). In collaboration with other parts of the Korean government, MEST has been concentrating on the adoption of policies and programmes pertaining to teacher training. MEST has also teamed up with local education offices and local schools to expand programmes and policies for multicultural children. While such concerted efforts have been beneficial, certain key concerns still remain.

One area of concern is the mastering of proper Korean language skills (both oral and written). Many multicultural children struggle to understand a new language, and to adapt to a different cultural setting during their early childhood. This is a very challenging undertaking for a developing child to experience. Furthermore, if a mother were the immigrant, the mother herself may be battling with a Korean husband's lifestyle and mode of communication. She may not understand at all why her husband may ignore her, what he wants her to do, or how she should behave towards her husband's family members. Due to lack of Korean language skills, a foreign wife can be shunned from raising her own child, the primary reason being that a multi-linguistic home setting is not encouraged by mainstream society. This practice produces what can be referred to as a 'without communication' state between the mother and child resulting in isolation on both sides. A multicultural child can be deprived of his/her mother's love, which is an essential element of early childhood development. As a direct consequence, this particular multicultural child grows up by himself/herself with limited support or help from its mother. The child may grow to be recessive, and this may result in poor academic performance due to lack of self-worth and self-confidence (Seol, 2005).

On the other hand, if a foreign mother were extensively involved with the child's education and development, it is inferred that the child is in a formative 'middle ground' because he/she does not have a firm understanding of either Korean or the mother's native language. In early childhood, a multicultural child loses the opportunity to form the foundations of language skills at the same level as indigenous children. This lack of fundamentals can unfortunately lead to difficulties with academic performance and maintaining certain developmental standards. This in turn may cause multicultural children to be classified incorrectly as 'developmentally challenged' because they have not attained the proper support and have simply been marginalized for something they had no control over from the outset. Research has shown that the reason for these multicultural children having learning disabilities or behavior difficulties is not based on actual skill sets or abilities, but on the lack of resources provided for these children to learn proper and timely Korean language fundamentals.

Bullying and group isolation comprise another set of factors that affect multicultural children's educational performance. While neither Korean children nor multicultural children are immune from bullying and group isolation, the reasons for bullying and group isolation are clearly different between indigenous Korean children and multicultural children. The primary reason for bullying among native Korean children is due to the superior attitude of others (29.4 per cent). On the other hand, for multicultural children the major reasons are that their mothers are foreigners (34.1 per cent), followed by the inability to properly communicate (20.7 per cent); without any special reason (15.9 per cent); different attitude and behavior (13.4 per cent); and different appearance (4.9 per cent) (Seol, 2005). Thus the timely development of language skills is fundamental for multicultural children to succeed in education.

Social adjustment is another serious issue that elicits great concern. Inherent difference of skin colour, varying minority nationalities and other pressures cause these children to have very severe emotional crises. The struggle for social acceptance becomes a key component in the child's life, and failure to cope with such elements can lead to juvenile delinquency, antisocial behavior, social alienation and criminal acts (Hong, 2010). There is, however, no established supporting system for these children, such as bilingual counsellors, multicultural teachers, social workers, therapists, child care or and legal and medical assistance. Table 10.4 outlines the type of programmes now offered in a multicultural family support centre operated by the Ministry of Health and Welfare in Korea. According to the table, multicultural family support programmes are well organized and operated, but these programmes are still not adequate because they do not address the real challenges and needs of everyday life for most multicultural families.

Economic hardship is yet another issue for multicultural children. Their mostly lower socioeconomic status makes it difficult for these children to reach

Table 10.4 Overview of programmes operated by the Ministry of Health and Welfare

Program	Descriptions
Educational Programs	• Korean language education • Education for families • Education on multicultural understanding • Capability development
Counseling Programs	• Counseling (residence, finance, employment, human rights, domestic violence and sexual violence) • Counseling on family affairs and marital relations, as well as counseling therapy
Programs for Children	• Childcare Information Center • Programs for the development of children's learning capability • Support for children's language development • Bilingual classes • Support for language education of multicultural children provided by local childcare centers • Learning support, through mentoring programs with college students
Programs for the Development of Marriage Immigrants' Capabilities	• Family volunteer club • Employment and business start-up programs, as well as cooperation with industry • Opportunities to serve as native language instructors, multicultural instructors, translators and interpreters
Improvement of Awareness and Opinions of Multiculturalism	• Relationship-building with mothers of marriage immigrants • Organization of self -reliance groups by nationality
Home Visiting Services	• Visiting child care support services • Visiting Korean language education services • Maternity guidance services

Source: *The Guidebook for Living in Korea for Foreigners* (Ministry of Health and Welfare, 2009).

and overcome the threshold of entering into higher education. Most multicultural families are in strained economic circumstances. Although international marriage partners may have professional degrees or higher educational studies from their native lands, obtaining regular employment is difficult regardless of their pedigree. If they do have a paid position, their wages may not meet the minimum cost of living in Korea. In fact, it is even very difficult for double-income Korean families to pay their children's higher education expenses. According to one study (Lee et al., 2008), 41.6 per cent of multicultural families earn monthly wages between 1,010,000 Korean won (KW) (equivalent to US$1000 approximately) and 2,000,000 KW (US$2000), and 26 per cent of them earn less than 1,000,000 KW (US$1000). This suggests that a significant proportion of all multicultural families earn less than 2,000,000 KW (US$2000) per month. Financial hardship thus creates barriers for these families, including their children. Such economic issues correlate with the lack of educational opportunities due to the lack of funds. Real opportunities could be made available, however, by government policies that would include the following: a) multicultural parents need support for the opportunity to further their own education in various subjects such as Korean language, computer skills, legal issues, medical services; b) multicultural parents need support for coping with the social and emotional adaptation they and their children are faced with; c) multicultural children must receive the same opportunities and appropriate treatment at the hands of their teachers as indigenous Korean children despite the cultural differences; and d) multicultural families must have an opportunity to improve themselves without bias against them. To meet and overcome all these challenges, including poverty, improved and relevant educational opportunities at all levels, but especially in early childhood, are essential.

Early Childhood Education Policy Strategies for Multicultural Children

As previously stated, the number of multicultural families in Korea has been increasing for the last two decades. This rapid growth now drives some educational policies and issues. Beginning in 2006, the Korean government has initiated many efforts for the benefit of multicultural families. But despite these efforts, the rapid demographic movement toward being a multicultural society has outpaced the policy strategies enacted in terms of educational, economic, political and socio-cultural programmes. The tenets of basic language skills, academic performance, emotional stability and economic soundness are the key to the educational development of a child in their formative years. As a result, it is critical to build firm strategies for developing and implementing educational policies. These policies must be analyzed on a number of distinct levels: the personal level, the family (parental) level, the societal level and the political (governmental) level.

First, an education policy strategy should focus on the advancement of multicultural children's capabilities on a personal level. Korean language proficiency is absolutely vital for multicultural children to overcome personal and family difficulties. A one-dimensional policy without consideration of personal needs would be unwise, as every multicultural family varies in their cultural background, economic and social circumstances, and their inherent abilities and skills. One must take into consideration personal circumstances. In order to do so, it is necessary to train Korean teachers, coordinators, mentors and helpers in understanding multiculturalism and to cultivate multicultural teachers who can provide adequate assistance to these children at the school level. Suitably targeted resources can play a significant role in educating multicultural children and Korean children simultaneously and to mutual advantage. In so doing, multicultural children can experience positive social adaptation, and academic excellence and achievement beyond their early childhood years.

Second, educational policy strategy needs to be focused on the family. Differences are likely to exist between a multicultural child who has a Japanese mother and the child who has a Mongolian mother. This sort of variance must naturally tie into the educational policies initiated and implemented. Another variation of note is the duration of habitation in Korea. For instance, the needs of a recent immigrant would vary significantly from those of a seasoned immigrant of, say, five years or more. Another variation that needs to be taken into account is different forms of marriage, such as a remarriage family, a single parent family, a family with adopted children or step-children and other variations.

Academic experience and qualifications are also an important variation. Professional skills and qualifications can be a great asset for multicultural parents as well as for Korean society in general. A medical doctor, international lawyer, social worker, public accountant or those who have professional skills would all contribute greatly to the public welfare in Korea. All these qualities are of significant benefit for Korean society and should not be regarded negatively. Special skills such as in arts, crafts and software programming can be helpful resources in Korea. The underlying reasons for immigrating to Korea also need to be understood. Intentions differ as with the other factors mentioned above. Some immigrate in search of increased income while others come because of marriage. Whatever the reason or circumstance, the most important need is to strengthen multicultural parents' skill sets, experience and knowledge so that they can: a) foster healthy and linguistically skilled children; b) further educate their children; c) add to Korean proficiency in general; d) acknowledge the mainstream Korean culture; e) discover and develop knowledge that involves the conversion of their qualification and academic experience to their new situation; and f) cultivate self-esteem and self-reliance as independent human beings.

On the societal and governmental level, educational policy strategies for early childhood should pursue the object of integration, so that multiculturalism is seen to be a normal component of South Korean society. The many organizations, policies and programmes that relate only to the indigenous majority culture need to accommodate this objective. This includes the formal education system with which many multicultural families are frustrated. Initiatives need to be developed that enable the Multicultural Support Centre to focus on individual needs in a flexible manner at whatever level is appropriate. The Ministry of Education, Science and Technology should be enabled to provide teacher-training programmes with proven methods that will enable multicultural parents especially to become bilingual. MEST can also concentrate on developing the curriculum for multicultural adults as well as creating and publishing a Korean language textbook suitable for multicultural children in early childhood. The Ministry of Health and Welfare could be enabled to recognize and treat conditions that multicultural adults and children may have but which need a different approach from the standard medical service.

As often happens with such issues in many countries, numerous informal and non-formal organizations are already actively playing vital roles in Korean society, such as parents associations and NGOs, such as MSF (Medicins Sans Frontieres), EWB (Educators Without Borders) and many others. Education needs to be seen in a holistic way (Brock, 2011). Formal institutions such as schools can work with the non-formal such as libraries, churches, support centres, community centres, cultural centres, continuing education centres, teachers; groups and counsellor groups. All these could collaborate and cooperate to produce policies and programmes that span the educational continuum and produce imaginative and creative leadership, which is a major political and professional challenge.

In a small town in Gyeonggi province, an incredible collaborative effort has taken shape successfully. The city council provided financial support while a primary school monitored the educational curriculum. It held Korean language classes for multicultural parents and children after school with many diverse programmes. Successful and positive outcomes are achievable if cooperation and concerted efforts are made with the right intentions and partners. It is not insignificant that the success of the Gyeonggi initiative has been achieved at the local level. That is the only scale at which cooperation of many partners is likely to happen, and it is up to national and provincial authorities to encourage it, rather than continue to foster conformity and larger-scale control.

Conclusion

Educational concerns relating to multicultural children mostly originate from their early childhood experiences, especially the lack of fundamental Korean language skills. This deficiency can lead to serious and lifelong social, economic, political and educational problems. At the present time, what such children experience in Korean society is not always good or desirable. Rather, it provokes dissatisfaction and conflict with the family, peers and others they interact with. Sometimes multicultural children break down emotionally, mentally and in other ways due to an identity crisis, group isolation or bullying. Like a vicious circle, this experience ultimately fosters poor academic achievement, emotional instability, social maladjustment and economic marginalization as they move through adolescence into adulthood. As described above, this is a significant and growing concern in South Korean society which has ramifications for its economic performance. It also has implications for the significant educational success of the country in certain elite forms of education such as international competition at secondary and tertiary level. Many so-called multicultural children and adults could further enhance these successes if they were enabled to cope with the challenge of living in two cultures. This is something already experienced in some other countries with longer histories of immigration, and on a larger scale, such as in Australia, the United Kingdom and the USA. Much could be gained in South Korea by looking at these cases: how they have been through phases of failure and success though successive generations of multicultural evolution in their societies. None of these countries has completely solved the problems of integration. There is no easy solution. But there does need to be a political will and a willingness of the majority host community, in this case native South Koreans, to cooperate at all the levels outlined above: cultural, social, economic and political. If such an effort is made and is successful, one day there will be a Prime Minister or President of the country coming from a immigrant family such as has happened in the USA, Australia and France in recent years. South Korea is no longer a single-race nation, and if it is to continue to grow and succeed it has to recognize that fact and the challenges it presents. The accommodation of the educational needs of the youngest members of the immigrant and multicultural community in South Korean is where that recognition has to begin.

References

Bennett, C. I. (2007). *Multicultural Education: Theory and Practice* (6th edn). Boston, MA: Allyn & Bacon.

Bray, M. (2009). *Confronting the Shadow System: What Government Policies for What Private Tutoring?* Paris: IIEP/UNESCO.

Brock, C. (2011). *Education As a Global Concern*. London: Continuum.

Brown, E. L. (2006). 'Knowing, Valuing and Shaping One's Culture'. *Multicultural Education*, 14 (1): 15–19.

Cheon, K. S. (2007). *A Study on Policy Methods of Multicultural Education*. Gyeonggido: Gyeonggido Family & Women's Research Institute.

Cho, Y. D. (2006). *A Research on the Actual Condition of Multicultural Family Children Education*. Seoul: Ministry of Education, Science and Technology.

—(2006). *A Study of Material Development for Supporting Multicultural Family Education*, Seoul: Korea Education Development Institute.

Eun, K. S., Kim, B. J., Oh, M. S., Kim, K. I, Cho, D. G. and Kim, B. S. (2007). *Multiculturalism in Korea: Current Situation and Issues*. Seoul: Doseochulpan Hannul.

Garcia, J. and Pugh, S. L. (2002). 'Multicultural Education in Teacher Preparation Programs'. *Phi Delta Kappan*, 47 (4): 214–19.

Griffis, W. E. (1882). *The Hermit Nation Korea* (revised edn. in 2004). La Vergne, TN: Lightning Source Inc.

Hong, B. S. (2010). *Juvenile Problem Theory: Understanding and Support Methods of Juvenile in Crisis*. Seoul: Gondongche.

Hong, Y. S. (2007). *Children Education's Problems and Implications of Multicultural Family in Korea*. Kwangju: Department of Education, Kwangju University.

Kim, H. W. and Kim D. J. (2007). 'Multicultural Phenomenon of Korean Society and Educational Tasks'. *Humanity Studies*, 34 (3): 153–76.

Kim, J. H. (2008). 'Multiculturalism and Education in Korean Society', *Philosophical Studies*, 106: 29–52.

Kim, K. R. (2006). *Influences of Multicultural Family Children's Self Identity and Social Support on Social Adaptation*. Seoul: Kukmin University.

Kim S. M., Hwang, J. M. and Yi, J.Y. (2007). *Establishment of Policy Paradigm for Transmission into Multi-ethnic & Multicultural Society (1): Current Adaption and Policy Task in Korean Society*, Seoul: Korean Women's Development Institute.

Kim, Won, Kim, B. S., Seo, D. H., Seo, J. N., Yu, S. Y., Seo, H. C., Oh, M. S. and Cheong, M. R. (2011). *Multiculturalism in Korea; Family, Education and Policy.* Seoul: Yimaejin.

Korean Legislation No. 8442 (17 May 2007).

—No. 8937 (21 March 2008).

Korean Women's Development Institute (2008). *Prospect and Policy Maneuver for Multicultural Society.* Seoul: Korean Women's Development Institute.

Lee, C. K. (2011). 'The Educational Life Histories of a Group of North Korean Defector University Students in South Korea', in l. Demirdjian (ed), *Education, Refugees and Asylum Seekers.* London: Continuum Books, pp. 38–77.

Lee, J. B., Kang S. W. and Kim, H. (2008). *A Research on the Educational Status about the Children of Multicultural Family – Based on the Families of International Marriage.* Seoul: Korea Education Development Institute. http://www.liveinkorea. kr/board/board_read.asp?pzt=ct&lng=kr&cc=mfsc&id=1231&gr=1239&sn=&sw= &sdate=20120402&num=2033561&pg=1 (Accessed 2 July 2012).

Ministry of Education, Science and Technology (2009), *09 Education Support Plan for the Reinforcement of Multicultural Student's Capabilities.* Seoul: Ministry of Education, Science and Technology.

Ministry of Health and Welfare (2009). *The Guidebook for Living in Korea for Foreigners.* Seoul: Ministry of Health and Welfare.

Ministry of Health and Welfare, Ministry of Justice, Ministry of Gender Equality and Korea Institute for Health and Social Affairs (2010) *A Research on Current Condition of National Multicultural Family in Korea in 2009.* Seoul: Ministry of Health and Welfare, Ministry of Justice, Ministry of Gender Equality and Korea Institute for Health and Social Affairs.

OECD (2006). *International Migration Outlook.* Paris: OECD.

Oh, K. S., Kim, H. J., Yi, S. O., Pak, H. S., Cheong, J. H. and Jung, H. S. (2007). *Current Circumstance and Tasks of Multicultural Education.* Seoul: Hakjisa.

Pak, S. H. (2007). *An Analysis Study on Current Scheme, Tasks and Achievement of Multicultural Education Policy in Korea.* Seoul: Ministry of Education, Science and Technology.

—(2007). *A Study on Analyzing Current Policies, Tasks, and Outcomes of Multicultural Education in Korea.* Seoul: Korea Education Development Institute.

Seol, D. H. (2005). *Current Research of Immigrant Women via International Marriage and Methods of Health and Welfare Supporting Policy.* Seoul: Ministry of Health and Welfare.

UNESCO APCEIU (Asia-Pacific Centre of Education for International Understanding under the Auspices of UNESCO) (2008). *Understanding of Multicultural Society: Current Situation and Prospect of Multicultural Education.* Gyeonggi: Doseochulpan Dongnyeok.

Unification Office of Korea (2008). http://www.unikorea.go.kr

Vital Statistics 2011 (27 June 2011). *Statistics Korea*. Ministry of Public Administration and Security. http://www.index.go.kr/egams/stts/jsp/potal/stts/PO_STTS_IdxMain. jsp?idx_cd=2430&bbs=INDX_001&clas_div=C&rootKey=1.48.0 (Accessed 2 July 2012).

Yi, H. K., Seol, D. H. and Cho, S. N. (2006). *A Research on Current Condition of Immigrant Women by International Marriage & Support Policy Methods in Health, Social Service*. Seoul: Ministry of Gender Equality and Family.

Yi, J. B. (2008) 'A Research on Actual Education Condition of International Marriage Family Children', in *Symposium of Multicultural Children*. Seoul.

Yi, S. S., Pak, J. S., Kim, P. S. and Kim, H. S. (2007). *Marriage and Childbirth Behavior of Immigrant Women by International Marriage & Policy Direction*. Seoul: Korean Institute for Health and Social Affairs.

Yun, H. Y. (2006). *A Study on the Outstanding Examples of Support for the Multicultural Family*. Seoul: Korea Education Development Institute.

Zirkel, S. (2008). 'The Influence of Multicultural Educational Practices on Students Outcomes and Intergroup Relations'. *Teachers College Record*, 119 (6): 1147–81.

11

South Korea: College Admissions System and Reform Issues

Soojeong Lee and Eul Sook Kim

Of all the educational policies in South Korea, that relating to the college admissions system could well be the most sensitive, not only for policy makers but also for the public. Most Korean people are very interested in how the college admission system works, probably due to the high profile of education in the culture, including the importance of gaining graduate status. That is why the Korea's college admissions system has gone through many reforms in the brief period since the time of the national liberation in 1945. The reform of the college admissions system is always complicated and ongoing. This is due to the diverse cultural, social and political factors that bear upon the whole system, its structure and operation. This chapter briefly overviews the characteristics related to the whole education system including the tertiary sector, and Korean society and culture, which have worked as backgrounds to the reforms to Korea's college admissions system.

Background of the Reforms of Korea's College Admissions System

High entrance rate for higher education

It has taken more than 50 years since national liberation in 1945 to reach the peak of universalization of higher education in Korea. In 2005, the advancement rate for universities was 82.1 per cent; it has since increased up to 83.8 per cent in 2008 (KEDI, 2011, pp. 26–7). The higher education entrance rate of Korea is now among the top echelon of OECD countries (OECD, 2010a). Table 11.1, which shows the overview of Korea's education system as of year 2007, shows

Table 11.1 School system (2007)

Classification		Schools				Students	Teachers
		Total	National	Public	Private		
Total		19,865	96	13,787	5982	11,883,628	506,682
Kindergartens		8294	3	4445	3,846	541,550	33,504
Primary Education (6years)	Subtotal	5757	17	5664	76	3,830,063	167,185
	Primary Schools	5756	17	5664	75	3,829,998	167,182
	Civic Schools	1	–	–	1	65	3
Middle School Education (3years)	Subtotal	3044	10	2372	662	2,067,656	108,195
	Middle Schools	3032	9	2371	652	2,063,159	107,986
	Civic High Schools	4	–	1	3	191	10
	Miscellaneous Schools	8	1	–	7	4,306	199
High School Education (3years)	Subtotal	2218	17	1246	955	1,862,501	120,585
	High Schools	1457	12	792	653	1,347,363	83,662
	Vocational High Schools	702	5	408	289	494,011	36,549
	Air & Correspondence High Schools	39	–	39	–	14,285	–
	Trade High Schools	12	–	–	12	3378	137
	Miscellaneous Schools	8	–	7	1	2,764	230
Special Schools		144	5	50	89	23,147	6256
Junior College Education (2years)	Subtotal	152	3	8	141	800,423	11,713
	Junior Colleges	148	3	8	137	795,519	11,685
	Colleges attached to industrial firms	1	–	–	1	39	3
	Distance Learning Colleges	2	–	–	2	4769	21
	Miscellaneous Schools	1	–	–	1	53	4

University Education (4years)	Subtotal	220	41	2	177	2,461,712	56,349
	Universities	175	23	2	150	1,919,504	52,763
	Teachers Colleges	11	11	–	–	25,834	855
	Industrial Universities	14	6	–	8	169,862	2190
	Technical Colleges	1	–	–	1	139	—
	Broadcast & Correspondence Universities	1	1	–	–	272,763	136
	Distance Learning Universities	15	–	–	15	72,454	386
	Colleges Attached to Industrial firms	1	–	–	1	95	1
	Miscellaneous Schools	2	–	–	2	1,061	18
Graduate School Education	Subtotal	36	–	–	36	296,576	2,895
	Graduate Schools at Universities	<1006>	<168>	<14>	<824>	291,215	2416
	Graduate Schools	36	–	–	36	5361	479

Notes
1. The number of faculty for graduate schools includes only full time professors.
2. < >reflects status of graduate schools and is excluded from the total figure.
3. Does not include branch schools.
4. Primary Education starts at age of 7.

Source: MEST (2012). http://english.mest.go.kr/web/1693/site/contents/en/en_0203.jsp (28 July 2012).

the number of schools, students and teachers (note that the population of the Republic of Korea is 50 million as of June 2012). A distinguishing feature of Korea's higher education is that most high school graduates, including from vocational high schools, can be admitted to all forms of colleges or universities if they wish to continue their education. Table 11.1 provides the background of the system of education as a whole.

The South Koreans were not prepared for the unexpected three-year-long war in 1950, and it left the country in a devastated condition. A total of 4776 schools, including primary, secondary and tertiary institutions, were destroyed, which comprised an estimated 17,375 classrooms (Lee, 2002, p. 250). However, the national education system never fully ceased during the war, and South Koreans by no means gave up on efforts to educate the nation's populace. The percentage of students attending elementary schools of age group 7–12 reached 89.9 per cent by 1956 and 96.4 per cent in 1959 (Lee, 2008a, p. 29). And within a half century after national liberation in 1945, the advancement rate for middle school and high school had reached nearly 100 per cent; in 1995, the figures for these benchmarks were 99.9 per cent and 98.5 per cent, respectively (KEDI, 2011, pp. 26–7). The following table shows the advancement rate to the next stage at each level from the 1980s until 2011.

Intense competition for admission to better high schools and colleges

Massive nationwide reforms have been instituted to alleviate the intense competition among students for being admitted to 'better' high schools and colleges. In 1969, as a part of the '7·15 College Admission Reform', the entrance examination for middle schools was abolished. According to Soojeong Lee (2006), the reasons are as follows. Until the late 1960s, all middle schools selected their own students through a competitive entrance examination. As a result, rankings among middle schools based on entrance examination scores were created and a few high-ranking middle schools emerged. Elementary school students, accordingly, competed intensely for the admission into high-ranking middle schools (Lee, 2006, pp. 18–19). Much evidence has proved that the abolition of the middle school entrance examination worked positively on the expansion of secondary education (Mason et al., 1980, pp. 352–4). As Soojeong Lee (2006) pointed out, it nonetheless causes a stiff and excessive competition for admission into a few high-ranking high schools, especially those which were considered to be routes for entering the most prestigious universities in Korea. This created an

Table 11.2 Advancement rate to the next stage at each level, 1980s to 2011

Division	Elementary to Middle School		Middle to High School		High School to Higher Education		General High School to Higher Education		Technical High School to Higher Education	
	Total	Female	Total	Female	Total	Female	Total	Female	Total	Female
1980	95.8	94.1	84.5	80.8	27.2	22.9	39.2	35.4	11.4	5.0
1985	99.2	99.1	90.7	88.2	36.4	34.1	53.8	53.5	13.3	9.9
1990	99.8	99.8	95.7	95.0	33.2	32.4	47.2	49.8	8.3	6.3
1995	99.9	99.9	98.5	98.4	51.4	49.8	72.8	75.8	19.2	17.2
2000	99.9	99.9	99.6	99.6	68.0	65.4	83.9	84.6	42.0	35.7
2005	99.9	99.9	99.7	99.8	82.1	80.8	88.3	88.8	67.6	62.0
2006	99.9	99.9	99.8	99.8	82.1	81.1	87.5	88.1	68.6	63.3
2007	99.9	99.9	99.6	99.7	82.8	82.2	87.1	88.0	71.5	66.6
2008	99.9	99.9	99.7	99.7	83.8	83.5	87.9	88.6	72.9	69.5
2009	99.9	99.9	99.6	99.7	81.9	82.4	84.9	86.3	73.5	70.8
2010	99.9	99.9	99.7	99.7	79.0	80.5	81.5	83.6	71.1	70.6
2011	99.9	99.9	99.7	95.3	72.5	75.0	75.2	78.6	63.7	62.9

Source: KEDI (2011). *2011 교육통계 자료집 [2011 Educational Statistics]*, pp. 26-27.

Notes
1.   From 2011, the data is based on the number of students who are enrolled as of 1 April (previous data were based on the number of students who were accepted to universities as of their graduation in February).
2.   The number of entrance examination repeaters is not included in the data.

additional issue of 'overheated tutoring', part of the so-called 'shadow system' in the subsequent competition to get into the top-ranked universities.

This, in turn, created a response to the growing problem of the searing competition for high school entrance. It was putting extreme amounts of pressure on young adolescents, and so the government abolished the entrance examination for high school in 1974, another major reform. Following a pattern established by the abolition of the middle school entrance examinations, the High School Equalization policy in 1974 was instituted in the two major cities, Seoul and Pusan. Although the crux of the policy was to allow students to attend randomly selected high schools rather than being required to take an examination for admission, the government expected that the intensified competition among middle school students for admission into the top-ranked high schools would disappear because of the abolition of the high school entrance examination.

By 2007, a total of 28 cities had adopted the policy, comprising 59 per cent of regular high schools, 73 per cent of students and 71 per cent of teachers distributed in those areas at that time (ibid.). The policy still exists, and according to a source provided by the Gyeonggi Province Office of Education, 31 cities, including Seoul, six metropolitan cities and 24 other cities, had adopted the policy by December 2010 (GPOE, 2010), and more cities are adopting the policy (Asiatoday.co.kr, 2011). Table 11.3 shows the number of high schools operating under the Equalization Law, and Table 11.4, the growing trend in high school education during the 1970s.

In the years since then, criticisms of the policy has included its limitation of freedom in choosing schools and the difficulty in teaching students at different learning levels. Yet scholars have pointed out that it has been paramount in alleviating the problems of excessive private tutoring expenditures; rankings-conscious high schools; educational quality gaps among students and teachers; and educational conditions in schools (Lee, 2008b, p. 22). Private tutoring services include a range of formal after-school academic activites, such as individual or group tutoring, instruction from for-profit *Hakwon* (the so-called

Table 11.3 Number of high schools and students under the equalization policy

	Equalization Region	Non-equalization Region	Total
Schools	694 (56.79%)	528 (43.21%)	1222
Students	851,318 (71.91%)	332,557 (28.10%)	1,183,875

Source: Education and Human Resource Department & Korean Educational Development Institute (2003) (reused in Kang, 2005. p. 173).

Table 11.4 Expansion of high school education since the 1970s

Year	General High Schools			Technical High Schools		
	Number of Schools	Number of Students	Number of Teachers	Number of Schools	Number of Students	Number of Teachers
1965	389	254,095	7894	312	172,436	6214
1970	408	315,367	9845	481	275,015	10,009
1975	673	648,149	20,415	479	474,868	15,340
1980	748	932,605	27,480	605	764,187	23,468

Source: Gang, Seong-Guk (2005). *Analysis on Educational Index of 60 Years of Korean Education Growth.* Seoul: KEDI (reused in Lee, 2008a, p. 38).

'cram schools'), self-study or practice exam sheets, internet tutoring and after-class lessons within regular public schools (Lee and Shouse, 2011, p. 212). However, the alleviation of the burden on private tutoring expenditures was not applied to high school students but only to middle school students. In other words, middle school students' reliance on private tutoring services was only reduced, but high school students' use of private tutoring services was boosted as described below.

Expansion in higher education and excessive spending on private tutoring as preparation for college entrance exams

Up until the beginning of the 1970s, South Korea's university entrance rate was similar to that of other Asian countries (Lee, 2008b, p. 27). According to S.-J. Lee's study (Lee, 2008b, p. 27), the period from 1945 to 1980 is divided into three terms; the term of 'let-alone' (1945–60); a term of repression of the maximum number (1961–72); and the term of partial expansion of the maximum number (1973–80).

The beginning of a mild expansion was found in the early 1970s, as the effects of the abolition of the middle school entrance examination and the beginning of the High School Equalization Policy became apparent. New problems stemming from this transition, however, included that the national college entrance examination was subject to a new level of competitiveness, especially for admission to top-ranked universities. There was also the economic burden of expenditure on private tutoring services for the examination.

'Education Fever' was manifested in Korean parents' desire to spend additional money on the private tutoring services for their children, which was expected to give them added advantages over students who did not use

Table 11.5 Growth of higher education

Year	Number of Schools	Number of Students	Number of Professors
1945	19	7819	1490
1950	55	11,358	1100
1955	74	84,996	2626
1960	80	81,519	4027
1965	157	142,629	5351
1970	168	201,436	10,270
1975	205	318,683	13,819
1980	237	647,505	20,662
1985	262	1,451,297	33,483
1990	265	1,691,681	42,911
1995	327	2,343,894	58,977
2000	372	3,363,549	57,632
2005	419	3,548,728	66,862
2008	405	3,562,844	73,072

Source: Ministry of Education, Science, and Technology, Korean Educational Development Institute (2008). *Educational Statistics Analysis Handbook*; Kim, Jong-Cheol (1979). *Research on Korea's Higher Education*. Seoul: Baeyoungsa (reused in Kim, 2008a).

private tutoring services in preparing for the national college entrance exam (Lee and Shouse, 2011). 'Education Fever' is a well-known Korean parental zeal for providing children with better educational opportunities (Lee and Shouse, 2008). In fact, as Soojeong Lee (2006) argued, Korean parents' 'Education Fever' is not a parental aspiration for simply providing their children with educational opportunities, but for providing their children with admission into top-ranked schools because actual educational opportunities for colleges or universities are not limited for high school graduates. It is also evidenced by the fact that more than 60 per cent of vocational high school students aimed to enter academic colleges (Lee, 2006, pp. 26–7).

The problem is the fact that the national college entrance examinations, like the College Scholastic Ability Test (CSAT), were used to rank universities according to the scores of the students which they admitted, and thus the competition for admission into the top-ranked universities made Korean parents willing to endure any amount of suffering in order to provide their children with private tutoring in preparation for the national college entrance exam (Lee, 2006, p. 1). Table 11.6 shows Korean students' participation rate in private tutoring services and parents' average monthly expenditures. These excessive expenditures and reliance on private tutoring services has left the public education system dysfunctional in many ways. Therefore, the government has constantly tried to enhance the function of public education by reducing the expenditure and reliance on private tutoring. For example, the government even banned private tutoring in 1980 as a part of the '7·15 College Admission Reform'. However, the government gradually retreated from this position and ultimately dropped the ban entirely when a 2000 court decision found that the ban was an infringement of human rights. It is notable, however, that even the ban on private tutoring did not stop students taking private lessons due to the endemic nature of 'Education Fever' in Korea. As we can see in Table 11.6, Korean parents' excessive spending on private tutoring services for their children's admission into high-ranked colleges and universities has been a serious and ongoing problem for the government.

Reform of the College Admissions System

From the time of national liberation in 1945 through to the present, the Korean college admissions system has been reformed more than 16 times. The many changes in this relatively brief period have been brought about for a number of complex reasons.

Most importantly, as previously mentioned, college admission in Korea is a very complex matter related to profound socio-psychological and cultural factors such as the 'Education Fever' and its intricate social structure (O, O-W., 2000; Seth, 2002). Distinctive to this country's system is, as Lee and Shouse (2011, pp. 213–14) pointed out, the manner in which most Korean high school students compete aggressively in order to be admitted to prestigious colleges and universities. According to them, Korean parents' zeal for providing their children with better educational opportunities is actually a parental aspiration for their children's admission to a few top-ranked universities and colleges (Lee and Shouse, 2008, p. 115; 2011, pp. 213–14). Such fierce competition among almost all high school students for the admission to the select few positions has caused a range of problems for Korean society. Among these were Korean parents' excessive expenditure on private tutoring services and the distortion of curricula, evolving into common practice in high schools throughout the nation. Therefore, the matter of college admission has been among the most sensitive issues for the country's policy makers and the general public. For these reasons the South Korean government has been under great political pressure to solve its problems once and for all. That is why the college admissions system has been constantly revised in an attempt to make it work (Joo, 2000; Lee, 2009; Lee and Shouse, 2008, 2011)

Table 11.6 Average monthly private tutoring expenditures per student and participation rate

Division	2007	2008	Fluctuation Compare to previous year	2009	Fluctuation Compare to previous year	2010	Fluctuation Compare to previous year	2011	Fluctuation Compare to previous year
Expenditure (10,000KRW, %)	22.2	23.3	5.0	24.2	3.9	24.0	-0.8	24.0	0.0
Elementary	22.7	24.2	6.6	24.5	1.2	24.5	0.0	24.1	-1.6
Middle	23.4	24.1	3.0	26.0	7.9	25.5	-1.9	26.2	2.7
High	19.7	20.6	4.6	21.7	5.3	21.8	0.5	21.8	0.0
General High School	24.0	24.9	3.8	26.9	8.0	26.5	-1.5	25.9	-2.3
Participation Rate (%,%p)	77.0	75.1	-1.9	75.0	-0.1	73.6	-1.4	71.7	-1.9
Elementary	88.8	87.9	-0.9	87.4	-0.5	86.8	-0.6	84.6	-2.2
Middle	74.6	72.5	-2.1	74.3	1.8	72.2	-2.1	71.0	-1.2
High	55.0	53.4	-1.6	53.8	0.4	52.8	-1.0	51.6	-1.2
General High School High	62.0	60.5	-1.5	62.8	2.3	61.1	-1.7	58.7	-2.4

Source: Stastics Korea (2011). 2011년 사교육비 조사 보고서 [*The Survey of Private Tutoring Expenditure 2011*]. Korea: Stastics Korea, pp. 18–19.

Note: Private tutoring expenditure includes total expenditures for a range of after-school academic activities, such as individual or group tutoring, instruction from for-profit *Hakwon*, self-study or practice exam sheets, internet tutoring and after-class lessons within regular public schools.

The Korean college admission system that has gone through revision a number of times, but the major changes since 1945 can be classified in a series of stages according to major criteria used for selection decision, as described in Table 11.7 (Kim, 2008a, pp. 48–50).

During the first stage, which lasted from 1945 to 1953, each university selected its own students by administering separate exams. In 1954, the government required applicants to take the 'national general university admission exam' in addition to the separate exams organized by each university and college. The government insisted that universities incorporate these scores into their decision-making process in order to ensure that all qualified students would be admitted. This began to change the college admissions' landscape.

During the third stage, which lasted from 1955 to 1961, the two-exam requirement was abolished and the system of using separate examinations by each university was readopted. This was because of issues such as the burden on students of taking two separate exams as well as the loss of educational opportunities for applicants who failed the national exam.

The fourth stage took place from 1962 to 1963. Since the system of using separate exams by each university caused problems, including the unfair admission of incapable applicants, the government began to require each college and university to use the new 'national exam for university admission qualification' as a selection criterion in the admission process. Under this policy, the number of applicants who passed the national exam was set at 110 per cent of the university population, while a 'national exam for graduation' was also administered to control the quality of graduates.

However, criticism arose that requiring a national exam restricted the freedom of colleges and universities. Therefore, from 1964 to 1968, the system of using separate exams by each university was once again adopted.

Yet the system of using separate exams by each university still caused problems such as excessive acceptance of unqualified students, unfair rejection of students and an overall inefficiency in managing the student population. As a result of these and other factors, in 1969 the government introduced the nationally-administered 'preparatory exam for university admission' in conjunction with separate exams by the universities, a system which remained in place until 1980. Initially, the preparatory exam was supposed to be a qualification exam, but later became utilized as more of a selection mechanism. The separate main exams of a few top-ranked colleges and universities were so difficult and competitive that they caused new problems. These included high schools distorting their curricula in order to help students prepare for these extreme tests, and students' excessive reliance on private tutoring again, with their parents paying exorbitant fees for such services.

The seventh stage occurred in 1981. In the period of 'the reform of July 30, 1980', the system of separate exams was abolished, and instead, both the preparatory exam for university admission as well as high school records were used as admission criteria for university entrance.

Next, however, this preparatory exam for university admission, with its nature as a licensing exam, was replaced by the 'college entrance exam', which was similar to a scholastic aptitude test, a system which prevailed during the period from 1982 to 1985.

In the next stage, an essay exam was incorporated, so that universities could better evaluate each applicant's high-level thinking abilities within the exam. From 1986 to 1987, applicants were allowed to include an essay along with their other application materials. Therefore, the three main factors considered for admission at this time were the 'college entrance exam', the high school record (GPA) and an essay exam by each university. The essay exam had to be taken at the university to which students applied.

In the years from 1988 to 1993, however, the essay exam was abolished and replaced by an interview, and thus the three criteria which now applied in relation to gaining admission to a university were the college entrance exam, the high school record (GPA) and the interview.

Yet some argued that an applicant's mental aptitude could not be measured by the college entrance exam. As this view took hold, from 1994 through 1996, the college entrance exam was changed into College Scholastic Ability Test (CSAT) and the interview was once again replaced by a separate exam by each university. Therefore, the three criteria of CSAT, the high school record (GPA) and the separate exam conducted by each university were used as selection materials for admission.

Since 'the reform of May 31, 1995', supported by the growing consensus that admission should be independently determined by each university, the government has gradually tried to give colleges and universities control over the admission process. This power includes the choice of screening materials and admission periods. This new direction has been manifested in two major reforms, known as 'The Reform Measures for the 2002 University Admission System' and 'The Reform Measures for the 2008 University Admission System'. As a result of the former, colleges and universities were given complete control over their own admissions policies. However, the government applied the 'three no's' policy. This rule forbids colleges from using the 'separate exams by university' system, emphasizing the Korean language, English, or maths; manipulating the high school rating system; or participating in a system of admission-by-contribution.

The 2008 reform built on the changes made in 2002. With the introduction of the 'Admission Officer System' since 2008, the government has made an effort to have colleges and universities voluntarily choose the admission policy best suited to their unique needs, as well promoting liberalization in college admission. The government has begun to encourage colleges and universities to apply the Admission Officer System to their admission process by allocating portions of the public budget to the endeavour. The Admission Officer System is also designed to use several additional criteria to evaluate applicants' potential and abilities (apart from exam scores such as the CSAT score and GPA score) in the admission procedure. Table 11.7 presents a summary of the changes since 1945

Major Issues in the Reforms

The were two main goals underlying the above reforms: a) to assure fairness throughout the college admission process, and b) to reduce the degree of competition among high school students preparing for the college entrance exam.

Fairness and equity in the college admission system

In the first stage of reforms, the government started officially to regulate the college admission process. The foremost purpose was to prevent colleges and universities from granting admission to unqualified students, and thus ensure 'fairness' and 'equity' in university admissions. As a major strategy, the government required all universities and colleges to strictly apply the nationally administered university entrance examination to their admission process. The government even instituted the Reform of 30 July 1980, abolishing separate exams by universities, which had previously fostered problems such as unfair admission, excessive acceptance of borderline applicants and the inclusion of incapable students. As a result, fairness and equity in university admission was considered to have been achieved for a short period. The national exam also proved to be a means to help solve, at least to some degree, the problem of corruption in college admissions (Lee, 2009).

Table 11.7 College admission system overview since 1945

Periods	Major Criteria for College Admission
1945–53	Separate exams by each university
1954	National general university admission exam and separate exams by each university
1955–61	Separate exams by each university
1962–63	National exam for university admission qualification
1964–68	Separate exams by each university
1969–80	Preparatory exam for university admission and separate main exams by each university
1981	Preparatory exam for university admission and high school record (GPA)
1982–85	College entrance exam and high school record (GPA)
1986–87	Three criteria: college entrance exam, high school record (GPA) and essay exam by each university
1988–93	College entrance exam, high school record (GPA) and interview
1994–96	College Scholastic Ability Test (CSAT), high school record (GPA) and separate exams by university
1997–onwards	Selecting methods decided by each university and introduction of Admission Officer System

Source: Kim, Y.-C. (2008a), pp.48–50 (rearranged).

Yet at the same time, several problems in other aspect of higher education began to rise to the surface, and grow to become ever more serious.

Reducing intense competition for the college entrance exam

Since a student's score in the national college entrance exam played such a critical role in the university admissions process, it profoundly influenced the course of high school education (Lee, 2003, pp. 31–2). That is, high school teachers started to focus their classes on how to prepare their students well for the national university entrance exam. The competition among students for getting ever higher scores in the national college entrance exam has grown increasingly intense. Since then, the following issues caused by the above phenomenon have been considered major problems that the Korean government should solve regarding its public education system.

First, because of this robust competition among high school students, high school students generally spend too many hours preparing for the national university entrance exam, sometimes even every day of their high school career. Therefore, it has been pointed out that requiring this test is actually stifling to the adolescents' normal mental and physical development (Kim, 1991).

Second, high school education in Korea has been criticized as being too focused on the knowledge-centred learning necessary for preparing for the national college entrance exam and not sufficiently concerned with the classical concept of 'education for the whole man'. Generally, this phenomenon has been referred to by Lee (2003, p. 27) as 'examination hell', as well as considered in the wider regional context by Zeng (1999). In particular, it has been pointed out that such knowledge-centred education was in fact caused by the initiation of the national college entrance exam as an evaluation method (Joo, 2000). While the government applied the relative evaluation method centred on multiple choice tests to the national college entrance exam in order to develop transparency and objectivity in university admission, the result of this decision is that students in high school spend more time learning how to do well on multiple choice tests than they do on 'learning how to learn', or acquiring further general knowledge on their own.

Third, according to many educators and scholars, Korean students' severe reliance on private tutoring services resulted from the bitter competition among them in preparation for the college entrance exam (Joo, 2000). A distinctive pattern that has been demonstrated by several studies is that most Korean students used private tutoring services, regardless of their achievement levels and of the quality of their schools (Lee and Shouse, 2007). As Lee and Shouse (2011) revealed, students who use private tutoring services do so because of the ruthless competition among those who wish to be admitted to a few top-ranked universities or colleges.

As a consequence, the Korean government, with the aim of eliminating the root cause of the aforementioned problems, has tried to reduce the fierce competition among high school students in their preparation for the college entrance exam. As a major policy initiative, the government has chosen to reform the national college admission system. In order to reduce the competition among students for getting better scores in the university entrance exam and parents' spending on private tutoring services for their children, and to normalize middle and especially high school education, several reforms have focused on which criteria are weighted for evaluation and how they should be applied to the university admission decision (Lee, 2011). The major issues arising are described below.

The reduced weight of the college entrance exam score and increased weight of the high school GPA

A major direction of the reforms in national university admission policy in recent years is to give a one-time decisive factor, such as the national college entrance exam and the College Scholastic Ability Test (CSAT) score, less weight in the evaluation process for an admission decision, and to give a long-term decisive factor, such as the high school GPA, increased weight. The government intention with this modification was to mitigate the intensity of students' competition in preparation for the entrance exam, as well as to normalize high school education by reducing the weight of the CSAT score as the criteria for evaluation in the university admission process. In particular, the aforementioned two big reforms regarding the national university admission system implemented since 2000, those in 2002 and 2008, were designed to decrease the weight of the CSAT score as the primary criterion for evaluation in the university admission process.

Diversifying the criteria for evaluation and ways of admission process

Another major direction of the reforms is to require universities to use several diverse criteria in the admission process so that they may evaluate high school graduates' varied aptitudes and abilities, creativity and potential, in addition to their scores in academic subjects. For this aspect of the admission assessment, the government judged that the method of subjective and qualitative evaluation needs to be applied to the national university admission system (Lee, 2011). And thus the government intended to diversify the 'criteria for evaluation'; the 'ways of admission process'; and 'times for applying' (screening periods) as announced in the two reform proposals of 2002 and 2008.

For example, the government has suggested that universities and colleges apply actively diverse methods of 'special admission' in their admission system. While CSAT scores and high school GPA are considered as the important criteria for screening in 'general admission', the entrance opportunities made available by way of 'special admission' would supposedly consider a few diverse yet important screening materials, such as a high school principal's recommendation, an essay exam and an interview or test conducted by the university.

Liberalization of college admission and introduction of the Admission Officer System

Arguably the most significant changes in the Korean college admission system might be the reforms for liberalization of the process and the introduction of the Admission Officer System. Liberalization of the college admission system was first announced in the 2002 reform. The core of this policy was to cede the government's controlling power in college admissions, so that various institutions would be given the liberty to choose their students freely without official intervention from the authorities. The reform movement liberalizing the college admission system, as one of the key efforts for college autonomy, was materially enhanced when the Lee Myung-Bak administration announced plans for the 'Three-stage Liberalization of the College Admission System'. In recent years the government has started to lend support to its stated goals by supplying some funds to universities and colleges that have introduced this Admissions Officer System to their admission process (Lee, 2009).

The major purpose of the introduction of the Admissions Officer System was to make universities and colleges use other diverse criteria to evaluate applicants' potential and abilities in addition to exam scores such as the CSAT score and GPA score in their admission process, in order to mitigate students' competition in preparation for the entrance exam and also to normalize high school education. Therefore, admission officers evaluate high school graduates' diverse aptitudes, abilities, creativity and potential using diverse criteria such as each student's personal portfolio, teachers' records about each student's school life, and an in-depth interview, without undue emphasis on achievement in CSAT and high school GPA scores. So the system rejects the idea of selecting students uniformly according to their test results, but supports the idea of choosing students by utilizing a holistic evaluation system that considers students' abilities, talents and potential through submitted documents such as a detailed three-year school record (including attendance, teachers' comments, books read, extra-curricular activities, grades, voluntary services and other information), personal essay, recommendations, along with any other relevant material. The implementation of the Admission Officer System is expected to strengthen, and in some cases revitalize, the high school education available to students. The expectation is that it will encourage teachers to provide a broader-based education rather than simply teaching toward one important admissions test. At the same time, it is anticipated that the reform will help alleviate the parents' burden of paying for private tutoring by excluding from consideration evaluation materials that are usually the result of private tutoring, such as TOEFL (Test of English as a Foreign Language) scores, TEPS (Test of English Proficiency) scores, volunteer work abroad, and so forth (Lee, 2009; KCUE/ EBS, 2012).

The current government, the administration of Lee Myung-Bak, has been strongly supportive of the Admissions Officer System. To this end the system has been reinforced by laws that have been newly implemented as of 26 January 2012. In addition, portions of the public budget have been allocated toward operating the new system (Ministry of Government Legislation, Higher Education Law, 2012). This year has been the fifth year for the government to support the Admissions Officer System since its official launch in 2008. The system has been taking hold in many universities, including the most prestigious schools throughout Korea, commencing with ten universities in 2007 and rising to 125 universities in 2012. This brings the intake to 46,337 students from among a total of 377,958 students for four-year universities, an increase of 7,406 students from the previous year (KCUE, 2012b). Notably, Seoul National University has now used the system for six years in a row since 2007, and this year it will select 79.4 per cent of its freshman students in this manner (Hankyung.com, accessed on 25 June 2012).

Table 11.8 Admissions Officer System in Korea

	2007	2008	2009	2010	2011	2012
Government Budget to support the System (currency in KRW)	2 billion	15.7 billion	23.6 billion	35 billion	35.1 billion	39.1 billion
Number of four-year Universities being supported by the Government within the Budget above	10	40	47	60	60	66
Number of universities using the System* (among 200 four-year universities)	10	41	90	118	121	125
Number of students (among four-year universities) selected through the System**	Not available	Not available	Not available	32,916	38,931	46,337

Source 1: KCUE (2012a). *Admissions Officer System Operation Support Project Administrative Training 2012.* Seoul: KCUE.
*Source 2: Admissions Officer System homepage. http://uao.kcue.or.kr/info/status.jsp (30 June 2012).
**Source 3: KCUE (2012b). *2013 School Year Early Decision Application Guideline Essential Particulars.* Seoul: KCUE.

Evaluation of Reforms

As mentioned previously, the major purpose of the reform of the college admission system since the 1990s, and most especially in the last several years, has been to reduce the intense competition among students preparing for the national college entrance exam and to normalize high school education.

Regarding the results of these recent reforms, however, there are already both positive and negative viewpoints emerging. Because of the recent nature of the changes, there is not yet sufficient empirical evidence to demonstrate whether there has been success in achieving either the goal of reducing the intense competition for college entrance via diminishing students' dramatic use of private tutoring services, or in normalizing high school education throughout the country.

Thus far most studies that have presented positive outcomes relating to recent reform of the college admission system have only evaluated opinions about policy directions and intentions as well as overall perceptions of the changes, primarily by people related to the system. According to the report presented by the Korean Education Development Institute (KEDI, 2010b), for example, it was revealed that most staff members of the admissions office in colleges and universities, including the admission officers, positively evaluated the purpose and meaning of the Admission Officer System reform aiming at normalizing high school education by comprehensively evaluating students by criteria that did not include test scores.

There are just a few research studies, such as a report by Chae et al. (2010) and Soojeong Lee's (2011) study, that substantially examine the effects of these reform policies on the normalization of high school education or the competition among students. Soojeong Lee's study, which longitudinally analyzes the reform of the college admission system since 2000, proves that those recent reforms were effective in reducing students' reliance on private tutoring services. It shows that high school students under the 2008 college admission system, where diverse criteria including high school GPA were given more weight compared to the CSAT score in the university admission process, used fewer private tutoring services than those under the previous system.

Conclusion

Since fairness and equity in university admission have been realized for a short period, the Korean government has kept reforming the college admission system for the purpose of reducing the intense competition among students preparing for the college entrance exam and limiting parental expenditure on private tutoring for exam preparation.

As Lee and Shouse (2011) explained, however, it is not such a simple matter to relieve the extreme competition among students to be admitted to a few prestigious top-ranked colleges or universities because the competition is very intricately connected with the complex matters of the entire social structure and culture, as well as the public education system. Therefore, it would not be possible by making changes only to the college admission system to solve the many other problems regarding the obsession of Korean parents for engaging in dramatic expenditure on private tutoring services for their children as they prepare for exams like the CSAT.

Another consideration to keep in mind is that it might, in any case, not be the right thing to do. The policy of college admission reform needs to be assessed in relation primarily to other values such as assuring 'equal opportunity' and selecting 'qualified students' for college education (Lee, 2009, 2011). Is it reasonable to expect a legislative reform that overhauls the college admission system to also be responsible for fundamentally altering long-standing trends and deeply ingrained cultural patterns without a broader change in social mores and perspectives? On the other hand, as Michael Seth (2002) mentioned, Koreans' distinctive 'Education Fever' might still be the greatest single asset in facing the upcoming challenges for the country.

At this time, the Korean government needs to do more to evaluate the effects of the reform of the college admission system discussed above. In other words, further studies are necessary to examine whether these reforms have indeed had a profound effect in reducing intense competition among students for university entrance opportunities and humanizing the high school experience.

Depending on the findings of such recommended studies, the government may be faced with a new, even greater, set of challenges. The government is necessarily the political deliverer of formal education, but it does not, and cannot, determine the culture in which education is embedded in all societies, differentially. Furthermore, cultures are dynamic, as shown in the previous chapter with regard to increasing multiculturalism in Korea. So the

problem on which this chapter is focused will continue to change in the future and will require ongoing vigilance on the part of successive governments. They may be assisted in meeting the challenge by encouraging international and comparative studies of university admission and financing procedures in other countries.

References

Asiatoday.co.kr (2011). 강원도교육청, *2013년부터 춘천.원주.강릉 '고교평준화'* 된다. [*Gangwon Province Office of Education: Chuncheon.Wonju.Gangneung adopting the High School Equalization policy from 2013*]. http://www.asiatoday.co.kr/news/view. asp?seq=577169 (Accessed 23 June 2012).

Admissions Officer System homepage. http://uao.kcue.or.kr/info/status.jsp (Korean) (Accessed 30 June 2012).

Gang, Seong-Guk (2005). *Analysis on Educational Index of 60 Years of Korean Education Growth.* Seoul: KEDI (reused in Lee, 2008a, p. 38.) (Korean).

Chae, C. G., Yu, H. G., Rhu, J. Y. and Lee, S. J. (2010). *Impact of Reforms of College Admissions System on Expenditures on Private Tutoring Services. A Study of Education and Human Resource Department and Korean Educational Development Institute.* Seoul: Ministry of Education, Science and Technology.

GPOE (Gyeonggi Province Office of Education) (2010). 경기도 고교 입시제도 개선을 위한 고교 평준화 실시 지역 추가 지정 계획. [*Plan of Expansion of the High School Equalization Policy in Kyeonggi Province for an Improvement on High School Entrance Examination*]. Korea: GPOE. http://www.google.co.kr/url?sa=t&rct =j&q=&esrc=s&source=web&cd=6&ved=0CEIQFjAF&url=http%3A%2F%2F cfile230.uf.daum.net%2Fattach%2F1734F0394D3CE7721399FA&ei=T8fuT8gL 1IytAZzr7I4C&usg=AFQjCNHwuJDftch1E4vOQBBwgeysJ4upSA&sig2=wtfy6l hN__j-Oqneylq9Dw

Hankyung.com. (2012). 서울대, 입학사정관제 *80%* 선발. [*Seoul National University, Admissions Officer System 80% Selecting Students*]. http://www.hankyung.com/news/ app/newsview.php?aid=2012062109151 (Accessed 25 June 2012).

Jeong, J. S. (2010). 대학서열체제와 그 해소방안, 역사비평 *2010년* 가을호, ['Hierarchical System of Universities and Measures of Its Resolution']. *Yuksabipyung, 2010, Fall):* 135–40.

Joo, C. A. (2000). 'The Entrance Examination System', in J. C. Weidman and N. Park (eds), *Higher Education in Korea.* New York: Falmer Press, pp. 89–107.

Kang, S. J. (2005). 'High School Equalization Policy in Korea'. *International Conference on 60 Years of Korean Education: achievements and challenges.* Seoul: KEDI, pp. 169–95.

KBMaeil. (2012). 대입 수시지원 최대 *6회...* 수시합격자 추가지원 못해. [*Maximum 6 Opportunities for Nonscheduled Admission... No more chances after 6 tries*]. http:// www.kbmaeil.com/news/articleView.html?idxno=257804 (Accessed 25 June 2012).

KCUE (Korean Council for University Education) (2012a). *2012년* 입학사정관제 운영지원사업 행정연수 [*Admissions Officer System Operation Support Project Administrative Training 2012*]. Seoul: KCUE.

—(2012b). 2013학년도 수시모집요강 주요사항 [*2013 School Year Early Decision Application Guideline Essential Particulars*]. Seoul: KCUE.

KCUE/EBS (2012). *2012 EBS-*대교협 학교방문 대입정보 설명회 [*2012 EBS-KCUE School Visit University Entrance Information Session*]. Seoul: KCUE/EBS, p. 87.

KEDI (2005) *International Conference on 60 years of Korean Education: achievements and challenges*. Seoul: KEDI.

—(2010a). 대한민국 교육정책: 과거·현재·미래 – 5·31 교육개혁 평가와 미래교육의 비전·전략 [*The Education Policy of Republic of Korea: The Evaluation of the 5·31 Educational Reformation and Vision and Strategy for future education*]. Seoul: KEDI.

—(2010b). *A study on development of outcome model for admissions officer system and improvement policy*. RR 2010-21-2. Seoul: KEDI.

—(2011). *2011 교육통계 자료집* [*Data of educational statistics 2011*]. Seoul: KEDI.

KFTA. (2008). 대입 자율화 방안의 쟁점 및 대안 [*The Issue and Alternative of the Liberalization of University Entrance*]. Seoul: KFTA (Korean Federation of Teachers Association).

Kim, A. N. and Lee, B. S. (2004). 한국 고등학교의 보편화에 따른 대학 재구조화의 현황과 정책방향 ['Restructuring of Higher Education Institutions: A Survey of Institutional Progresses and Policy Directions']. *Journal of Korean Education*.

Kim, Ki Su (1991). 'A Statist Political Economy and High Demand for Education in South Korea'. *Education Policy Analysis Archives*, 7 (19): 1–25.

Kim, S. T. (2010). 한국거버넌스학회보 *17권* 제*1*호. 입학사정관제도와 사교육의 연관성에 관한 소고 [*The Continuity between Admission Officer System and Private Education*]. Seoul: Korea Association for Governance (KAG).

Kim, Y. (2004). 한국의 교육과 경제 발전: *1945–1995* [*Education and Economic Development in Korea: 1945–1995*]. Paju: Korean Studies Information Company.

Kim, Y.-C. (2008a). *Understanding Korean Educational Policy Vol. II: Universalization of Tertiary Education*. Seoul: KEDI.

—(2008b). 고등교육의 보편화 [*Universalization of Tertiary Education*]. Seoul: KEDI.

Kim, Y. G. (2008). 입학사정관제도의 운영상 문제점 및 발전방안 ['The Operational Problem of Admission Officer and Improvement Plan']. *Journal of Korean Educational Forum*.

Lee, D. (2002). 해방후 *1950*년대의 경제 [*1950s Economy After Liberation*] Seoul: Samsung Economic Research Institute.

Lee, Ki-Bong. (2003). *The Best of Intentions: Meritocratic Selection to Higher Education and the Development of Shadow Education in Korea*. Doctoral dissertation, Pennsylvania State University.

Lee, Sang-Jin (2008a). *Understanding Korean Educational Policy Vol. I: National Development Strateg and Education policy*. Seoul: KEDI, p. 29.

—(2008b). 국가발전전략과 교육정책 [*National Development Strategy and Education policy*]. Seoul: KEDI.

Lee, Soojeong (2006). *Prestige-oriented view of college entrance and shadow education in South Korea: Factors influencing parent expenditures on private tutoring*. Unpublished doctoral dissertation, Pennsylvania State University.

—(2007). 명문대 중심 대입관과 사교육비 지출간의 관계 분석: 사교육 원인에 대한 사회심리적 접근 *Vol. 25, No. 4* ['The Analysis about the relationship between a Major University Entrance Perspective and Expenditure of Private Education: Social

Psychological Approach about Cause of Private Education']. *Journal of Educational Administration*, 25, 4: 455–84.

—(2009). *A Study on the Relationship of Criteria for College-Admission Decision and Normalization of School Education*. A paper presented at the 2009 Korean Comparative Education Studies (KCES) Annual Conference. Korea: Seoul.

—(2011). 'A Study on the Impact of Changes of College-admission Policy on Korean High-school Students' Use of Private Tutoring Services'. *Journal of Economics and Finance of Education*, 20, 1, March: 121–41.

Lee, Soojeong and Shouse, R. C. (2007). *Does 'Low-Quality' Schooling Cause Students' Reliance on Private Tutoring?: Prestige-Orientation in the Korean K-12 education*. 2007 American Educational Research Association (AERA) Annual Meeting, Chicago, April.

—(2008). 'Is education fever treatable? Case studies of first-year Korean students in an American university'. *KEDI Journal of Educational Policy (KJEP)*, 5, 2: 113–32.

—(2011). 'The Impact of Prestige Orientation on Shadow Education in South Korea'. *Sociology of Education*, 84, 3: 212–24.

Mason, E. S., Kim, M. J., Perkins, D. H., Kim, K. S. and Kim, Q. (1980). *The Economic and Social Modernization of the Republic of Korea*. London: Harvard University Press.

Ministry of Education and Human Resources Development (1998). *The Reform Measures for the 2002 University Admission System*. Seoul: MEST.

—(2004). *The Reform Measures for the 2008 University Admission System for Normalizing Schooling*. Seoul: MEST.

MEST (Ministry of Education, Science, and Technology) (2012). *Education System –Overview*. http://english.mest.go.kr/web/1693/site/contents/en/en_0203.jsp (Accessed 28 July 2012).

Ministry of Government Legislation (2012). 고등교육법 제34조2-3(입학사정관 등) (입학사정관의 취업 등 제한) [*Higher Education Act 2nd and 3rd of 32th (about Admission Officer System, Limitation of Admission Officer System)*]. http://www.law.go.kr/LSW/lsEfInfoP.do?lsiSeq=122381#0000 (25 June 2012).

O, O. W. (2000). *Education Fever of Korean Society*. Seoul: Kyoyukgwahaksa.

OECD (2010a). 'Tertiary education entry rates', *Education: Key Tables from OECD*, No. 2. doi: 10.1787/20755120-2010-table2. (June 18, 2012).

—(2010b). 'Tertiary education graduation rates', *Education: Key Tables from OECD*, No. 1. doi: 10.1787/20755120-2010-table1 (June 18, 2012).

President Transition Team 17th (2008). 대입 3단계 자율화 방안 [*The Three Steps Plan for Liberalization of University Entrance*]. Seoul: 17th President Transition Team.

Seth, M. J. (2002). *Education Fever: Society, Politics, and the Pursuit of Schooling in South Korea*. Honolulu: University of Hawaii.

Special Project Team of National Administration Briefing (2007). 대한민국 교육 40년. [*40 Year History of Korea Education*]. Seoul: Hanmedia.

Stastics Korea (2011). *2011 년 사교육비 조사 보고서* [*The Survey of Private Education Expenditure 2011*]. Seoul: Stastics Korea.

Zeng, K. (1999). *Dragon Gate: Competitive Examinations and their Consequences*. London: Cassell.

12

Taiwan: Trends and Agendas in Education Reform

Hsiao-Lan Sharon Chen

Introduction

Education reform is a social enterprise and a political process. It is not value-free but carries ideological assumptions of 'educational vision' influenced by politics, economics, culture and philosophy. In most cases, education reform policies are shaped and negotiated through the exercise of power in which political, social and educational issues are closely intertwined. Situated in a rapid transforming society, and confronted with the development of new social order and political ecology, the educational development in Taiwan, a small island-nation with remarkable economic growth, is a particularly complex and crucial undertaking in which the education reform efforts are worthy of exploration and analysis.

Due to remarkable economic development and political modernization, education in Taiwan, being intertwined with the complexities of a transforming society, has encountered dramatic changes throughout the years. Especially, in the past two decades, there have been numerous grass-roots movements active in Taiwan, advocating education reforms and school innovations. Based on the related analyses, the struggles for democratization, liberalization, internationalization, localization and the pursuit of 'national' identity are reflected by the various controversies/dilemmas of Taiwan's education reforms (Kwok, 2010; Law, 2002; Tu, 2007; Yang, 2001). To help grasp the overall picture of how Taiwan's education reforms came into being during a period of democratic transition, this chapter introduces the social and educational context of Taiwan, the major education reform policies concerning primary and secondary education since 1988 (after the cessation of martial law), and the driving forces of education reforms. To avoid being read like propaganda, this chapter also reflects the trends and agendas of education reforms in Taiwan to highlight the critical issues of, and necessary considerations for, educational change.

Social and Educational Context of Taiwan

Located in eastern Asia and the western Pacific, Taiwan is an island with only 36,000 square kilometres of land but 23 million people living on it. Less than 2 per cent of the population are indigenous peoples from 14 different aboriginal tribes, but over 98 per cent are Han Chinese, the descendants of immigrants from the various provinces of mainland China, including the early immigrants (since the seventeenth century) who are often referred to as 'Taiwanese' (70 per cent Holo and 15 per cent Hakka), and immigrants who moved to Taiwan with the Republic of China (ROC) government in 1949, generally referred to as 'mainlanders' (13 per cent). As a new culture indigenous to Taiwan has been gradually emerging, Taiwan's indigenous people, the early Holo and Hakka immigrants, and the recent immigrant 'mainlanders', have all played a role in Taiwan's development. Although lacking an internationally recognized legal status as a nation, Taiwan has achieved worldwide noteworthy economic and socio-political transformation. In search for her own cultural identify and striving for global competitiveness through education, Taiwan has been continuously confronted with the challenges brought by the trends of internationalization and problems caused by her historical fate (Yang, 2001). To appreciate better the relationship of education reforms and the social transformation in Taiwan, it is necessary to briefly review how Taiwan's transitional past and present form the perspective of education.

Historical tracks

Taiwan had a long history of colonization, having been ruled a) by the Dutch (1624–62); then b) China (1662–1894), – Cheng Cheng-kung, a general of the Ming dynasty, ousted the Dutch and established a Han Chinese political administration in 1662, then in 1683 conquered by the Ch'ing dynasty; then c) Japan (1894–1945), – ceded to Japan as the Ch'ing government was defeated in the Sino-Japanese war. At the end of World War Two, after 50 years of Japanese colonial rule, Taiwan was returned to the ROC in 1945 under the leadership of the Kuomintang (KMT). In September 1945, the National Meeting of Post-war Education was held and strategies of decolonization were aimed at removing

Japanese cultural influences and promoting 'education for nationalism'. Not only was 'Chinese culture education' emphasized, but also Mandarin Chinese became the official language. The use of Japanese and Taiwanese dialects in schools and the media was prohibited.

In 1949, the KMT-ruling ROC government moved its site to Taiwan after their defeat in the civil war on the Chinese mainland (which is now ruled by the Chinese Communist Party under the country name of the People's Republic of China or PRC) and began to consolidate its centralized power of the party-state and to maintain the dominance of mainlanders over Taiwanese. To keep its political stand and national security, and to continue its Sino-centric hegemonic governance, the KMT declared the rule of martial law. Under the KMT one-party rule, which lasted for about four decades, political opposition was suppressed, academic freedom was hindered and a unified version of textbooks was instituted. Meanwhile, with a view to promoting economic development, efficiency-based economic rationalism and competency-based education were emphasized in education policy. As the economy grew, the education system in Taiwan also advanced considerably so that compulsory education was extended from six years to nine years in 1968, and the number of schools and student enrolment at all levels continued to increase.

Due to economic growth, political stability and a succession of movements staged to pursue democracy, martial law was lifted in 1987. Taiwan then launched into being a more democratic and open society. Democratization, pluralism and liberalization have hence become the core values, and been sought after in every social sphere (Yang, 2001). Political transformation resulted in the springing up of new social groups. The Democratic Progressive Party (DPP) gained its legal status and became the major competitor to the KMT. In cultural development, besides traditional Chinese culture and Western culture being reflected in various perspectives of Taiwanese society, a movement toward valuing the indigenous elements in Taiwanese culture became prevalent. In educational praxis, triggered by the democratization, the liberation of individuals as well as the educational system, and the diversification of curriculum content, were the core issues that education reform has been trying to address to meet the demands of a changing society (Tu, 2007).

In the 1990s, under pressure from various civil education groups at the grass roots, the bureaucratic Ministry of Education (MOE) was forced to carry out a series of education reforms. As researchers noted (Kwok, 2010; Law, 2002), the year 1994 was a turning point in Taiwanese education. The civil education groups used different strategies to air their views and to strive for their rights of participation in shaping education reform. On 10 April 1994, Taiwan's middle-class citizens organized and staged a mass demonstration demanding education reform. The main appeal of the 10 April Education Reform Alliance was to demand the removal of all unreasonable controls and restraints imposed on education by the authoritarian government. Reformists, by cooperating with legislators from various parties, forced the government to make concessions on the issues of educational reform and legislation. A Cabinet-level Commission of Education Reform (CER) was established in September 1994 as a 'political buffer' (Law, 2002) to review the whole education system and to set the framework for education reform. The CER's *General Advisory Report*, released in 1996, identified not only the major directions for large-scale governmental reform in education, but also priority items to be addressed by educational legislation and administration.

By opening up the polity and society in the late 1980s, and introducing the direct electoral system in the 1990s, Taiwan has established its foundations of democratic civil society and brought forth the peaceful transfer of power between parties, from the KMT to the DPP in 2000 and from the DPP back to the KMT in 2008. The whole society is becoming more democratic, but the electorate is split into two ideological camps. Education reform issues have opened up more political debates and engendered more legitimized public participation or opposition at various levels. Although the CER's manoeuvre initially helped maintain a cross-party consensus on education in Taiwan, and head in a direction of decentralized, deregulated educational decision-making and practices, education reform policy has involved more complex power struggles. Education issues, in particular textbook reform, curriculum reform and the promotion of national identity, have remained as major fault lines between the KMT and the DPP, as well as various pressure groups competing for electoral pay-offs afterward (Kwok, 2010). For better or worse, education in Taiwan is entrapped in a culture of continuous change that is vibrant and difficult to predict in detail and in its consequences.

The current school system in Taiwan

As the above historical tracks show, the education system in Taiwan used to be a highly centralized, top-down system. The MOE played the major role in determining financing, policy and curriculum. After a series of education reforms following the abolition of martial law, the education system is heading in a direction of a bottom-up decision-making approach, encouraging decentralized, site-based management. The current education system basically supports 22 years of academic study, including two years of pre-school education, nine years of compulsory education (including six years of elementary school and three years of junior high school), three years of upper secondary education (students can choose to study at a general senior high school for an academic track or to enter a vocational high school or junior college for a vocational track), four–seven years of college or university programmes (undergraduate programmes basically require four years of study, but some specialized fields such as medicine mostly take six–seven years, including one year of internship), one–four years for a master's degree programme and two–seven years for a doctoral degree programme (depending on students' academic research and performance). In addition to the above-mentioned levels, the MOE also promotes supplementary education (including basic education, advanced education and short-term continuing education) to provide all citizens with opportunities for lifelong learning.

Based on past education reform efforts, the gross enrolment ratio at elementary and junior high schools has remained at more than 97 per cent since the late 1970s, and the illiteracy rate in Taiwan has declined from 12.7 per cent in 1980 to 2.0 per cent in 2010 (MOE, 2012). Also, senior secondary education and higher education were expanded in the 1980s and 1990s so that the number of schools, and student enrolment at all levels, increased dramatically up to over 5.3 million students in 2000–1. However, due to the effects of the falling birth rate in the past decade, the total number of students in 2010–11 dropped to 4.97 million (MOE, 2012). According to the latest 2012 educational statistics, a total of 4.86 million students are receiving education at 8100 education institutions throughout Taiwan (see Table 12.1).

To further enhance educational development in Taiwan, the MOE proposed to extend the length of time for compulsory education from nine to 12 years by school year 2014, along with promotions to raise the standards and quality of teachers. Though pre-school education in Taiwan is not included in the compulsory education system, in order to take care of underprivileged children the MOE has offered free tuition for children living in outlying areas and in indigenous townships since 2010. Currently, the central government is providing subsidy support for private kindergarten students (up to NT$30,000) and free tuition for children that qualify at public kindergartens. Also, a reforming plan is being implemented to help accommodate the effect of the declining birth rate and in support of smaller class sizes (MOE, 2012).

Being aware of the global as well as the domestic challenges that Taiwan has

Table 12.1 Summary of Education at All Levels—SY 2011–2012　Unit: Person

	No. of Schools (school)	No. of Teachers	No. of Classes (class)	No. of Students	No. of Graduates in 2011	Students Per Teacher
Total	8,100	271,480	155,820	4,860,034	1,213,643	26.41
Kindergarten	3,195	14,918	9,335	189,792	–	13.39
Primary School	2,659	98,528	58,008	1,457,004	271,625	19.08
Jr. High School	742	51,188	27,645	873,220	316,904	18.64
Sr. High School	336	36,407	10,119	401,958	128,967	23.43
Sr. Voca. School	155	16,976	8,847	366,449	109,837	29.45
Jr. College	15	1,691	2,356	101,300	20,463	28.94
Uni. & College	150	48,662	32,251	1,250,925	292,758	25.71
Special Edu. Sch.	27	1,829	640	7,014	2,038	3.8
Supp. School	819	1,204	6,286	197,384	67,694	–
Open University	2	77	333	14,988	3,357	–

Source: Department of Statistics, Ministry of Education, 2012.

been facing, such as global competition, repercussions from the digital era, a widening societal economic gap, the growth of local citizen groups, a falling birth rate, an ageing society, and so forth, the civil education groups from the bottom and the Executive *Yuan* from the top all pushed very hard for the MOE to come up with a timely educational development blueprint and action plans to address these concerns.

Driving Forces of Education Reform

Concerning education reform policies, there have been many forces influencing the decisions of the MOE and related authorities in Taiwan. They include legal requirements imposed by legislatures, ethical and political constraints, availability of funding, and expectations and pressures from various interest groups. To highlight a few as examples, categorized as socio-political forces and systemic-educational forces, it may help understand their co-constructed impact on education development in Taiwan.

Socio-political forces

Generally, people in Taiwan value education highly, regarding it as the capstone of a nation and the key factor for social advancement. Looking back over the past six decades, education in Taiwan has indeed made great progress both in quantity and in quality. The success of its educational development has contributed substantially to Taiwan's vibrant economic development and democratic movement. However, the traditional Chinese value of 'academic rationalism' results in serious problems for a culture of schooling where studying hard, passing examinations and then entering university become the supreme goals for students. Many schools have retained as their major function the aim of pressing for the intellectual growth of the students in the academic courses. Confronting these long unsolved problems, gradually more and more progressive parents and reformists have begun to advocate new ways of educating in order to free students from a bureaucratized, test-driven template.

Basically the social drive behind education reform began to gain momentum in the 1980s and has continued to do so. As described above, after the abolition of martial law in 1987, Taiwan launched into a socio-political transition from authoritarianism to democratization of the polity and the strengthening of civil society. The government began to deregulate education by sharing its control with other agencies, and thereafter the civil education reform movements began to flourish. Every kind of private group was founded one after another, advocating various reform goals. For examples, the Humanistic Education Foundation demanded the normalization of education; the Association for Teachers' Human Rights sought to liberalize the educational system to protect teachers' working rights. The Homemakers Unified Foundation aimed to exert parental educational rights; and the Zheduo Scholar's Association promoted autonomous professional bodies for teachers. Parents' organizations were also set up. These civil education reform groups cooperated in holding an educational conference and formed an alliance, demanding autonomy for schools at all levels.

In the early 1990s, the Legislative *Yuan* became an important battleground for civil education reform groups, many of which were founded by the DDP. It was a period of popular education being promoted in legal cases. Many views were formed in opposition to those of the KMT and the presiding educational bodies, and many issues under debate became a contest between the DDP and the KMT. By the end of 1993, the University Act and the Teacher Education Act went through the third reading in Legislative *Yuan*, and the Teachers' Acts were passed, which brought Taiwan's grass-roots reform of educational system to an unprecedented peak. Later in 1994 the most notable 10 April Demonstration for Education Reform made up the largest education reform movement in Taiwanese history, aiming not only at the MOE, but demanding that national administration agencies and congress adjust the education budget on a large scale, reallocating and redistributing the nation's resources. In their appeal for reform, the 410 Educational Reform Alliance loudly voiced their demands to a) reduce the class size and school size of elementary schools; b) establish more high schools and universities; c) promote the modernization of education; and d) draft the fundamental laws of education, which have become the core agendas for the subsequent education reforms.

As the democratization process is one of the greatest social changes to have occurred in Taiwan in the past two decades, as Kwok (2010) describes, education reform in Taiwan was an outgrowth of the democratization that had been ongoing, and which opened up political debate and legitimized public participation and political demonstrations. It is interesting to see that most of the reform initiatives were initially advocated by civil education groups from the bottom that forced the bureaucratic MOE to reform the entire education system, and the major emerging reform policies were not interrupted by the changes in regime (i.e. no matter whether the KMT or DPP were in power).

Systemic-educational forces

Pressed by the various civil education groups urging educational change, the MOE held the Seventh National Education Conference in June 1994, and based on its conclusions the ministry released its *Report on ROC Education* in February 1995, outlining a plan for Taiwan's educational reform into the twenty-first century. Two main areas of reform were proposed in the report: promoting a more liberal education, and alleviating examination pressure through providing diverse ways of entering high schools and universities. Meanwhile, in order to divert the strong pressure put on the MOE by civil education groups, the Commission on Educational Reform (CER) was established in September 1994, given a mandate to reform and support by the Executive *Yuan*. Creating a supra-ministerial reform agency, the CER, outside the traditional educational bureaucracy, reflected a political compromise for bridging the government and civil education groups, thus marking a new milestone in educational reform efforts from the government. After two years of careful study and analysis, the commission released its *General Report on Educational Reform* in December 1996. The report listed five major reform targets: a) deregulating education; b) engaging every student; c) broadening the accesses to higher levels of schooling; d) raising education quality; and e) establishing a society of lifelong learning, as well as eight key reform tasks (CER, 1996).

Combining the recommendations of the general report and the ideas proposed for long-term policies – such as those in the *Report on ROC Education – A Vision Toward the 21st Century*, the *Report on ROC Education for the Disabled*, and the *Report on ROC Education for the Aborigines* – the MOE then mapped out the *Curriculum Guidelines for Compulsory Education*. Also, the MOE selected priority projects from the *General Report on Educational Reform* by the CER and the *Guidelines for Compulsory Education Reform*, and came up with an educational reform action plan. To implement the reform proposals, an inter-ministry Education Reform Taskforce was then organized under the Executive *Yuan* in January 1997 with the mission of monitoring the progress of actualizing the reform proposals. In April 1998 the Taskforce approved the proposal of Twelve Education Reform Mandates, allocating a special budget of US$5 billion, later finalized by the Executive *Yuan* and Legislative *Yuan* in May 1998, for the mission to be accomplished in five years. The approval of the budgeted Twelve Education Reform Mandates was so important that it was 'leaving greater leverage for unprecedented education changes in Taiwan' (Li, 1999). Consequently, the Twelve Education Reform Mandates has become the most widely-acknowledged blueprint for education reform in Taiwan and served as the major guideline for the educational reform policy-making of the MOE. The Mandates are as follows:

a) Revamping national education projects, K-12.
b) Fostering pre-school and kindergarten education programmes.
c) Renovating teacher education and in-service training programmes.
d) Promoting impeccable diversified vocational education.
e) Pursuing excellence in higher education and its development.
f) Advocating lifelong learning projects.
g) Strengthening educational programmes designed for the handicapped.
h) Enhancing educational programmes for the native Taiwanese (aboriginals).
i) Expanding access to colleges and universities.
j) Creating a new system integrating teaching, guidance and counselling.
k) Increasing the educational budget for the enhancement of educational research.
l) Accelerating the promotion of family values/ethics through parental education.

Examining the driving forces of the education reforms in the past two decades in Taiwan, it is interesting to see the power struggles as well as the exercise of politics between various civil interest groups and the central government and between the KMT and DPP parties. The whole developmental process, just as Law (2002) has pointed out in his analysis, involved applying 'a pincer approach' to force the bureaucratic MOE to reform the entire education system, the 'pincers' being the pressure from bottom-up civil education groups and the top-down supra-ministerial reform agency, CER. It has been quite obvious that these three bodies competed with each other over the agenda and the course of education reform.

Overview of Major Education Reform Policies

Since the 1990s there have been numerous successive education reform efforts at all levels, from mandates to legislation and from legislation to concrete measures (Yang, 2001). The spectrum of education reform includes pre-school education, compulsory education, higher education, teacher education and lifelong learning, as well as educational internationalization. Focusing on primary and secondary education, only the related major reform policies are introduced below.

Educational Fundamental Act

In 1994, the 410 Educational Reform Alliance initiated their demand to formulate fundamental education laws. Soon after that, some DPP members of the legislature proposed a new draft of the Education Fundamental Act. After six years of discussion on legislation, and passing through the hands of three Ministers of the MOE, in June 1999 the Educational Fundamental Act was finally promulgated with 17 articles. The content primarily included: a) declaring the subject of educational rights and the purposes of education; b) defining principles of pedagogical implementation; c) ensuring equal educational opportunity for all; d) demanding liberal budgets for education and reasonable distribution of resources; e) keeping education neutral; f) encouraging participation of the private sector in education; g) protecting students' rights of learning and parents' rights to choose schools; h) the education authority and obligations of the central government; i) formulating local education review boards, extending national basic education and proper planning for small schools and small classes; j) developing a modern education system by conducting experiments and strengthening research and assessment; k) keeping the rights of requesting an academic attainment test and availing of needed legal assistance for teachers and students to protect their rights and autonomy.

This Fundamental Act was very effective among education ordinances and was the basic constitution for all of the other education laws. As the 16th article of the Educational Fundamental Act states: 'after this Act takes effect, relevant education regulations and rules shall be amended, annulled, or formulated in accordance with this Act'. It is important to note that the Act makes up for the insufficiency in the constitution regarding education principles. It provides the guiding principles for education in Taiwan, providing legitimacy for many reform initiatives or measures that have been included in the education reform mandates, and marks the start of a more just and humanistic era for education.

Teacher Education Act

For years, teacher quality in Taiwan had been highly controlled by a monopoly system of teacher education. Institutions for training prospective teaches, teachers colleges for primary school teachers and normal universities for high school teachers, used to be rather parochial, conservative and uniform in their milieu. They were often criticized for their training programmes and education modes, which had to cater to the totalitarian government's policies. Influenced by the movement demanding the liberalization of education, the new Teacher Education Act was passed in 1994 to promote the policy of pluralism in teacher recruitment. Upon approval, any university is now allowed to set up its own teacher-training programme and to offer it to interested students. The Teacher Education Act has brought great changes with regard to the supply pool for teachers and the method of employing them. In other words, the training of teachers has moved from a planned system to a reserve system, in the hope that the sources for school teachers can be diversified and the market adjust supply and demand.

It was believed that competition arising from the diversity of the teacher education programme might enhance the quality of teachers and bring a dynamic energy into classrooms. However, after it has been in operation for more than 15 years it has given rise to oversupply. There are not only issues raised about the uneven quality of the programmes in the various universities, but a phenomenon has appeared of so-called 'vagrant teachers' trekking island-wide to compete for a dwindling number of teaching posts.

Curriculum Guidelines for Compulsory Education (1–9)

Among all the education reforms, one of the most challenging and most influential innovations has been curriculum reform. On the basis of the Education Reform Mandates ratified by the Executive *Yuan*, the MOE has undertaken innovation in the curricula at all levels. In September 1998, just five years after the 'New Curriculum Standards' was promulgated, a newly reformed *Curriculum Guidelines for Compulsory Education (1–9)* was announced (MOE, 1998). It underwent trial implementation in 2000 and officially began to be put into practice nationwide since the school year 2001 at elementary schools, and in 2002 at junior high schools. Drawing upon ideas from contemporary curriculum and instructional theories, the *Curriculum Guidelines* (often called the Nine-Year Integrated Curriculum) reconstructed the traditional subject-based curriculum into seven broad study fields to strengthen the continuity from elementary to junior high, and to promote curriculum integration (e.g. merging the subjects of history, geography and citizenship into one social study field), school-based curriculum development and alternative evaluation.

In line with world trends, the *Curriculum Guidelines* also identified information technology, environmental education, gender education, human rights, life education and home economics as six major topics, along with basic ability indicators, to be integrated in each study field. It was intended to turn away from the traditional approach of helping students to build a body of knowledge, to a more constructivist approach of fostering basic skills that students can take with them. It brought about not only structural changes of the curriculum but also substantial changes of pedagogy. To a certain degree, it appears to be a revolution of curricular practices.

Deregulation of the textbook market

In Taiwan, the political control over education in the past during the KMT party-state era was reflected in the unified school curriculum in primary and secondary education. Since nine-year compulsory education was enacted in 1968, textbooks at all levels had been compiled and edited by the National Institute of Compilation and Translation (NICT). In the early 1980s the MOE, along with introducing the NICT-approved system, began to liberalize the textbook market so that non-government publishers were able to compile and publish textbooks of non-academic subjects for high schools. From the 1990s, under pressure from civil education groups, the MOE further opened up the textbook market to the private sector and separated the processes of editorship and evaluation. In response to the call for deregulation, the gradual open textbook market policy was set in 1996, commencing with textbooks for all subjects in primary education first, then textbooks for non-examination subjects in junior high schools in 1988, and then textbooks for the six remaining restricted academic subjects in senior high schools in 1999. At the same time, in the name of quality control, the NICT continued to compile textbooks on academic subjects for primary and junior high schools. In 2001, with the *Curriculum Guidelines for Compulsory Education (1–9)* being implemented nationwide, all subjects for all levels were completely opened to the market and the NICT ceased its compilation of school textbooks, though it still played the role of evaluator in reviewing and approving textbooks.

Although the incorporation of market forces into the textbook market does not necessarily mean the complete removal of the government's intervention in textbook production, it does mark another important stage in 'curriculum deregulation' in Taiwan. In the pursuit of liberalization and diversification of education, the opening up of the textbook market has not only created more choices for schools and teachers but more importantly has to some degree reduced the government's political control over education.

Multiple entrance approaches to high school and college

Taiwan society has been deeply influenced by traditional Chinese examination culture, praising the examination system for its impartiality. For many years the joint entrance examination has been the only path to senior high school. Many students have suffered significant disadvantage by such a narrow measure. To alleviate the examination pressure involved in entering schools of a higher level and to promote a more liberal education to rectify the distorted, test-driven pedagogical practices, the 1995 *Report on ROC Education* first announced that the system controlling entrance to senior high school was to be reformed and that multiple ways of entering high schools were to be established. In 2001 the achievement test, the traditional entrance examination to senior high school, was abolished. It was reformed into the Basic Competence Test which aims to evaluate students' fundamental knowledge and skills. Also, the MOE adopted the Multi-Track Admissions Programme to separate the examination and the admission process, including entry on the basis of Basic Competence Test results, recommendations, applications, admission via registration and placement, and the special provision of entry for gifted students. Consequently, the decades-old method of admitting junior high school students to senior high schools through annually held joint entrance examinations is no longer the only option.

Under the multi-track admission system, students can apply for admission based on their performance in the Basic Competence Test as well as records of their other talents and performances. This should be a relief for students and their parents. However, student discontent has remained high and the alternative admission approaches seems to lack equity. Many parents raise doubts about the effectiveness and fairness of the multi-track admission programme, and some even advocate it might be better to restore the old system of joint entrance examinations.

Curriculum guidelines for senior high school education

Since the *Curriculum Guidelines for Compulsory Education (1–9)* was implemented, the continuity and coherence issues of curricular and pedagogical practice have kept emerging. In line with the concern of continuity issues, the MOE moved forward to reform the high school curriculum. Because it involves preparing students for higher education that will lead to different specialized academic tracks as well as vocational choices, the task of reconstructing the high school curriculum was in fact far more challenging. In August 2004, the Ministry of Education announced a partial curriculum revision in the form of the *Temporary Curriculum Guidelines for Senior High School Education (10–12)* in which the subject areas of history and sciences were not included because conflicts over the content were just too difficult to settle. It was not until January 2005 that the complete curriculum guidelines were promulgated for senior high schools nationwide to be put into practice in the school year 2006. These guidelines are outlined in the document *Temporary Curriculum Guidelines for Senior High School Education (10–12)* (MOE, 2005), for a three-year experimental stage. The revised 'formal' version of the curriculum guidelines was initially intended to be finalized and announced in 2009, but because of the reorganization of the revision task force committees as a result of the return of the KMT to power, the announcement was delayed until 2010 and without inclusion of the subjects of history and Chinese. Battle continued for another year over revision of the content of the history curriculum and the inclusion of classical Chinese culture readings as an elective course, but a complete formal *Curriculum Guidelines for Senior High School Education* was finally agreed and announced in 2011.

The *Curriculum Guidelines for Senior High School Education* (MOE, 2011), involving 23 subjects, was one of the largest curriculum reform projects in Taiwan and arguably the history curriculum guidelines was one of the most controversial subjects (Chen, 2008). The heated debates about restructuring the history curriculum, or adding Chinese culture readings, were ideological ones related to national identity issues that always return to the realm of the political. Though the ideological battles in the media appeared chaotic and irrational, it reflected the power struggles in curriculum making in a democratic society. It also provided a very good opportunity for more people to participate in thinking about history education and language education. To have fairer curriculum decisions for high school students, however, it is necessary to examine these questions concerning the high school curriculum below the surface level of the political struggles covered in the media – to dig into more profound pedagogical concerns.

Twelve-year compulsory education

To raise the quality of the labour force in the interest of national competitiveness, the idea of extending compulsory education was first raised in the 1980s. A consensus was reached at the 2003 national education development conference to phase in 12-year compulsory education. Since then, the 12-year compulsory education project has been seriously discussed and planned. However, due to operational concerns about redistribution of resources (equity issues), standards (quality issues) and power (efficiency issues), the project was delayed. To achieve the goal of promoting equal educational opportunity and to prepare for the implementation of 12-year compulsory education, the MOE set six core guidelines: a) keeping students' welfare as the focus; b) emphasizing multi-tracking and matching students to schools; c) encouraging students to choose their nearest school; d) ensuring the rights of disadvantaged students; e) adopting admission methods according to the needs of particular school districts; and f) implementing the reform in a gradual and flexible manner. In 2009 the MOE began expanding an Open Admissions Programme for general high school, vocational school and five-year junior colleges, with a gradual increase in numbers of students catered for under the programme. It is expected that in 2014 12-year compulsory education will be fully implemented and that about 70 per cent of students will be able to enter high school, vocational schools or five-year colleges under the Open Admissions Programme. Also, the Basic Competence Test will then be replaced with one grand examination, the results of which will only serve as a reference for the students and no longer be the deciding factor for admission.

Most parents agree with the goals and direction of 12-year compulsory education, but are wary of the practice of open admissions to senior high schools. How should a school select its students? Most parents believe open admission is not easy to achieve and varied comparison and ranking methods are not always fair. They are afraid that the competition for getting into a superior high school will be overwhelming and that open admission will turn out to be 'a hundred texts for high-school entry'. Students will not only have to do well in all the tests held in junior high, but also participate in various competitive activities in order to gain extra points, which might be even more difficult than preparation for the Basic Competency Test. At the time of writing, disputes about the equity and justice of the Open Admissions Programme are still going on.

Reflection on Trends and Agendas

Based on the above survey of the major education reform policies in the past two decades, we may find that the trends of education development in Taiwan are very much linked to political evolution. Democratization, liberalization, decentralization, deregulation and diversification have become key elements of education reform agendas. It will be helpful to review the trends and agendas of education reform in Taiwan from a critical perspective, so that we can better see the issues and challenges in educational change. The following are the most distinctive, influential and controversial factors.

Civil participation

As mentioned above, education reform in Taiwan was an outgrowth of democratization since 1988, and the reform initiatives were initially suggested by civil social groups, including civil education groups and other interest groups. There have been many such movements, for example university professors campaigned for university autonomy, school teachers fought for teachers' rights and empowerment, parents and different interest groups initiated reforms of the school system and entrance examinations, and so forth. Basically, the participation of stakeholders and various social groups has helped to diversify the sources of opinion on education reform and has forced the MOE to take up initiatives for reform rather than maintain the status quo. In other words, civil participation has changed the political ecology of education administration and policy making at the school, local and central levels. However, inevitably it often turns out to be a power struggle between political parties or among different interest groups, according to their political standpoints or ideological assumptions.

Protecting plurality and neutrality

Through the collective efforts of different civil education reform groups, together with a readiness to compromise on the part of the government and help from legislators of different political parties, redefinition of the legal framework to protect plurality and neutrality in education was achieved and led to revision of education laws and regulations. The efforts include the revision of the University Law (1993) to protect university autonomy, the enactment of the Teacher Act (1995) and the Law for Education of Aboriginal Peoples (1997) to protect the rights and autonomy of teachers and aboriginal peoples, and the most significant one, the enactment of the Educational Fundamental Act (1999) to reduce the domination of the MOE and the political influence on education. The redefinition of the legal framework represents a replacement of rule by leaders by the rule of law. With the redefined legal framework for

education, a new common rule has been set in the educational game for stakeholders to operate within and to provide guiding principles and criteria for all
activities. Yet, to make the legal framework more complete, continuous revision
of existing education laws and regulations need to be carried out in accordance
with the Educational Fundamental Act.

Incorporating market forces

Infusing market mechanisms into the educational process has forced government
to reduce its control over education. One typical example was deregulation of
the textbook market. Before the 1990s, the MOE prescribed the contents
of curriculum and textbooks, compelling students to take in political and
ideological information. From the 1990s, the government began to deregulate
education by sharing its control with other agencies. The market has been
allowed to play a part in the provision of textbooks, and the role of the law in
the governance of education has been strengthened. These developments have
reduced the MOE's administrative control over education. In consequence,
there has been a reallocation of power among teachers, principals, the education
authorities and even the parents. As civil society becomes more empowered, the
educational choices created by market forces become more decisive. Through
competition, negotiation and compromise, education becomes less dominated
by the government, more self-determined and more open to other social
agencies.

Encouraging flexibility and multiplicity

Brought about by the liberalization of education, reforms such as the freedom
extended to private publishers to compile and publish textbooks and the
establishment of a multi-track admission programme to admit students to
higher levels of schools are a significant departure from previous policies
and measures, which allowed only one definite set of textbooks and only one
unified way of admitting students. Also, influenced by the decentralization of
education, the reform of the curriculum at all levels encourages flexibility in
school-based management and curriculum development; deregulation relating
to private schools allows more variety in educational programmes; and adjustments to educational administration promotes more creative pedagogical
innovations. However, with so many deregulated educational practices on the
way and so many curricular and pedagogical initiatives available, it is somewhat

overwhelming for administrators, teachers, students and parents. Inevitably, there have been doubts and complaints about chaotic situations arising as a result of the continually evolving educational landscape.

Promoting equity and social justice

Through the empowerment of civil society, the market and law, it becomes obvious that striving for equality of education, valuing the humanistic spirit, attaining liberty and diversity and promoting self-determination are primary goals of the current educational reform movement in Taiwan. Many efforts, from central government to the local governments and schools, have been made to achieve these goals, including implementing the multi-track admission programme, extending compulsory education, encouraging school-based curriculum development, promoting multicultural education, designating Educational Priority Areas for financial aid, and so forth. They all targeted at making education at every level more equally accessible and students are more able to develop according to their disposition, thereby moving toward a more just society where appropriate education for all is possible. In actual practice, of course, the most compelling challenge lies in decreasing educational disparities, between the urban and rural areas and populations, and between the elite, the mass and the disadvantaged.

Refocusing national identity

In the past decades, Taiwanization of education has been concerned with the reallocation of power between the state, society and education, and the pursuit of 'national' identity. In order to form her own national and cultural identity, Taiwan takes every opportunity to move away from mainland Chinese affili-ations and towards respecting local ethnic identity and culture. The aim is to construct Taiwan as the new political and cultural identity of its people. Under persistent pressure from social groups and local governments, the MOE began, in the early 1990s, to shift the focus of the school curriculum from a Sino-centric curriculum to a more Taiwan-centric one, involving homeland studies and mother languages. The recent curriculum reforms for compulsory education as well as for high school education have created space for local identities, local history, multiculture and ethnic languages to help build up ethnic solidarity and foster a common and shared identity. However, the presentation of Taiwan as a new collective identity in the school curriculum is not without resistance.

It often becomes an issue of contention between the political parties and civil social groups.

With so many vibrant but forceful ongoing reform efforts, education in Taiwan is full of promising possibilities and stressful challenges. Beyond the afore-mentioned trends and agendas in Taiwan's reform efforts, there are serious ideological issues and practical problems in terms of reform, caused by conflicting educational interests and discordant political views. For example, differences over the concepts of competition for excellence and social justice for all has created dilemmas in applying the current Open Admissions Programme to support the implementation of 12-year compulsory education. As the open admissions policy does not necessarily mandate what really matters to parents and students, it will be exceedingly difficult to change actual practice at school level. As a matter of fact, the nature, amount and pace of change at school level is actually far beyond the control of the MOE. If the 12-year compulsory education and open admissions policies are still endorsed on the rhetorical level, they will remain the subject of scepticism and criticism in terms of actual practice.

For another example, the imbalance of power between social groups, parents, schools and government has brought about endless disputes and struggles over education agendas. Politics has been central to education reform in Taiwan, and in many cases, education reform has interacted closely with electoral politics, as seen in attempts to alter and mould the preferences of the masses, particularly in relation to the subjects of language and history. After the assumption of power by the DPP in 2000, there was a rupture in education reform, with a shift in emphasis from the pursuit of plurality to the pursuit of Taiwanization. Furthermore, political rhetoric had been applied to reformist measures on education such as democratization, localization, Taiwanization and de-Sinification, downplaying the factors of economic and global capitalism (Kwok, 2010, Yang, 2001). In turn, when the KMT returned to power in 2008, the political rhetoric of education reform policy then shifted back to pursuing plurality, internationalization and revival of Chinese culture, in addition to democratization. It is evident that political rhetoric and the pursuit of 'national' identity interplay very closely in both education and the broader civil society of Taiwan.

Whatever problems have occurred, or issues emerged, it is undeniable that the past civil education reform efforts have contributed to the liberalization of education in Taiwan. After the liberalization of education and prior to the full establishment of a pluralistic value system, society at large has not yet been able to adjust itself to these changes. Inevitably, periods of chaos arising from disappointed expectations have been a consequence of the period of reform. The changes in the education system, curriculum guidelines, examinations and school admissions have required the general public to adapt its modes of thinking or even its traditional value systems. It is very true that education reform in Taiwan is not simply reform in the classroom or in the school. Education reform in Taiwan is also social reform, a challenge to cultural traditions and a means to redefinition of belief and of identity.

Conclusion

No matter that education reform in Taiwan is perceived as 'the rejuvenated national goal' (Li, 1999), as 'a means to enhance school effectiveness' (Pan and Yu, 1999), as 'a journey of searching for "national" identity' (Law, 2002; Tu, 2007), or as 'a political game between stakeholders and interest groups' (Kwok, 2010), it is amazing that this country where everyone embraces education reform and education policy making. Tracking the historical background, current trends and agendas of Taiwan's education reform in the past helps us understand how this reform has had far-reaching consequences, leading to a more just, more liberated educational practice. Situated in a somewhat paradoxical state of affairs, it is important to realize that education reform is not about one aim but many, and that its development will continue through many contrasting stages. As the wheels of education reform keep rolling, whether the goal is to sharpen the nation's competitive edge, further develop its society and culture, elevate the collective identity of its citizens, or raise the overall quality of education for all, we can expect to see more struggles and changes, as well as unprecedented miracles in Taiwan's vibrant education development.

References

Chen, H. L. (2008). 'A critical reflection on the reform of high school history curriculum in Taiwan'. In D. Grossman and T. Y. Lo (eds), *Social Education in the Asia-Pacific: Critical issues and multiple perspectives.* Charlotte, NC: Information Age Publishing, pp. 87–110.

CER (Commission on Educational Reform) (1996). *General Report on Education Reform.* Taipei: Executive *Yuan.*

Kwok, K. H. (2010). *Politics, social change and education reform in Taiwan, 1994–2008.* Unpublished PhD dissertation, University of Hong Kong.

Law, W. W. (2002). 'Education reform in Taiwan: A search for a "national" identity through democratisation and Taiwanisation'. *Compare: A Journal of Comparative and International Education*, 32 (1): 61–81.

Li, C. C. (1999). 'Sweeping educational reform in Taiwan: From primary education to lifelong and global learning'. *Educational Policy Forum*, 2 (1): 1–32.

MOE (Ministry of Education) (1998). *Curriculum Guidelines for Compulsory Education (1–9)*. Taipei: MOE.

—(1999). Educational Fundamental Act. http://edu.law.moe.gove.tw/EngLawContent. aspx?Type=E&id=58 (10 July 2012).

—(2005). *Temporary Curriculum Guidelines for Senior High School Education (10–12)*. Taipei: MOE.

—(2011). *Curriculum Guidelines for Senior High School Education (10–12)*. Taipei: MOE. http://www.edu.tw

—(2012). *Education in Taiwan*. Taipei: Department of Statistics, MOE. http://www.edu.tw

Pan, H. L. and Yu, C. (1999). 'Educational reforms and their impacts on school effectiveness and improvement in Taiwan, R.O.C.'. *School Effectiveness and Improvement*, 10 (1): 72–85.

Tu, C. S. (2007). *Taiwan's educational reform and the future of Taiwan*. Invited speech at the London School of Economics and Political Sciences, 10 January. http://english.moe.gov.tw/fp.asp?xIterm=70457ctNode=369&mp=2 (Accessed 11 June 2012).

Yang, S. K. (2001). *Dilemmas of education reform in Taiwan: Internationalization or localization?* Paper presented at the 2001 Annual Meeting of the Comparative and International Society, Washington, DC, 13–17 March.

13

Taiwan: Examinations

Pei-tseng Jenny Hsieh

> During the testing period each July, public attention is riveted on the students. In the days just before the test, certain temples are filled with families asking the gods for assistance. During the test period, newspapers and TV news reports run images of the students filing grimly into the exam halls, and columns with advice for students and parents. The local governments allow families with exam-related emergencies to call for police assistance. The officers give police escort to students caught in morning traffic jams or rush students back home to retrieve forgotten admission tickets. Doctors are on hand at all exam sites around the island, and many parents and other family members gather outside the buildings to offer the young people cold drinks, snacks, massages, and advice during the breaks … (Cheng, 1995)

Such a description is so vividly part of the memory of my years as a student in Taiwan. As it is in most East Asian countries, the entrance examinations that qualify students to the next level of education plays one of the most significant roles in the education system in Taiwan. 'One test determines one's entire life' is a popular saying in Chinese and portrays without much exaggeration the role of entrance exams. While similar forms of exam exist in other parts of the world, the extent to which individual students and their families' lives are related to the preparation and outcome of entrance exams in most of the East Asian countries is beyond the scope of comprehension for many outside of the system (Zeng, 1999). Before we can begin with the discussion of exams in Taiwan, it is crucial to appreciate and understand the context as a whole.

Historical and Contextual Background

Taiwan, also known as the Republic of China (ROC), has a relatively short yet unique history, and has been one of the most popular cases for discussion in almost every textbook of international relations. An interesting feature in contemporary Taiwan is the valuing of education in its participation in the global race, which has led to a series of major education reforms aiming to achieve such goals. The uniqueness of Taiwan's history, geopolitical position and economic development shapes the prevailing ideology regarding education in Taiwan. These special features were discussed in the previous chapter and some aspects will be further elaborated in this chapter.

The political status of Taiwan and the evolution of Taiwanese identity

Well known by the name Formosa, Taiwan, the Republic of China (ROC), is one of several countries in the world, together with Kosovo, Palestine and Vatican City, that are not member countries of the United Nation. In the 2012 Olympics, the Taiwanese flag hung for three days in the streets of London with others and was removed before the opening ceremony as a result of political protests. Many around the world are puzzled by the status of Taiwan, while mainland China, also known as the People's Republic of China (PRC), has sought every opportunity to declare Taiwan a province destined for reunification with the Chinese mainland. The PRC has never hesitated in announcing its determination to resolve the 'Taiwan problem' by military force if necessary.

As a matter of fact, both the PRC and ROC regimes maintained that they were the sole legitimate government of the whole of China until the 1990s. Before the early 1970s, many of the world's most powerful nations recognized Taipei, rather than Beijing, as the legitimate government of China, and the Taiwanese government maintained control of the Chinese seat in the United Nations Security Council. This global recognition helped the political party in charge at the time, the Koumintang (KMT), to consolidate Taiwan's establishment and its Chinese legitimacy. This vision was promoted by the effort of maintaining China's 5000-year-old history and culture on the island. While mainland China suffered from the Cultural Revolution during the years 1966 to 1976, Taiwan encouraged, and managed to preserve, the cultural traditions more than any other region of Chinese heritage. The revival and the maintenance of Chinese culture and life were portrayed as the special mission of Taiwan's Chinese population.

The 1970s is considered the turning point for the international status of Taiwan. Following the Sino-Soviet split and the ensuing rapprochement between the Americans and the communist regime in mainland China, the ROC was forced to withdraw from the United Nations in 1971. The United

States of America formalized its diplomatic relations with the PRC in 1979, and thereafter many other countries followed and withdrew their diplomatic relations with the ROC government.

Meanwhile, within its own territory, Taiwan went through a transition from authoritarianism to democracy in a relatively short period under the leadership of Chiang Kai-Shek's son and political successor, Chiang Ching Kuo. An awareness of 'Taiwaneseness' emerged as the government initiated a policy of integration of the people in Taiwan by sharing power with the Taiwanese born and raised on the island. In addition, the government also modified its political system by institutionalizing and legalizing opposition parties and introduced popular elections at local and national levels. On President Chiang Ching-kuo's death in 1988, Lee Teng-hui succeeded, becoming Taiwan's first native-born President. In 2000, Chen Shui-bian of the Democratic Progressive Party (DPP) won the presidential election and ended the KMT's 50-year rule. The alternation in power of political parties led Taiwan's democracy to a new stage that further distinguishes it from mainland China (Rubinstein, 1999).

This strengthening of Taiwanese consciousness was reflected in school curricula. The curricular content shifted from being highly China/Chinese-centred to being supportive of specifically Taiwanese history, culture and dialects in the 1980s and 1990s. At the same time, regardless of these efforts, Taiwan's international status faced increasingly severe challenges as the PRC became politically and economically stronger and even more determined to claim its 'ownership' of Taiwan.

The more eagerly Taiwan asserts its distinctive identity internationally, the more strongly the PRC insists on its 'One China Policy' and opposes the movement towards complete independence for Taiwan. The ongoing issue regarding the national identity of Taiwan is a complex one and emerges constantly with the increasing cross-strait interaction and communication. Most people in Taiwan have a sense of dual or mixed identity, describing themselves as 'both Taiwanese and Chinese' with different weights (Schubert, 2004; Hsiao, 2004, 2008). Some people perceive themselves as Chinese in the ethno-cultural domain and as Taiwanese in the political domain. Some accept that Taiwan is/was geographically part of China, but nevertheless hold a strong sense of a distinctive 'Taiwaneseness'. For many, perhaps most of the Taiwanese people, Taiwanese identity is about – as some scholars have detected – a growing sense of civic nationalism, in which 'Taiwaneseness' is defined not primarily in nationalist, ethno-cultural or even linguistic terms, but more broadly and inclusively as a sense of belonging to and affection for the 'breeding land',

Taiwan (Hughes, 1997; Liu, 2005; Hsiao, 2008). It is not expedient here to explore further the complex political and national identity issues of Taiwan. Yet what is clear from the discussion above is the necessity for Taiwan to raise its international profile and visibility – if not through political means, through any other means possible. The tension with the PRC and the resulting diplomatic isolation of Taiwan in the international society are crucial in understanding the governmental ideology regarding education policies in Taiwan.

Economic development

Taiwan has worked hard to overcome very poor initial economic circumstances: overpopulation, a small domestic market, scarce indigenous resources and rampant inflation. Until the 1950s, Taiwan was still a 'less developed country' and had a per capita gross national product (GNP) of US$170, placing its economic ranking close to the sub-Saharan countries. By the 1990s Taiwan's per capita GNP, adjusted for purchasing power parity (PPP), had soared to US$20,000, contributing to a Human Development Index similar to that of European countries such as Spain, Portugal and Greece. At the same time, Taiwan's economic structure has shifted emphasis from agricultural to industrial production in less than three decades. Foreign investment helped to introduce modern and labour-intensive technology to the island in the 1960s. The emphasis has changed from production of consumer goods for export to more sophisticated heavy industry and technology-intensive products. Since then Taiwan has transformed itself into one of the newly industrialized countries. Foreign trade has been a major factor in Taiwan's rapid growth, as exports provided the primary impetus for industrialization. The value of exports grew rapidly during the 1960s and the value of trade roughly tripled in each five-year period and increased nearly sixfold between 1975 and 1990. Nearly 90 per cent of the industrial goods are for export, and imports are dominated by raw materials and capital goods (*The Economist*, 2008).

It is now recognized that, while Taiwan may be in a rather weak diplomatic position, the development of the territory has relied, and will continue to rely greatly, on international commerce. Excluded by the United Nations and its related organizations, including the supposedly less political organizations such as UNESCO and the World Health Organization, Taiwan earned its place as a member of the World Trade Organization in 2001. How to sustain its international visibility through global economic competitiveness is therefore a priority for the government of Taiwan.

Today, Taiwan has a dynamic capitalist economy with gradually decreasing state involvement in investment and foreign trade. While once the most well-known country for exporting goods, traditional labour-intensive industries have now reduced significantly in scale, with more capital and technology-intensive industries in place. Taiwan has also become a major investor in many other Asian countries. Indeed, regardless of the political sensitivity in the cross-strait relationship with the PRC, it is the largest foreign investor in mainland China, with around 50,000 Taiwanese businesses established there. The trade surplus is substantial, and its foreign reserves are the world's fifth largest. Taiwan's current Gross Domestic Product (GDP) is US$504 billion, ranking 21st in the world (*The Economist*, 2011), and its GDP by purchasing power is US$876 billion, placing it at 19 in the world ranks (International Monetary Fund, 2011).

The so-called 'Taiwan Miracle' refers to the rapid industrialization and growth in the economy during the second half of the twentieth century, in particular the period from the 1960s to the 1980s. Because of its parallel rise with that of several other East Asian economies, by the 1980s, together with Hong Kong, Singapore and South Korea, Taiwan became one of the 'Four Dragons' or 'Asian Tigers' (Lau, 1986).

Although the most rapid development of the economy springs only from the 1960s, the 'Taiwan Miracle' actually established its base prior to the end of World War Two. Japanese governance at that time introduced public and compulsory education in Taiwan. Many believe this was the most significant element in driving the rapid economic growth of Taiwan, as education has always been highly emphasized in the economic strategies of successive governments (Armer and Liu, 1993; Rodrik, 1995; Lin, 2003).

The global economic downturn at the turn of the millennium, combined with poor policy coordination by the new administration and increasing bad debts in the banking system, pushed Taiwan into its first recession since 1947, in 2001. Due to the relocation of many manufacturing and labour-intensive industries to mainland China, home unemployment also peaked at 5.85 per cent in 2009 (International Monetary Fund, 2011). This problem became one of the major issues in the political elections and is also related to new directions in education policies and strategies. In addition, Taiwan has launched an ambitious project to promote itself as an Asian-Pacific Regional Operational Centre. Education is one of the keys to economic success and one area where the state has usually taken the lead. The economic miracle in Taiwan could be said to be the consequence of the ambitious educational goals set by Taiwan's government as an integral part of its economic strategy. To re-create a miracle like this, within the development of an operational centre in Asia, the government is again looking to the field of education.

Education in Taiwan

As noted above, education has played a prominent part in shaping the status and development of the country.

In Taiwan, the state has played a critical role in education. It decides who should be educated and provides either the schools themselves or the financing for the schools. Although the Taiwanese government is currently criticized for its ill-planned contemporary education policies, state education planning was once the biggest contribution to society.

The development of the education system

In 1968, the introduction of the Nine-Year Compulsory Education System for both boys and girls commenced the expansion of schooling and significantly increased the number of junior high school graduates. The quality of the labour force improved with the increase in the average years of formal education. In 1964, the population of workers with a university degree or above was only 3 per cent, while those who completed a primary school education consisted of 83 per cent. By 2000, more than 60 per cent of workers had at least a senior high school degree, and nearly a third of the workers had obtained a college degree. In 2009 some 39 per cent of the Taiwanese population had a HEI degree, while the percentage of those younger than 40 years old and with a degree was 55 per cent (Ministry of Interior, 2011).

Taiwan's economic development has relied especially on governmental policies that increase human capital in the labour force. This strategy is implemented at different levels of schooling. Even when compared to the other Asian Tigers, the rate of growth of public expenditure on education was highest in Taiwan. The expenditure on education grew at a rate nearly four times as fast as the growth of GNP and by the early 1990s public expenditure on education amounted to nearly 7 per cent of GDP. At the time of writing, education expenditure is 5.7 per cent of GNP (MOE, 2012a) and 20.5 per cent of total government expenditure.

Education expansion in Taiwan occurred in a sequential nature. In the early stage of growth and industrialization the expansion of primary education took priority. A much smaller proportion of expenditure was on secondary and tertiary education, and enrolment in these sectors was a small proportion of the relevant age group. Subsequently, however, motivated both by changes in the economy and by the rising expectations of parents whose children were completing their primary schooling, first secondary and then tertiary education became the focus for expansion.

By 1965 the enrolment rate for primary education in Taiwan was already 97.15 per cent of the official estimated age cohort. Widened access to basic education was reflected in the levels of literacy and in the rapidly reducing discrepancy that had existed between male and female access to education opportunities and therefore their respective levels of education. The general effect of the expansion of primary schooling was the steady flow of literate and numerate citizens into the workforce at a time of rapid industrialization.

Before the Nine-Year Compulsory Education System was introduced in Taiwan in 1968, secondary education (three years of junior high school and three years of senior high school) was elitist. The schools were highly academically oriented and admissions extremely competitive. They were key steps closer to the top of a social pyramid, one of their goals being to prepare a minority of pupils for entry to the tertiary stage of formal education.

In response to public demand and to the government's own desire to invest in human and political capital, secondary education expanded rapidly with the introduction of the Nine-Year Compulsory Education System. By 1986, the enrolment rate for junior high schools in Taiwan was already 92 per cent (Morris, 1996). Yet the entry to senior secondary schooling remains a main source of pressure for pupils nowadays due to the entry exam requirements and the competition to get into the top public schools.

Taiwanese education systems have always been highly competitive. As far as the nature of the primary school curriculum is concerned, the stated goals have been to provide pupils with high levels of achievement in basic literacy and numeracy and to promote social cohesion and a sense of national identity. Nonetheless, an underlying and very much focused-on goal is to maximize their educational chances and academic capability in relation to accessing entry to a prestigious secondary school. In the junior secondary sector, the focus is again on academic achievement and selection to the next stage of education. The labour market and parental expectations favour a highly academic school curriculum, and the government's attempt to place a large proportion of pupils in technical streams has only served to reinforce the degree of competition.

Each level of educational attainment is perceived as helping ensure a higher rate of future/lifetime earnings, access to a job in the cities or in the government and higher social status.

After its success in expanding primary and secondary education, the government of Taiwan moved quickly to the expansion of tertiary education, which, in the early period of industrialization and growth in the 1960s, was a very small and elite sector providing a highly academic curriculum. By 1986, enrolment rates in tertiary education had grown to 33 per cent. Students in private higher education institutes accounted for more than 70 per cent of the overall number in the tertiary sector. While the private universities/colleges are providers of a substantial proportion of the tertiary sector, the public universities are at least twice better resourced by government expenditure. They remain more prestigious, and entry to them is more competitive. With regard to the nature of the government's relationship with tertiary education, there are high levels of state control related to central manpower planning. What makes Taiwan different from other East Asian countries is this strong reliance on government manpower planning in a period after initial industrialization, with a strong focus on technical and vocational education.

The government has explicitly linked educational provision at all levels to the needs of the economy. Nonetheless, the mismatch between industrial demand and education supply in Taiwan has become a problem and a feature of political discussion in the recent years. As tertiary education expands, the mismatches between educational output and employment needs have become more pronounced. On the supply side, the educational institutions and students have responded to market forces which much preferred the general education stream. On the demand side, employers indicate the need for employees with appropriate technical skills, but in practice are often in favour of students from the public higher education institutions. Parents and their offspring follow the signals of the labour market in which general education produces the highest return, and strive to enter into this mainstream. By contrast, government seems to have been more successful at channelling students into technical and vocational streams in which the status of the schools remain low, because those who enrol are considered to be those who fail to obtain a place in the more academic general secondary schools.

As part of the reform projects in the 1990s, technical colleges around the island were transformed into technical universities, and a significant number of private universities have been established by private enterprise.

Teacher status

There is no doubt that in all of the above discussed education levels, teachers play an important role in determining the quality of service provision. Teacher professionalism and teacher education have been recognized by many scholars and governments as the keystone for social and economic development (Cheng, Chow and Tsui, 2001; Johnson and Maclean, 2008). Only quality education and quality teachers can train the highly qualified and skilled workforce driving economic success.

While many countries increasingly encounter problems of teacher shortage, with difficulties in attracting academically able students into the teaching profession, Taiwan has enjoyed a long tradition of recruiting highly talented people and retaining them (Leavitt, 1992; Williamson and Morris, 2000; Fwu and Wang, 2002). This unusual phenomenon and an overall greater satis-faction of teachers with their jobs than their international counterparts might be attributed to the relatively high social status enjoyed by teachers in Taiwan. The amount of occupational prestige and authority assigned to teachers by the public indicates the importance of education and the degree of respect for the teachers within Taiwanese society (Lin, 1992; Fwu and Wang, 2002).

While sharing similar social origins, gender distribution and teacher–student ratio with teachers internationally, Taiwanese teachers are of a relatively higher academic quality and have a more positive role image than most others. This contributes to their advantageous standing in society. Well thought through teacher education, recruitment and retention policies have attracted and retained academically able candidates in the teaching profession. The roots of these favourable government policies and initiatives for teachers are in the cultural, historical and political development of Taiwanese society. The Chinese cultural tradition, Japanese colonization and Nationalist rule have all played a role in shaping the relatively high social status of teachers in Taiwan. Beliefs embedded from Confucian ideology further stress the value of education and portray the teacher as 'a role model and learned scholar' (Fwu and Wang, 2002; Wu, 2005).

Before the Teacher Education Act and teacher unions were introduced in 1994, under governmental initiatives teachers were already enjoying continuous improvement in salaries and benefits. The reason stated by the government for providing such generous support for teachers was that it was 'necessary to upgrade teachers' living standards, provide them with secure job prospects and elevate their social status, so that they would be fully devoted to educating the next generation' (Ministry of Education, 1957, p. 27, cited in Fwu and Wang, 2002). In Taiwanese society, teachers have traditionally been respected for their 'morally and intellectually superior' image and this view still exists in the public's mind today. The status of teachers may change over time with the transformation of political and cultural contexts in society, yet at least at present they remain well-respected figures in Taiwanese society (Lin, 1992; Fwu and Wang, 2002). Teachers possess a great amount of authority in the classroom and the majority enjoy a generally supportive working environment with cooperation from parents and students (Biggs, 1999; Lin, 1999; Aldridge and Fraser, 2000). During the reform of education, Taiwan has undergone a major transformation in the education of teachers and definition of their roles, yet the social status of teachers has remained relatively stable.

Supplementary tutoring

Private supplementary tutoring (cramming) cannot be overlooked when discussing teaching and learning in the Taiwanese education system.

Cramming is huge in Taiwan and is especially prominent at the transition points at which students have to prepare for the entrance exam to the next stage of education. Even when pupils can easily meet the learning demands of education systems without tutoring, many families still invest in tutoring in order to be sure that their children have a competitive edge. As discussed at the beginning of this book, cramming is extremely popular and coexists with the mainstream education in East Asia; in recent years it has also it has grown dramatically in other parts of the world. The reasons underlying the growth of private tutoring vary, but in all settings it has major implications for learning and livelihood, especially in a context like Taiwan where future life chances are closely linked to academic performance.

Cramming reflects the competitive ethos in the educational process, which shapes the patterns of teaching and learning. The transfer of knowledge and skills to pupils in cramming institutions has focused on what is perceived to be necessary for the public joint examination. The prosperous private cramming institutions cater for all levels of students, from children in the first year of primary school with parents worrying that they may 'lose at the start of the race', to repeaters wishing to gain access to the mainstream education system or the more prestigious schools (Kwok, 2004; Wu, 2004; Silova and Bray, 2006).

Financially capable families are able to secure not only a greater quantity but also a better quality of private tutoring. Not surprisingly, children receiving such tutoring do often perform better in school. Access to cramming may determine not only achievement at specific levels of education but also access to subsequent stages of the education system and to better lifetime earnings (Bray, 1999, 2006; Wu, 2004). In Taiwanese society, cramming has far-reaching implications and deserves considerably more attention from both policy makers and researchers.

Globalization in education

Although education in Taiwan is by many standards a success and contributes greatly to the development of the country, due to issues indicated above, there have long been calls for sweeping reform of the system. With the current international awareness of all aspects of human development, emphasis has been placed on the issue of 'globalization'.

Globalization broadens people's social and occupational perspectives beyond conventional geopolitical borders and cultures. In recent decades, educational and curricular reforms worldwide have been focused on preparing citizens for the economic and social challenges of globalization. In the 1990s, Taiwan authorities began referring to globalization in their discussion of long-standing educational problems in the country (such as examination pressure on students). Globalization was invoked as a justification for reform of all sections of the education system including curricula. In the reform of Taiwan's education system within this context, the joint entrance examinations especially have come in for severe criticism. Such a highly competitive system places tremendous stress on students, especially when educational qualifications are so critical for an individual's lifetime earnings. The joint exams place a great emphasis on rote memorization of texts. Students are forced to memorize vast amounts of disconnected detail, regurgitated during the exams and then often forgotten. Critics of the system believe this type of learning has denied students the opportunity to develop creativity and independent thinking, and therefore diminishes their global competitiveness (MOE, 2004).

The overwhelming criticism of the joint entrance exams initiated Taiwan's education reform in the 1990s, and the government argued that the review of the school entry system and curriculum would contribute to the globalization of Taiwan. However, the reform act has probably encouraged more the global competitiveness than global awareness. New directives in education have been formulated to 'enhance professionalism to help the nation with meeting the world competition and sustain national growth' (MOE, 2004). The intent is to transmit the government's worldview to students through the school curriculum. The curriculum standards of elementary and junior secondary schools refer to love for the world as a quality of good citizens' cultural exchanges and manners on international occasions. Nonetheless, the issue of 'global awareness' is not such an important theme in school (Law, 2004)

One reason why Taiwan is constrained in its development of global awareness is the fact that the Taiwanese school curricula have to first respond to contemporary socio-political changes, primarily in relation to mainland China (PRC). The most recent education reforms have emphasized generic and transnational skills, such as English proficiency and information technology, and developed tripartite frameworks for citizenship education at local, national and global levels. At the same time, schools have incorporated local languages, histories and identity into the curricula to express a different relationship with the PRC with a focus on national identify. In sum, schools have been paying more attention to local and national than to global concerns (Law, 2004). For many of the Taiwanese people, the focus of 'Global' education is primarily on English language learning and achievement in international rankings to 'better prepare students for the world' (MOE, 2004).

Entrance Examinations in Taiwan

In the 1992 International Assessment of Educational Progress (IAEP), which tests mathematics and science knowledge in students from 20 countries, Taiwan's nine and 13-year-olds were top in the rankings. Although organizations in charge of international surveys have always asked countries to be careful in using the results of the survey, especially in the ranking for comparison, it is nevertheless one of major reasons, if not the most important, for governments to take part in such surveys. Subsequently, Taiwan has continued to top various international achievement surveys. Table 13.1 shows the performance of Taiwanese students in the recent surveys it has taken part in.

Before we can discuss the students' performance in international achievement surveys, it is important to bear in mind that there are differences between examinations and international assessments. In a rather narrow definition, examinations are normally criteria-referenced tests following closely the curriculum; the tests are normally designed for the purpose of ranking for selection or exclusion (e.g. deciding who goes to the next level of education). Assessments are norm-referenced tests with the purpose of diagnosing problem

Table 13.1 Ranking and scores of Taiwanese students in international achievement surveys

	PISA 2006	PISA 2009	TIMSS 1999*	TIMSS 2003	TIMSS 2007	TIMSS 2011
Reading	16 (496)	23 (495)				
Mathematics	1 (549)	5 (543)	3 (589)	4 (585)	1 (598)	4 (591)
Science	4 (532)	12 (520)	1 (569)	2 (571)	2 (561)	6 (552)

*Result of 8th Grader

areas in the curriculum, exploring factors that may contribute to the learning outcomes and tracking progress of achievement over time. Examination results are released for individual students while assessment results aim to provide an overall picture of the education system.

The Programme for International Student Assessment (PISA) and the Trend in International Maths and Science Study (TIMSS) are possibly the two most popular and often discussed international surveys in recent years and very much favoured by governments in East Asia. While they both seek to assess specific knowledge and skills of students at a particular age group or school grade, organizations in charge argue that there are fundamental differences in the two assessments.

The PISA framework proposes that it is based on real-world application and tests problem-solving skills to 'assess how well 15 year olds are prepared for life challenges' (OECD, 2003, p. 20). TIMSS on the other hand is based on classroom mathematics knowledge and curriculum content and aims to 'improve the teaching and learning of mathematics and science by examining the relations between achievement and different types of curricula and context' (IEA, 2003, p. 13). PISA items are considered more application-based of real-life experience and culturally bound while TIMSS items are more universal. Some argue that this is the reason why Taiwanese students are not performing as well in PISA, while others challenge the reliability of identifying real-life challenges in 60 countries. We cannot explore this issue in detail in this chapter but there is little doubt that Taiwanese students belong to the high achieving groups in all international surveys.

Results that are similar to Taiwan's can be seen in many other countries in the East Asia Pacific Rim and have attracted the attention of governments and researchers wishing to 'cherry pick' the practices that contribute to the success of these countries. In a review aiming to tease out the contributing factors behind successful performance in mathematics education, the Nuffield Foundation,

UK, revealed that high attainment, as defined by the results of international achievement surveys, 'may be much more closely linked to cultural values than to specific maths teaching practice … being born into a culture that highly values success in mathematics establishes a "virtuous cycle" of continuing success (Askew et al., 2010, p. 12).

While there are fundamental differences between the design of entrance examinations in Taiwan and assessments like PISA and TIMSS, it would seem naïve to discard the connection. One thing we can be sure of is that Taiwanese students are more experienced test takers than many of their counterparts in other countries. In a context where examinations play such a significant role, the degree of central control over the curriculum, related policies, selection procedures for students to move up in the school system and the intensity of after-school cramming are all related to how exam results are valued and inevitably affects the outcomes when it comes to other types of tests.

Examination results and credentials

As mentioned above, in Taiwan the curricula of primary and secondary schools are strongly controlled by the state, resulting in a uniform national curriculum. In addition, the national systems of assessment closely follows the curriculum and plays a critical role in selecting and allocating pupils through highly competitive and norm-referenced public examinations (Marsh and Morris, 1991).

Within selective systems, teaching and learning are viewed instrumentally with regard to the goal of maximizing success in highly competitive public examinations. When provision of education became universal, the examination performed the function of determining the stream of education (i.e. academic/general or technical/vocational) or the status of the institution (e.g. an elite metropolitan university or a private higher education institution). The selective function of education still prevails even under mass provision at all levels of education.

The entrance exam system in Taiwan has been repeatedly criticized by people concerned with education there. But many problems in education do not originate within the education system but are a reflection of concepts and ideologies in society. The pressure arising from the transfer from one level of the system to the next is such an example.

The biggest problem in Taiwan's education system is probably the obsession with 'credentialism' and 'academic elitism'. This is illustrated by the amount of emphasis people put on getting into prestigious universities and obtaining a legitimate credit from them. Graduate certificates, especially those from a good university, are considered the most important keys for one's access to jobs. This is an aspect of the 'meritocracy' emphasized by Confucius when he suggested that government officials and bureaucrats should be selected on the 'merit' of examination in the classics (Ho, 1967). It is believed that once one obtains the proof of credit, the doors to an ideal career will be opened for them. Such an ideology has a long history in Chinese culture, for example the local government election exams in the Han Dynasty, the civil service nomination Nine Rank System from around AD 200, the popular *Ke Gu* system for the selection of government officials in the Suei and Tang Dynasty, and, after the establishment of the Republic of China, the creation of the Examination *Yuan*. One would not be surprised to see primary or junior high school teachers with doctoral degrees and the Taiwanese Parliament actually contains the highest percentage of members with doctoral degrees of any legislature in the world. This is part of the reason why entry to the next level of education is so crucial and the students' utmost goal, and examination is considered the fairest way to provide equal opportunity for all.

Joint entrance exams have a long history in Taiwan and have been the gatekeepers for students wishing to continue to secondary and tertiary education. The entrance exam systems have received a tremendous amount of criticism in recent years and are considered the main cause for student burnout. Nevertheless, the joint entrance exams were once considered the fairest way to admit college students as all the tests are administered and marked anonymously and the tests are the same for all students, thus eliminating the traditional advantages enjoyed by children from a wealthy or powerful background.

The joint entrance exam for junior high schools was only abolished at the time when junior high schools became part of the nine-year compulsory education system in 1968. Joint entrance exams for senior high schools and vocational schools were introduced in 1958 and abolished in 2000 as part of the education reform plan. In this chapter, we will focus the discussion on the Joint College Entrance Exam (JCEE) in trying to explain the development of the entrance exam and admission system currently in place in Taiwan.

The JCEE was first introduced in 1954 by the Ministry of Education, and the four most reputable and historical higher education institutions (HEIs) at the time (National Taiwan University, Taiwan Provincial Teacher's College, Taiwan Provincial College of Agriculture and Taiwan Provincial College of Technology) were the first ones to take part. The development and administration of the JCEE was rigid, well designed and monitored. There was a carefully selected steering committee with a membership that altered annually. A different university was in charge of monitoring and implementing at different stages of the exam process each year. Every year new test items were selected from a pool contributed by high school teachers and the test was drawn up by a team of university professors. The items were based on the standardized textbooks used at all Taiwanese high schools. When the draft tests were ready, some top-ranking college freshmen would take part in the pre-test to provide feedback on the difficulty level. All people who have viewed the tests are sequestered before the exam takes place. The JCEE system quickly gained public acceptance because of of its perceived fairness. In 1956, private universities and career schools (including military schools) also began to take part and the number of students participating in the exam increased significantly over time. In 1972, career colleges introduced their own joint exams so the JCEE became solely the entry path for the universities and colleges. To prepare for JCEE, students are divided into subject area groups normally in the second year of senior high school. The *Jia* Group is for those interested in studying science and engineering subjects in universities; the *Yi* Group is for humanities; the *Bien* Group is for those interested in medicine, zoology and plantation; and the newly established *Ding* Group is for those intended to be law and business majors.

Some of the most compelling arguments against the entrance exams have come from Lee Yuan-tseh (李遠哲). Once the president of Academia Sinicar, Taiwan's top-ranked research institute, and a Nobel Prize winner in chemistry, Lee is one of the nation's most respected scholars and one of the people who led the revision of the exam system. New and alternative means of entry to high schools and colleges/universities have been introduced since the early 1990s and there have been numerous proposals and reform plans aimed at reducing the pressure on students and normalizing the education system. The College Entrance Examination Centre (CEEC), consisting of all the principals of HEIs in the country, was formed in 1989 to review the university admittance system and oversee and monitor the joint exam process. In 1992, CEEC first proposed to the MOE the multiple admission system as a replacement of the entrance exam system. In 1997, CEEC ceased to publish the minimum requirement score of individual HEI courses in order to break the myth about departmental and school ranking and encourage students to pursue subjects they were genuinely interested in. In 2002, JCEE was formally abolished and replaced by the multiple entry system (Hsu, 2001).

Compared to the old system, the current pathways for admission to senior high schools and colleges are extremely complex.

High school entrance

The year 2001 marked the occasion of the replacement of the Joint High School/ Vocational School Entrance Exams by the multi-track admission system. With the new system, junior high school students can be admitted to senior high school or vocational schools through three paths; a) student registration, whereby students will be judged and assigned to particular high schools according to their school performance; b) school recommendation, whereby schools nominate selected students to take tests for specific high schools; and c) student application, whereby students apply themselves to high schools of their choice. Except for around 5 per cent of the places that are offered without entrance exam, admission is often based solely on the result of the Basic Competency Test (BCT), which tests Chinese, English, mathematics, natural science and social science abilities.

In 2010, the Taipei City government launched an exam-free senior high school entrance scheme as part of the effort to implement a 12-year compulsory education system. Graduating junior high school students whose average grades are in the top 40 per cent in their schools are eligible for the 'Stars Programme'. This allows students in less competitive junior high schools the chance to enter senior high school or vocational schools, including the more prestigious ones. The MOE expected that this would also improve the overall quality of senior secondary education.

In April 2012, the MOE announced the plan to extend compulsory education from nine to 12 years. The new programme will commence in 2014, although attending senior secondary education was already the norm for the majority of Taiwanese society. In 2011, for example, 97.67 per cent of junior high school graduates continued into senior secondary education. The impact of 12-year compulsory education is likely to be further elimination of the role of entrance exams. BCT will be replaced by the 'Joint Junior High School Education Test', which will grade students on broader achievement levels rather than raw scores.

College entrance

Lee criticized, in particular, the joint college entrance exam system, and in 1994 stated publicly that the exam system was unfair, that it constrained the ability of students to think creatively and that he would like to see the JCEE discontinued before the end of the twentieth century. Lee recommended that the JCEE system be replaced by a two-part system similar to the US Scholastics Aptitude Test (SAT) and the UK's former O-level exam – students first take a general test and then individual tests developed by the HEIs. He believed that this would allow students to make academic choices according to their interests and aptitudes.

Soon after the joint high school entrance exam was abolished, in 2002, the JCEE was replaced by a multiple college entrance programme. High school students take the General Scholastic Ability Test (GSAT) and a separate subject test required by individual university departments. In the following years, there were proposed changes in various aspects of the system, calling for combining these two tests into one or keeping only the GSAT and taking into account reference letters and individual students' special talents and skills.

At the time of writing in 2012, there are three paths to enter HEIs. The 'Stars Programme', similar to the new admission methods for senior secondary schools, was also introduced at the college admission level to give students who are not in elite high schools the opportunity to enter some of the best universities. Any high schools or vocational schools can recommend students whose academic performances are in the top 5–10 per cent to universities that have taken part in the programme. Students will be judged upon their academic performances in the first two years in senior high school and the result of the GSAT. Universities can admit a maximum of one student per school through this programme.

Under the current system in 2012, students' paths of entry depend on their choices on the type of examination:

a) Having participated in GSAT, students can choose the entry methods of *Stars Recommendation* and *Individual Application*, the former having evolved from the original Stars Programme while taking into account results of interviews, reference letters and proof of students' additional performances and skills.
b) Students who choose to only take subject-specific tests can only apply for the limited number of HEI departments not requiring the result of GSAT.
c) Those who choose to take both the GSAT and subject-specific tests could be admitted through both the application and exam results.

Examination distribution is similar to the traditional JCEE; if students fail the recommendation and screening process, it gives them a second chance to enter a HEI course based on their performance in this entrance exam. Students are assigned to courses by the Exam Centre and have less freedom in choosing what they are interested in.

Yang's (2004) study looked at the phenomena of student burnout in the technical-vocational track after the introduction of the multiple enrolment programme. He suggests that the various enrolment programmes do link to student burnout. Students who enter school via admission application have the least stress, followed by students who enter via the recommendation and screening process; the entrance exam does give students the most stress at the time of the entry. However, those who have the option of admission application tend to be students who are high academic achievers, and the ones using exam distribution tend not to be. Admission application also gives students the most freedom to choose their desired HEI courses (whether that choice is their parents' or their own).

Generally speaking, students should have more choice in terms of admission methods. However, the majority of the students (and parents) would opt for the exam route, that is, taking as many exams as possible to ensure they can be admitted to the higher ranking or more recognized HEI courses.

If the reform process is successful, the MOE estimates that by 2014 more than 80 per cent of students will gain admission to university through applications that take into account more dimensions of student performance than simply a single, one-off test score. Nevertheless, top-notch schools would still retain the right to require students to take additional exams if they so wished.

Conclusion

When a child is in the last year of junior high [9th Grade], it's as if the whole family is living with a time bomb that ticks down to the day of the test. The whole clan centres on the needs of that child.

This was quoted from a newspaper article entitled 'The Joint Entrance Exam Monster is Dead! Now What?' The article was an interview of a mother whose son was going to take the Joint Entrance Exam for senior high schools in 2000. This was the year before the high school Joint Entrance Exam was abolished and replaced by the multiple-track admission system. A decade later, most would agree that these sentiments still accurately describe families with children in the admission process of going to the next level of education.

It is clear that the Taiwanese government has made a considerable effort in trying to prepare a labour force that is adequate and competitive for the country in the early twenty-first century. The reforms of the entrance exam system aim to deal with what is considered one of the major obstacles in being a forward-thinking society. There is a clear need to lessen the pressure of exams, reduce urban–rural differences, widen access to higher education and normalize the junior and senior high school educational system. Many viewed the abolition of the joint entrance exams as a revolution in the education system of Taiwan. Nonetheless, many also believe that it is still admission by means of examination but with a different name. Other critics fear that these changes would eventually dispose of the fundamental ideology and tradition underpinning the exam/selection process, that is, fairness, and favour students from wealthier backgrounds.

As a matter of fact, currently in Taiwan it is not at all difficult to enter a HEI. As people strive for ways to obtain graduate certificates, private HEIs offer such an opportunity, and normally with lower entry requirements. In recent years, the supply of HEI courses/spaces has actually exceeded demand, while the top notch universities have little problem attracting the most academically gifted students. Many private HEIs, especially in programmes that are less popular, are lowering the entry requirement that were already relatively low. In 2011, there were 173 HEIs in Taiwan, consisting of 158 universities (including two Open Universities and seven special universities/academies for the training of the police and military) and 15 vocational colleges (MOE, 2012a), which is quite a significant number for a small island with a population of 23 million. In 1995, less than 45 per cent of college applicants gained admittance to a local college or university. In 2007, it was estimated that 96 per cent of university entrance exam takers would be eligible for a university place and there are undergraduate programmes with minimum entry requirements of around 5 percentage marks in exam scores. While this is a rather extreme case, it shows why many began to question the quality and usefulness of a university degree. Nonetheless, when it comes to job applications, industries and employers still base their judgement mainly on the certificate (Hsieh, 2011).

At the other end of the spectrum are the elite schools, as people always tend to prefer schools that are highly competitive in the next level of exams. The route of entry to high schools is still highly competitive. Even with the many reform acts that have been introduced to tackle the problem brought about by high-stake examinations, while the system can be changed, the mentality underpinning the significance of success in the exam cannot be transformed so easily. It will take some years before we can see any significant changes brought by the new admission systems and by 12-year compulsory education, especially in relation to student workloads and the even grander goal of 'raising the global competitiveness' of Taiwan. Whether the reforms above will succeed in all these objectives, from those at local level of the individual and their families to those of the government in the international sphere, remains to be seen.

References

Aldridge, J. M., Fraser, B. J., Taylor, P. C. and Chen, C. C. (2000). 'Constructivist learning environments in a cross-national study in Taiwan and Australia'. *International Journal of Science Education*, 22: 37–55.

Armer, M. and Liu, C. (1993). 'Education's effect on economic growth in Taiwan'. *Comparative Education Review*, 37: 304–21.

Askew, M., Hodgen, J., Hossain, S and Bretscher, N. (2010). *Values and Variables: Mathematics education in high-performing countries*. London: Nuffield Foundation.

Biggs, J. B. (1999). 'Western misperceptions of the Confucian-Heritage learning culture', in D. A. Watkins and J. B. Biggs (eds), *The Chinese Learner: Cultural, Psychological and Contextual Influences*. Hong Kong: CERC.

Bray, M. (1999). 'The shadow education system: private tutoring and its implications for planners'. *Fundamentals of educational planning*. Paris: UNESCO International Institute for Educational Planning.

—(2006). 'Private supplementary tutoring: comparative perspectives on patterns and implications'. *Compare*, 36: 515–30.

Cheng, J. (1995). 'Exam under Examination'. *Taiwan Review*. http://taiwanreview.nat. gov.tw/ct.asp?xItem=108&CtNode=1358 (Accessed 20 July 2012).

Cheng, Y. C., Chow, K. W. and Tsui, K. T. (2001). 'In Search of a New Teacher Education: International Perspectives'. In Y. C. Cheng, K. W. Chow and K. T. Tsui (eds), *New Teacher Education for the Future – International Perspectives*. Hong Kong: Kluwer Academic Publishers.

Chern, C. L. (2002). 'English language teaching in Taiwan today'. *Asia-Pacific Journal of Education*, 22, 2: 97–105.

The Economist (2008). *The World Fact Book 2008*.

—(2011). *The World Fact Book 2011*.

Fwu, B. J. and Wang, H. (2002). 'The social status of teachers in Taiwan'. *Comparative Education*, 38: 211–24.

Ho, P. T. (1967). *The Ladder of Success in Imperial China – aspects of social mobility 1268–1911*. New York: Columbia University Press.

Hsiao, H. H. (2004). 'Taiwan's dual election: democracy and national identity'. *Open Democracy*.

—(2008). 'Taiwan identity and China: 1987–2007'. *Open Democracy*.

Hsu, M. J. (July, 2001). 'When JCEE paced into history'. *National Policy Foundation Research Report*. National Policy Foundation.

—(2009). 'The Emergence of the entrance examination system, its associated problems and necessary reforms'. *National Policy Foundation Research Report*. http://www.npf.org.tw/post/2/6175 (Accessed 25 July 2012).

Hughes, C. (1997). *Taiwan and Chinese Nationalism: National Identity and Status in International Society*. New York: Routledge.

IEA (International Association for the Evaluation of Educational Achievement) (2003).

TIMSS Assessment Frameworks and Specifications 2003. Chestnut Hill: TIMSS International Study Centre.

International Monetary Fund (2011). *2011 World Economic Outlook*. http://www.imf.org/external/data.htm (Accessed 23 July 2012).

Johnson, D. and Maclean, R. (eds) (2008). *Teaching: Professionalization, Development and Leadership*. London: Springer.

Kwok, P. (2004). 'Examination-oriented knowledge and value transformation in East Asian cram schools'. *Asia Pacific Education Review*, 5: 64–75.

Lau, L. J. (1986). Introduction', in L. J. Lau and L. R. Klein (eds), *Models of Development: A Comparative Study of Economic Growth in South Korea and Taiwan*. San Francisco: Institute for Contemporary Studies Press.

Law, W. W. (2004). 'Globalization and citizenship education in Hong Kong and Taiwan'. *Comparative Education Review*: 253–73.

Leavitt, H. B. (1992). 'Introduction'. In H. B. Leavitt (ed.), *Issues and Problems in Teacher Education: An International Handbook*. New York: Greenwood Press.

Lin, J. F. (1999). *Taibeishi Guoming Xiaoxue Zishen Jiaoshi Gongzuo Manyiduzhi Yanjiu* [*Investigating the work satisfaction of senior primary school teachers in Taipei*]. Unpublished master's thesis, National Taipei Teachers' College, Taipei, Taiwan.

Lin, Q. J. (1992). *TaiBei Shi Fiao Shi ZhiYeSheng Wang Yu Zhuan Ye Xing Xiang Zhi DiaoChaYanJiu* [*A survey study of the occupational prestige and professional image of teachers in Taipei*]. Taipei: Ministry of Education.

Lin, T. C. (2003). 'Education, technical progress, and economic growth: the case of Taiwan'. *Economics of Education Review*: 213–20.

Liu, C. N. (2005). *From Chinese national identity to Taiwanese consciousness: an examination of the cultural elements in Taiwan's democratization during the Lee Teng-hui era and its legacy, 1988–2004*. Robina, Australia: Faculty of Humanities and Social Sciences, Bond University.

Marsh, C. and Morris, P. (1991). *Curriculum Development in East Asia*. London: Falmer.

Martin, M. O., Mullis, I. V. S., Foy, P. and Stanco, G. M. (2012) TIMSS 2011 International Results in Science. Chestnut Hill, MA: TIMSS & PIRLS International Study Center, Boston College.

Ministry of Interior (2011). *Statistical Yearbook of Interior Population of 15 Years and Over by Educational Attainment*. http://sowf.moi.gov.tw/stat/year/elist.htm (Accessed 15 January 2013).

MOE (Ministry of Education) (2004). *Taiwan Year Book*: Ministry of Education. http://www.gio.gov.tw/taiwan-website/5-gp/yearbook/.htm (Accessed 1 November 2011).

—(2012a). *2012 Educational Statistical Indicators*. http://english.moe.gov.tw/ct.asp?xItem=12710&CtNode=816&mp=11 (Accessed 23 July 2012).

—(2012b). *101 Nien Guochung Biyehshen Duoyuan Jinlu Hsuendau Shoze* [*2012 Multiple Admission Methods Promotion Booklet for Junior High School Students*]. Taipei: MOE.

Mo, Y. C. (2009). 'Taipei to start exam-free senior high admissions'. *Taipei Times*, 4 June, p. 2.

Morris, P. (1996). 'Asia's four little tigers: A comparison of the role of education in their development'. *Comparative Education*, 32: 95–110.

Mullis, I. V. S., Martin, M. O., Foy, P. and Arora, A. (2012) The Timss 2011 Results in Mathematics. Chestnut Hill, MA: TIMSS & PIRLS International Study Center, Boston College.

OECD (2003). *The PISA 2003 Assessment Framework*. Paris: OECD.

Rodrik, D. (1995). 'The dynamics of political support for reform in economies in transition'. *Journal of Japanese and International Economies*, 9: 403–25.

Rubinstein, M. (1999) (ed.) *Taiwan: A New History*. Armonk: M. E. Sharpe.

Schubert, G. (2004). 'Taiwan's political parties and national identity: The rise of an overarching consensus'. *Asian Survey*, 44: 534–54.

Silova, I. and Bray, M. (eds) (2006). *Education in the hidden market place: monitoring of private tutoring*. New York: Open Society Institute.

Teng, S. F. (2000). 'The Joint Entrance Exam Monster is Dead! Now What?' *Taiwan Panorama*, May, p. 6.

Williamson, J. W. and Morris, P. (2000). 'Teacher education in the Asia-Pacific region: a comparative analysis'. In P. Morris and J. W. Williamson (eds), *Teacher Education in the Asia-Pacific Region: a comparative study*. New York: Falmer Press.

Wu, J. A. (2005). '*Linching Shidia Taiwan Shuyuan Jiaoyu de Ruxue Xixiang*' ['Confucian thoughts of Taiwan academy education during the Ching Dynasty']. *Yuntech Journal of Chinese Studies*, 1: 111–31.

Wu, L. (2004). 'Disaffection and cramming: the story from Taiwan'. *International Journal on School Disaffection*, 2: 15–20.

Wu, M. (2010). 'Comparing the Similarities and Differences of PISA 2003 and TIMSS'. *OECD Education Working Papers*, No. 32. http://dx.doi.org/10.1787/5km4psm13nx-en (Accessed 20 August 2012).

Yang, H. J. (2004). 'Factors affecting student burnout and academic achievement in multiple enrolment programs in Taiwan's technical-vocational colleges'. *International Journal of Educational Development*, 24: 283–301.

Zeng, K. (1999). *Dragon Gate: Competitive Examinations and their Consequences*. London: Cassell.

Index